Public Finance Administration

Public Finance Administration

SECOND EDITION

B.J. Reed
John W. Swain

SAGE Publications
International Educational and Professional Publisher
Thousand Oaks   London   New Delhi

For information address:

SAGE Publications, Inc.
2455 Teller Road
Thousand Oaks, California 91320
E-mail: order@sagepub.com

SAGE Publications Ltd.
6 Bonhill Street
London EC2A 4PU
United Kingdom

SAGE Publications India Pvt. Ltd.
M-32 Market
Greater Kailash I
New Delhi 110 048 India

Printed in the United States of America

Library of Congress Cataloging-in-Publication Data

Reed, B. J.
    Public finance administration/B. J. Reed and John W. Swain—
2nd ed.
        p. cm.
    Includes bibliographical references and index.
    ISBN 0-8039-7405-1 (acid-free paper)
    1. Finance, Public. 2. Administrative agencies—Finance.
3. Public administration. I. Swain, John W., 1948- . II. Title.
HJ141.R45   1997
350.72—dc20   96-25311

This book is printed on acid-free paper.

    99 00 01 10 9 8 7 6 5 4 3 2

Acquiring Editor:	Catherine Rossbach
Editorial Assistant:	Nancy Hale
Production Editor:	Astrid Virding
Production Assistant:	Karen Wiley
Typesetter/Designer:	Danielle Dillahunt
Cover Designer:	Candice Harman
Print Buyer:	Anna Chin

Contents

Preface

The title of this book, *Public Finance Administration,* signifies its focus on administrative activities associated with the handling of public monies for all kinds of public organizations, including nonprofit organizations and entities at the local, state, and federal levels of government. Administrative activities of concern here are the less visible day-to-day handling of public monies and related technical support activities rather than the more visible political activities associated with public budgeting.

This book is distinct from others by its exclusive and comprehensive focus on the administration of public finances. The singular focus on public finance administration makes it possible to be comprehensive and fully discuss relevant areas. Most other books in this area are less comprehensive and discuss many of the same topics in a more abbreviated fashion within the context of public budgeting. Comprehensiveness is apparent from the number of diverse topics covered by chapter titles, as well as in the broad treatment of topics within the chapters. Along with breadth, a singular focus makes for greater depth and full explanations of the basic concepts, concerns, and processes. The thrust of this book is toward the basics rather than the esoteric because there is far more specialized rather than basic literature available in the area.

This book is meant to be easy to use. We wrote it from the premises that our readers would not be experts in the area, that it should be readable, and that it takes a public administration perspective. The stress, therefore, is on defining terminology, framing conceptions, showing steps in processes, explaining purposes, and examining common controversies. We assume readers have little or no background, but we also provide much detail for those with some background. The readability is a function of a writing syle that is as relaxed as the topics allow and down-to-earth rather than academic in tone. We have worked in the public sector and regularly teach and train in-service public administrators. The resulting public administration perspective is somewhat unique in this area, as much of the literature is produced by persons with different perspectives, especially policy and economic perspectives. Most texts in this general area use a theoretical perspective divorced from concerns of practical administration. Here, theoretical conceptualizations are related to practical situations.

The changes in this revised edition include updating the content and examples, adding discussion questions at the end of chapters, and creating an Internet site relevant to point to places on the Internet relevant to particular chapters. A wide variety of such sites can be accessed from a World Wide Web home page created for that purpose: http://www.unomaha.edu/~wwwpa, fsite.html. If you have any problems accessing this site, e-mail B. J. Reed at Breed@fa-cpacs.unomaha.edu.

Acknowledgments

W e would like to thank especially those who helped in the preparation of this text. First and foremost, Joyce Carson's, Nancy Krzycki's, and Jan Pugh's willingness to spend long hours word processing the manuscript helped make the effort less painful. We would also like to thank Greg Delone, who served as a graduate assistant involved in this revision at the University of Nebraska at Omaha, and Linda Royster and Jon Steigman at the University of Alabama, who provided research and review assistance on the text. We would like to thank Nancy Krzycki for her efforts in establishing and maintaining the World Wide Web Site for Public Budgeting and Finance at the Department of Public Administration, University of Nebraska at Omaha. Finally, we would like to thank Donald Baum, Bob Blair, Kathy Swain, and the anonymous reviewers who gave of their time to review all or parts of the manuscript.

B. J. REED
JOHN W. SWAIN

Introduction

What is public finance administration? The need for carefully considering public finance administration as a topic area arises because it lacks any clear-cut technical or commonsense definition. Rather than present readers with a bland and overqualified topic definition that is a relief to forget, we want to make public finance administration a topic of some meaning beyond a mere book title by approaching the topic through common conceptions about the area. The most common conceptions of public finance administration include the notions that public finance administration is dull and obscure, that it deals with numbers and calculations that are sometimes esoteric, that it is about money, and that it is technical in character. Some of these conceptions are correct, whereas others are partially or totally false. The listing of news stories in Table 1.1 provides a starting point for assessing what public finance administration is about.

The news stories display the excitement of major political, personal, and organizational drama when large amounts of money are being handled in interesting ways. The regular flow of such stories, and general public interest, do not allow public finance administration to be obscure. The interesting ways that public monies are handled or mishandled have significant impacts on every citizen in the form of taxes, public services, and public policies. Such a topic—and, we hope, this book—is neither obscure nor uninteresting.

Clearly, numbers, calculations, and money play an important role in public finance administration. Numbers represent measurements of money or monetary value in real situations. The 2.5 million residents, and their government officials, in Orange County, California, saw 1.7 billion dollars of real investment losses in 1994, approximately $680 per resident. Residents' concern with garbage collection fees and other public revenues is no mere fascination with numbers but instead reflects a very real concern for meeting their living costs. The calculations here, as is overwhelmingly the case in public finance admini-

TABLE 1.1   Public Finance Administration News Stories

Orange County loses $1.7 billion because of risky investments, and treasurer pleads guilty to six counts of fraud, consulted astrologer

Mercedes Benz economic incentives package ruled unconstitutional and renegotiated

U.S. Federal Emergency Management Agency works to ensure timely payments to disaster victims

County weighs sports stadium investment with cost-benefit analysis

A former treasurer of Episcopal Church embezzles 2.2 million dollars, says actions cry for help, church against prosecution

Alabama state legislators try to find way to get state pension despite constitutional ban

IRS refuses to return man's check when he grossly overpaid because of two year statute of limitations

U.S. Representative promotes taxpayer bill of rights

City sets sights on collecting loans originally made for economic development

City police radio system contract award stopped by court

New York City bond rating lowered

UN auditor cannot find $40 million of physical assets when concluding Cambodian peace mission, no guidelines for financial liquidation of mission

U.S. Department of Defense experimental purchasing program cuts regulations and costs for buying weapons

Spy agency hoards money to build building

Spy agency lost track of $2 billion

Bill for garbage collection goes up

Florida spaceport fails to take off in state-sponsored commercial space program

United Nations seeks tax

---

stration, are simple, straightforward arithmetic. The reason for precise meas-urement of monetary values is the importance attached to money as a medium for measuring the value of resources available for exchange. People pay attention to money, precise measurements of monetary value, and calcula-tions concerning monetary values because money is a marker for all things of material value.

Numerical representations of money and related calculations represent more that just material values. Other real issues and ideas are very much involved in the realm of public finance administration. Examples from the listing of news stories include an international organization eyeing possible revenue sources, a federal agency experimenting with purchasing regulations, a state economic development project, a city collecting debts, and a church losing more than two million dollars to embezzlement. Often, questions arise in public finance administration regarding what is fair, what is appropriate, and what is good public policy.

The conception of public finance administration as technical is wholly correct. *Technical,* despite connotations to the contrary, means the way things are done. Public finance administration concerns how things are done with money, and is, therefore, at the heart of the administration of public organi-zations. Each item in the list of news stories represents a problem or situation that public officials responsible for public finance administration have to deal with in some fashion. Officials' concerns in these and countless other situations involving public monies are what to do and how to do it.

Public finance administration is based on very diverse concepts linked by the common idea of handling public monies. In other words, public finance administration is concerned with the handling of public assets and liabilities, and making relevant information and insights available to public officials so they can make informed decisions. (These two sentences represent our closest approach to a formal, concise definition of public finance administration.)

Public entities, such as governments and nonprofit organizations, are responsible for the flow of tremendously large amounts of money every year. Federal receipts and payments are calculated in the hundreds of billions of dollars. Often, states handle billions of dollars. Local governments and nonprofit organizations collectively deal with hundreds of billions of dollars. Few public administrators deal directly with the overall financial operations of their public organization; many do have firsthand dealings with public monies in their own responsibility areas. Nonprofit housing officials, local public works directors, state development specialists, and federal park rangers are all involved in some aspects of public finance administration. All public administrators, generalists as well as those specializing in public finance functions, deal with public finances on a daily basis.

Public finance administration is concerned with how monies are handled as they flow into, within, and out of various public sector organizations. Interest in this area has grown increasingly in recent years among the general public, policymakers, public administrators, and concerned academics. Few areas intersect so many aspects of public organizations as does public finance administration. The "how" of public finance administration, which incorporates a wide variety of topics, is the central focus of this book.

WHAT PUBLIC FINANCE ◆ ADMINISTRATION IS NOT

Although public finance administration has been generally described, it can also be distinguished from what it is not. Public finance administration is not private finance administration, public finance, macroeconomics, or public budgeting. Although each of these areas has relevance for public finance administration, each can be distinguished from the major focus of this text.

Private finance administration is concerned with handling the assets and liabilities of individuals and businesses to gain income and profits through the sale of goods and services. Private-sector finance administration deals differently with products, taxes, and constraints than does public finance administration. In the private sector, income comes from the voluntary exchange of money for goods and services, and taxes are paid to governments. The products of the private sector are provided on the basis of market demand and profitability, and taxes are involuntary payments. The constraints on private organizations are the factors of production (e.g., capital, labor, and land) that are available, legal restrictions on economic activity, taxes, and market conditions. Though many analytical concepts are useful for both private and public finance administration, the two use quite distinct practices.

Macroeconomics and public finance are theoretical fields in economics. Public finance as discussed by economists is concerned with economic principles as they relate to public sector impacts on the private economy, specifically the allocative, distributive, and regulatory impacts of public budgets. Macroeconomics deals with the behavior of national economies and is the basis for fiscal and monetary policy recommendations. Neither focuses on the administrative activities of public organizations.

Public budgeting is concerned with the planned acquisition and use of resources by public entities. It involves the decisions of what revenues to collect and what expenditures to make. Public budgeting and public finance administration are closely linked, but they are separate functions. Public budgeting is concerned with policy decisions related to obtaining and using resources, and public finance administration is concerned with providing relevant information on which to make budgetary decisions, implementing such decisions, and other aspects of handling public monies. How they relate is discussed in Chapter 2.

◆ THE KEY ELEMENTS OF PUBLIC FINANCE ADMINISTRATION

The key elements necessary to understand and practice public finance administration include a basic comprehension of public organizations and how they function, an understanding of major finance concepts, and a detailed knowledge of particular techniques.

Public Organizations

Throughout this book, certain characteristics of public organizations are emphasized for their relation to public finance administration. These characteristics include legal constraints, political circumstances, and the peculiar character of most public services.

Legal Constraints

Various laws require, authorize, and prohibit public finance administration activities. For example, Article I of the U.S. Constitution authorizes Congress to lay and collect taxes (Section 8) while restricting that power (Section 9). State constitutions restrict both state and local governments in raising and spending public funds. Thousands of federal, state, and local laws affect financial actions of public organizations. Examples of requirements laws include requiring checks to be signed by three different officials, public referenda for school bonds, and certain procedures to be followed in obligating a government to make a purchase. Authorizing laws allow governments to hoose to do certain things, for example, use particular revenue sources, offer conomic development incentives, or borrow money to build roads. Likewise, aws prohibit certain activities. Prohibited activities include spending more noney than is collected and investing public monies in certain securities. Nonprofit organizations are subject to relevant laws as well as their own ylaws and regulations.

Political Circumstances

Because their activities depend on long-term popular support of the citizens they represent and because elected representatives are concerned with etting votes in the next election, public organizations are politically sensitive. n the United States, citizens elect representatives to exercise control of overnments. Within the constraints of law, elected officials determine the ctions of governments. Because of the support needed from the public, lected officials may make decisions based on political pressures as well as ther factors. Public administrators must consider political circumstances ecause their activities are overseen by elected officials. Nonprofit organizaions are no less sensitive to political pressure from their supporters, including overnments that charter and regulate nonprofit organizations and in some ases provide them with grants and contracts.

Public Goods

Public organizations primarily produce public goods. Public goods display he characteristics of indivisibility, nonsubtractability, or both. Indivisibility neans that a good cannot practically be divided up into pieces and, therefore, s generally available to all within a given area. (National defense is a public ood from which all members of a nation benefit or suffer.) Nonsubtractabily means that one person benefiting from a good does not subtract from or eny others benefit of that same good. (National defense and lighthouses are lear-cut examples.) Private organizations do not provide public goods beause doing so is not profitable.

Financial Concepts

Financial concepts are discussed throughout the book within the context f particular topic areas. Some concepts appear in many places, others appear nly once. Within the various topic areas, financial concepts are explained and llustrated in relation to the practical application of particular techniques. bstract concepts are introduced for the purpose of developing an understanding of the practice of public finance administration.

Particular Techniques

Particular techniques are discussed with their meanings and purposes, najor elements and concepts, and steps in carrying out the technique. Each chapter starts out at a general level showing what a technique is about and how it fits into the operations of public organizations. More detailed discussions ensue, illuminating the specific details and actions involved in using particular techniques and providing specific, concrete examples. Also, some of the following chapters provide lists of "Suggested Readings" at the end for readers desiring to pursue a topic in greater detail.

◆ THE BASES OF PUBLIC
FINANCE ADMINISTRATION

Bases refer to situational factors determining what can be done. The bases of public finance administration include relevant laws, political circumstances, techniques, and organizational arrangements. Laws provide requirements, authorizations, and prohibitions. Political circumstances provide general (and on occasion very specific) guidance, often through the budgetary process. Techniques, though they are basic and available to all public officials, may or may not be used in a given situation. For example, the most basic of all public finance administration techniques is public accounting. Yet, accounting is not fully used by public organizations despite its critical importance. (A sad and amusing case of such non-use is the actual statement of a public administrator, upon having a check bounce, that "someone ought to keep track of these things.") Various techniques are used to a greater or lesser extent in given situations. Organizational arrangements established by constitutions, laws, and other policies vary considerably. The division of responsibilities among public officials generally includes (1) overall financial guidance from policymakers who are elected legislators and elected or appointed executives, (2) one or more specialized finance offices or agencies, and (3) responsibilities allocated to operating agencies. Responsibility for financial activities is divided in various ways between and among political and administrative officials. Among the political officials, responsibilities are divided depending on the relative powers of legislators and executives and the number of elected executives who have financial responsibilities. For administrative officials, the responsibilities are divided among one or more specialized finance offices and the operating units. For the specialized finance office or offices, the possibilities range from one person handling an organization's finances to a host of specialized offices. Common specialized organizational responsibilities include revenue collection, accounting, expenditure disbursement, treasury, purchasing, debt management, pension administration, and risk management. Operating units can have more or fewer finance activities delegated to them in different situations. Such diversity in the organization of public finance administration results from tradition and circumstances, though recent years have seen a trend toward greater centralization.

Politics, laws, knowledge of particular techniques, and organizational arrangements all constrain or determine what occurs in a particular situation. On occasion, a particular practice more favorable on technical grounds is made impossible by one of these factors. The most common difficulty is political circumstances.

ORIENTATIONS IN PUBLIC ◆
FINANCE ADMINISTRATION

Public organizations display three orientations: control, management, and planning.[1] Although public organizations reflect all three orientations in varying degrees, particular organizations tend toward a greater emphasis on one of the three. A control orientation is reflected in a concentration of effort to ensure that the organization completes specific tasks and that organization members do not deviate from official policies. A management orientation is reflected in a concentration of efforts to achieve efficiency and effectiveness in day-to-day operations and, hence, pronounced attention to operational details. A planning orientation is reflected in a concentration of efforts on determining organizational goals and the choice of means to achieve goals. Each of the different orientations is also reflected in the relevance of different kinds of information. The control orientation requires information about whether certain actions are taken or not. The management orientation requires measures of input-output relationships and accomplishments. The planning orientation requires projections of future events, visions of possible futures, and means of achieving possible futures.

A public organization invariably expresses its orientation in its public finance administration activities. Certain finance techniques are emphasized or used in particular ways in association with particular orientations. Also, because the orientations typically require information congruent with their purposes, the techniques are used on different information or used to develop different kinds of information. A control orientation is associated with greater attention to accounting, auditing, and expenditure administration; a management orientation with cost analysis, purchasing, cash management, and risk management; and a planning orientation with financial predictions and capital budgeting. Despite the affinity between certain techniques and orientations, any of the techniques can be used to serve any orientation. Throughout this text, the themes of control, management, and planning will be used to put the techniques and practices in perspective. Knowing what a technique or practice is oriented toward accomplishing can help us understand how an accomplishment is obtained.

These varying orientations are examples of Miles' Law: "Where you stand depends on where you sit."[2] Frequently, understanding different perspectives helps in understanding the specifics of public finance administration.

SYSTEMS IN PUBLIC ◆
FINANCE ADMINISTRATION

Public finance administration techniques are applied in differing degrees, though not always in a predictable pattern. For example, although the federal government might be thought to be more systematic, local governments are actually more systematic in their use of capital budgeting and cash management.

Technique applications range from complete systems to principles applications to single practice applications. Complete systems provide regular procedures, generally represented by written policies, for all relevant areas covered by a technique. Also, complete systems are generally reviewed periodically to make appropriate changes. Complete systems show a high degree of effort. Principles applications use one or more technique principles as practical rules of thumb to govern certain aspects of a technique area. For example, in the area of cash management, federal officials generally follow the principle that collections and payments should be made in a timely fashion. Finally, some public organizations use one or more particular practices or actions in a technique area. For example, many local governments make regular checking account deposits, a practice found in the cash management technique area.

Applications of public finance administration techniques vary because of public official interest, the utility of particular applications, or both. Public officials, both policymakers and administrators, have varying knowledge of and interest in various technique areas. Knowledge and interest can produce systems applications by themselves. The utility of technique applications can be estimated in political and monetary terms. Politically, because of problems, perceptions, or opportunities, a technique can be presented as having high utility, particularly where a problem is perceived. For example, Orange County, and many other public organizations, reviewed their investment policies because of the highly and widely publicized losses. Monetarily, applications can be valued by estimating monetarily valued costs and benefits, as in the case of the county looking at the investment in a sports stadium. In many cases, complete systems are not justified by reasonable estimates of advantages to a public organization, and principles or practice applications are more useful.

Computer systems are one example of complete system applications. The use of computers in various areas of public finance administration continues to grow and to become routine. Although computer usage affects various technique areas, however, computer applications are not discussed extensively in this text because the material on technique areas is more fundamental. Computers make more and faster computations possible but do not make them more easily understood or more appropriate. Basic understanding of the techniques makes understanding the usage of computers in the various areas intelligible.

◆ THE ORDER OF THIS BOOK

The chapters in this book are arranged by logical precedence—earlier chapters provide a basis for understanding one or more later chapters. For example, the next chapter describes relationships between public budgeting and public finance administration, which provides a comprehensive overview of the handling of public monies. The chapter on public sector accounting provides an understanding of financial information storage and retrieval and explanations of various important terms. Understanding information systems and key terms makes later chapters more intelligible. This arrangement does not lend itself to a set of multichapter book sections that stand alone. All public finance administration is intertwined, both conceptually and practially. The book, though, can be thought as having four parts. First, the initial our chapters provide a broad introduction to public finance administration, including its relationship with public budgeting, the crucial area of public ector accounting that provides many concepts used in tracking the flow of esources in and out of public organizations, and a discussion of the economic oncepts of money and value. Second, the next five chapters focus on revenues nd expenditures, how they are administered, and the importance of forecast-ng and cost analysis in dealing with revenue and expenditure flows. Third, he following seven chapters deal with various less visible, but not less impor-ant, technical areas that focus on managing cash flow, investments, debt, risk, urchasing, capital budgets, and financial components of human resource management, especially pensions. Fourth, the last three chapters take a roader and more evaluative perspective while looking at the techniques in uditing, assessing financial conditions, and the emerging use of development inance.

DISCUSSION QUESTIONS

1. What do you expect to see and be concerned about in public finance administration?
2. Why bother with the details of handling money or assets and liabilities?
3. How does public finance administration relate to other aspects of public administration? Personnel, information systems, intergovernmental re-lations, and urban governance?
4. Why did you sign up for this course?

NOTES ◆

1. This section is an adaptation of ideas initially expressed in R. N. Anthony (1965). *Planning nd control: A framework for analysis*. Boston: Division of Research, Graduate School of Business dministration, Harvard University, and expanded upon in A. Schick (1966). The road to PPB. *ublic Administration Review, 26*, 243-258.

2. R. C. Miles (1978). The origin and meaning of Miles' Law. *Public Administration Review,* 8, 399-403.

WORLD WIDE WEB SITES ◆

Note: This general site will lead you to other more substantive sites. This is public finance administration and budgeting home page created by the lepartment of one of the authors. Because of the rapid changes in technology nd content providers, other more specific web and other site connections vill not be listed here but can be found at the first web site listed below. If you ave any problems with accessing that site, e-mail B. J. Reed at 3reed@fa-cpacs.unomaha.edu.

http://www.unomaha.edu/~wwwpa/fsite.html

◆ SUGGESTED READINGS

J. Richard Aronson and Eli Schwartz (Eds.). (1987). *Management policies in local governmen finance* (3rd ed.). Washington, DC: International City Management Association.

John L. Mikesell (1995). *Fiscal administration* (4th ed.). Pacific Grove, CA: Brooks/Cole.

John E. Petersen and Dennis Strachota (Eds.). (1991). *Local government finance: Concepts an practices*. Chicago: Government Finance Officers Association.

Budgeting and Finance Administration

How public finance administration relates to public budgeting puzzles many people. Both areas are public and involve money. To many people, the terms overlap. This impression is reinforced by texts used in the general area. Public budgeting, public finance, and mixed topic texts cover the same and divergent topics without any apparent order, rhyme, or reason. This chapter clarifies what public budgeting is and how it relates to public finance administration. The two areas are highly interrelated and not completely separable. Public budgeting is the process of making decisions about public revenues and expenditures; public finance administration concerns the techniques used in dealing with public monies. The two are only clearly distinct in concept.

PUBLIC BUDGETING ◆

Public budgeting can be defined as the planned acquisition and use of resources by public entities, similar to what individuals and households do when making and spending money. This simple definition obscures the numerous highly complicated and interrelated phenomena that constitute public budgeting, such as the following:

- The large number of people involved
- The fact that budgets deal with public or communal concerns about which people have different viewpoints
- The extended time periods, typically a year
- The fact that budgets are binding
- The technical difficulties of the subject matters (e.g., nuclear waste disposal, health research, and economic relationships)
- The sheer size of the resources involved

Budgeting proposals and results are recorded in documents that are plans for gathering and spending money over some time period. One distinctive feature of public budgeting is the number of different documents that are used by a variety of persons, at different times, and for different purposes. The number of documents reflects the fact that public budgeting is a formal process used to coordinate the activities of large numbers of people. Individuals and households budget only for themselves; public organizations budget for themselves and their constituents.

Personal and household budgets can be for any point in time to any other point in time, from formal to very informal, and from rigid to flexible to the changing at any point in time. Because public budgets involve numerous people and are binding for fixed time periods, they proceed through a formalized process with distinctive beginnings and endings and definite intermediate steps.

The public budgeting process is described as having four general stages, which are given various names:

1. Preparation or formulation
2. Submission and approval, policy making, legal enactment, or formal approval
3. Implementation or execution
4. Audit and review, audit, audit and evaluation, or review

The first stage involves preparing estimates of revenues and expenditures for a specific, future time period. The beginning is found in *the call* or *call letter* that directs various officials to fulfill budgeting responsibilities. The timing of the call can be fixed by law or can be a matter of administrative or executive convenience. Estimating revenues and expenditures is undertaken in various places. Usually, and especially with taxes, estimates of revenues are made by central administrative officials. Estimates of expenditures are made by operating units under the general direction of instructions found in the call letter. Estimating expenditures generally involves considering what activities or policies to propose, what things should be purchased to carry out organizational activities or policies, and what the prices are likely to be. The operating agencies are proponents of spending, and the central officials are proponents of economizing and of care in the selection of spending choices.

The second stage of the budgeting process begins when the chief executive or administrative officer submits a proposed budget to the policy-making or legislative body. Policymakers look at the information in the proposed budget along with other information available to them. A proposed budget is treated as another proposed policy or law. The process is one of gathering information, looking at alternatives, and voting on preferred policies. This stage concludes when the proposed budget with any changes is approved as a policy or policies, or as a law or laws that provide authorizations to operating officials to collect and spend money.

The third stage of the budgetary process is the period when money is spent and collected: The approved budget plan is carried into action. This stage is

he primary reason that budgets exist: to fund the provision of public-sector
;oods and services.

The fourth stage of the process involves auditing and reviewing the ap-
•roved budget's implementation. Both reviews and audits involve looking at
hings to ascertain that an organization is performing well. People within
•ublic organizations conduct reviews, usually informally, although annual
eports are formal yearly reviews. Reviews answer questions concerning how
vell or appropriate the budget and the organization meet their obligations
nd opportunities. Audits are technical reviews culminating in a formal
eport, usually conducted by persons outside of the organization, that speak
o specific questions. Examples of such questions include whether the organiation followed standard accounting rules, complied with budget decisions,
,ad procedures to guard resources and the accuracy of financial data, and
•erformed in an economical, efficient, and effective manner. Audits are fre-
uently required by laws or by persons outside of the specific organizational
nits being audited.

Public budgeting is highly political; it determines whose policy preferences
•revail. Decisions on whether to raise or lower taxes or expenditures, to build
•ombers or provide health care for the poor, and to hire police or social
vorkers are all public budget decisions, as is any other public sector decision
bout the collecting or spending of money. Politics are especially evident in
he first two stages of the process. Federal officials debate issues of taxes,
lefense, and social spending. State officials predominantly choose among
axes, education, highways, prisons, and welfare. Local government spending
hoices abound whereas easy revenues elude officials. Expenditure opportu-
ities for nonprofit organizations exceed their revenues as well.

Public budgeting can be viewed from a wide variety of perspectives. Already,
t has been discussed as being a plan, a process, and a matter of politics.
ikewise, budgets can be seen as control, management, and planning devices.
'arious other identifiable participants provide perspectives useful for under-
tanding the process. For politicians or policymakers, decisions on revenues
nd expenditures fulfill their responsibility to act for public organizations and
o meet constituent concerns. From a constituent's perspective, the budget
nay or may not reflect public service and revenue preferences. For econo-
nists, budgets allocate resources, distribute costs and benefits, and stabilize
conomies, as well as represent choices under conditions of scarcity. For
•perating officials, budgets represent constraints that restrict their activities
•y controlling the provision of resources to operate (i.e., the budget within
vhich they have to stay).

Expenditure budgets are prepared using a variety of different approaches.
A *budget approach* refers to a general way of doing a budget that includes
•articular ideas and reflects different concerns. Approaches use different
nformation and organize information differently to answer different ques-
ions. Lump sum budgeting, the simplest approach to public budgeting, was
ised widely until this century. This approach presents expenditure decisions
.s lump sums to fund public organizations or organizational units. It answers

the question, "How much for each organizational unit?" The line item ap
proach is currently the most common one in the United States. All the thing
to be purchased, the objects of expenditure, are listed, one to a line, fo
example:

Paperclips . . . 10 cases (10,000 to the case) . . . $50.00.

The line item approach answers the questions of how much a public organi
zation will be buying at what price. This is the most familiar approach and th
one most people describe when asked to describe a budget. Three late
approaches emphasize other concerns: Performance budgeting focuses atten
tion on what activities are performed and the relative efficiency with whicl
they are performed (i.e., "bang for the buck"). Program budgeting focuse
attention on effectiveness by looking at the predicted results from budgets
Zero-base budgeting focuses attention on choices by providing budget alter
natives.

A variety of techniques is used in public budgeting, some used in differen
fields and some mostly or exclusively in budgeting. Cost-benefit and cost
effectiveness analysis, trend analysis, operations research, and regression analysi
are widely applied analytical techniques that are sometimes used in budgeting
Multiyear financial projections, crosswalks of budget information from on
form of organization to another, and financial capacity evaluation are analyti
cal techniques generally used in connection with public budgeting concerns
These examples show a few of the many techniques used in public budgeting
This text deals with public finance administration techniques, all of whicl
bear some relationship to public budgeting.

◆ RELATIONSHIP BETWEEN PUBLIC BUDGETING
AND PUBLIC FINANCE ADMINISTRATION

How public budgeting and public finance administration relate can b
viewed from a conceptual and a practical viewpoint. Public budgeting focuse
on the issues of alternative choices, typically at a broad level of detail. From
conceptual viewpoint, public budgeting relates to all areas of public financ
administration, but it does so in a general sense. Public budgeting provide
the arena for the large decisions, the what. Public finance administration deal
with the smaller decisions, the how. Public budgeting encompasses and brack
ets public finance administration. Public budgeting is the activity carried ou
by political actors and upper-level administrators to determine the outcom
of public revenue and expenditure decisions; public finance administratio
activities are carried out, principally, at and by lower levels of public organi
zations. This distinction between making budget decisions and carrying then
out may not provide a perfectly unambiguous dividing line, but it shows th
different thrusts of the areas. When a government decides that a dam acros
a raging river is the appropriate response to a perceived need for flood contro
that decision is a budgetary one and is recorded in budgeting documents. A
the handling of monies after the budgetary decision is made falls into th

realm of public finance administration, which is concerned with carrying out organizational functions by applying particular techniques. In a sense, public finance administration can be seen as involving the detail work underlying and following budget decision making.

Much like the distinction between politics and administration, public budgeting and finance administration may not be irrevocably separable. The distinction may be only conceptual and, practically, a question of focus. Public budgeting decisions set the agenda for public finance administration activities. Public finance administration processing techniques are used to gather information for conducting and analyzing budgetary debates and issues. Like the politics-administration dichotomy, the public budgeting and public finance administration distinction may break down ultimately where public budgeting at the higher levels and its associated politics come into contact with the work of the public organization and public finance administration at the lower levels.

Practically, public finance administration involves techniques. Many techniques can be grouped together in various ways. Techniques can be grouped under the themes of control, management, and planning; into management and analysis groups; into asset and liability management groups reflecting an accounting viewpoint; and into groups for the budgetary process stages. For the sake of clarifying the relationship between public budgeting and public finance administration, particular techniques are listed in Table 2.1 under the stage of the budgetary process with which each is most closely associated.

The preparation stage of budgeting involves predicting future events and analyzing budget choices. Therefore, relevant techniques and related topics are discussed here. Still, techniques generally more relevant to other budget stages can be used or considered during this stage. The preparation stage is a time to forecast revenues and expenditures. How much will be collected and how much will be spent provides the basis for budgetary discussions. The amount of money collected in revenues is the typical limiting factor on expenditures. How much a particular policy, program, or other budget entity is expected to cost affects its consideration. Preliminary estimates of revenue and expenditures are the starting points for serious budget decision making. This is a technical area of great political consequence, as estimates form the political terrain for budgetary politics, with some of the various forecasts being technically plausible but also politically convenient.

Cost analysis is used to weigh alternatives so choices can be made. These analytical techniques are used to choose and support expenditure choices. Simple cost analysis is similar to expenditure estimation. In cost-effectiveness analysis, the benefits of options are assumed and the cost per unit produced is estimated to choose among alternatives. In cost-benefit analysis, costs and benefits of policies, projects, or operating methods are compared to facilitate making an informed choice. Arguments and information from these analytical techniques often find their way into budget approval sessions. These kinds of analyses also are commissioned in the budget implementation stage for later decision on issues in the approval stage of the next budget cycle.

Capital budgeting, which has various manifestations, is done both in connection with and separately from the regular budget process. Capital items are

TABLE 2.1   Public Budgeting Stages and Public Finance Administration
           Techniques

Stages	Techniques/Areas
1. Preparation:	Forecasting revenues and expenditures, Cost analysis, Capital budgeting, Debt administration, Risk management, Pension administration and other personnel issues, Assessing financial conditions, Economic development and development finance
2. Approval:	Policymakers look at information developed in preparation stage and revenues
3. Implementation:	Accounting, Revenue administration, Expenditure administration, Purchasing, Cash management, and Investment
4. Audit and Review:	Auditing

investments in physical assets with extended utility (e.g., buildings, roads, vehicles, and other equipment), which are treated differently from regular, recurrent items of expenditure (e.g., personnel, transfer payments, and expendable supplies). Where budgets are divided into an operating budget and a capital budget, the capital budget represents a multiyear plan for expenditures on capital items. Usually, expenditures are authorized simultaneously for both budgets for a one-year period. Where there is not a separate capital budget, capital items are often given extraordinary treatment in criteria for selection of capital items, purchasing processes, approval for inclusion in a proposed budget, and analysis. Often, cost analysis is applied to capital items.

Debt administration involves acquiring and paying back borrowed money. Debt is usually incurred as a result of capital projects that are funded separately from regular budgets. Debt is paid for in each regular budget, however. The federal government, of course, is exceptional in debt (perhaps phenomenal resonates better), because debt has been used more for economic policy and political reasons than as a means of funding capital projects.

Debt administration is characterized by multiyear expenditures, a characteristic shared by two areas—risk management and pension administration—that are sufficiently closely related for all three to be called liability administration. All three areas also involve multiyear obligations, that is, future monetary obligations.

Risk management, minimizing the adverse consequences of "the slings and arrows of outrageous fortune," affects regular operating budgets in two general ways: decision about what to do and not to do and paying for or financing risks. First, certain programs, policies, procedures, facilities, and expenditures may not be chosen or may be handled differently as a result of risk management analysis. Risks and their potential costs can be too great to justify doing something or can justify additional expenditures to make things safer. Second, operating budgets show funding for risks. Risks are potential losses that may or may not occur. Funding can take the form of insurance payments, the transfer of monies to contingency accounts to pay for risk losses, or expenditures to pay for actual losses (e.g., replacement of items or damage claims).

Pension administration, which involves making arrangements for payments to be made to employees or their dependents when they are no longer employed by an organization, should show up in regular budgets as a cost of operating. Unfortunately, this is often not the case. Despite the fact that pensions are financed out of the same revenue sources as other expenditures, pensions are paid out over an extended time period. Currently employed personnel will be paid pension benefits in the future, and these payments are often left out of budgets. This is a serious omission, as pensions are a significant portion of expenditures for personnel, which is most frequently the largest public organizational expenditure. At the state and local level, personnel expenditures are frequently more than half of the expenditures made. To predict future budgetary costs accurately, one has to predict the cost of pensions as well as other personnel costs, such as direct wage payments, fringe benefits, collateral expenditures, and raises.

An assessment of the financial condition of a public organization contributes to budget preparation by determining areas of financial strengths and weaknesses. For example, an organization with insufficient revenue flows might avoid debt, or a government with excessive cash balances might lower taxes. Such assessments can be used to guide operating and capital budgeting decisions.

Development finance is concerned with using the financial tools available to public organizations, principally governments, to increase favorable economic activity. It is a part of the general area of economic development that is generally concerned with increasing economic activity. Public organizations participate in development finance by providing financial incentives to encourage persons to engage in favored economic activities. These financial incentives provide means by which projects can occur that otherwise would not be possible. The key here is that incentives change the situation. Incentives include tax incentives, public organization financial participation in projects, and a variety of innovative financing techniques to assist entrepreneurs in accumulating capital for a project.

The approval stage of the budget process involves the policymakers looking at all of the relevant information presented in budget proposals, along with any gathered during budget hearings. At this stage, policymakers often consider policy issues having to do with revenues for the sake of making adjustments. Revenues are interesting in the budget process principally as a funding mechanism and as a matter of political controversy. Revenue measures define an art form concerned with separating people and money. Also, revenue characteristics are relevant to revenue administration. Policymakers figure out what to do to acquire revenues, and administrators have the pleasure of finding out how to make revenue policies work in practice. This reminds some revenue administrators of the mice's proposal to bell the cat.

The budget implementation stage includes the technique areas of accounting, revenue administration, expenditure administration, purchasing, cash management, and investment. Public-sector accounting involves making records of financial activities that occur during the implementation stage. The records developed in this stage—measurements of actual revenues and actual expenditures—form the basis for estimates of expenditures and revenues

during the next budget preparation stages, audits and reviews of the implemen
tation of the budget, and financial decisions during budget implementation.

Revenue administration deals with finding the revenue base, assessing it
value, and collecting money from individuals and organizations. It require
providing information to people to persuade them to send money to publi
organizations.

Expenditure administration handles making payments for spending com
mitments. Unlike a personal situation, where an individual or family spend
money by making choices and paying by cash, check, or through some credi
arrangement, public organizations extend the process of spending money
Typically, certain people decide what money to spend (budgeteers); someone
buys something or makes transfer decisions, usually under the supervision o
some superior (operating officials); someone else pays the bill (treasur
officials); and someone else will later review the expenditure (auditors). A
emphasis on controlling behavior to ensure that public monies are not mis
used, which necessitates voluminous accounting records, characterizes expen
diture administration.

Although expenditure administration focuses on actually spending mone
and how it changes hands, purchasing deals with the actions associated wit
buying goods and services other than hiring personnel. Purchasing involve
figuring out what, when, and how to buy, with particular attention to decidin
what to buy and what costs to incur.

Cash management relates to implementing both sides of a budget. In cas
management, one attempts to predict and adjust the flows of cash to benefi
a public organization. This involves bringing revenue into the treasury in
timely fashion, paying bills on time, and investing money.

Public organizations make investments from money on hand (e.g., mone
from cash management or borrowing), and from money put aside for futur
purposes (e.g., pensions and risk management). Money on hand that is no
otherwise used serves a public organization best by being invested becaus
investments provide revenues. Of course, the situation in which money i
being invested determines the choice of investments. Basically, money i
invested in either an obligation (debt) or an equity (ownership) situation. A
obligation or debt situation occurs when money is loaned or entrusted t
another party, which creates a debt obligation with some interest paymen
being the investment benefit; an equity or ownership situation occurs whe
money is used to purchase some valuable thing that is expected to produc
income, an increase in value, or both.

The fourth and final stage of the budget process, the audit and review stage
appears to be relatively simple but is actually one of the most complex areas
The complexity stems from the wide variety of audit purposes and technique
because those techniques require collateral actions during the preparation an
the implementation stages, because some auditing can take place in th
implementation stage or at any point or period of time following the comple
tion of budget implementation, and because audits take place while othe
budget stage activities are taking place. Performance auditing is one kind o
audit. In performance auditing, certain activities are defined as performance
before budget implementation, recorded during budget implementation, an

analyzed during the audit stage. Other kinds of audits include ones concerning accounting systems and reports, management procedures, and effectiveness. Audits guide the other budget stages. Likewise, reviews of and reports on an agency's or organization's budget year using various methods of analysis can be quite complex.

CONCLUSION ◆

Although public budgeting and public finance administration are conceptually distinguishable, in the world of practice one can always be said to be dealing with a public budget when one is engaged in public finance administration activities. The reader has been shown the conceptual and practical distinctions between the technical focus of public finance administration and the political focus of public budgeting. Budgeting activities can be thought of as the tip of the iceberg that is most visible; finance activities are less visible and a larger portion of the whole set of connected activities. As with icebergs, one is well advised to pay attention to the submerged as well as exposed portions of public organizations' finances.

DISCUSSION QUESTIONS

1. How do you think public budgeting contributes to public finance administration?
2. What technique areas do you think of as being most important for public budgeting?
3. What information do public budgeting and public finance administration share?

SUGGESTED READINGS ◆

Donald Axelrod (1995). *Budgeting for modern government* (2nd ed.). New York: St. Martin's.
Robert D. Lee, Jr. and Ronald W. Johnson (1989). *Public budgeting systems* (4th ed.). Rockville, MD: Aspen Publishers.
Thomas D. Lynch (1995). *Public budgeting in America* (4th ed.). Englewood Cliffs, NJ: Prentice-Hall.
Irene S. Rubin (1993). *The politics of public budgeting* (2nd ed.). Chatham, NJ: Chatham House.

Public-Sector Accounting

Accounting, despite a great deal of mystique, can be understood as the recording and reporting of financial information. Part of accounting's mystique stems from the professional accounting jargon. One example of such jargon is the commonly used definition of "fund":

> A fiscal and accounting entity with a self-balancing set of accounts recording cash and other financial resources, together with all related liabilities and residual equities or balances, and changes therein, which are segregated for the purpose of carrying on specific activities or attaining certain objectives in accordance with special regulations, restrictions, or limitations.[1]

A fund can be described less technically and more intelligibly as a separate set of accounts established to keep track of particular things. Separateness fundamentally defines a fund. Here, accounting terms and concepts are presented and explained with a minimum of technical jargon.

Another part of accounting's mystique has to do with numbers, a math phobia if you will. Fortunately, the mathematics actually involved are adding and subtracting. One does not have to penetrate the mysteries of secret accounting rituals nor enter the higher realms of mathematics to understand public-sector accounting (henceforth referred to as public accounting). Knowledge of the purposes, concepts, and practices of public accounting and basic arithmetic is sufficient to understand public accounting thoroughly.

Accounting is important in public finance administration because accounting systems primarily provide financial information for public organizations when decisions concerning money are made. The accounting system provides answers to such questions as

- How much money is on hand?
- What can be spent on personnel?
- Has money been collected and spent as it was budgeted?
- How much does it cost to . . . ?

Accounting systems can be said to serve the control, management, and planning purposes of public finance administration. Public accounting emphasizes control. Budgeted expenditure information, that is, how much money can be spent by what organizational units for what, is introduced into accounting systems to control expenditures. For example, a particular office budget may allow $1000 for office supplies. Not only is that information in the accounting system but also how much has been spent and how much remains available to be spent (the balance). The person authorized to expend the $1000 for office supplies, the accounting office, and higher-level officials have the same information available to them. This use of accounting prevents improper spending. The same sort of information for the entire budget is available to oversight authorities and the public of the various governmental jurisdictions. The availability of budgetary information in the accounting system makes it possible to track actual expenditures in relation to budgeted expenditures, which is a prerequisite for control.

Accounting systems provide information to make managerial decisions of an operational and financial character. If money available for office supplies is running out, that information could lead to decisions aimed at conserving such supplies. Likewise, accounting information showing a surplus in another account and a dwindling office supplies account might lead to shifting money into the office supplies account. Management decisions concerned with money are based on accounting system information.

Accounting systems provide information that allow people to make financial plans. Plans are usually based on predictions that the future will be much like the past. Budgets, for example, are plans based primarily on the experiences of previous years as recorded in the accounting system. Cash management provides another example of using accounting information for planning, where one uses past years' revenue and expenditure patterns to anticipate the current-year pattern. How public accounting supports these three purposes will become more clear as particular examples are discussed in later chapters.

ACCOUNTING: ◆
PUBLIC VERSUS PRIVATE

Public accounting differs from private accounting in many respects. The key distinction involves the uses to which accounting information can be put. Private accounting information is oriented toward showing net worth and profits. Public organizations are never sold nor do they make a profit; therefore, net worth and profit are pointless for public organizations. Public accounting is oriented toward showing flows of money—generally revenues and expenditures—particularly in relationship to budgeted amounts. The control orientation reflects the fact that public organizations are bound by budgetary authorizations to collect revenues and to make expenditures. Also, because both have the same information categories, public accounting systems are said to "mirror" budgets. To overspend a budget is a violation of budget law or policy as well as a demonstration of political insensitivity. Public organizations prevent that by tracking their budgets in their accounting systems, which is one reason for public accounting systems primarily showing concern with the control of public funds. Many specific differences in concepts and practices reflect these fundamental differences between public and private accounting.

Two noteworthy differences in the public sector are the diverse kinds and sources of accounting rules (more formally "the authoritative sources of accounting standards"). Businesses have one basic set of accounting rules from one source. In contrast, the six categories of areas covered by differing accounting rules are colleges and universities, hospitals, voluntary health and welfare organizations, nonprofit organizations, state and local governments, and the federal government. Each of the different categories has two or more sources of accounting rules.[2] Also, over the last several years, various sources keep developing new accounting and reporting rules, which have caused some consternation in public organizations as they became required to do new and different things. Some of the new rules require recording and reporting the value of employees' accumulated leave, nonprofit organization pledges, and performance measures.

◆ FINANCIAL REPORTS—
THE END RESULT OF ACCOUNTING

The purpose of accounting is to make financial information available. Information comes out of accounting systems in financial reports. Here, by starting with the end results, financial reports, the reader can see what all of the hoopla along the way is about.

Accounting systems use a wide variety of standard accounting reports and countless other optional reports. Reports vary by time period, scope, and level of detail. Differences in reports are determined by the people for whom they are prepared. An administrator concerned with $1,000 appropriated for office supplies wants to know how much money has been spent and how much can still be spent (the balance), whereas governing officials do not care about those office supplies and use much less detailed reports. For the most part, those using accounting reports find them tailored to their needs, however imperfect that tailoring may be.

The time periods involved for various reports are a year or series of years; a quarter, which is the first, second, third, or fourth set of three-month period in a year (e.g., January 1 to March 31 is the first quarter); a month; and any specifically requested period or point in time. Yearly reports are almost universal, and quarterly or monthly reports are common in all but the smallest organizations. The particular period or point in time reports are used to reach specific decisions; for example, whether we have money to buy more office supplies.

The scope and detail of reports vary. Generally, the broader the scope, the less detail there is; conversely the narrower the scope, the more details there are. The administrator of an office uses a detailed accounting report for that office, whereas a governing official uses a more general report covering all the various organizational units. The scope of reports ranges from a particular transaction, through a particular account or set of accounts to an organizational unit, to a comprehensive report of all financial information for a public organization. Likewise, the level of detail varies. Some degree of summarization of detail is necessary to make the reports useful. The greatest detail possible includes all information in all the accounts in the accounting system. Generally, the most detailed reports are for the expenditure accounts for the lowest level of organizational subdivisions; those reports show the appropriation, the amount expended in some fashion, and the balance (the amount still available to spend for expenditure accounts). Revenue reports are as detailed, but only the central finance offices have many of those accounts. Also, there are many more expenditure accounts than revenue accounts. In revenue accounts, one finds estimated revenues, revenues collected in some fashion, and the balance (revenues remaining to be collected). Normally, reports for officials at higher organizational levels are less detailed and summarized by different categories such as organizational unit, objects of expenditure, and the like. The following discussion of the different report users shows the variety in accounting reports.

The users of financial reports are administrators, governing officials, the public, and the financial community. Each of these groups has fundamentally different information needs because they have different purposes and do different things. Administrators need the most specific reports to make operational decisions and detailed plans. Governing officials, unless they are probing or reviewing a very specific question, are concerned with the overall financial position of the whole organization. The public takes a perspective similar to governing officials except that the public is not usually as interested. The financial community's interest focuses on the creditworthiness of governments to make decisions about lending money to public organizations. Other groups, such as special interest groups, researchers, and employee unions, generally use the reports intended for the public.

Managers need the most specific information to make day-to-day decisions. The lower the level of the organizational subdivision, the greater the detail that is needed. For example, an office manager is likely to get a monthly report detailing the balances in all the accounts for that office, including the office supplies account. Part of that report would include the following:

Account	Budgeted	Spent	Available to Spend
Office Supplies	$1,000	$500	$500 (balance)

The office manager can see the situation for all of the office accounts in a straightforward fashion. If the report comes early in the fiscal year, the manager may have a problem in the office supplies account because half of the appropriation has been spent. If the report is late in the fiscal year, the manager has some flexibility. Occasionally, lower-level managers need more specific information and keep their own records or request specific information.

Higher-level managers receive less detailed reports but also have access to the more detailed reports distributed to lower-level managers. For example, a manager responsible for three organizational subdivisions is likely to receive less detailed reports than the managers of those three subdivisions.

Such reports might include the following:

Organizational Unit	Budgeted	Spent	Available for Expenditure
Unit X	$30,000	$15,000	$15,000
Unit Y	$43,000	$26,000	$17,000
Unit Z	$37,000	$17,000	$20,000

This report shows the financial situation of the three organizational subdivisions. The manager receiving this report is likely to look further into the situation of Unit Y, unless already known, because that unit is spending money much more rapidly than the other two units, which marks it as having an unusual situation, if not some problem. The two options for the higher-level manager are talking to the Unit Y manager or looking at the more detailed Unit Y report, which this manager may or may not receive on a regular basis. In addition, higher-level managers frequently receive *exception reports*. An exception report is made when certain specific exceptions to what is expected occur. For example, for Unit Y, an exception report might be a copy of Unit Y's detailed report going to one or more upper-level managers because its spending exceeded one half of its budget before the fiscal year midpoint. Another kind of exception report might be a listing by organizational unit of every account that shows expenditures in excess of one half of the budgeted amount during the same time period. The result is the same. Upper-level managers are apprised of exceptions as they occur. Exception reports are one way of tracking compliance with administrative directives. The regular reports distributed to managers in public organizations become less specific at the higher levels of organizations, except in small organizations, because too many details are not very useful. The less detailed, broader reports along with exception reports make it possible to track the organizations' finances without requiring managers to wade through page after page of detailed reports. The higher managerial levels are not concerned about the $1000 office supplies situation unless it poses a particular problem.

Governing officials receive regular reports that are comprehensive in breadth and not particularly detailed. Elected officials look to accounting reports that show budget plans in broad outline to see that they are being implemented as planned. An example for a governing official might appear as follows:

	Second Quarter, 1997	
	Estimated	Actual
Revenues	$4,000,000	$4,012,383
Expenditures	$3,840,000	$3,785,000

Organizational Unit	Budgeted	Spent	Available for Expenditure
Agency A	$100,000	$ 50,000	$ 50,000
Agency B	$149,000	$ 72,838	$ 76,162
Agency C	$211,000	$110,050	$100,950

Deviations from the budget signal a need to gather more detailed information and perhaps a need to alter the budget plan. When budgetary changes are contemplated, more detailed information is used by governing officials to make policy decisions. One prime example is found in budget proposals submitted to elected officials, which usually contain at least one previous year and the current year's information for most categories in a budget. An example might look something like this:

Budget Proposal: Unit X

Requested	Budgeted This Year	Budgeted Last Year	Year-to-Date Expenditures
Office Supplies			
1300	$1000	$900	$1000

The public uses very general annual reports to form an overall impression of a government's or nonprofit organization's operations. Constituents receive information on public organizations through the medium of news reports, more often broadcast than print ones. The information received by the public typically includes revenues by source, expenditure by function or organizational subdivisions, the financial results of operations (surplus or deficit), and debt. Sometimes, such reports represent figures in bar graphs and pie charts. Such information shows in a general way what an organization is doing and where it stands financially. An example of information for the general public from accounting reports might look like this:

Mudville Finances, 1997

Revenues by Source

Sales Tax	$ 2,000,000
Property Tax	$ 7,000,000
Miscellaneous	$ 1,500,000
Total	$10,500,000

Expenditures by Function	
Administration	$ 500,000
Public Safety	$ 4,500,000
Public Works	$ 3,000,000
Recreation	$ 1,500,000
Total	$ 9,500,000
Surplus	$ 1,000,000
Outstanding Debt	$ 3,000,000

The financial community reviews financial reports of public organizations, primarily state and local governments, as a way to evaluate organizations ability to repay loans. State and local governments "sell" bonds, which are nothing more than legally binding promises to repay the price of the bond (the principal) plus interest at some future time. As with other credit situations, the people lending money have an intense interest in being certain that they are lending money to someone who has the ability to meet the payments. Annual financial reports are an important component of the information used by financial institutions and ratings services to evaluate creditworthiness. Some of the measures used are overall indebtedness, revenue capacity, and operating results (surpluses or deficits). Financial community member concerned with lending money to Mudville would look at the same information provided to the public but also at other indicators of financial condition including multiple years of annual financial reports. In that manner, the financial community can observe whether Mudville's financial position is improving or declining and, more important, judge whether Mudville can pay back its loans. Though the financial community starts with accounting system information, it looks at many other things.

The whole range of possible reports and suggested reporting requirement staggers the imagination. In addition to internal reports for differing time periods, organizational units and levels, and degrees of detail, external report show the same information arrayed in different ways along with even more information not in accounts. An illustrative example of such an external report, a Comprehensive Annual Financial Report, in *Governmental Accounting, Auditing, and Financial Reporting,* has a table of contents of approximately four and one-half pages and more than 129 pages of reported data and text.

◆ ACCOUNTING CYCLE AND ACCOUNTING DOCUMENTS

So far, public accounting has been discussed in general terms and for the final product of accounting, financial reports. Let us now focus on the practices of accounting, that is, how accounting is done.

All accounting operates on a general cycle of events that begins with the recording of a financial transaction and ends with reports. The cycle consist of four steps:

1. Financial transaction and evidence of that transaction
2. Entering the transaction into a journal
3. Posting journal entries to a ledger
4. Obtaining information in a ledger for reports

These terms will become familiar as each stage of the accounting cycle is described; most have to do with the written documents produced at each stage of the cycle. Because computerized accounting systems use a slightly different cycle and are harder to understand, we will use the traditional cycle and documents and afterward briefly discuss how computerized accounting systems differ. The typical documents include

1. Evidence of a transaction (receipt, voucher, budget)
2. Journal (general and special journals)
3. Ledger (general and special ledgers)
4. Reports

For the sake of illustration, a single *transaction* can be followed through the cycle. A transaction means an event about which information is gathered. Suppose that a transaction involves a supplier of paper selling 10 cartons of paper to a government agency. When that occurs, the variety of documents produced can include a purchase order, a shipping or delivery voucher, and a receipt. Among all these documents produced, the public organization uses one or more to record the transaction. This occurs according to specific rules, often using forms designed for a specific type of transaction for a particular public organization. The rules cover what constitutes a financial transaction, when to record it, and what information to record. Everything a public organization wants to know about any transaction has to be recorded; hence special forms are used. At a minimum, the government records the date, the amount, what was purchased, and who was paid. Many more items could also be recorded; most commonly included are an account number signifying the organizational unit and the source or category of budget authority. An example of a voucher (a payment authorization) for this transaction would be that for Mudville, as shown below.

Payment Voucher 347   Date: January 30, 1997

Account Number: 03-231-003
Item(s) Purchased: 10 Cartons of Paper   Price: $300
Supplier: Ajax Paper Company
Payment: Warrant 73005   Signed:_____

By looking at this document closely, we can find what is being recorded in the accounting system. Mudville refers to the public organization, in this case the City of Mudville. From left to right, one first finds the term *Payment Voucher 347*. *Voucher* is a term meaning a supporting document, usually for expenditures. In this case, the voucher was designed to collect accounting system information and indicate that the items purchased have been received. The number "347" is a unique, usually preprinted, number that identifies this particular payment voucher. All the payment vouchers are filed in numerical order, and if someone decides to review this financial transaction, 347 can be found after 346 and before 348. Documents in an accounting system are designed for cross-referencing for the sake of double-checking. By using document numbers, any and all transactions can be traced through the accounting cycle. When documents have no numbers, they are filed by date. The date "January 30, 1997," provides information for the time dimension of financial reports as well as uniquely identifying the transaction as occurring on this particular day and no other, which distinguishes it from all similar transactions.

The account number "03-231-003" represents one of the most unnecessarily mystifying aspects of accounting. All that an account number signifies is a name; any account number is simply a shorthand way of naming something. Your name identifies you just as numbers on team members identify them (e.g., number 34, Shaquille O'Neal). An account is an information category. The numbers identify in which account (information category) to record gathered information. The numbers here indicate the expenditure (03), Administrative Services Office (231), and Office Supplies (003) account.

The "items purchased" is self-explanatory. The "price" indicates the amount of money involved. The signature on this document might be either the person processing the transaction or the person who is authorized to spend money. The requirement of signatures on accounting documents is used to locate responsibility for an action. With a signature, it is practically impossible for a person to deny doing or knowing about something. The "Payment: Warrant 73005" is an entry made by the finance office when the payment was made to the vendor. The term *warrant* refers to a government check. The number, again, is used for cross-referencing. All of this information indicates that the paper transaction has occurred and that the vendor has been paid.

The next event in the accounting cycle is entering the evidence of a financial transaction into a journal. *Entering* simply means writing, and *journal* refers to a document created by entering evidence in a particular, systematic way. The key feature that organizes journals is that evidence is entered in chronological order, that is, by date. For transactions that occur frequently, often special journals are used to record one particular kind of transaction (e.g., payroll, warrants, and property tax payments). Periodically, special journal information is summarized and entered into the general journal. The general journal is a record of all transactions for an organization. The idea behind special journals is that detailed information of a particular kind should be kept together and that the general journal should not become crowded with minute detail. Journal entries include pieces of information similar to the original evidence documents; however, the information is systematically organized and augmented in the journal. One version of a general journal entry for the illustrative paper transaction might be as follows.

General Journal

Transaction Date	Document Number	Number		Accounts	Debit	Credit
May 1	4711	Voucher	347	03-231-003	$300	
		Warrant	73005	01-231-003		$300

The heading indicates that this is the General Journal. The date is self-explanatory. The transaction number 4711 is a unique number for this journal entry, which identifies it. Later in the accounting cycle, this number can be used to trace this particular transaction. The document numbers are the same as those on the payment voucher discussed earlier. The account numbers show our old friend 03-231-003 and a closely related number, 01-231-003. The only difference in the account names is in the first two digits, 01 instead of 03. As you remember, 231 stands for Administrative Services Office, and 003 stands for Office Supplies. The first, 01, stands for Cash, and 03 stands for Expenditure. The accounts shown are "Cash-Administrative Services Office-Office Supplies" and "Expenditure-Administrative Services Office-Office Supplies." This practice is more precise, less time-consuming, and less confusing compared with using full account names. The two accounts are listed here because the financial transaction being accounted for affects them. The cash account, 01, is listed because a warrant was written against that account and sent to the vendor. Just as for a personal checking account, the warrant amount is recorded to keep track of the balance available in the cash account. Likewise, the expenditure account, 03-231-003, is listed to keep track of this expenditure. It should be noted that the documents—the voucher and the warrant—are listed on the same line as the accounts that they affect; the warrant affects the cash account and the payment voucher affects the expenditure account.

This brings us to the point that the dreaded *debits* and *credits* can be introduced. Take a deep breath and listen closely. As unbelievable as it may sound, debits and credits are no big deal. Exhale. To the uninitiated, this may come as a wild surprise. If you understand the following four words, you can understand the meaning of debit and credit: *left, right, add,* and *subtract.* Let's start with left and right. Debit means left, and credit means right. As you can see in the journal example, the debit entry is on the left and the credit on the right. Debit and credit entries are on separate lines and on the left and right to ensure that they are entered correctly. Debits always are entered in the left-hand column and credits in the right-hand column. Debits and credits also indicate whether the amount listed is to be added to or subtracted from something. In the example here, $300 is added to an expenditure account, 03, and $300 is subtracted from the cash account, 01. In this example, why the particular addition and subtraction are made is easily understood: $300 paid to Ajax Paper Company means $300 less cash, so subtract from the cash account; $300 spent on paper means $300 more expenditure, so add to the expenditure account. Deciding what to debit and what to credit, that mysterious accounting rite, goes by the name of *analysis.* In any accounting system set rules determine what accounts to debit and credit in particular circum stances (add to or subtract from). The difficulties associated with learning about debits and credits primarily arise from learning the rules for what accounts to debit and to credit in different circumstances. Because each entry involves at least one debit and one credit entry concerning the same transac tion, confusion can easily occur. How the adding and subtracting aspects of debits and credits work will be developed later. Whenever a transaction is entered, at least one debit and one credit entry are always made.

Finally, it should be noted that the journal entry omits some information on the payment voucher, namely the 10 cartons of paper and Ajax Paper Company. If anyone ever wants to find out what was purchased or who the supplier was, they can track back to it using the payment voucher number 347.

Taking a broad look at the journal entry, we can see that no truly new information has been added to the accounting system by anything other than manipulation or processing evidence of the original transaction. The trans action number is an arbitrary name given to the journal entry. The debit and credit record the adding and subtracting of the amount on the payment voucher and warrant. A journal is principally a means of organizing all the original evidence in a systematic order for the purpose of having it recorded and available in one place as a record and as a basis for posting the information to a ledger.

Accounts are found in *ledgers,* which is where the information from the general journal is placed, which is called *posting.* In some cases special ledgers are kept for the same purposes as special journals, and in the same fashion information summarized from special ledgers is posted to the general ledger. The organizing concept for journals is *date,* and the organizing concept for ledgers is *account.* An account is any defined set or category of financial information. Most accounts are fairly standard. The most common varieties of accounts are discussed below. The ledger entries for the paper transaction are shown in two versions, the first using "T" accounts, used in the teaching of accounting, and the second representing the appearance of actual ledger accounts, which use typical abbreviations for debit, credit, and balance.

"T" Accounts

| Expenditures—03-231-003 | | | Cash—01-231-003 | | |
Debit		Credit	Debit		Credit
Balance	1000		Balance	1000	
4711	300		4711		300
New Balance		1300	New Balance	700	

Ledger Accounts

Transaction Number	Other Accounts	03-231-003			01-231-003			Other Accounts
		Dr	Cr	Bal	Dr	Cr	Bal	
4711		300		1000		300	1000	
				1300			700	

The ledger accounts are used to record the financial impact of transactions and to accumulate that information to show their results over time. Put another way, ledgers are used to prepare reports showing the effects of financial transactions over time (e.g., monthly, quarterly, and annual reports). In the two versions of this example, information brought forward from the general journal entry includes the transaction number from the general journal, the account numbers, and the debit or credit status of the entries. In both examples, the accounts show a balance reflecting information previously posted to the accounts. In both cases, the $300 is posted to an account as a debit or a credit, and the $300 is added to or subtracted from the previous balance. The $300 is added to the expenditure balance and subtracted from the cash balance. Although this may seem mysterious, it makes sense in two ways, common sense and accounting sense. In commonsense terms, an additional expenditure of $300 is added to the balance showing the amount of expenditures and subtracted from the balance showing cash on hand. In accounting-sense terms, there are two rules:

1. Debit an expenditure account to show an expenditure
2. Credit a cash account to show a cash outlay

The visual impression in a "T" account makes it very easy to decide whether to add or subtract when debiting and crediting. If an entry is on the same side of the line dividing debits and credits for an account, it is added; if it is on a different side, it is subtracted. Although this can appear confusing, debits and credits will become clearer as they are discussed and illustrated in more detail.

The two versions of ledger accounts are visually rather than conceptually different. The "T" accounts example merely shows the accounts as physically isolated. In actual practice, as illustrated in the ledger accounts example, that is not the case. Paper-based systems and printouts of computer-based systems show several accounts across each sheet of paper, which is visually more detailed and much more practical because it takes up less space and is easier to use.

The next and last step in the accounting cycle is extracting information from the accounts to create reports. Of all the information in all the accounts, information appropriate to particular reports is selected. The only information from accounts used for reports are balances, except in those rare instances where specific transaction information is desired. Balances are used either to report a total result to the current point in time for a fiscal year or to report the financial impact of operations for a specific period, which is reflected in the changes in balances between one point in time and another. An example of this can be seen by using the paper transaction example and assuming (1) that the balance of $1000 in both accounts existed after three months of the fiscal year, (2) that the $300 transaction occurred in the fourth month, and (3) that the new balances were unchanged through the fourth month. After four months, the balances are $1300 and $700, showing more expenditure and less cash than the previous month's balances. To show what occurred during any particular period, take the beginning balances and compute the difference between those balances and concluding ones. A visual example of such a report may make this more clear.

Report: Fourth Month		
	Expenditure Account	*Cash Account*
Third-Month Balances	$1000	$1000
Fourth-Month Balances	$1300	$ 700
Change in Balances	+ $ 300	- $ 300

So, account balances are used to prepare reports, but how can one tell which accounts to choose? The accounts chosen are those appropriate for the report users. Reports are selected by using the account numbers. For example, upper-level administrators and elected officials find expenditure and cash accounts information in their reports, and the administrator of the Administrative Services Office finds all accounts for that office in accounting reports. The various accounts are identified and selected by using the account numbers: (01), Cash; (03), Expenditures; and (231), Administrative Services Office. Cash account balances show available cash; expenditure account balances display what was spent; and Administrative Services Office account balances indicate remaining expenditure authority. Any categorization of information that is part of the account codes can be used. For example, if someone wanted to know how much had been spent on office supplies by the whole organization, that could be computed by adding all of the Office Supplies accounts, those with the account codes 03-###-003. Information, however, can only be extracted from an accounting system or any other information system after it has been entered into the system in some fashion. For our example, account codes, the first two digits are the most noticeable and are used to identify cash and expenditures, often the most important accounts in public accounting systems. The administrative unit code comes next, and the object of expenditure code, Office Supplies, comes last because it is the most detailed and the least important aspect of the transactions that are coded.

Computerized accounting systems differ from the traditional cycle by sometimes capturing (gathering) transaction information when the first evidence of a transaction is recorded (when the transaction is done on-line) and sometimes having the information input from original evidence documents. Once information is input, usually it can be shown organized as a journal,

:dger, or report by particular commands based on conceptions of traditional ccounting systems. Computerized accounting systems are basically database rograms with built-in routines.

Although this description of events in the accounting cycle answers the uestion, "What happens in the accounting cycle?" and shows examples of ccounting documents, the illustrations of the different information catego-ies have been left incomplete for the sake of laying out the cycle. This brings s to the accounting jargon necessary to understand public accounting, the irgon that identifies the information categories. Accounting involves processing iformation; the key is understanding the information categories used.

INFORMATION CATEGORIES ◆

Categories used to organize information are central to any information ystem. Words are used to categorize reality, and the concepts underlying ords are used to organize physical things (e.g., socks are found in the sock rawer or spices in the spice rack). In information systems, abstract state-ients are used to maintain records, for example, the record in a checkbook. iformation systems rely on abstract definitions and defined operations that re implied by the definitions or are carried out according to some set of rules. or example, a checkbook record uses the categories of balance, deposit, hecks, and service charges (checks and service charges are subtracted from ie balance and deposits added). Information systems are based on conven-ions or customary practices. Accounting information systems are more com-licated and harder to grasp because of the large number of categories and ules and because they are not based on familiar, everyday experiences. Jonetheless, in public accounting most information categories and their rules re simple derivatives from six central concepts: fund, the accounting equa-on, account types, debits and credits, bases, and account classifications.

Here, a brief preview might help introduce concepts and make the extended iscussion more intelligible.

- A *fund* is the initial division of public accounting systems; funds are used to keep particular information separate. An example is a highway fund used to record transactions for revenues and expenditures for highways.

- An *accounting equation* is used for each fund to organize all of the accounts and to guide the mathematical operations.

- The *account types* refer to the fundamental categories or kinds of accounts that are used to record information.

- *Debits and credits* involve adding and subtracting entries to the accounts accord-ing to set rules.

- A *basis* refers to different conceptions of when to record entries, that is, when a transaction has occurred.

- *Account classifications* are numbering systems that define all of the accounts, such as 03-231-003.

Briefly, a public accounting system is divided into funds, each of which use
its own accounting equation to organize the various types of accounts, which
are given numerical names in the account classification. All the operations—
debits and credits—are determined by rules depending on the basis and th
account type. Accounting concepts fit together very tightly, but they have t
be taken apart to show the information categories.

Funds and Account Groups[4]

Public accounting is often called *fund accounting.* In the private sector, a
organization's accounting is done as part of a unitary whole. In contrast
public organizations' accounting systems are divided into distinct parts: fund
and account groups. All the information found in a public accounting system
is found in its funds and account groups. Basically, a fund is a separate grou
of accounts. The cash and other financial resources accounts show the *asset*
what the organization owns; the *liability* accounts show what the organizatio
owes; and the residual balance or *fund balance* accounts show what th
organization "owes" to itself, which is the difference between total assets an
total liabilities.

Public organizations have funds primarily because of legal restrictions o
the use of revenues and to collect different types of information. Preferabl
entities use as few funds as possible to avoid unnecessary work and confusio
There are various reasons for legally restricting the use of certain revenue
Revenues can be earmarked for particular expenditures, such as highways o
social security; money from grants can be restricted to a particular func
revenues from bequests can be restricted to ensure compliance with the term
of the bequest; or revenues from the sale of bonds can be restricted to ensur
that the money is used for legally allowable purposes. Likewise, other revenue
can be restricted to particular funds to collect information useful for runnin
a public organization. Funds used for this reason include funds used to recor
debt payments and charges for services provided by one organizational subun
to other subunits.

The types of funds used in public accounting fall into three categorie
governmental, proprietary, and fiduciary. Governmental funds segregate par
ticular resources and show how they are used. Proprietary funds measure th
income position of services where fees are collected by relating expenses t
revenues. Fiduciary funds, also called *trust and agency funds,* show that respon
sibilities to others are being carried out. The fund types used by state and loc
governments are

- Governmental: General, special revenue, capital projects, and debt service func
- Proprietary: Enterprise and internal service funds
- Fiduciary: Expendable trust, nonexpendable trust, pension trust, and agenc
  funds

In addition, some local governments use funds to account for special assess
ment projects, even though those kind of funds are no longer recognized. Th
federal government and the various kinds of nonprofit organizations us

similar types of funds, even though some have different names. The number of funds used by public organizations varies from one to many funds. A general fund is always used.

One *general fund* is used by all public organizations to account for a large portion of their transactions. Any financial transactions not restricted to another fund are found in the general fund, including the many transactions for ordinary operations.

Special revenue funds are used where revenues from a specific source or sources are restricted to expenditures for particular purposes. Federal taxes on gasoline, for example, go into a federal fund from which expenditures are made to provide for transportation systems. Likewise, because many grants can only be used for certain purposes, many recipients establish grant project funds. Often unpopular revenue sources are sold politically by restricting the revenue to "good" purposes, for example, state lottery revenues for education.

Capital projects funds are used to account for construction of physical facilities because of legal restrictions or a desire to focus attention on one or more capital projects.

Debt service funds can be used to account for the accumulation of resources for and payment of general obligation long-term debt (i.e., an overall public organization debt to be paid off in future fiscal years). Other kinds of debt can be accounted for in a debt service fund also. Short-term debt and revenue bond debt are accounted for in the fund to which the debt is attributed, however.

Enterprise funds are used in accounting for businesslike activities or in other situations where payments are made for services that benefit identifiable consumers. Publicly owned utilities, zoos, universities, parking lots, hospitals, and airports are typical enterprise services. Enterprise funds are used to track the degree to which such services are self-supporting or subsidized. Enterprise funds are particularly useful in ensuring that services requiring expensive capital investments are being priced at an appropriate level to pay for the capital investment.

Internal service funds are used when a public organization subunit provides measurable services to another subunit. Copying centers and motor pools are typical examples. The use of internal service funds makes it possible to attribute service expenses to particular organizational units or programs.

Fiduciary funds or *trust and agency funds* are used when a public organization is handling someone else's monies in the capacity of a trustee or an agent. *Trust funds* involve managing resources by making decisions as public organizations execute a trust placed in them by someone else; *agency funds* involve holding resources for others as an agent when the others are expected to reclaim their resources. The financial transactions are segregated to a separate fund to ensure proper handling of the monies. *Expendable trust fund* means that the resources in the fund can be spent on particular purposes, for example, cemetery expendable trust fund. A *nonexpendable trust fund* means that the original principal placed in the fund cannot be spent; some such funds can allow expenditure of the investment return, for example, an endowed scholarship fund, but others might require that no part of the fund be spent, for example, a fund that has revolving loans. *Pension trust funds* are used to account for the accumulation, investment, calculation, and payment of pension benefits. *Agency funds* are used to hold monies owned by other entities; generally, this type of fund is used to account for the temporary custody of the monies and not their ownership or use, for example, utility customer deposits or property taxes held by a county for a school district.

In addition, two sets of *account groups* contribute to showing a public organization's financial situation. Unlike funds that are used to record separate or restricted revenues and particularly the expenditure of such revenues, the two account groups maintain a record of fixed assets and long-term debt not associated with particular funds. In some cases, fixed assets and long-term debt are attributed to and recorded in particular funds, for example, enterprise funds and internal service funds. Although this can seem confusing in theory, the practice is relatively simple because what is accounted for in the account groups is limited and governed by clear-cut rules. The two account groups are General Fixed Assets and General Long-Term Debt.

The *General Fixed Assets Account Group* includes a listing of all general fixed assets and their monetary cost. Fixed assets include property of a lasting character—land, buildings, equipment, and the like. It does not include assets that are "liquid," money or things easily convertible to money, such as stocks, bonds, and the like. In accounting for general fixed assets, their purchase is recorded as an expenditure in the relevant fund whereas the ownership of such assets is recorded in the General Fixed Asset Account Group.

The *General Long-Term Debt Account Group* is used to record outstanding debts owed by the public organization that are not attributable to any particular fund. This account group lists the amounts and types of debt. Often, the purpose and due dates for debts are recorded also. In accounting for general long-term debt, the monies received to create the debt are treated as revenue in one or more funds while the debt itself is recorded in the account group.

The funds and the account groups are the broad areas within which public accounting takes place. Within the funds, accounting is done in the context of accounting equations.

The Accounting Equation

An equation is a statement of a mathematical relationship (e.g., $1 + 1 = 2$). The most familiar form of equation expresses the concept of mathematical equality: One side of an equation equals the other. As long as the same thing is done to both sides of an equation expressing equality, the equation always has equal mathematical values on both sides of the equation. Modern, double-entry accounting is characterized by always having at least two entries for every accounting transaction and by the rules of accounting operating in such a way that the accounting equation, which expresses equality, is always in balance (i.e., one side of the equation always equals the other). All additions to and subtractions from accounts are such that no entry is allowed by the rules to disturb the relationship of equality. Additions and subtractions have an equal effect on the total value of both sides of the equation. The various accounts and the rules of adding and subtracting (the dreaded debits and redits) are organized to maintain "balance." Also, this approach highlights mathematical errors because errors throw an equation out of balance.

All accounting equations, accounts, and rules (debits and credits) are logical developments from the basic accounting equation: Assets = Equity. Assets refer to resources owned, and equity refers to resources owed. In the practice of accounting, assets and equity are two aspects of the same concrete phenomenon. For instance, if you were to account for bananas and you had two of these yellow fruit, your basic accounting equation would be 2 bananas = 2 bananas. Your assets and equity would be the same. If you gave one away or traded a banana for an apple, your accounting equation would show 1 banana = 1 banana or = 1 banana + 1 apple = 1 banana + 1 apple.

All possible transactions are recorded in a way that keeps an accounting equation in balance.

All accounts are theoretically derived from assets and equity and can be found either on the asset side of the accounting equation, which is the left side, or on the equity side of the accounting equation, which is the right side.

Using the accounting equation concept, you add to both sides of the equation:

$$2 = 2$$
Add: 1 $2 + 1 = 2 + 1$
$$3 = 3$$

Subtract from both sides of the equation:

$$2 = 2$$
Subtract: 1 $2 - 1 = 2 - 1$
$$1 = 1$$

Or add and subtract on one or both sides of the equation in such a fashion that the equality relation is maintained:

$$+ 1 = 1 + 2$$

Transfer: 1 from one asset account to another

$(2 - 1) + (2 + 1) = 2 + 2$
$+ 3 = 2 + 2$

The rationale behind all the rules is "Keep the equation in balance."

Debits and credits are used because they represent left and right and provide means of adding and subtracting. The simplest way of expressing this is through working with a basic accounting equation: Assets = Equity. If you start with two bananas, the basic equation is

Assets = Equity
2 bananas = 2 bananas

By using "T" accounts, we get

Assets		=	Equity	
Debit	Credit		Debit	Credit
2 bananas				2 bananas

For accounts on the left side of an accounting equation, a positive balanc or an addition is debit, and debit means left. For accounts on the right side o an accounting equation, a positive balance or addition is a credit, and credi means right. Debit and credit are abbreviated as Dr and Cr respectively.

The "T" accounts show adding and subtracting relationships visually. W add to or subtract from an account on one side of an accounting equatio differently than we add to and subtract from an account on the other side o an equation.

The left side of the accounting equation is sometimes referred to as the asse or debit balance side, and the right side is referred to as the equity or credi balance side. The asset and equity labels derive from the fundamental charac ter of the accounts on each side of the accounting equation, and the debit an credit balance labels are because those are the normal balances on the respec tive sides of an accounting equation.

Add: one banana

Assets		=	Equity	
Dr	Cr		Dr	Cr
2 bananas				2 bananas
1 banana				1 banana
3 bananas				3 bananas

Subtract: one banana

Assets		=	Equity	
Dr	Cr		Dr	Cr
2 bananas				2 bananas
	1 banana		1 banana	
1 banana				1 banana

The rules for adding and subtracting are as follows:

Addition:	debit on the left side of an equation
	credit on the right side of an equation
Subtraction:	credit on the left side of an equation
	debit on the right side of an equation

We know whether to debit or credit depending on whether we are addin to or subtracting from an account and whether the account is on the left o on the right. The act of deciding what to debit and what to credit is calle *analysis.* To do analysis is to determine which accounts are affected and in what way. In other words, we are determining from where and to where resources are going. One way of knowing whether to debit or credit accounts is to know the account types. The various account types are invariably on one side or the other of an accounting equation.

The account types come in three groups: *real, nominal,* and *budgetary* accounts. The real accounts are the only ones found on the balance sheet and can be said to reflect "real" impacts on the financial condition of an organization. Nominal accounts show the flow of monies during a fiscal period. Budgetary accounts are used to record budgetary decisions.

Real account types include assets and two types of equity accounts: liabilities and fund balance. Typical asset accounts include cash, short-term and long-term investments, and payments due from others. Equity accounts include liability accounts, which show what an organization owes to others, and fund balance accounts, which show what an organization "owes" itself. For the most part, one fund balance account is used in an artificial manner to keep an equation in balance. Hence, the numbers in a fund balance account are not particularly meaningful and merely reflect the difference between the total assets and total liabilities. Liability accounts include payments due to others, short-term debt, and in enterprise funds, long-term debt. These account types form the basic accounting equation reflected on the balance sheet, which is a report. When a fiscal period accounting system is put into service, the previously blank pages of the journal and ledgers are said to be *opened* when the balances of these account types are taken from the balance statement for the end of the last fiscal reporting period and entered into the journal and posted to the ledger. Conversely, one *closes the books* when all the other account types are closed and the balances in these accounts are recorded on the balance statement. These account types provide a slightly expanded accounting equation:

Assets = Liabilities + Fund Balance

The nominal account types—revenue and expenditure—are used to record the impact of operations during a fiscal period, that is, to show the flow of monies. Although accounting theory explains the location of these accounts in an accounting equation, it suffices here merely to show the locations:

Assets + Expenditures = Liabilities + Fund Balance + Revenues

Typical revenue accounts include revenues by various sources (e.g., income taxes, sales taxes, property taxes, import duties, and parking meter collections). Expenditure accounts reflect the budgetary categories, such as the organization unit (Administrative Services) and object of expenditure (Office Supplies).

The budgetary account types—estimated revenue and appropriation—are used to record the budgetary decisions of an organization. The estimated revenues are those predicted in the organization's budget and that the organization is authorized to collect, and the appropriations are authorizations to spend money. They are used to relate actual revenues and expenditures to their corresponding budgetary estimates and limits. Because expenditures are limited by budgetary law or policy, the appropriation accounts are used to control expenditures. The specific estimated revenue and appropriation accounts use exactly the same titles as the revenue and expenditure accounts except that budgetary accounts show the budgeted amounts and the nominal accounts show the effects of actual operations. The expanded accounting equation, without theoretical justifications, is

$$
\begin{aligned}
\text{Assets} \quad &= \quad \text{Liabilities} \\
+ \text{Expenditures} \quad & \quad + \text{Revenues} \\
+ \text{Estimated Revenues} \quad & \quad + \text{Appropriations} \\
& \quad + \text{Fund Balance}
\end{aligned}
$$

Virtually all transactions affect only the Asset, Expenditure, Revenue, and Liability accounts. The budgetary and the fund balance accounts are used in opening and closing the books, and in between those events, the budgetary accounts are used as benchmarks or guides against which the revenue and expenditure accounts are measured. The only other time you have budgetary account transactions during a year is when a budget is changed.

Finally, accounts are subdivided into *control accounts* and *subsidiary accounts.* This is surely an unwelcome but necessary complication because most accounting information is in subsidiary accounts. The control accounts are the accounts in the general accounting equation discussed earlier (e.g., Assets, Expenditures, Revenues, and Liabilities). The subsidiary accounts usually include information from two or more control accounts. Also, the control accounts are broad in character, and the subsidiary accounts are very specific. The control accounts are few in number, whereas subsidiary accounts are numerous.

Subsidiary accounts contain detailed and partial information from one or more control accounts. An example of a subsidiary account is a Personnel Expenditure Subsidiary Account, which has the Expenditure Account as its control account. The subsidiary account in this example is only used to record transactions having to do with personnel expenditures whereas the control account is used to record all expenditures. There are three purposes served by having separate accounts for partial information. First, subsidiary accounts provide detail. Second, they bring together specific budgetary and nominal account information in one place. Third, they leave the general accounting equation free of excessive detail, which makes it easier to determine if the equation is in balance.

The use of both control and subsidiary accounts is done by entering control and subsidiary account information into the journal and posting that information to both ledger accounts. It works in such a way that the same information posted to a subsidiary account is also posted to a control account. How this works and how subsidiary accounts serve the purposes listed can be seen by way of examples. An example of journal entries for a control and a subsidiary account can show how this is accomplished.

Journal Example

First Version:	Debit	Credit
Expenditure	$100	
Administrative Services-Office Supplies		
Cash		$100

or

Second Version:		
03-231-003	$100	
01-231-003		$100

Both versions of the journal example have Expenditure, 03, as the control account. In the first version, the subsidiary account, Administrative Services-Office Supplies, is listed below the control account. In the second version, both the control account and subsidiary account are indicated by the numerical code. The Cash Account in this example, as in general practice, is not a control account. A number of subsidiary accounts can be listed under the control account. This is appropriate when, for example, an organization made a payment to an office supplies firm for supplies being delivered to different organizational subunits with their own subsidiary accounts. The journal entry in such a case shows the control account entry and then various amounts for the different subsidiary accounts. In turn, the journal entries are posted to the ledger accounts as shown here.

Ledger Accounts

Control Account:

Expenditures (03)

	Dr	Cr
Balance	$1000	
	$ 100	
New Balance	$1100	

Subsidiary Account

Administrative Services-Office Supplies (231-003)

	Dr	Cr
Balance	$ 200	
	$ 100	
New Balance	$ 300	

It is easy to see how subsidiary accounts provide detailed information. Expanding the example of the Personnel Expenditure Subsidiary Account, we can look at subsidiary expenditure accounts for personnel, supplies, and contracts for three organizational units. The control account is the Expenditure Account.

| | Expenditure Account | |
	Dr	Cr
Balance	$100,000	

Subsidiary Expenditure Accounts (Debit Balances)

	Unit A	Unit B	Unit C	Row Totals
Personnel	$22,000	$25,000	$23,000	$ 70,000
Supplies	$ 6,000	$ 2,000	$12,000	$ 20,000
Contracts	-0-	$ 2,000	$ 8,000	$ 10,000
Column Totals	$28,000	$29,000	$43,000	$100,000

The sum of the balances in the subsidiary accounts is equal to the balance of the control account. The subsidiary accounts show details relevant to the organization using the accounting system. As in the earlier Office Supplies example, the people using the accounting system can see how their organizational subunit stands in respect to particular categories of financial information.

Subsidiary accounts also bring specific information from two or more control accounts together in one place. For the most part, this results in showing the relationship between the budgeted and actual amounts in specific categories and the remaining balances. In this way the subsidiary accounts show how the details of operations relate to the budget. The subsidiary accounts record transactions for the different types of control accounts and a subsidiary account balance. An example most simply shows how this works.

Control Accounts

| | Expenditures | | Appropriations | |
	Dr	Cr	Dr	Cr
Balance	$100,000			$200,000
	100			
	$100,100			

Subsidiary Accounts

Administrative Services-Office Supplies

Expenditure	Appropriation	Available for Expenditure Balance

Dr	Cr	(Cr)
	$1000	$1000
$100		$ 900

In this example, $100 is posted to both the expenditure control account and the subsidiary administrative services-office supplies account. The subsidiary account shows an initial credit balance of $1000, which occurred when the budgetary appropriation of $1000 was posted to the account. The posting of the expenditure of $100 as a debit results in a new balance of $900 when the debit amount is subtracted from the credit balance. This subsidiary account shows the amount of the remaining budget authority, which is the difference between the amount appropriated—the budgetary account category—and the amount expended—the nominal account category. The balance remaining is what can still be spent on office supplies by the Administrative Services Office.

The previous examples show how the purpose of keeping the number of accounts in the general accounting equation to a minimum is served. By using the control accounts to determine that the equation is in balance, bookkeepers and accountants save a lot of time. If all the entries and postings are done correctly, the sum of the balances of the control accounts is equal to the sum of the balances of the subsidiary accounts because exactly the same information is posted to the control and subsidiary accounts.

Bases of Accounting

Bases of accounting are concerned with when to record financial transactions and, hence, what really constitutes a transaction. The bases use different rules to record transactions. For example, only an encumbrance-basis accounting system uses "encumbrance" accounts that reflect the recognition of an accounting transaction at a particular point in time. The bases determine which of a large number of sequential events are recorded by when a transaction is recognized. There are four bases and one modified version: cash, accrual, modified accrual, encumbrance, and cost. Two or three bases can be used at the same time.

Cash basis accounting is the easiest to understand and use. In using the cash basis of accounting, you record a financial transaction when money or its equivalent changes hands. Individuals account for their personal checking accounts using this basis. The cash basis is intuitively appealing and easy to use. The cash basis has two major faults: First, by manipulating the flow or recording of cash transactions, the financial picture of an organization can easily be distorted. The classic example is an organization not paying bills for goods or services and carrying them from one year to another to hide the implicit debt such bills represent. Second, the cash basis provides the latest possible recording of financial transactions for collecting information. Events are irreversible by the time they are recorded. Accounting is taught using another basis, the accrual basis.

Accrual basis accounting uses the notion of legal obligation to record financial transactions. Under this basis of accounting, financial transactions are recorded when a legally binding financial obligation has occurred. Ten cartons of paper arriving with a bill and someone billed for a tax payment are two different examples of events recorded in accrual-based accounts. Accrual basis accounts are those with the words *payable, due,* and *receivable* in their account names. Cash transactions are also recorded in an accrual-based accounting system. Enterprise and internal service funds ordinarily use the accrual basis.

Modified accrual basis accounting is like accrual accounting in its central notion of legal obligation. It differs from accrual accounting primarily with respect to the accrual of revenues. Because public revenues are unpredictable and not easily measured, modified accrual basis accounting requires that revenues be both measurable and available during the current fiscal period before they can be recorded as obligations due to a public organization. According to authoritative accounting standards, most funds should use the modified accrual basis. Both accrual and its modified version provide information on financial transactions, particularly expenditures, earlier than a cash basis system.

Encumbrance basis accounting relies on the notion of commitment. Financial transactions are recorded when a commitment is made. This basis is used only for expenditure accounts. Rather than wait until an order of goods or services is received, the encumbrance basis can be used to record commitments when orders are placed or even when spending decisions are made. By accounting for decisions to spend, you can set aside monies already committed and thereby have the earliest possible information about expenditures, some of which may be reversed. Like accrual accounting, encumbrance-based systems also record financial transactions concerning the actual transfer of money. An accrual or a modified accrual basis and an encumbrance basis can be used concurrently.

Finally, and least important for public organizations, *cost basis* accounting relies on the notion of use or consumption of resources to recognize a financial transaction. The purpose of cost accounting is to record the costs of providing goods and services. Cost accounting is almost always an addition to an accounting system rather than a primary basis for gathering information. An example of a cost being incurred is the use of a carton of paper to produce tax bills. When the carton is used, it would be recorded as a cost. Public organizations seldom engage in cost accounting, though cost accounting can be very useful in some situations, particularly in connection with the pricing of goods and services sold by public organizations. For example, nonprofit hospitals may need to determine the actual expenditures for different treatments to accurately price them. The key aspects of the bases are summarized in Table 3.1.

Differences among the commonly used bases are the timing of recording, the accuracy of reports, and the work involved. The encumbrance basis provides the earliest record of expenditures, followed in order by the accrual basis, the cash basis, and the cost basis. Encumbrance information includes intentions, whereas accrual information is firm legal obligations. Accrual-

ABLE 3.1   Accounting Bases

asis	Time Dimension (Key Idea) Earlier to Later	Example
ncumbrance	Commitment	Order placed for paper
ccrual & Modified Accrual	Obligation	Paper and bill received
ash	Money moves	Paper paid for
ost	Use	Paper consumed

ased accounting frequently includes accounts showing obligations and cur-
ent assets not normally found in accounting systems using other bases,
icluding depreciation, receivables, payables, and inventory. These accounts
rovide a greater breadth of information and make it possible to obtain a more
recise understanding of an organization's current financial position. For the
mount of work involved, the cash basis requires the fewest entries and takes
ie least work to train people to keep the books and to understand reports.
To basis of accounting neglects recording of cash transactions; they only
iffer in what else is recorded. Accrual-based accounting probably involves
ie most work because it is harder to understand, which makes training people
iore difficult. Any accrual transaction requires two sets of entries, one for the
bligation and one for the cash transaction that eliminates the obligation.
ncumbrance accounting appears to be slightly less difficult than accrual
ccounting because it is easier to understand and to train people. It uses three
ets of entries for every transaction: one for the commitment and two when
ie record of the commitment is eliminated and the cash payment sent.

Larger public organizations, those more reliant on debt financing, and
iose with more professionalized staff use the modified accrual and accrual
ases. In many cases, states require that certain local government activities be
ccounted for using an accrual basis, for example, enterprise fund activities.
ome financially conservative public organizations, particularly municipali-
.es, use the encumbrance basis, sometimes in conjunction with an accrual
asis.

Smaller public organizations, those with less professionalized staff, and
iose less reliant on debt financing use the cash basis, except where required
o use an accrual basis. Although professional accounting groups rail against
iis practice and insist upon the superiority of the accrual bases, the use of
ie cash basis makes sense in organizations relying heavily on part-time and
olunteer labor or in geographically isolated places. In such organizations, the
osts of training for and using an accrual basis are high, and the staffs have
lenty of other things to claim their attention.

Account Classification[5]

All accounting systems use a variety of accounts for their reporting needs.
Because of the length of many account titles and for greater accuracy, accounts

TABLE 3.2   Anatomy of an Account Code

10-01-415.121-300

Number	Category	Example
10	Fund	General Fund
01	Organizational Unit	Avalanche Alert Department
4	Account Types	Expenditure
415	Function	Financial Administration
415.121	Detail	Accounting
300	Object of Expenditure	Consulting Services

are assigned a numerical code. The listing of all accounts and their assigned codes is called the *chart of accounts.* The chart of accounts is functionally equivalent to the program at a sporting event, just as keeping score is different kind of accounting. Charts of accounts vary essentially in the degree of detail based on how detailed the accounts are themselves. To have sufficient coding system, we have to have a designated set of codes for every aspect of the account that is recorded. A very simple accounting system with only nine accounts is easy to code with a single digit for each account, 1-9. Very complicated systems can use more than 10 digits to code an account. As a rule, public organizations have more complicated systems because of control and details. Table 3.2 provides a relatively complicated example of an account code that can be understood through the following discussion of account classifications.

The best way to illustrate charts of accounts is to construct one to show what goes into such an enterprise. North Snowshoe lost its accounting system and bookkeeper in an avalanche, so we can construct one for them. First of all, codes can be established for funds. It makes sense to assign a two-digit code for funds because of the number of different kinds of funds. Though all types of funds are not used everywhere, frequently there are several of one fund type. If we used a one-digit code, 1 to 9, and then found we needed a tenth fund, we would have to revise the whole system. The fund codes:

10—General Fund
20—Special Revenue Funds
    21—Disaster Relief Grant
    22—Tax on Avalanche Insurance
30—Capital Projects Funds
    31—Avalanche Retaining Wall
40—Debt Service Fund
50—Special Assessment Funds
    51—Paving District #3 (Blizzard Hills Subdivision)
60—Enterprise Funds
    61—Icehouse
    62—Sewer

70—Internal Service Funds
  71—Snowmobile Motor Pool
80—Trust and Agency Funds
  81—Frostbite Cemetery Expendable Trust
90—Account Groups
  91—General Fixed Assets
  92—General Long-Term Debt

The first two digits of all of the account codes for North Snowshoe show the fund, for example, 10 for the general fund or 90 the account groups.

Next, organizational subdivisions are used to ensure compliance with appropriate legislation. In most instances appropriations are granted to organizational units. This budgetary information is recorded in accounting systems by organizational unit codes: 01—Avalanche Alert Department. Such designations are necessary to ensure control of expenditures. Taking the previous example one step further, all general fund accounts for the Avalanche Alert Department start with the account code 10-01.

Next, in descending level of detail, are codes for account types. Although different systems are theoretically possible, the standard recommended in *Governmental Accounting, Auditing, and Financial Reporting* (listed in chapter notes) and used by most public organizations is a four-type system.

1. Assets
2. Equities (Liabilities and Fund Balance)
3. Revenue
4. Expenditure

The budgetary account types are not coded because they are mirrored by the revenue and expenditure accounts and are accounted for in revenue and expenditure subsidiary accounts. Also, the account types can be further subdivided to include specific account categories. Asset accounts show the kind of asset, 101-Cash. Equity accounts show different kinds of liabilities and fund balance accounts, 201-Accounts Payable and 253-Fund Balance. Revenue accounts are categorized by the source of revenue: 310-General Property Tax. The expenditure accounts are generally classified by function or program and activity: 415-Financial Administration. More detailed codes can be used to designate function or program; for example, the account code for accounting for the Avalanche Alert Department is 10-01-415.121.

Another aspect is the *character* of expenditures that focuses on time period: current operating expenditures, capital outlays, debt service, and intergovernmental transfers. Often in practice, this recommendation is ignored because the effort required to gather and record this information is thought to exceed its value.

Finally, accounts are coded to show objects of expenditure, that is, goods and services for which money is spent. For example, depending on how detailed the chart of accounts is, the object code for the cost of our consulting service in setting up their chart of accounts could be 30 or 300. Following the previous example, the whole code for accounting consulting services for the Avalanche Alert Department is 10-01-415.121-300. As with organization subunit codes, object of expenditure codes are used to designate accounts for the purpose of budgetary control. Generally, account codes for every kind of expenditure in a public organization's budget occur at the same level of detail. If the budget uses Personnel as an appropriations category, the account codes show a personnel appropriation and expenditure code. If the budget shows further detail for personnel expenses by type of employee or type of expense, the code of accounts shows those same details as account codes because there are subsidiary accounts for every budget category.

To review and extend our view of charts of accounts, account codes represent account titles; they supply short, precise names for accounts. The account codes are arranged in groups to facilitate recording information that the designers of an accounting system decide is useful. The account codes illustrated here are those most commonly used.

As you may have noticed already, the expenditure account codes are the most detailed because of the preoccupation of public organizations with control and, hence, accounting for expenditure as appropriated. Likewise, for management or planning purposes, the expenditure accounts are the most often used accounts. The other account types are relatively few in number, primarily because of the use of organizational subunit and object codes. Except for expenditure codes, accounts are coded only by fund and account types. For example, 10-310, which signifies general fund-general property tax, is sufficient to identify that account.

Nonetheless, account codes used in conjunction with expenditure transactions are parallel, or echoes of expenditure codes, despite the fact that the other account in the transaction can be identified by a single code. For example, the expenditure code of 10-01-415-30 (general fund-avalanche alert department-financial administration-accounting services) appears in accounting documents along with 10-01-101-30 (general fund-avalanche alert department-cash-accounting services). In the case of 10-01-101-30, only two of the four sets of numbers designate the actual account, which is general fund-cash (*10*-00-*101*-00). Likewise, a revenue code could appear as 10-00-310-00 (general fund-general property tax). The use of essentially dummy or meaningless account codes serves two purposes—maintaining consistency in code patterns and length of code and providing a second account code to check against the first. In other words, this practice fosters precision and accuracy.

Also, it should be noted that the account codes discussed here are merely the common and recommended ones. Any other characteristic or aspect of a financial transaction that can be conceptualized can be the basis for a set of account codes. The most common one not previously discussed is that of *cost center*. Cost centers refer to any set of expenditures that can be identified and grouped (e.g., activities, projects, or programs). Using such a code, you can develop and use figures on different cost centers, primarily for managerial purposes. In some cases, cost center codes are not part of the formal accounting system but are developed and used within organization subunits. In such cases, letters of the alphabet are used to avoid confusing the central accounting ersonnel (e.g., 10-01-415-30a). Account codes are only limited by one's imagination.

Information categories discussed here, whether funds or expenditures, reflect information used in the practice of public finance administration. Even though a few concepts are limited to accounting practices alone (e.g., the accounting equation and debits and credits), most information categories discussed here reflect very real information necessary to administer public finances.

SPECIALIZED USES OF ACCOUNTING ◆

Virtually all public organizations engage in the generic accounting practices discussed so far. In addition, many use specialized accounting for other aspects or purposes of financial administration. Generic accounting is oriented toward tracking revenues and expenditures in relationship to budgets and recording the resulting balances, assets, and liabilities. Most needs for financial information are sufficiently served by generic accounting. Specialized accounting serves other information needs. Specialized uses of accounting include internal control, cost accounting, personnel accounting, financial disclosure, and inventory accounting.

Internal Control

Internal control, which results in internal control systems or internal controls, refers to procedures that control how accounting and related financial matters are handled in an organization. Internal control procedures are designed first of all to safeguard an organization's assets from mishandling, whether by accident or on purpose. Although internal control serves this central purpose, it also ensures compliance with legal requirements (budgetary and others), supports the accuracy of accounting systems records, generally follows good management practices, and helps employees avoid temptations to misuse organizational resources. Internal control is discussed under the heading of accounting because it is usually a part of accounting system and procedures design, even though most areas of financial management are concerned to some degree with safeguarding resources. Principles of internal control are built into the design of accounting systems.

The practice of internal control relies on the central ideas of fixing responsibilities and reviewing the exercise of responsibilities. Responsibilities are "fixed" in two senses. First, responsibilities in the sense of everything required and prohibited is specified in written policies and procedures. These include such things as when to record what information and physical safeguards for assets. Second, responsibilities for particular individuals are specified by linking particular individuals to particular actions by signature, by job assignment, or both. Associated with individual responsibilities is the notion that personnel should be competent and trustworthy and adequately trained for their responsibilities. Reviews are built into an accounting system by procedures that divide transactions responsibilities between two or more persons (often with a routine of comparing totals between or among those persons) accounting reports, management reviews of transactions, and internal and outside audits of the accounting system. The same kind of internal control procedures, sometimes referred to as administrative controls, can specify routines, responsibilities, and reviews for any area of an organization. Most frequently internal control is applied to public finance areas with high values especially purchasing, investment, cash management, pensions, expenditure administration, and revenue administration.

Not only is it necessary to have internal control procedures, it is also necessary to follow them. Not having and not following are functionally equivalent. Orange County, California, was a case of both in different respects the county lacked internal control procedures on borrowing for investment and specific investments, and the treasurer violated accounting system rules by committing fraud. Another example of an organization that did not practice internal control is an Iowa village that lost hundreds of thousands of dollars when the village clerk wrote and cashed 40 or 50 checks to herself over a two-year period while forging another official's signature. The loss was discovered when the clerk moved to Arizona. Apparently, no one bothered to check the balance in the village's bank account against accounting reports.

Cost Accounting

Cost accounting, a separate basis, can be used where attributing costs to particular category is necessary or helpful. Categories used in cost accounting include particular services, functions, programs, projects, or organizational subunits. Through the use of cost accounting, one can determine what something costs totally and by components. Knowledge of costs, both total and component costs, supports managerial and policy decisions as to allocation of resources in budgets, prices of services, and choice of operating methods.

Personnel Accounting

In addition to personnel records dealing with the personnel process itself personnel accounting involves accounting for financial transactions concerning personnel. Personnel accounting deals with all manner of payment involving personnel, primarily in relation to payments to or on behalf of employees or because of employees.

Personnel accounting is specialized because of the need for more detailed information than is easily accommodated in a general accounting system Summary entries from personnel accounting systems are entered into general accounting systems based on the personnel journal entries.

The amount of detail in personnel accounting stems from the primary information category and the variety of information recorded. The primary information category is the individual employee payment record, for which all manner of payments are recorded whether the payment is to the employee on behalf of the employee, or on account of the employee. Employees are paid regular wages and salaries as well as other special payments. Taxes and other payments are made on behalf of employees and based on payroll deductions. Public organizations make payments to other organizations on account of particular employees (e.g., payroll taxes on employers, worker's compensation insurance, and pension and health plan payments). Because personnel accounting records are organized by individual employees and show payments made for each employee, these records show the fulfillment of legal obligations with respect to each employee.

Financial Disclosure

Many public organizations desiring to issue bonds have found themselves required by state laws or the practical requirements of investor concern to make financial disclosure. Financial disclosure statements commonly include the following:

1. Standard accounting report information, such as total revenues and total expenditures
2. Information based on accounting reports, for example, available debt capacity (debt limit-current debt)
3. General economic conditions, such as unemployment rate
4. Specifics of bond issue, for example, revenue source for repayment

Because financial disclosure statements rely partially on accounting systems, the persons responsible for the accounting are also given the responsibility for maintaining specialized financial disclosure records and preparing financial disclosure statements.

Inventory Accounting

Inventory accounting deals with keeping track of materials and capital equipment. The reasons for inventory accounting are reduction of waste and loss, maintenance of necessary inventories to operate, and minimization of purchasing costs. Inventory accounting supplies useful information for budget preparation.

ACCOUNTING AND MANAGERS ◆

Accounting information is a key ingredient in managerial decision making. Although managers in public organizations deal with finances, people, programs, operations, and organizational relations, the management of finances is frequently overlooked in discussions of management. Organization finances concern some of the most important realities that managers face, particularly for the use and availability of resources. In dealing with finances, most managers' exposure is to accounting information.

When managers are in a control relationship, whether being controlled or controlling others, their attention is on subsidiary expenditure accounts. Financial control through an accounting system is one of the most effective means of organizational control: no money, no action. Management decisions about how to operate are based on reviews of accounting information or costs, expenditures, and the balances available for expenditure. A good example of this is found in cases where managers look at their accounts to determine where to focus their attention. In public organizations, usually personnel is the overwhelming user of resources. If an organization's resources are primarily personnel, the focus of management attention should be on the efficient and effective use of personnel rather than on other more minor resources. Cost and expenditure information is particularly useful in choosing between alternative operational practices. Financial management decisions particularly those having to do with cash, debt, and investment management rely heavily on past accounting data. Planning relies on information from the near past for projections into the future for budgets, capital budgets, and service plans. When managers have decisions to make, they frequently draw on financial information provided by an accounting system.

◆ CONCLUSION

As promised in the introduction, you have not been turned into an accountant This chapter, however, provides a basic understanding of public accounting and penetrates into and illuminates some of the mysteries of accounting. The key facets covered here encompass accounting reports, the accounting process, the kinds of information recorded, various specialized uses of accounting, and an appreciation of how accounting relates to management. Later chapters provide examples of how accounting supports other financial administration techniques.

DISCUSSION QUESTIONS

1. What good is accounting? How does it contribute to public budgeting and other public finance administration areas?
2. How does the accounting cycle work?
3. What accounts would you want to pay attention to in your actual or an imaginary organization?
4. What kind of reports would you want to see? Those oriented to control management, or planning? What should those reports contain?
5. Consider how a nonprofit charitable organization might account for pledges? Would they be recorded as pledges and then as revenue, and how would those that did not materialize be dealt with?
6. Is using funds a good idea?

NOTES ◆

1. Government Finance Officers Association (1994). *Governmental accounting, auditing, and financial reporting*. Chicago: Government Finance Officers Association, pp. 11-12.

2. Government Finance Officers Association, pp. 4-10; more comprehensive discussions and istings can be found in Joan W. Norvelle (1994). *Introduction to fund accounting* (5th ed.). icson, AZ: Thoth Books, pp. 3-7, 13-25; and Robert J. Freeman and Craig D. Shoulders (1993). *overnmental and nonprofit accounting* (4th ed.). Englewood Cliffs, NJ: Prentice-Hall, pp. 12-17, 1, 642, 681-683, 732-735.

3. Government Finance Officers Association, pp. 411-553.

4. This section draws on *Governmental accounting, auditing, and financial reporting*, pp. -17, see pp. 35-177 for more details and illustrations.

5. Examples used here are drawn from *Governmental accounting, auditing, and financial porting*, Appendix C: Illustrative Accounts, Classifications and Descriptions, pp. 361-410.

SUGGESTED READINGS ◆

arry Anderson (1989). Budget accounting. *Public Budgeting & Finance, 9,* 94-101.

homas J. Cuny (1995, Fall). The pending revolution in federal accounting standards. *Public Budgeting & Finance, 15,* 22-34.

obert J. Freeman and Craig D. Shoulders (1993). *Governmental and nonprofit accounting* (4th ed.). Englewood Cliffs, NJ: Prentice-Hall.

overnment Finance Officers Association (1994). *Governmental accounting, auditing, and financial reporting*. Chicago: Government Finance Officers Association.

an W. Norvelle (1994). *Introduction to fund accounting* (5th ed.). Tucson, AZ: Thoth Books.

CHAPTER

4

Money and Values:
Monetary Values

M onetary value is the one thing that unifies public finance administration if public finance administration had a song, it would start, "Money, money money." Concern for money relates to concern for serving the public. Monetary values are important in the public sector because monetary values measure both human values and resources.

Money is a scorekeeping device used to express values and allocate resources. We cannot always reflect our real values with money, just as some things cannot be monetarily valued. Monetary values are, however, the most commonly used and most accurate measuring device in the public sector. Once the character of monetary value is understood, it is much easier to use.

In this chapter, we explore money values for the meaning of money and its relation to values generally, the manner in which money prices work in making decisions, how costs and benefits substitute for prices in the public sector, how money values are estimated for public decisions, and how monetary values fluctuate with time.

◆ VALUES

All people place value on things. Some values are positive: I like puppies and celery soup. Other values are negative: Murders are horrible. Values can be a means to an end or ends themselves. Many words describe placing values on things: *good, bad, want, need, desire,* and *cheap,* for example. Values placed on things may or may not involve money. Values not involving money are generally outside the scope of public finance administration, but nonmonetary values do impinge on public finance administration.

Money is the measure of things in public finance administration. Key terms revolve around monetary value: *money, prices, revenues, expenditures, per sions, cash, costs,* and *benefits. Money* is basic whereas the other terms are derivative versions of monetary values.

Valuing as a human activity involves judging the goodness and badness of things as a basis for action. Monetary value refers to the money value a person assigns to something—Herb says, "My celery soup is worth $1 a cup." Definitions of monetary value appear circular because the valuing depends on individual judgments. Something has such monetary value as a person gives it. Other people can see the celery soup as being more or less valuable (i.e., are willing to make an exchange for more or less money).

MONEY ◆

What is money? Money is not primarily the physical manifestations with which we are familiar: coins, dollar bills, checks, or plastic charge cards. These are particular forms of money. Fundamentally, money is an abstraction; its meaning does not relate to any specific object. Money is purchasing power: that which is given and taken in exchange for other things. Money is valued for its use; people are willing to exchange goods and services for money. The true value of money is its exchange value. Historically, money evolved from commodities to pieces of paper representing commodities to pieces of paper that are recognized and accepted as money. Currency in the United States is "legal tender for all debts, public and private," a statement that appears on all dollar bills. Currency and all other forms of money convertible to currency are acceptable as money in exchange for goods and services because the U.S. government will accept dollar bills and legally enforce payment of debts with them. Acceptability of currency money is based on governmental backing. As a medium of exchange, current forms of money have the advantages of being highly divisible, measurable, storable, and portable.

A money economy is quite important to the private sector and has been instrumental in modern economic growth. Money is useful in the private sector for facilitating exchanges and communicating information. It is easier to make indirect exchanges of goods and services in money and to have money prices register the relative values of goods and services. For example, you probably bought this book with money. The bookstore took your money for the book and used money to pay the publisher for the book and the bookstore employees for their labor. Goods and services exchanges are much more difficult to make. For example, if you paid for this book with a piglet and 10 pounds of onions, would you have gotten change in celery? What would the publisher and the bookstore employees have gotten? How much is the book valued at in other commodities or services?

Money is particularly useful for the private sector, and it also assists the public sector. Though the public sector does exist to supplement the deficiencies of the private sector by providing necessary goods and services that the private sector cannot, will not, or should not provide, it uses money as a prime measure of values. Monetary value has several advantages.

First, money value as a measure is highly communicable. If someone says, "10 dollars," everyone else knows what is meant. Second, much of public-sector financial administration involves voluntary exchanges that are equivalent to private-sector exchanges. Third, when the resources are extracted from the population in the form of taxes and other payments, usually money is taken rather than goods and services. Fourth, in many cases, money is the only useful way to assign values. Despite the expression to the effect that an individual would give a right arm for something, it is seldom done. Fifth, money is a measure of available resources. All these reasons are instrumental. Public organizations are necessarily judged and valued by their decidedly nonmonetary ends. In the public sector, preferences are expressed in the political process; however, intervening measures are frequently made in monetary terms. For example, saving lives is a generally accepted goal in the public sector. If method A saves lives at the cost of one billion dollars per life and method B at the cost of two billion per life, clearly method A is preferable (more highly valued) because it saves twice as many lives as method B for the same cost. Money measures.

◆ PRICES

Prices express monetary value. A price is merely what one offers or requires in exchange for a good or service, the money involved in buying or selling something. Setting of prices is a reflection of what people value things at monetarily.

The money prices applied by the buyer and seller of the book overlap. The price set by the bookstore and the price you were willing to pay were coincidental. If the price set by the bookstore or what was an acceptable price to you changes, however, then one of you will have more money if an exchange is made and one less, or one of the parties will refuse to make the exchange. The prices set by the parties determine whether an exchange will take place and whether more or fewer resources will be applied toward a particular product. Generally, prices cover a range of values and vary among individuals; exchanges take place when the price ranges of buyers and sellers overlap. As prices change, individuals choose whether to buy or sell goods and services. What an individual buys and sells is a reflection of the money values placed on those items; that is, what preferences an individual has. Continuing with the book example, if this book were priced at $10,000, then you probably would not have purchased it and would be willing to sell it now. If you had not purchased this book, you would have more money to spend on other things, and the bookstore would have less.

All things that are monetarily priced can be compared. The same money used to purchase this book could have been used to buy celery, haircuts, beer, clothes, or a book for a different course. Prices, then, serve individuals as measurements of different choices for their use of resources. Prices do the same thing for all individuals; they help them to make choices of goods and services to buy and sell. Just as individuals choose celery or books, public rganizations choose between different goods and service options; both use rices as key pieces of information.

Prices are determined by a number of factors. These factors are generally rouped under the headings of supply and demand. Factors associated with upply are quantity, scarcity, uniqueness, costs involved in supplying, and xpectation of demand. Factors associated with demand are quantity, per- onal preferences, income level, and availability of similar goods or services. n effect, buyers and sellers assess the relative merits of an exchange and put money price on their side of an exchange.

The merits of an exchange can be thought of in terms of benefits and costs, ositive and negative features respectively. Usually, prices are monetary, but ven nonmonetary exchanges can be measured in money, even if there are onmonetarily measured benefits and costs. In a price situation, all the enefits and costs for individuals on either side of a possible exchange are ffectively expressed in a price or price range.

A few examples may be helpful. The opportunity to acquire a small animal—a uppy—without paying any monetary charge is common. The direct money rice of the exchange would be zero. Despite the apparent attractiveness of uppies, many people choose not to accept a free puppy. The nonmonetary enefits are readily apparent: a warm, cuddly, affectionate companion. The osts, both monetary and nonmonetary, however, are more than many people are to incur. The money costs typically include food, supplies, and veterinary are, and can include greater housing costs for renters. The nonmonetary osts, which can be priced, are typically time and trouble: the time to feed, xercise, and care for a pet, and the trouble caused by a dog's resistance to ousebreaking, tendency to bark loudly at inappropriate times, or desire to etch the postal carrier. These costs help explain why free puppies are not cceptable to some people. Conversely, some people place a higher value on aving a dog than on the costs discussed here. Indeed, some people pay ubstantial prices to obtain certain kinds of dogs.

Another example is the price decision of a person who is selling a restaurant. Ierb inherited a restaurant in a good location without inheriting any skill or nowledge of the restaurant business. He took a personal hand in running it nd misread demand. It now appears that he will have to sell his beloved Herb's 'elery Soup Emporium to pay off his overdue business loans for advertising. Ie is choosing to sell voluntarily rather than to have his restaurant foreclosed y his banker, who refused to extend his loans and to eat in his restaurant. ccording to his commercial real estate broker, the restaurant is worth $100,000. Ierb has been offered $90,000, which is more than enough to pay off his usiness loans. Should he take the offer or hope for a better one? The only two iings that matter to Herb are the money and the mental anguish he is uffering from seeing his restaurant fail. The benefits of a sale at the present me are $90,000 and the end of mental anguish. The costs are the loss of the estaurant and, possibly, a lower price. The decision comes down to Herb's ersonal preference for attempting to get a higher price for the restaurant ompared with his preference for ending his mental anguish. What would you o in Herb's place?

Opportunity Cost

Any price or choice situation reflects the fundamental economic notion of opportunity cost.[1] *Opportunity cost* is the notion that a cost or consequence of any decision is the rejection of other possibilities. Every choice represents an opportunity to choose between what is better and worse, and a cost of any choice is the rejection of other particular possibilities. The notion applies to both benefits and costs. Price is a measurement of the opportunity cost. Money spent on anything is no longer available to be spent on other things, and money gained from selling something reflects the choice of one selling opportunity over others. The acronym "tanstaafl," which stands for the statement "There ain't no such thing as a free lunch," emphasizes the notion of opportunity cost. Even if someone else pays for your lunch, the time has been used and is no longer available.

Opportunity cost applies to public organizations as much as to any other entity. Money or any resource handled in any particular way is no longer available for other uses. Examples in the public sector start with the decision to collect money from people with the presumption that a public organization can do something more useful with the money. Each expenditure of money or other resources results in opportunity costs by the public organization. The concept of opportunity cost is a basis for all decisions. Public organizations sometimes fail to recognize opportunity costs adequately. For example, city councils choose to create new roads through their own parks because they do not have to buy the land; unfortunately, the real cost is the loss of parkland.

Prices are said to assist in allocating resources "efficiently." This is largely because prices represent opportunity costs. Economists believe that things are produced and consumed according to the values placed on them and the means necessary to produce them. By definition, more highly valued things are produced and consumed in greater quantity than less highly valued things. Prices organize production and consumption of goods and services. Producers and consumers determine how much of a good or service to offer for sale or to buy by reference to the prevailing prices. Of course, prices and buying and selling decisions vary for different individual producers and consumers.

The collective community of buyers and sellers creates a prevailing price for a good or service. This discussion ignores quite a few technicalities, which are treated in the field of microeconomics. Generally, suppliers (sellers) continue to supply and even increase their supply of a good or service as long as the price they can get is greater than the prices they paid to produce a good or service and greater than other alternative uses of those resources. Similarly, demanders (buyers) will buy more of a good or service when the value of the things at that price is greater than alternative uses of money. If the price goes down, consumption of a product tends to go up in quantity. As prices go up, suppliers are willing to supply more, and demanders are willing to buy less. Prices, therefore, act as signals.

The relevance of the price mechanism to the public sector is fourfold. First, it explains money and money values more clearly. Second, expenditures in the public sector are purchases of goods and services from private-sector individuals and organizations; knowledge of prices helps in these situations

Third, public organizations sell some things and benefit by seeking the highest reasonable prices for what they sell. Fourth, public organizations exist to provide goods and services where the price mechanism does not work. Economists characterize these situations as involving "market failure."[2] Although market failure can become terribly complicated, such situations can be described as those in which a valued product would not be produced, would be produced at an inappropriately high or low level, or would be inappropriately distributed if relying solely on the price mechanism. Public organizations use different guiding principles rather than prices. For example, courts operate on the basis of law. The consequence of not using the price mechanism is that public organizations determine the demand and supply of certain goods and services and, consequently, the amount of resources devoted to them. Public goods provision is best understood by seeing its difference from situations involving the price mechanism.

Costs and Benefits

Because of market failure, public-sector decision making is not usually predicated on price. Valuing and choosing continue, but the whole situation is changed. The two key differences are the use of cost and benefit valuation and the attenuation of the factors ordinarily found in a price decision situation. Attenuation means separation; in this context, it means that things ordinarily found together are somewhat separate. Although the use of costs and benefits is of greater consequence in public decision making, the attenuation of the price decision factors is discussed first because it makes benefit and cost valuation necessary.

Both sides in a private-sector transaction assess the relative merits of an exchange to put a price value on it. All aspects of the situation are summed up in prices, and the two sides' prices determine if an exchange will be made. In extreme contrast, public-sector decisions are not marked by a two-sided assessment of costs and benefits resulting in a definitive price value. They are marked by much looser assessments of costs and benefits.

Public-sector decisions are made on behalf of collectivities instead of individuals. Decisions are framed by what is better or worse for this community rather than by "my" preferences as a buyer or a seller.

Public-sector decisions are made by representatives rather than by the persons bearing the costs and receiving the benefits, as happens in the private sector. Representatives make value assessments for a collectivity rather than for themselves, which makes valuing more difficult.

Public-sector decisions frequently involve the separation of those bearing the costs and those enjoying the benefits of a situation. Also, the decision makers usually are neither the prime beneficiaries nor those primarily burdened by the costs of their decisions. This contrasts with the private sector, where individuals decide for themselves and reap the consequences of their decisions. Also, public decision makers take the place of both buyers and sellers in the private sector by setting levels of demand and supply of public goods.

Because of the attenuation of the decision situation, most public-sector decisions are not reached through setting prices. What is being valued frequently has moral and political dimensions. Public organizations do not just produce another line of products similar to other products. They represent moral and political values for themselves and attempt to impose those values on others. The ultimate basis of public-sector actions is the goodness or rightness of the actions. The signers of the Declaration of Independence stated this eloquently when they pledged their "lives, fortunes, and sacred honor" to the cause of independence. They wanted to do the right thing. It was a priceless decision in that no monetary value was placed on the decision. Today, as always, many public-sector decisions are priceless ones that are properly decided in light of various moral and political standards.

Public-sector decisions are determined by considering costs and benefits. Public-sector decisions tend to be rather messy affairs in comparison with private-sector situations. In public-sector situations, one finds varying views on costs and benefits, their relative importance, and their relative consequences. Even in cases where nonmonetary costs and benefits are not at issue, monetary values are obscured by the attenuation of the decision-making situation. Consequences of decisions are difficult to predict for collectivities. Monetary values are hard to estimate for groups of people. Because of the costs and benefits separation, there are incentives to misrepresent one's preferences to secure benefits and to avoid costs through the political process. Also, moral and political values matter. Where moral and political values are not at issue, assessments of costs and benefits of various alternatives can serve public-sector decision makers in a way similar to prices. Though estimation of monetary costs and benefits is imperfect, systematic and explicit estimates can very well be better guides than implicit and uninformed guesses. Also, remember that prices are individuals' estimations of value that are personal judgments.

◆ ESTIMATING MONETARY VALUES

One estimates monetary values in the public sector for a variety of purposes—to influence behavior, to gauge prices, and to make informed decisions. The situations in which these purposes are pursued include the budget process, regulatory decisions, and any other policy or operational choice situation.

For exchanges, prices are estimated for either the buying or selling of goods and services. As a seller, a public organization benefits by setting prices that produce the greatest return consistent with public purposes. If a public organization is selling something without any public good consequence, that public organization should obtain a fair market price. Otherwise, underpriced goods and services are a benefit to those purchasing them at the expense of all other financial supporters of that organization.

If public purposes are involved, then a public organization is simultaneously collecting a price and providing a public good. Swimming pools are a good example of this. In most cases, the fees for swimming do not and are not intended to cover the complete costs of providing the service.

As a buyer, a public organization estimates likely prices for purchases to minimize the monetary costs of organizational activities. This generally means avoiding paying too much for goods and services. As a buyer of goods and services, a public organization is well advised to have a healthy respect for market imperfections. On the negative side is the price gouging that some people attempt in dealing with governments (for example, the periodic bid rigging cases where highway contractors collude in bidding on state road contracts). On the positive side is the recognition of a monopsony position, where one or several public organizations are the exclusive or predominant buyers of something, usually a labor service such as nursing or teaching. The short-run situation is one in which relatively low wage costs are a possibility; however, the long-run prospects involve the adequacy of a supply of sufficiently trained and qualified personnel in such labor fields. Even though labor service is hard to value and predict over time, a monopsony position can start with low pay and lead to a lowering of the numbers and quality of people available to a public organization.

In estimating values for analyzing policy options through cost analysis, estimates are made to stand for the values individuals themselves would place on a particular thing. Costs and benefits are estimates of the prices individuals might place on the things in question; estimates of costs and benefits in this sense are often called shadow prices or proxy prices. This puts public organizations in the position of trying to determine whether to provide some good or service that the private sector does not provide on the same evaluative basis as used in the private sector, by individual valuation. This undoubtedly is the most difficult area for the estimation of monetary value.

To Influence Behavior

In estimating monetary values for the purpose of influencing behavior, a public organization is putting a price on desired and undesired behaviors. Money penalties or rewards are placed on specified behaviors.

Penalties for undesirable behavior are generally set at a sufficiently high level to discourage the behavior. Penalties that are seen as being less costly than the undesirable behavior is beneficial do not discourage. For example, easily payable five-dollar fines for speeding do not deter most people from speeding. On the other hand, penalties set very high are not likely to be enforced vigorously. Hanging violators for speeding would not be enforceable for political and administrative reasons.

In an intermediate position, one may find behavior that is both desirable and undesirable. Usually this involves using publicly provided goods. It is desirable that the goods be consumed, but it is possible that use above a certain level would cause the quality of a good to deteriorate because of crowding effects or would increase the cost of the good to a level that would be excessive to the public organization involved. In such cases, there are frequently either charges for the goods involved or some nonmonetary barrier that serves the same purpose: rationing the good. Goods for which charges are applied include those where nonpayers can be excluded from benefiting and where beneficiaries are identifiable; examples include toll roads, zoos, colleges and

universities, and parks. In some cases, nonmonetary costs are imposed o
individuals claiming public goods where a monetary change is not feasible
Recipients of welfare services are frequently subjected to long lines; th
waiting time can be seen as a nonmonetary charge.[3]

Finally, there are positive rewards given for desirable behavior, includin
contingent and monetary rewards. The Nobel Prizes are the most prominen
examples of contingent rewards. Contingent rewards are too uncertain an
of too little monetary value to substantially affect behavior. General reward
influence behavior because of their greater certitude. For example, deduction
for charitable contributions and other desired behaviors affect choices tha
people make.

Predicting the precise results of attempts to influence people's behavior i
difficult because of other influences. Penalties, rewards, and charges ar
typically estimated, applied, and the resulting behavior is reviewed for possi
ble adjustment.

All assessments of the proper monetary value to influence behaviors are
matter of judgment and reasoning by analogy. The judgments concer
whether a particular value will have the desired effect. When we reason b
analogy, we first find something equivalent to that which is not priced. The
we price the equivalent item. By this procedure, we can estimate opportunit
cost. For example, a five-dollar fine for speeding is not an effective deterren
to speeding because most people believe the time saved by speeding is wort
more than the five-dollar fines they will pay for speeding. To reason by analog
to set a speeding fine, we have to figure what is a sufficiently high fine tha
people will save paying the fine and other penalties by driving within the spee
limits. We could start with an estimate of the value of an individual's time an
predict an adequate monetary fine. Reasoning by analogy also leads to th
suggestion that increasing the time costs of speeding by holding speeder
alongside the road or in a jail or requiring them to appear in court will succee
in cases where the motive of speeding is to save time.

To Gauge Prices

Prices are estimated on things bought and sold by public organizations. Th
estimating of prices breaks down into situations involving typical private
sector exchanges and those with some degree of "publicness." In a typica
private-sector exchange, a public organization behaves in the same fashion a
private individuals. The marketplace governs prices of exchanges. In case
with some degree of publicness, the "price" is oriented toward both a
exchange and the provisions of some public benefit.

In typical private-sector exchanges, demand and supply determine price
Such prices are easiest to estimate when there is an ongoing market. Beside
the product features affecting price, the most common concern is pric
movements over time. Time is particularly relevant because prices are esti
mated for transactions that take place months from when estimates are mad
(e.g., budget expenditures).

Where there is not an ongoing competitive market, three sources of relevan
information exist for prices. First are frequently analogous products an

markets. The price of one thing can be measured or estimated by the price of a similar thing. Second, we may gain information through experience in offering to buy or to sell something at different particular prices. Finally, there are opinions as to what something is worth.

Prices are attached to things with a degree of publicness when there are identifiable beneficiaries of a voluntary exchange. Commonly, the purposes served by prices in such situations include one or more of the following: gathering information, rationing a scarce product, influencing behavior, acquiring revenue, and recovering costs. First, prices attached to publicly provided products help us gather information on the degree of demand for those products. The number of units sold by period is a measure of demand.

Second, though all price products are scarce in some sense, some are relatively scarcer relative to demand, for example, national parks, toll roads, and public universities. Under conditions of overcrowding or deterioration as a result of high demand usage, prices and price increases can affect a situation in a desired manner.

Third, prices influence behavior. Examples include grants, tax advantages, fines, and bounties for predators. An interesting example is found in Germany, where pollution behavior is regulated by effluent charges, which are prices put on units of different kinds of pollution.

Fourth, some activities undertaken by public organizations, particularly governments, are justified partially as serving a public purpose but are also treated as opportunities for raising revenue. State liquor stores and state gambling operations are justified by states for regulating the sale of alcohol and providing citizens with sanitized gambling opportunities. Efforts by state officials to entice people into gambling or buying liquor at their outlets, however, are very obviously aimed at generating revenue. Various state gambling operations advertise heavily and seek to maximize outlets. One state was uncertain about which side of an interstate highway to put a liquor store. It compromised by building two stores, one on each side of the highway.

Finally, prices are attached to recover costs where the primary public benefit is that a public organization carries out the activity. Examples in this area are health and safety inspections, which serve the public by being conducted by a public organization but which are priced to recover the costs of the service.

Depending on the particular purpose served, prices are set or estimated in different ways. Prices for information are set as low as possible, though high enough to offset collection costs. Prices set for influencing behavior and rationing scarce products are necessarily set and adjusted in a manner that relates to experience. Prices set for revenue production resemble private-sector exchange prices in that the positive difference between income and expenses is as high as possible.

Finally, where cost recovery is the purpose, we can do some version of cost accounting and adjust the charge for service as the costs change. Cost recovery can be partial or complete, depending on the degree of publicness. With minimal publicness, cost recovery should be complete or close to complete. For goods that are mostly public, however, the cost recovery should be only a portion of the cost approximately equal to the benefit to the private beneficiary. For example, if college students personally derive approximately one third of the benefit of their college education with two thirds of the benefit going to rest of the people in the United States, then their appropriate tuition costs would be about one third of the cost of providing their education.

To Make Informed Decisions

Decision makers in public organizations estimate costs and benefits to make decisions for their organizations. Regardless of their self-consciousness, public-sector decision makers perform some version of cost analysis when they make decisions. The degree of formality, sophistication, and explicitness varies, but the basic process considers the same questions:

1. What are the options?
2. What are the consequences of the various options?
3. What are the costs and benefits of the consequences?
4. Which option has the most favorable configuration of costs and benefits?

A key concern is the explicitness of the costs and benefits analysis. Whether the costs and benefits are monetary or nonmonetary, explicit treatment of costs and benefits tends to reduce errors caused by sloppy reasoning or a partial viewpoint by bringing the values involved into the open where they can be discussed.

Policy options usually fit one of three patterns: to begin or to continue a policy, to increase or to decrease the level of a publicly provided good, and to choose among alternative means of pursuing a particular goal. Though often an area of dispute, we have to specify the consequences of the various options because the consequences involve costs and benefits. The consequences of a policy option are easier to specify retrospectively rather than prospectively. In retrospective analysis, one specifies consequences caused by the policy options in prospective analysis one is predicting, which necessarily involves a greater margin of error.

Cost consequences can be broken down into costs to a public organization and costs to the relevant public. Costs borne by public organizations include actual expenditures and tax expenditures, which are foregone revenues. Costs borne by the organization include monetary expenses and anything else valued that is diminished. Estimating public organization costs is easier than estimating costs to the public. Benefits also can be divided into benefits accruing to a public organization and to its public. Benefits to a public organization include revenue gains and expenditures or costs avoided. Benefits accruing to a relevant public include monetary income and things the public values, whatever those things may be.

A key point to remember in estimating costs and benefits, one that appears to be frequently forgotten in the public arena, is that the costs and benefits are collective for a public organization and its constituents. Shifting money between a public organization and its public or within its public is neither a benefit nor a cost to the collectivity. State aggressiveness in selling gambling

hances and liquor to nonresidents is partially explained by the expectation
hat any sale will bring a net benefit to the state involved.

The problems associated with estimating things valued by the public are
ruly heroic in nature. How is this done? However it can be done. After
pecifying the consequences of a policy option, one has to sort out the
ignificant from the insignificant. In estimating costs and benefits, one must
raw a line between those costs and benefits that are sufficiently important or
alued to be estimated and those that are not. Though at some point this
ecessarily becomes a matter of judgment, some criteria are helpful: intended
onsequences, an identifiable market, and a public outcry. When any of these
riteria are met, something is probably worthy of being estimated. For other
hings excluded from analysis, one assumes that they are trivial in scale, offset
y countervailing factors, or both. Next, costs and benefits are listed and their
nagnitudes calculated.

The estimation of monetary values can be broken down into estimation of
ctual prices and shadow prices. Actual prices refer to situations where money
vill be changing hands; these include expenditure and revenue changes for
ublic organizations and expense and income changes for individuals and
rivate organizations. As an example, a state highway project could involve
xpenditures for construction, reduced expenditures for maintenance, and
ossibly greater sales tax revenue because more nonresidents would use the
ighway and make purchases at businesses adjacent to the highway. Also, the
roject could initially reduce income for affected businesses during the period
f construction and increase it later as a result of increased volume of traffic.
ctual prices are estimated using expenditure and revenue estimation tech-
iques for public organizations and expense and income estimating tech-
iques for businesses or economic models where individuals or economies
re involved.

Shadow prices are harder to estimate because we are attempting to place a
nonetary value, a price of sorts, on something that will not be exchanged.
hadow prices are usually estimated by analogy. This thing that is not bought
r sold is like that which is bought and sold. For highways, time saved by
eople using the highway is valued by analogy with some wage rate in that
rea, despite the fact that all the people's time that is saved is not salable. A
eautiful view at point A can be valued by the difference between the price of
ousing with a similar view at point B and similar housing without a view at
oint C. A human life, which is priceless to some and relatively cheap to others,
an be and is valued by observing human behavior to see what income
ifference there is for working in life-threatening jobs, for example, coal
nining.[4] Estimates of the value of lives do not devalue life but, rather, assist
n making choices.

In estimating costs and benefits, the preference is for estimating as much
s possible on actual markets and on actual behaviors rather than imagined
r hypothesized markets and behavior. Although it may be possible to ap-
roach costs and benefits estimation by asking people what value they place
n different things, talk is extremely cheap and not necessarily accurate.
ehavior is more revealing of what value is placed on something. Some of the
ame people who say life is priceless also drive death-dealing automobiles

without the use of seat belts. Such people place more value on travel time and mobility than they do on the possibility of being killed or injured in an automobile accident. Admittedly, the realm of behavior involves habit, deficiencies in information, and less than rational decision making. How people actually behave and choose, however, is largely protected by laws in the United States within bounds placed on some harmful behaviors (e.g., speed limits and drug use). The rational-person approach to estimating costs and benefits would be appropriate only for a society of totally rational people, which is not found in our world, except in my office on Thursday afternoons. Costs and benefits are estimated for real people to the extent possible.

◆ MONETARY VALUE AND TIME

Time and value are highly interrelated; that is, time affects the value of things. Time effects on value are important in the arena of public finance administration. Specifically, time affects prices, costs, and benefits. Five kinds of time effects on values concern the public sector:

- Ordinary change
- Price fluctuations
- Money supply change
- Rental value (time value of use)
- Risk of changes

Ordinary change refers to the regular, anticipated changes. Automobiles, houses, roads, and other physical structures gradually lose value over time because of physical deterioration. Some things gain in value for a period of time and then diminish past a certain point: aged meats, wines, and cheeses. Some things do not change in value in relation to time, for example, diamonds, gold, spouses, and land.

Ordinary change over time of physical objects that ordinarily diminish in value over time affects the public sector, for example, physical structures, equipment, and furniture. This is reflected in public-sector accounting in funds that use accrual or modified accrual accounting. Ordinary change in the value of physical items (depreciation) is used to measure the costs of operations in enterprise and internal service funds to assist in setting accurate prices for services.

A second effect of time on value is price fluctuation as a result of market changes in supply and demand. Some formal markets and public-sector organizations deal with this phenomenon. Several commodity markets even have "futures" trading, where delivery of commodities at some period in the future is specified. You would use these markets for buying and selling the future delivery of something. For example, brokers trade futures in June wheat on the Chicago Board of Trade, which are commitments to buy or sell wheat in the succeeding June. Public organizations recognize and deal with this when making purchases that extend over time. Contracts that provide for price changes in a good or service can do so on a cost basis or on the basis of some benchmark or standard that is possible to verify. Also, when a price changes rapidly, vendors and public organizations will often try to make an adjustment even when there is a fixed-price contract.

The third time effect on monetary values is caused by changes in the money supply, which is influenced by the U.S. government. Those interested in the mechanics of this can find the details in any introductory economics text that covers macroeconomics. Basically, the relationship at issue is the rate of change in the money supply related to the rate of change of the sum total of goods and services produced in the United States. If the money supply grows faster than the supply of goods and services, more money is available to purchase goods and services than previously. The result is inflation, an increase in prices. If the sum total of goods and services grows faster than the money supply, there is relatively less money to purchase goods and services. The result is deflation, a decrease in prices. Changes in the money supply are interesting because that has had the greatest influence on apparent monetary values. Since the 1982-to-1984 period, prices as measured by the consumer price index have increased on average more than 150%. An average item costing $1.00 in 1982-1984 would cost more than $1.50 today. Any kind of analysis of values over extended periods requires some treatment of price inflation. In dealing with prices or other values relative to the past, analysts equalize them by picking a base year and decreasing values in subsequent years at a rate equal to some measured inflation rate. If an item was priced at $1.00 in the base year and increased at a rate of 10% over the next two years as did prices generally, then item prices of $1.10 in the first subsequent year and $1.21 in the second subsequent year merely reflect inflation.

To erase the effects of inflation for purposes of analysis, we use a price deflator, which uses an index of price changes to provide a general measurement of price changes. The most familiar index is the CPI, the consumer price index. Prices of certain items are added to create an index; changes in the total of the index are considered reflective of general price changes. To equalize prices from different periods, we divide a particular price by the index to get a price equivalent to the base year of the index.

For example, using the example of the $1.00 item and general inflation of 10% over two years, we could construct an index and equalize the prices of the item over time. Table 4.1 shows the price deflators and the deflated prices for a cup of celery soup. Remember that price deflators are intended only as a means of removing the effects of price inflation caused by changes in the money supply. Other changes in prices should still appear. Price deflators or indexes can be used in an organization's financial condition analysis, cost analysis, analysis of past expenditures, and multiyear revenue and expenditure estimation.[5]

A fourth effect of time on value is the rental value of something. The value of something varies by whether it is purchased completely (lock, stock, and barrel, as was said about guns, or the whole nine yards, as for a bolt of cotton) or its use is purchased for a period of time. Both outright purchases and rentals of things have advantages that differ under different circumstances. The price of a rental item varies by the length of time involved as well as by any other

TABLE 4.1 Price Deflation for a Cup of Celery Soup

Base	Year	Year Two	Year Three
Sticker Price	$1.00	$1.10	$1.21
Inflation Rate	-	10%	10%
Price Deflator	-	1.10	1.21
Deflated Price	$1.00	$1.00	$1.00

NOTE: Sticker Price/Price Deflator = Deflated Price.

significant factors involved. Paradoxically, one major reason for the rental of things by the public sector is that such transactions typically confer federal income tax advantages on private vendors, which can be partially captured by public organizations. These range from what appear to be blatant rip-offs to ordinary business transactions. According to some, an example of a blatant rip-off was a city selling its buildings to a private firm, which in turn rents them to the city on a lease-purchase basis. In this case, both the city and the business benefit at the expense of the federal treasury.[6] An example of an ordinary business transaction is a business routinely deducting the depreciated expense of equipment leased to a public organization.

The most pervasive use of rental value is for money. Private individuals rent money from others when they take out loans or use charge cards, and rent money to others when they deposit money in an interest-bearing account. Many transactions are partially evaluated by the better choice based on the rental value of money. Private individuals choose to pay charge card bills costing 16% or more per annum rather than retain the same money in an interest-bearing account paying 8%. Similarly, a public entity choosing between the outright purchase or the rental of a piece of equipment considers the rental value of money, the value of the money not spent on buying the piece of equipment.[7]

The last factor affecting value over time is risk, the chance that something negative can occur. With a longer period, the probability of untoward events increases. This affects values. Risks can be shared or shifted to someone else. For example, a purchase of a commodity such as gasoline over a year at a fixed price means that the vendor is assuming the risk of price fluctuations. Because of budgeting inflexibility, particularly among governments, public organizations avoid risks. Someone has to receive some value to take on the risk, however. The gasoline vendor will require a higher price for doing so.

The utility of understanding the relationship between time and value lies in each of the particular areas of public finance administration as monetary value runs through all of them. An area in which time and monetary value relations is particularly important is cost analysis. Also, the time value of money is particularly important in areas where handling money is a focus (debt management, cash management, investments, and purchasing, for example). The time value of money is a reflection of three time factors that affect monetary values. Those factors are (1) the rental value of money, (2) estimates of risk, and (3) anticipation of changes in the money supply. These three

actors are considered in markets where money is rented. These markets
rovide a basis for valuing things over time. Once you have a monetary value
r price for something at one point in time, you can use that value and relevant
market rates to compute a *net present value*. Net present value is merely a
measure of the estimated current value of something.

The net present value is calculated by discounting some future value by
some discount rate. A discount rate measures the opportunity cost rate of
return that is demanded and received in the money markets for the amount
f money at issue for the time period at issue. For example, one million dollars
elivered to you a year from now is worth one million dollars minus one
million dollars multiplied by the discount rate; this is the measurement of
what a million dollars could earn in interest income in the intervening period.
Typically, discount rates are used to calculate discount factors that are then
multiplied by the dollar amounts involved. A discount rate is generally se-
ected from among the various money market rates, which represents what
ou could get in interest income on the amount in question. For example, a
ederal Treasury Note rate for one year would provide a relatively risk-free
iscount rate whereas a one-year-high-grade corporate note rate would reflect
moderate degree of risk. You could use one of these two or some other money
market rate. For one million dollars discounted at 5% for one year, the
alculations are as follow:

$1,000,000 - ($1,000,000 x 5% [discount rate]) =
$1,000,000 - $50,000   = $950,000

r

$1,000,000 x (100% - 5%)   =
$1,000,000 x .95 [discount factor] = $950,000 [8]

One million dollars a year from today is worth approximately $950,000 today
when the appropriate money market rate is 5% per year.

Over multiple years with compound interest, the change in values is
astonishing. At the rate of 12% for 6 years or 6% for 12 years, a value is cut in
alf. At either rate over the specified period, a million dollars would be worth
bout one-half million dollars. Conversely, one-half million dollars invested
oday at 12% for 6 years or 6% for 12 years would be worth a million dollars
t the end of the period, which would give us the future value of some specific
monetary value. One value is the flip side of the other; each represents a
market value of money at different periods of time, considering the relevant
actors affecting value over time. Recognizing interest rates and discount rates
s manifestations of the time value of money makes it possible to make value
omparisons when time is a factor.

A discount rate is a quantified measurement of the opportunity cost of
using money for a period of time. The money markets pay interest on money
nd are an alternative use for money, whether publicly or privately held. Also,
s the markets determine values, the interest rates are perceived as accurate.
Discount rates can be used to make comparisons between private and public

use of resources and between alternative public use of resources. For example, a typical cost-benefit study compares the value of current expenditures with future benefits. One aspect of such studies is computing the net present value of both costs and benefits to decide whether to implement particular projects. Where the net present value of benefits is less than the costs, leave money for the contemplated project in private hands or use it for a better public project or purpose.

What discount rate to choose is often controversial. Theoretically, the controversy tends to be about what degree of risk of various investments to use for a discount rate basis. Relatively risky investments pay higher rates than less risky investments. Investments made by public organizations tend to be less risky. Investments in public organizations tend to be less risky and often have federal income taxation exemption and, therefore, pay a lower interest rate. On one hand, governments as investors or borrowers deal with low rates. On the other hand, corporate borrowers pay a wide range of interest rates based on risks. According to some, corporate investment rates are more realistic than governmental investment rates. Others take the opposite viewpoint. At the practical level, discount rates selected affect the results of net present value calculations. A relatively high discount rate diminishes the net present value of an investment. This issue will be explored more fully in Chapter 8, Cost Analysis.

◆ CONCLUSION

Monetary values are important in public finance administration. This chapter has explained the meaning of money and values; the related concepts of prices, costs, and benefits; how money is used to value things and to make decisions; how monetary values are estimated; and how time affects monetary values. The chapter contains economic ideas in the forms most intelligible from a public-sector viewpoint. This is a stepping-stone for understanding how money and values operate in particular public finance administration areas.

DISCUSSION QUESTIONS

1. How do time and money matter in relation to each other in public finances?

2. Do most values in public organizations get reflected in money terms or not?

3. Do people in public organizations think too little or too much about money?

4. How do different individuals' values get reflected in money?

NOTES ◆

1. Steven E. Rhoads (1985). *The economist's view of the world: Government, markets, and public policy*. Cambridge: Cambridge University Press, pp. 11-24.

2. Rhoads, pp. 66-67; Anthony Downs (1967). *Inside bureaucracy*. Boston: Little, Brown, 2-36; Joseph E. Stiglitz (1986). *Economics of the public sector*. New York: Norton, pp. 83-94. Also, many economists recognize a reciprocal situation in which governmental programs can be expected to fail to operate well. These situations are referred to as "government failures." See Rhoads, pp. 67-81 and Stiglitz, pp. 6-8.

3. Downs, p. 188; Jeffrey Manditch Prottas (1981, September/October). The cost of free services: Organizational impediments to access to public services. *Public Administration Review*, 1(5), 526-534.

4. Rhoads, pp. 127-128.

5. Francis J. Leazes, Jr. and Carol W. Lewis (1984). Now you see it, now you don't. In Carol . Lewis and A. Grayson Walker III (Eds.), *Casebook in budgeting and financial management* (pp. 39-194). Englewood Cliffs, NJ: Prentice-Hall.

6. For the compulsively curious, the story is found on page 1 of *City and state: Crain's newspaper of public business and finance* (Chicago), July/August 1985.

7. For an example of such a case, see Edward A. Dyl and Michael D. Joehnk (1978, November/December). Leasing as a municipal finance alternative. *Public Administration Review, 38*(6), 57-562.

8. For the compulsively precise, one can compute the discount factor for any situation with the following formula:

$$1/ (1 + \text{Interest Rate})^{\text{time in years}}$$

For example,

$$1/ (1 + 0.05)^1 = 1/1.05 = 0.952$$

for one year hence:

$$1/ (1+.05)^2 = 1/1.1025 = 0.907$$

for two years hence; and

$$1/(1 + .05)^3 = 1/1.157625 = 0.864$$

for three years hence.

SUGGESTED READINGS ◆

Steven E. Rhoads (1985). *The economist's view of the world: Government, markets, and public policy*. Cambridge: Cambridge University Press.

Joseph E. Stiglitz (1988). *Economics of the public sector* (2nd ed.). New York: Norton.

Public Revenues

5

Revenues are resources—principally money but also land, equipment facilities, and labor—gathered by public organizations. Revenues ar gathered primarily to enable public organizations to act. Revenue gatherin enables public organizations to act through expenditure of resources. Othe purposes include regulating behavior, allocating resources, distributing cost and benefits, and, for the federal government, regulating the national economy

Both recognized and self-proclaimed experts write much on revenue Some economists specialize in studying revenues. Many accountants specia ize in helping individuals and businesses legally avoid contributing greatly t the revenues of public organizations. Here, a nonspecialized approach focuse on revenue concepts, sources, evaluative criteria, and the pattern of publi revenues in the United States.

◆ REVENUE CONCEPTS

The most important revenue concepts include revenue, revenue measure tax, base, base measurement, exemption, deduction, rate, revenue liabilit credit, revenue structure, revenue expenditure, delinquency, incidence, pro gressivity, elasticity, nonneutralities, and earmarked revenues.

Revenue Measure

A revenue measure is a specific law, policy, regulation, or program fc gaining revenue. Governments, for example, have laws that authorize revenu collection. Without legal authorizations, governments cannot collect reve nues. Similarly, nonprofit organizations develop policies and plans and mak specific decisions for gathering revenues. Revenues do not appear magicall specific efforts must be made to gather them.

Tax

A tax is a required payment. Taxes are involuntary in the sense that governments compel payment. If individuals do not pay taxes, money and other assets can be legally taken from them, and they can also be penalized through civil and criminal court actions. Governments require compulsory tax payments to fund services that are predominantly public goods. Governments compel tax payments because people otherwise would not pay for the services. Governmental revenues are primarily tax revenues; other government revenues are nontax revenues. All revenues of nonprofit organizations are nontax revenues because only governments can use taxes.

Base

Base refers to something on which revenue is collected. Identifying a base from which or on which to collect revenue is necessary. Bases can be physical items, events, conditions, or activities. Bases have to be defined rather precisely to make it possible to collect revenues appropriately. The most common tax bases include income, sales, and property. These bases require more precise definition to determine clearly what is taxed to facilitate tax administration.

Base Measurement

Bases are measured to determine how much revenue to collect, typically in three ways. First, the measuring method used for major taxes is *ad valorem*, according to value." This refers to dollar value. When things are ordinarily measured by dollar values for other purposes, that valuation can easily be used for base measurement. Second, bases can be measured in numbers of units. The bases for cigarette taxes and lottery tickets are measured in this manner. Third, bases can be grouped into classes by some criterion. The area of permits or permissions particularly uses this type of base measurement. Driver license fees for various types of vehicles provide one example of this method.

Exemption

An exemption, which is sometimes called an exclusion, refers to something excluded from a revenue base. Exemptions are releases from obligation for things or people. Some things are exempted from bases because they are thought to be inappropriate to include in a base or are seen as being beneficial. Many states exempt food and drugs from sales tax bases because legislators accept the argument that taxes on the necessities of life adversely affect lower-income people. Also, exemptions can be given to persons generally or on specific criteria. Examples of both are found in federal personal income taxes—everyone filing has a certain amount of income exempt for each person covered by that form, and special income exemptions exist for people who are older than age 65 and those who are blind. Often, nonprofit organizations are exempt from paying sales and property taxes. Several groups receive partial property tax exemptions (e.g., home owners, veterans, veterans' spouses, and older persons). Exemptions are almost always associated with government revenue collection and taxes, though not all taxes have exemptions.

Deduction

A deduction is a reduction in a base contingent on some specific event or condition. Unlike an exemption, which involves exclusion of something from a base, a deduction is an adjustment in an already defined base. Deductions are similar to exemptions in that they are provided for things that are seen as inappropriate in a base or as particularly meritorious. The costs of earning income to some degree are deductible, as are the costs to businesses of collecting sales taxes in some states. Deductions on meritorious grounds include charitable contributions, medical expenses, taxes, and home mortgage interest expenses.

Rate

A rate is the value charged for whatever base measurement for taxes or other revenue. Many rates are ad valorem and involve a percent of the base measurement. Other rates are applied against specific units of the base—so many dollars or cents per unit. Both ad valorem and unit rates can be used on a sliding scale basis, with the rate changing, either on a percentage or unit basis with changes in the size of the base. The rate can increase or decrease as the base increases. The rates found in a formal statement of revenue policy are called *face rates.* On the surface, these appear to be the applicable rates. Because of exemptions, deductions, and other adjustments, however, actual rates paid are significantly different. What is actually paid is referred to as *effective rate*; that is, what the rate would have been if no adjustments had been made. To compute effective rates, the revenue liability is divided by an overall base before exemptions and deductions.

Revenue Liability

Revenue liability refers to the amount of revenue owed. For a particular revenue source, this is a function of the adjusted base and rate. *Adjusted base* means exemptions and deductions have been subtracted from the gross or total base. The adjusted base multiplied by rate equals liability. In practice, this is complicated by base measurement, exemptions, deductions, and sliding scales.

Credit

Credits are much like exemptions and deductions. The primary difference is that credits apply against revenue liability. In other words, we can subtract a credit directly from the liability. If we are liable for $50 and have a credit of $25, our liability is reduced to $25. Credits are relatively more direct in affecting how much is owed than are exemptions and deductions. A credit

TABLE 5.1 Basic Revenue Measure Structure

Commonsense understanding of base - *Exemptions* = Gross *Base*
Gross Base - *Deductions* = Adjusted Base
Adjusted Base x *Rate* (or *rates*) = *Revenue Liability*
Revenue Liability - *Credits* = Adjusted Revenue Liability, which is the revenue owed

results in a forgiving of revenue liability on a dollar-for-dollar basis. Exemptions and deductions vary in value depending on the face rates.

Revenue Structure

Revenue structure refers to the relationships of different elements or features of a revenue measure. Change in one or more of a revenue measure's features changes its structure. Table 5.1 displays a basic scheme for the structure of revenue measures.

Revenue Expenditure

A revenue expenditure, which is most commonly a tax expenditure, is a revenue loss that results from a policy choice not to collect a particular revenue; revenue expenditures are also revenue or tax preferences because they give preferential treatment to particular persons or situations. An example of a revenue expenditure is the federal income tax deduction for the interest portion of home mortgage payments. All exemptions, deductions, variable rates, and credits can be viewed as revenue expenditures. A revenue expenditure necessarily requires some assumption of a normal revenue measure and a differentiation between that normal measure and the actual revenue measure. As many have noted, the revenue expenditure notion appears to presume that revenues not collected are somehow owned by the public organization. Regardless of the legitimate owner of resources, this concept helps to identify foregone revenues to analyze their impact.

Revenue expenditures are politically expedient because they are not as visible as direct payments. Therefore, legislators can provide greater benefits in the form of revenue expenditures than they could in the form of direct payments. Tax expenditures are also politically preferred because revenue provisions tend to be somewhat permanent and less controllable than budgeted expenditures. Revenue expenditures are implemented through exemptions, deductions, credits, special rates, or any other device reducing current revenue liability. Residential housing provides an excellent example of this. The federal government forgoes far more revenues on the deduction from personal income taxes on home mortgage interest expenses than it directly spends on all other housing programs, principally subsidized low-income housing. These two programs have dissimilar policy impacts. Tax expenditures constitute programs with substantive policy impacts that also affect public budgets by decreasing resources available for other programs.

Delinquency

Delinquency refers to situations where people fail to pay revenue liabilities. Some delinquency is temporary with payment made after some delay, and some delinquency is permanent, with no reasonable way to collect money owed. Delinquency is important in revenue estimation because delinquency affects how much money is actually collected, as can be seen in the following equation: Total Adjusted Revenue Liabilities - Current Delinquent Payments + Past Delinquent Payments = Revenue Yield.

Incidence

Incidence refers to the relative shares of persons who bear the burden of revenue measures. The person directly paying a revenue or a tax may be able to pass some or all of that cost on to someone else. The clearest case of shifted incidence involves payments by corporations, entities that are legally treated as if they were persons. For example, a corporation that pays corporate income taxes does not ultimately bear the tax burden because corporations are artificial persons. Some real persons will ultimately bear the tax burden by having fewer resources at their command. The people affected by taxes on a corporation include the consumers of the corporation's products, the owners, the employees, and the suppliers. The same thing can occur when real people pay revenue measures; they can shift the burden to someone else when possible. Property owners who rent property shift property taxes to renters to some extent. Business operators also shift some of the costs of their taxes to others.

Progressivity

Progressivity refers to the relative incidence of a revenue measure or revenue system on individuals at different economic levels. Different economic levels are usually measured by income but also can be measured as wealth. A revenue measure or system can be said to be progressive, proportional, or regressive. *Progressive* means that people at higher economic levels pay a greater percentage of their income or wealth in revenue than do those at lower economic levels. *Proportional* means that a revenue measure or system takes approximately the same percentage from people at different economic levels. *Regressive* means that people at lower economic levels pay a greater percentage of their income or wealth in revenue than do people at higher economic levels. These terms are descriptive. Degrees of progressivity or regressivity can be measured by the different percentages collected from different-level economic groups. In practice, measuring progressivity is difficult because of the number of different economic groups and the difficulty of measuring incidence. Table 5.2 shows the numerical relationships involved.

Difficulties abound in assessing progressivity in particular situations. First, one measure or one revenue system does not stand alone. An adequate measure of revenue progressivity requires comprehensiveness. The easy argument is that what is excluded can be the opposite of what is included. If some measures are progressive and others regressive, only a comprehensive assessment

TABLE 5.2 Progressive, Proportional, and Regressive Relationships

Low-Income Persons	High-Income Persons
Person 1	**Person 4**
Income: 10,000	Income: 100,000
Tax: 1,000	Tax: 10,000
Tax Rate: 10%	Tax Rate: 10%
Person 2	**Person 5**
Income: 10,000	Income: 100,000
Tax: 1,100	Tax: 11,000
Tax Rate: 11%	Tax Rate: 11%
Person 3	**Person 6**
Income: 10,000	Income: 100,000
Tax: 900	Tax: 9,000
Tax Rate: 9%	Tax Rate: 9%

Progressive Relationships:
Person 1 (10%) to Person 5 (11%)
Person 3 (9%) to Persons 4 (10%) and 5 (11%)

Proportional Relationships:
Person 1 to Person 4 (10%)
Person 2 to Person 5 (11%)
Person 3 to Person 6 (9%)

Regressive Relationships:
Person 1 (10%) to Person 6 (9%)
Person 2 (11%) to Persons 4 (10%) and 6 (9%)

nent of revenue measures provides an adequate description of progressivity. Second, because revenues do not stand alone in affecting people, an argument can be made for including the relative impacts of expenditures on individuals by economic-level groups also. Third, assumptions about incidence are crucial in assessing progressivity. For example, the degree to which the cost of property taxes is shifted to renters and customers of businesses is central to determining whether those taxes are progressive or regressive. Finally, one can find that the relationships between different-level economic groups are inconsistent, which is to say that we can simultaneously find revenue measures to be progressive, proportional, and regressive between particular economic-level groups. An extremely simple but not unrealistic example may clarify this:

Group	Income Level	Effective Tax Rate
	$10,000	30%
	$20,000	20%
	$30,000	30%
Progressive:	Group 2 to Group 3	
Proportional:	Group 1 to Group 3	
Regressive:	Group 1 to Group 2	

Elasticity

Elasticity refers to the rate of change in one thing relative to another thing that is, how one thing changes when another thing changes. Some revenue measures vary relative to general economic activity. As economic activity increases, so do income, sales, and property tax amounts increase. Income and sales taxes are relatively elastic; they increase and decrease more rapidly than economic activity; conversely, property taxes are inelastic and change less than the change in the level of economic activity. When economic activity increases or decreases by 10%, income and sales tax revenues change by more than 10% and property tax revenues by less than 10%.

Nonneutralities

Nonneutralities refer to the impacts revenue measures have on behavior Whatever the revenue measure, its existence has an impact on personal and business behavior. For example, income taxes decrease the value of income and thereby increase the relative value of leisure time. A more interesting example is the tax on windows enacted in England in 1696, which appears to have been an attempt to tax the wealthier portion of the community. A nonneutrality was that people built houses with few windows.[1] Oftentimes tax measures produce unanticipated nonneutralities.

Revenue measures are primarily instituted to collect revenues, and their exemptions, deductions, credits, and special rates may be used to attempt to influence behavior. In some cases, though, revenue measures are instituted with the avowed or actual purpose of regulating behavior. Penalty payment and forfeitures are obvious examples of regulatory-oriented revenue measures. Sin taxes—selective sales taxes on noncriminal vices, such as alcoholic beverages, tobacco products, and gambling—are often justified on the basis of behavior modification, even though they appear to be more revenue-oriented. Some revenue measures are used to gain criminal jurisdiction for tax evasion. Federal involvement in restricting illegal drugs is sometimes based on tax evasion, such as the tax on marijuana (obviously not a big money raiser). Charges for services are used to modify consumption patterns by making some goods and services higher priced to reduce demand. In some cases, more money is saved in reduced expenditures to provide a service than is gained in revenue (e.g., a false burglar alarm fee).

Earmarked Revenues

To earmark a revenue means to limit its use to one or more particular purposes. Earmarking is used most extensively at the state level, for a few programs at the federal level, and infrequently at the local level. More than one third of federal revenues are earmarked, primarily social security revenue but also motor fuel taxes and postal charges. States earmark extensively, most commonly in the areas of highways, education, debt, and intergovernmental transfers.

PUBLIC REVENUE SOURCES ◆

Revenues, like rivers, have sources from whence they flow. The sources of revenues are bases. To collect water from a river, you merely have to have access to some portion of it. Collecting public revenues requires locating a revenue base. Revenue measures can be described using a variety of categories. A discussion of revenue sources categorized by bases follows:

Base Categories:

1. Income taxes
2. Consumption taxes
3. Wealth taxes
4. Business activity taxes
5. Interorganizational transfers
6. Quid pro quo payments
7. Penalty payments and forfeitures
8. Gifts
9. Debt

Base categories can be grouped in various ways. The first four categories are composed of tax bases and the last five are composed of nontax revenues. The first three categories provide the most revenues in the United States, the middle three are next in importance, and the last three are least important for governments.

Income Taxes

Although "the" income tax is understood as the federal personal income tax, many other taxes are based on income. Another federal income tax on individuals funds the Social Security Administration. More than 40 states have a personal income tax. Eleven states allow one or more local governments to tax personal income.[2] Income taxes are collected on the existence of income; most frequently the rates are percentages of income after exemptions and deductions. The beauty of income taxes lies in four parts. First, the extremely large volume of income means that the revenue yield can be very large at relatively low rates. Second, especially at the federal level, such taxes can be used for implementing policy through tax expenditures. Third, they have relatively low administrative burdens. Fourth, collection occurs regularly throughout a fiscal year.

Consumption Taxes

Consumption literally means to use up. Consumption taxes are divided into two categories: general sales taxes and specific measures. The most well known measures are state and local "general sales tax" measures, which are not as general as they first appear. Typically, in addition to specific exemptions too numerous to detail here, such taxes do not generally apply to wholesal purchases and services, can exempt food and pharmacy purchases, and i: some cases exempt clothing purchases. The general sales tax is usually a ta on nongrocery and nonpharmacy physical goods purchased at the retail leve with specific exemptions. The various exemptions for general sales taxe represent political and technical concerns. States are making efforts to exten general sales taxes to some services as services become an increasing portio of economic activity. A problem with sales taxes on services is politica resistance by powerful groups. Watch this area in the coming years.

Specific measures include custom duties and selective sales taxes. Custom duties are charges laid on goods imported into the United States (e.g., car shoes, and steel). Selective sales taxes are called various things, including excis taxes, luxury taxes, sin taxes, and sumptuary taxes. Selective sales taxes ar taxes on specific things or specific groups of goods or services. These taxes ar extremely prevalent. Examples of selective sales taxes include

- Meals
- Lodging
- Amusements
- Amusement devices
- Gambling activities
- Marijuana
- Motor fuels
- Motor vehicle parts
- Tobacco products
- Alcohol products
- Public utilities (telephone, transportation, natural gas, water, and electricity)

Use taxes accompany general and selective sales taxes. Use taxes are levie on goods purchased in another jurisdiction but brought into the taxin jurisdiction for use. Sales taxes apply to purchases within a jurisdictio whereas use taxes apply to use within a jurisdiction. Use taxes are otherwis identical to sales taxes. Use taxes were introduced to prevent people fron avoiding sales taxes by making purchases outside of sales tax jurisdictions. Us taxes provide a legal basis for taxing products imported from jurisdictions no charging sales taxes. Use taxes are not generally enforced except on big-ticke items.

The *value-added tax* is a consumption tax used in Europe and occasionall considered in the United States. The State of Michigan experimented with version of one for a year. Despite many complicated variations, the value added tax is the sum of taxes on the "value" added to a product at each stag of production, paid by each producer, and recouped in the sale price of th products.

An extremely simple example may clarify how it works: Producer A spend $1,000 on factors of production to make a product that will be sold for $2,000 The value added is the difference between the cost of the factors of productio and the price of the product, $1,000. Assuming no previous value-added taxe have been paid and a 10% rate, the value-added tax would be $100. Producer A would charge $2100 for the product ($2000 for the product and $100 for the value-added tax). If the purchaser was the final consumer of the product, the value-added tax would work exactly as a retail sales tax. If another producer purchased the product, however, that purchaser would receive documentation that producer A had paid the value-added tax. When second- and later-stage producers or vendors are assessed value-added taxes, they receive credit for value-added taxes paid earlier in the production process. Value-added taxes can be collected from the earliest stages of production and provide incentives for compliance. They are used where a high rate of tax evasion might occur on a retail sales tax.

Wealth Taxes

Wealth taxes can conjure notions of great wealth but actually involve moderate and modest wealth more frequently. Wealth taxes involve the ownership or the transfer of ownership in property. The particular measures are real property taxes, personal property taxes, variously named death taxes, and gift taxes. All property can be divided into *real property,* which is land and anything attached to the land, and *personal property,* which is anything movable. Real property is the leading base for wealth taxes. Real property is assessed to assign it a monetary value, and various, usually local, jurisdictions apply tax rates on an ad valorem basis. Personal property taxes have declined in popularity in this century because of the difficulties of assessment and the ease of avoiding assessment. Personal property taxes have been repealed extensively and administratively avoided where laws have not been repealed. Personal property taxes are collected on registered vehicles, however, including motor vehicles, trailers, planes, and boats. Technically, the personal property tax can be assessed on particular personal property items themselves or assessed generally on a person using registered items as a basis for assessment.

The variously named death taxes, including estate and inheritance taxes, are taxes on the transfer of wealth on death from one person to another. These taxes represent an expression of antipathy toward hereditary wealth, as well as a target of revenue opportunity without a politically active constituency except in a few jurisdictions. These taxes give new meaning to the saying "Nothing is certain but death and taxes." People are taxed when they die. The taxes work differently in the precise point in the process of transferring that taxation occurs. Inheritance taxes are paid after transfer whereas estate taxes are paid before transfer. Since 1987, federal tax on estates started at 37% for estates greater than $600,000. The federal tax code provides a credit for state death taxes to a certain amount. This encourages states to use death taxes because the taxes will be paid, either to the federal or a state treasury.

Once death taxes were instituted, it became apparent that one sure way to beat them legally, aside from being poor, which many people cleverly contrived, was by transferring wealth before death. The tax countermeasure is a gift tax, which is designed to minimize wealth shifting before death without impinging on ordinary gift giving. Gifts of as much as $10,000 per recipient per year are not taxed. After that, complicated rules embedded in the federal personal income tax code apply.

Business Activity Taxes

Many business activity taxes resemble income, consumption, and wealth taxes applied to individuals. The key difference is the identification of businesses or business activities as the basis for taxation. Businesses and business activities are seen as targets of opportunity. Such taxes include corporation income and excise taxes, occupation taxes, employee-related taxes, gross receipts taxes, inventory taxes, and severance taxes.

Income from business activity pursued outside of corporations is subject to personal income taxes. Corporate income is taxed through corporation income taxes and corporation excise taxes. Corporation income taxes work essentially like personal income taxes; the corporation is treated as a person with income, exemptions, deductions, credits, and the like. Income to individuals from corporate dividends on sale of corporate stock is also taxed (with some arguing against the practice because it constitutes double taxation). Corporation excise taxes vary by the level of income. For state corporation income taxes, the portion of a corporation's income to be taxed in any given state is based primarily on calculations using sales, property, and payroll in that particular state as a portion of the corporation's total operations.

Occupation taxes are applied to corporations and individuals who engage in specified business activities. Tree trimming, law, and operating a roller rink are examples of business activities subject to these taxes. Occupation taxes are typically a set amount per year for being in a particular business. Of course, the amount of tax varies by business activity.

Employee-related taxes include the employer portion of social security, unemployment, disability, worker's compensation, and head taxes. These taxes principally fund programs for employees. The social security programs, officially called the Old-Age, Survivors', Disability, and Health Insurance system, primarily provide income for retirees but also fund Medicare. Unemployment, disability, and worker's compensation (temporary disability income) taxes are used to pay for these programs. Head taxes are taxes on business by employee, so much per employee, which are used at the local level to raise revenue.

Gross receipts taxes are levied on the total payments made to a business. These taxes can apply generally to corporations or businesses or can be specific to one business activity, for example, insurance companies.

Inventory taxes are levied on the value of business inventories held at a particular point in time. These taxes have been used less frequently as businesses learned to reduce inventories at tax time to avoid paying and as their uneven impact on various business activities became apparent.

Severance taxes are taxes levied on the extraction of natural products from the ground or water. Oil and natural gas are the most important objects of severance taxes, but they are levied on a wide variety of other mineral resources, timber, and fish.

Interorganizational Transfers

Interorganizational transfers refer to revenues obtained by public organizations from other public organizations. The two forms of these transfers are shared revenues and grants.

Shared revenue occurs when one government decides to give other governments some portion of a revenue that the one government has levied. Generally, states share revenues with counties, municipalities, and school districts as a form of general financial assistance and as a political device to secure local official support for tax measures. Income and sales taxes can be used. This is unlike a situation in which a local government levies a tax on the same tax base. That is not a shared revenue. The distinguishing characteristic of shared revenues is that recipient governments do not have to do anything to be entitled to the revenue.

Grants are payments from one organization to another without a specific benefit accruing to organizations making the payments. Grants are better known and involve much more money than shared revenues. Grants are not contracts for purchases. Grants are "given" to help others—the other organizations or their clientele. Grants are given because the granting organization sees a need for the recipient organization to have additional resources or because the recipient organization can do something that helps clientele. Much intergovernmental aid is based on a perceived imbalance between revenue-raising capacity and expenditure needs. Also, in many cases, a larger geographic unit will provide financial support for services that create benefits for constituents inside and outside of the smaller unit. For example, primary and secondary education, generally produced in smaller territorial units, generates economic benefits to entire states and the nation; for that reason, the state and federal governments provide grant funding. The geographically larger federal and state governmental units are seen to be legally and circumstantially more capable of collecting revenues than smaller ones, whereas the smaller state and local units have immediate and obvious expenditure needs. Grants to nonprofit organizations appear to be made with specific programming in mind.

Grants can be given on the basis of a direct appropriation, a formula, or on application. A specific amount given to one or a few organizations is typical of local government support of nonprofit organizations. Formula grants include weighted factors that determine how much money grant recipients will be given. Formula grants are entitlements, and all entities meeting the criteria set out in the relevant laws and regulations can obtain them. Project grants are awarded on a competitive basis in response to specific applications.

Quid Pro Quo Payments

Quid pro quo is a Latin phrase that means something for something. Someone pays money as a fee or charge and gets something in return. Such payments include a wide variety of payment situations in which the person or entity making a payment to a public organization receives some specific benefit. These payments can be categorized into payments associated with business-oriented situations, which are often spoken of as user fees, and primarily regulatory-related activities.

Public organizations are involved in a variety of business-oriented situations. First, they own businesses that they or their agents run as ordinary businesses. Second, they run businesslike enterprises where payments are required. Third, they engage in other business activities. Here, understanding the situations is more important than memorizing these terms. Businesses are separate from public organizations and are taxed. Any remaining revenue goes to the public organization after taxes. Tax-exempt public organizations conduct businesslike enterprises. Common examples of businesslike enterprises include liquor stores; public utilities such as electricity, water, sewage, garbage, and natural gas service; parks and other recreational sites; health and hospital services; gambling; and transportation facilities, such as airports, highways, and bridges. Other business activities that are not businesslike enterprises but involve payments include investments and the sale or rental of capital assets such as land, mineral rights, buildings, and equipment. These business oriented situations usually appear to be more oriented to revenue generation than to public purposes. They are distinguished by private entrepreneur engaging in the same activities.

Regulatory-oriented situations are more public purpose-oriented. In such situations, payments are associated with providing some service to benefit the public in some general fashion in addition to the person making the payment. Licenses, permits, and inspections are prime examples. Fees are required for licensing to ensure that the people being licensed meet some minimum standard of competence. Permits are required to ensure that people comply with relevant regulations (e.g., building and nuclear waste disposal permits). Inspections of food-preparing establishments and elevators tend to prevent mass poisoning and plummeting. In these cases, the payments approximate the costs of the regulatory services.

Penalty Payments and Forfeitures

Penalty payments and forfeitures result from some infraction. These include fines for felonies and misdemeanors; administrative fines for late payments and return of library books; and fines for corporate wrongdoing in complying with laws concerning restraint of trade, pollution, false advertising, and employee health and safety. Forfeitures are loss of property. A government takes possession of property that was acquired with ill-gotten gains, including tax evasion, or used illegally. Generally, these penalties are meant to deter undesirable behavior more than generate substantial revenue yields.

Gifts

Gifts come in the form of money, resources, and services. The gift of time is a gift of resources that would otherwise not be available or would require expenditures. Many gifts are tangible resources such as land, buildings, equipment, food, and blood. Various entities issue requests for gifts; some issue gift

:atalogues, which list and show, along with prices, what public organizations vant as gifts. Money and securities, such as stocks and bonds, which can be :onverted into money relatively easily, are a major source of revenue for some ionprofit organizations. Also, people give money to governments, especially tate universities. The gifts spoken of so far are voluntary ones, which can :ome with legal restrictions on their use. In some cases, gifts are refused)ecause the conditions are excessive.

Involuntary gifts, which sounds wrong, occur when gifts are given as a result)f circumstances that require them. There are two kinds of involuntary gifts. :irst, developers are usually required to "give" land and facilities (for instance, treets, sidewalks, and curbs) to local governments as a condition for approval)f requests for platting, subdivision, and zoning. The local governments do iot have the legal authority to take the land without paying for it but can ndirectly compel gifts. Second, when a person with property dies without ieirs, many states give the estate to themselves.

Debt

Debt is not often thought of as revenue. Debt initially produces revenue ind then is an obligation to be repaid.

EVALUATIVE CRITERIA ◆

Revenues have long been a source of interest and have drawn countless :valuations. Though specific disagreements abound, commonly enunciated :valuative criteria exist. Each criterion is partial and concerns itself only with)ne or a few aspects of revenue measures. Because each of the criteria tends o be based on a partial view of revenues, the criteria tend to conflict in)ractice.

The various evaluative criteria, which can be seen as answers to the question, "what characterizes a good revenue measure?," can be discussed under he headings of

1. Yield
2. Political expediency
3. Ease of administration
4. Consistency with economic and social goals
5. Equity
6. Directness

This ranking reflects the order in which policymakers appear to value the :riteria.

Yield

Policymakers do not pay attention to revenue measures generally unless :hey have the capacity to produce large amounts of revenue. Aside from specific regulatory-oriented revenue measures, yield is the first reason for having revenue measures. Certain things contribute to yield, including the size of the base, the accessibility of the base, elasticity, and inflation-driven bracket creep. A large base provides a greater potential amount of revenue than a small base. Also, very large bases make small rates feasible. For example, a 3% general sales tax is a small rate with a big base compared to a 30% selective sales tax on cigarettes. Yield is a function of the base and the rate. When taxes are "lowered" or "raised," generally only the rates are referenced. Changes in the base also affect the yield. This occurs frequently with local property taxes. Tax assessors make the property tax base larger by adding new properties and increasing assessed values, and other local officials heroically maintain or lower tax rates. A more accessible base makes it possible to collect more revenue by discouraging tax evasion. Elastic revenue measures have the advantage of generating more revenue over time as the level of economic activity increases. Finally, where a progressive rate structure is applied on an ad valorem base, inflation produces increases in revenues above the rate of inflation as the effective revenue rate increases. This phenomenon is known as bracket creep.

Political Expediency

Political expediency means choosing something that is politically acceptable. If a revenue measure is not sufficiently acceptable, given all the alternatives, the policy-making process can be used to overturn it. Few revenue measures create wild enthusiasm, but few stir up much negative excitement either.

Political expediency appears to be a function of popularity of the idea of the revenue measure and the relative pain of paying. The popularity of a revenue measure to most members of the public seems to involve taxing or collecting revenue from someone else. Also, things frowned on make popular tax bases. Taxes assessed at higher rates on persons outside of a state or local jurisdiction have been repeatedly struck down by the federal courts as interfering with interstate commerce. Taxes on outsiders, luxuries, sins, large corporations, and the wealthy tend to be most popular.

The other aspect of political expediency involves how much pain is felt by the person paying. Large, direct, and infrequent payments pain most people. Small, indirect, and frequent payments are less painful. Sales taxes, a few pennies at a time, benefit most by this situation, but withholding of income taxes by employers also increases the popularity of income taxes, as does escrowing of property taxes on a monthly basis with house loan payments. This aspect of political expediency is reminiscent of a biology experiment that tests the functioning of frog nerve endings. A frog placed in boiling water immediately jumps out. A frog placed in cold water that is gradually heated eventually becomes a boiled frog, however. Members of the public are much like frogs in being more sensitive to large changes and less sensitive to gradual ones.

Ease of Administration

Ease of administration concerns the administrative and compliance costs, the technical difficulties, and collection problems associated with a revenue measure. The administrative cost of collecting a revenue affects that revenue measure's net gain for a public organization. The more it costs to collect revenue, the less revenue is available to carry out an organization's purposes. Income and sales taxes have low administrative costs because they are administered primarily by individuals and businesses, whereas property taxes have high administrative costs. On the other hand, property taxes require little expense by taxpayers, whereas income and sales tax compliance costs are high because taxpayers have to do a lot to comply with the tax laws.

Technical difficulties involve interpreting and applying revenue measures to particular situations. The federal personal and corporate income taxes have whole professional areas of law and accounting devoted to them. On the other hand, most sales taxes are easy to interpret and apply.

Finally, collection problems can exist where it is difficult to part people and money without using a crowbar. The most pronounced area of difficulty is real property taxes. The process of collecting overdue property taxes involves taking possession of the property in question and selling it. This can take several years. On the other hand, sales taxes are easily collected by governments because businesses do most of the work at the point of payment.

Consistency With Economic and Social Goals

Revenue measures, as noted above, have nonneutral impacts on human behavior. From an economic perspective, revenue measures affect allocation, distribution, and regulation. A tax on oil tends to give other energy sources a slight advantage. Any tax measure changes resource allocation in some way. Any revenue measure changes the relative propensity to supply or demand particular products. Any revenue measure, along with expenditures, has a distributive impact on the relative well-being of different groups of people, not only among income levels but also geographically and by any other aspects on which people can be grouped. Also, any revenue measure potentially can regulate economic activity by encouraging or discouraging it. Of most concern are taxes that suppress or shift economic activity. The questions raised by economic nonneutralities tend to be matters of degrees rather than of direction. Is the economic impact of a revenue measure so great that it will be more harmful than helpful or more harmful than alternative revenue measures? Consistency with economic goals is evaluated as people compare their economic goals with the predicted results of various revenue measures.

In contrast, social nonneutralities tend to be appreciated and cultivated. Taxing sin and giving special tax treatment to charitable contributions are two of many possible examples. Consistency with social goals is generally evaluated on the face value of measures; preferential tax treatment is given on the basis of what appears to be socially good. With respect to both economic and social goals, economists tend to distinguish between situations where economic efficiency can be increased through nonneutral taxation (i.e., increase the net fulfillment of individual preferences) and situations where values are imposed on others as a form of paternalistic meddling.

Equity

Equity is frequently talked about but less often dealt with. Equity concerns tend to take a back seat to other conflicting concerns, the previously discussed evaluative criteria. Equity can be viewed in both horizontal and vertical forms. Vertical equity concerns people in unequal economic circumstances. Horizontal equity concerns people in approximately equivalent economic circumstances.

Vertical equity is a matter of debate between two schools of thought, which advocate either the ability-to-pay principle or the benefit theory. First, based on the ability-to-pay principle, some argue that those with more income or wealth have the ability to pay more and, therefore, should pay more. Often this view is actually based on the unstated assumptions that a person's ability to pay increases faster than income because of declining marginal utility of income (i.e., the last dollar of income is less valued than previous dollars). Advocates of this view argue for progressive taxation. Also, the ability-to-pay principle justifies politically popular schemes of taxation said to "soak the rich." Another aspect of the ability-to-pay school of thought is a preference for some reduction of differences among people for well-being, whether measured by the overall value of all income and services, after-tax income, or wealth. Second, based on the benefit theory, some argue that there should be a relationship between the amount of revenues paid and the benefits derived. This theory particularly applies where quid pro quo payments are involved, but it is also raised in contexts where there appears to be some reasonable connection between taxes and benefits. (Examples include taxes dedicated to highway programs, social security taxes, and property taxes funding police and fire services.) Generally, adequately assessing the benefits of all revenues in a comprehensive manner is practically impossible. Proponents of this view argue, however, that a reasonable assumption is that benefits accrue to individuals proportionally to their income or wealth and that revenue measures should be proportional. Neither of the two schools of thought is adequate to guide practical decision making. In addition to the questionable assumptions of the two viewpoints, determining the incidence of particular measures is difficult.

Horizontal equity is based on the ability-to-pay principle because it involves a relationship between persons' economic circumstances and revenue payments rather than a relationship between benefits and payments. As applied, the principle is that people in essentially the same economic circumstances be taxed about the same. Different patterns of income, wealth, consumption, and behaviors interact with the various associated deductions, exemptions, credits, and special rates to undercut horizontal equity, although some deductions can be seen as enhancing horizontal equity (e.g., personal income tax deductions for medical care or casualty losses).

TABLE 5.3 U.S. Public Revenues (in billions) FY 1991

	Own Source Collections		Total Government Collections		Total Public Sector Collections Total Public
	Amount	Government %[a]	Amount	Government %[b]	Sector %[c]
Federal	1,201	52.3	1,204	45.6	36.8
States	552	24.0	695	26.3	21.2
Local Government	542	23.6	744	28.1	22.7
Totals	2,294	100%	2,643	100%	
Nonprofit Organizations	631[d]	27.5	631	23.9	19.3
Grand Totals	2,925		3,274		100%

Sources: U.S. Bureau of the Census, *Governmental Finances in 1990-1991*, Series GF91-5, U. S. Government Printing Office, Washington, DC, 1993, Tables 4 and 6, pp. 4 and 7 for governments and the sources cited for nonprofit organizations in Table 5.8.

Note: Numbers are rounded to the nearest billion dollars or tenth of a percentage. Details and totals may not be consistent because of rounding effects.

a. Excludes intergovernmental transfers; the percentages are based on the government total for the column of 2,294 billion.

b. Includes intergovernmental transfers; the percentages are based on the government total of 2,643 billion.

c. Based on total collections of 3,274 billion.

d. This is a conservative estimate.

Directness

Directness simply means the degree to which a revenue measure visibly affects individuals. People can identify how much they pay in direct measures to a public organization. Some claim that this is an advantage because it encourages people to examine revenues and expenditures of public organizations. Direct measures are less politically expedient and more likely to lead to tax protests.

THE AMERICAN REVENUE SYSTEM ◆

The pattern of revenue collection by public organizations in the United States has four component parts: federal, state, and local governments, and nonprofit organizations. All four components draw their revenues from and serve the same people. They differ in functions. The federal government is primarily concerned with the nation's economy, international affairs and defense, and individual rights. To the extent that the federal government has extended itself into other areas, it has done so on general welfare legal principles and spendable federal grant monies. For example, highway speed limits are state responsibilities that are "influenced" by federal highway grant monies. On the other hand, state and local governments primarily concern themselves with exercising "police" powers, which involve dealing with the health, education, safety, welfare, and morals of their residents. States delegate

TABLE 5.4   Federal Revenues (in billions) FY 1991

Source Category	Amount	Percent	Subcategory Amount	Subcategory Percent	Subcategory Amount	Subcategory Percent
Individual Income Taxes	468	39.0				
Corporate Income Taxes	98	8.2				
Insurance Trust						
Revenues	388[a]	32.3				
Charges and Miscellaneous	167	13.9				
Charges:			86	7.2		
Postal service					43	3.5
Natural resources					16	1.3
Miscellaneous:			81	6.7		
Interest					11	0.9
Consumption Measures	58	4.9				
Custom Duties			16	1.3		
Selective Sales						
and Gross Receipt Taxes:			38	3.1		
Motor fuel					17	1.4
Alcoholic beverages					7	0.6
Public Utilities					7	0.6
Tobacco Products					5	0.4
Death and Gift Taxes	11	0.9				
Intergovernmental Transfers	3	0.3				

Source: U.S. Bureau of the Census, *Governmental Finances in 1990-1991*, Series GF91-5, U.S. Government Printing Office, Washington, DC, 1993, Table 6, p. 7.
Note: Numbers are rounded to the nearest billion or tenth of a percent. Subcategories are illustrative of what is included in the more general category and not exhaustive. Details and totals may not be consistent because of the effects of rounding.
a. Insurance trust revenues include income-based taxes to fund Social Security programs primarily and also a modest amount of employee retirement contributions, unemployment compensation, and other insurance trust revenues.

police power authority to local governments to act within relatively small geographic areas. Local governments are called subdivisions of states. Non-profit organizations are particular or specific in purpose. They are created and operated to serve some goal, whatever their geographic scope.

The amounts of revenue collected by public organizations shown in Table 5.3 are impressive. The revenue collected accounts for a little more than half of the Gross Domestic Product in 1991 (2.9 of 5.7 trillion dollars respectively). Notice the distribution of revenue collection. State and local governments together directly collected only slightly less than the federal government (own source collections) and directly spend slightly more than the federal government (total collections). Also, nonprofit organizations raised more than either state or local governments.

Federal Revenue

As shown in Table 5.4 the bulk of federal revenues flows from taxes on incomes. In addition to personal income taxes, insurance trust revenues are

nostly social security payments, which come about equally from taxes on
personal income and taxes on businesses based on employees' personal income. Corporate income taxes provide the least revenue of the three income-
based tax categories. A large amount of business activity income taxes is
collected under the heading of personal income taxes, however, most notably
for unincorporated businesses. The three income tax categories account for
about 80% of federal revenues. Other revenues are related to specific functions
or purposes. Postal service charges are associated with financing the postal
system; customs duties are used to regulate international trade; taxes on
motor fuel are used primarily for interstate highways; and death and gift taxes
were initiated to regulate state use of these taxes.

State and Local Revenue Systems

The reason for 50 state and local revenue systems is that local governments
depend on states for legal authority, including legal authority to collect
revenues. Each state chooses to give particular revenue measures and intergovernmental aid to its local governments and to retain particular revenue
measures for its own exclusive use. These decisions determine the characteristics of each state and local revenue system. Also, the distribution of service
responsibilities makes a difference. For example, the State of Hawaii provides
education, which reduces the need for local government revenues for that
purpose. Tables 5.5 and 5.6 show revenues by respective levels of government
separately.

State Revenues

States rely on diverse sources. The two leading revenue measures are general
sales taxes and income taxes, which are widely but not universally used.
Additional measures of general usage include intergovernmental transfers,
selective sales taxes, and charges and miscellaneous. After that, diversity prevails,
with property taxes, state-run liquor stores, and corporate income taxes.

Each state has a unique revenue system that developed from its circumstances and history. For example, Alaska relies on corporate income taxes,
Louisiana on severance taxes, Oregon on income taxes, and New Hampshire
on selective sales taxes. Alaska and Louisiana tax the oil and natural gas
industry as a means of exporting their tax burden. Oregon voters oppose a
general sales tax, and New Hampshire voters steadfastly oppose any broad-
based tax on income or sales.

Local Revenues

The approximately 83,000 local governments are extremely diverse. Their
common features are delegated legal authority and substate territorial extent.
For revenue, they rely most heavily on intergovernmental transfers, property
taxes, and charges and miscellaneous, which are used at the local level in all
states. Other revenue measures, such as income and sales taxes, are unevenly

TABLE 5.5   State Revenues (in billions) FY 1991

Source Category	Amount	Percent	Subcategory Amount	Percent	Subsubcategory Amount	Percent
Consumption Measures	154	23.3				
General Sales and						
Gross Receipts Taxes			103	15.6		
Selective Sales and						
Gross Receipts Taxes			50	7.6		
Motor Fuel					21	3.1
Public utilities					7	1.0
Tobacco products					6	0.9
Alcoholic beverages					3	0.5
Intergovernmental Transfers	144	21.7				
Individual Income Taxes	99	15.0				
Corporate Income Taxes	20	3.1				
Insurance Trust Revenues	102	15.4[a]				
Charges and Miscellaneous	98	14.8				
Charges:			47	7.2		
Education					26	3.9
Hospital					11	1.6
Miscellaneous			50	7.6		
Interest					28	4.2
Licenses[b]	19	2.9				
Utilities and Liquor Stores	6	1.0				
Property Taxes	6	0.9				
Severance Taxes	5	0.8				
Death and Gift Taxes	4	0.6				

Source: U.S. Bureau of the Census, *Governmental Finances in 1990-91,* Series GF91-5, U. S. Government Printing Office, Washington, DC, 1993, Table 6, p. 7.
Note: Numbers are rounded to the nearest billion or tenth of a percent. Subcategories are illustrative of what is included in the more general category and not exhaustive. Details and totals may not be consistent because of the effects of rounding.
a. Insurance trust revenues collected by states are primarily employee pension monies, 71 billion, but also include unemployment compensation, 18 billion, and worker's compensation.
b. License revenues include motor vehicle licenses, operator licenses, and corporation licenses.

available to local governments. This is primarily because of states' desire to retain these measures for themselves.

Local government responsibilities have grown over this century, and their own revenue sources have not kept pace. Intergovernmental transfers have filled the gap. These revenues appear to have peaked around 1980, however leaving local governments in an uncomfortable spot. Real property is their prime tax base because of its immobility, but tax protest has been most effective in placing limits on property taxes, and property taxes are inelastic

TABLE 5.6 Local Revenues (in billions) FY 1991

			Subcategory		Subsubcategory	
Source Category	Amount	Percent	Amount	Percent	Amount	Percent
Intergovernmental Transfers	201	33.0				
Property Taxes	162	26.4				
Charges and Miscellaneous	125	20.4				
Charges:			78	12.7		
Hospitals					23	3.7
Sewerage					54	8.7
Education					10	1.6
Housing and community development					14	2.3
Airports					5	0.8
Parks and Recreation					3	0.5
Miscellaneous:			47	7.7		
Interest earnings					31	5.0
Utility and Liquor Store Revenue	54	8.9				
Consumption Measures	32	5.2				
General Sales and Gross Receipts Taxes			22	3.6		
Selective Sales and Gross Receipts Taxes:			10	1.6		
Utilities					5	0.9
Insurance Trust Revenues[a]	16	2.6				
Individual Income Taxes	10	1.6				
Corporate Income Taxes	2	0.3				
Licenses	1	0.1				

Source: U.S. Bureau of the Census, Governmental Finances in 1990-1991, Series GF91-5, U.S. Government Printing Office, Washington, DC, 1993, Table 6, p. 7.
Note: Numbers are rounded to the nearest billion or tenth of a percent. Subcategories are illustrative of what is included in the more general category and not exhaustive. Details and totals may not be consistent because of the effects of rounding.
Insurance trust revenue is almost completely employee pension monies.

Charges usually do not cover anything more than the cost of services provided for the charges, if that. Other revenue sources will either increase, or local governments will match expenditures to their revenues by reducing them.

The revenue pattern among local governments found in Table 5.7 is complicated by the diversity of purpose, delegated authority, and outside funding. Mostly, revenue patterns vary by local government type. Counties and municipalities—general purpose units—have the broadest range of revenue sources. Though they rely primarily on property taxes and charges, they collect significant revenues from intergovernmental transfers, charges for utilities, sales, and income taxes. Townships, a general purpose category used in approximately 20 states, rely more on property taxes than counties or municipalities, except in the New England states, where towns are virtually indistinguishable from municipalities.

TABLE 5.7 Local Government Revenues by Governmental Types (in billions) FY
          1991

Type of Government	Amount	Percent
County	142	23
Municipal	210	34
Township	20	3
School District	188	30
Special District	65	10

Source: U.S. Bureau of the Census, *Governmental Finances in 1990-1991,* Series GF91-5, U.S. Government
Printing Office, Washington, DC, 1993, Table 6, p. 7.
Note: Numbers are rounded to the nearest billion dollars or percentage point. Details and totals may not be
consistent because of the effects of rounding. The amounts here exclude duplicative transfers.

School districts are the primary recipients of intergovernmental transfers.
They also use property taxes and, to a lesser extent, charges. Special district
tend to rely on three revenue sources: charges, property taxes, and intergov
ernmental transfers. The precise character of special districts services tends to
determine their sources. They charge for services when they can; service
desired by the federal and state governments are funded by transfers, and
others are funded by property taxes.

Nonprofit Organization Revenues

Nonprofit organizations are extremely diverse and derive their revenues in
a variety of ways, shown in Table 5.8. Some nonprofit organizations are simply
not identifiable. The ones that can be identified are churches (approximately
360,000 in 1991) and nonprofit organizations registered with the U.S. Interna
Revenue Service (approximately one million in 1991).[3] There are undoubtedly
many more nonprofit organizations that have not registered with the IRS.
Information on revenues for nonprofit organizations is extremely sketchy.
The three identifiable categories are churches, nonprofit charitable organizations, and private foundations and charitable trusts; the total for all of them
is relatively conservative and based on money and things convertible to
money. Not even seriously considered as revenue are the many hours of
voluntary labor that could be estimated as having a value in the billions of
dollars.

Revenue figures available for churches include only estimated contributions of $54 billion in 1991. Although the estimate appears large, it includes
only contributions and not the also large but indeterminate amounts of
money collected by churches through educational institutions, social service
grants, or unrelated business income.

Nonprofit charitable organizations are the largest category of nonprofit
organizations and enjoy the greatest flow of revenues, though most of the
revenue is handled by large organizations. In 1991, revenues to these organizations were primarily program service revenues, which are charges for services, totaling $380 billion. Contributions, gifts, and grants totaled $92 billion,

TABLE 5.8 Estimated Nonprofit Organization Revenues (in billions)
FY 1991

Revenue Category	Amount	Percent
Program Service Revenue	$380	60
Contributions, Gifts, and Grants	$153	24
Return on Ownership and Sale of Assets	$62	10
Dues and Assessments	$28	4
Other	$9	1

Sources: Various sources were used to compute a conservative estimate of the FY 1991 revenues of nonprofit organizations. The sources and the amounts by organization type are $552 billion for nonprofit charitable organizations (mostly from those coming under section 501(c)(3) but also including sections 501(c)(4)-(9) as well) with revenues of $25,000 or more in fiscal year 1990 in *Statistics of Income Bulletin, 14*, (2) Internal Revenue Service, Fall 1994, pp. 131-138; $25 billion for private foundations and charitable trusts in fiscal year 1991 in *Statistics of Income Bulletin, 14*(3) Internal Revenue Service, Winter, 1994/95, p. 141-152; and $54 billion estimated for gifts to religious organizations in 1991 in U.S. Bureau of the Census, *Statistical Abstract of the United States: 1994* (114th edition). Washington, DC, 1994, p. 389, Table 610.

Note: Numbers are rounded to the nearest billion dollars and percentage point. Details and totals may not be consistent because of the effects of rounding.

whereas dues and assessments, which tend to be implicit service charges, were $28 billion. Grants were slightly less than one quarter of the contributions, gifts, and grants in 1991.

Charges exceeding gifts appears anomalous because nonprofit charitable organizations are associated with charity, which is associated with giving. A quick scan of the largest revenue-producing types of nonprofit charitable organizations helps explain this. The four largest categories of nonprofit charitable organizations, which account for the bulk of nonprofit revenues, rely heavily on revenues from fees. Hospitals, educational institutions, and organizations supporting charitable organizations derive a majority of their funding from fees. Only the category of publicly supported organizations gets less than half of its revenues from fees; such organizations are what we think of when we think of charities (e.g., United Way Organizations and the American Heart Association). Organizations supporting charitable organizations include pension and health insurance organizations and overarching service units, such as the National Collegiate Athletic Association. These support organizations provide goods or services with identifiable beneficiaries.

Private foundations, which are exempt from federal income taxation, and charitable trusts, which are not exempt, are financially based on contributions that are then managed for future income. Approximately 43,000 of these entities filed required returns with the IRS in 1991, showing total revenues of $25 billion, of which $7 billion were from contributions, gifts, and grants and $18 billion were from returns on the ownership and sale of assets.

CONCLUSION ◆

Revenues collected by the public sector are large in scale, numerous, and diverse in characteristics. Revenue concepts help make discussions of revenue more meaningful. The categorization of revenue measures by their base provides evidence on their scope and character. The discussion of evaluative criteria assists in addressing the question of what revenue measures to prefer. The pattern of revenues to public organizations in the United States shows their scale and diversity. All together, the various topics in this chapter provide a brief and extremely cursory overview of public revenues from a nonspecialized viewpoint.

DISCUSSION QUESTIONS

1. What is your favorite revenue measure? Why?
2. What is the most important evaluative criterion for assessing revenue measures?
3. How is your state's revenue system structured?
4. How would you change your state's revenue system if you could?
5. How would you change the federal revenue system if you could?

◆ NOTES

1. Joseph E. Stiglitz (1988). *Economics of the public sector* (2nd ed.). New York: Norton, pp. 17, 328.

2. J. Richard Aronson and John L. Hilley (1986). *Financing state and local government* (4th ed.). Washington, DC: The Brookings Institution, pp. 149-150.

3. For information on nonprofit organization finances, see the sources cited in Table 5.8: Daniel F. Skelly (1994). Tax-based research and data on nonprofit organization. *Internal Revenue Service Statistics of Income Bulletin, 14*(1), 81-88; and Virginia Ann Hodgkinson, Murray S. Weitzman, Christopher M. Toppe, and Stephen M. Noga (1992). *Nonprofit almanac 1992-1993. Dimensions of the independent sector* (4th ed.). San Francisco: Jossey-Bass.

◆ SUGGESTED READINGS

J. Richard Aronson and John L. Hilley (1986). *Financing state and local government* (4th ed.). Washington, DC: The Brookings Institution.

Joseph E. Stiglitz (1988). *Economics of the public sector* (2nd ed.). New York: Norton.

Revenue Administration

Managing the flow of revenue into any public or nonprofit organization is a difficult task that requires varying types of skills and abilities, depending on the revenue source itself and the particular aspect of revenue administration involved. What collection system does a nonprofit agency put in place to ensure fees will be paid on time? Who decides how much your house is worth in determining property tax value? How does the federal or state government determine whose income tax returns will be audited? How does a state or local government ensure that all retail sales are taxed appropriately? How does a state go about informing its citizens of changes in a tax code? How does a city decide what a service such as refuse collection is worth? These are all revenue administration issues, and each presents a number of options and problems to public agencies.

As discussed in Chapter 5, revenue sources vary in their base and their structure. They also vary in how they are administered, how revenue authorizations are interpreted, and how the public is informed of the requirements associated with revenue collection. Administration of revenues generally includes several elements: (1) finding the base; (2) placing a value on that base; (3) determining a revenue rate to charge against the base; (4) actually collecting the revenue; (5) monitoring collection procedures to determine that what should have been collected was, in fact, collected; (6) handling complaints or appeals from the payers of the revenue; and (7) enforcing revenue collection. In the process, communicating policies and procedures and interpreting the law are also of key importance. This chapter will focus on the major revenue sources and how each is affected by these steps in the process of revenue administration. In addition, specific issues will be raised that affect revenue administration, including how agencies organize, the costs associated with compliance, and how to ensure fairness of administration.

◆ FINDING THE BASE

The first responsibility of government or nonprofit agencies is to locate th revenue base for collection purposes. This will depend on the specific laws o regulations that affect that revenue source. State laws define the property ta base and the items included under a sales tax. The federal government define income bases through the process of exclusions. User fee bases are also define by statute or law and, for nonprofits, through a policy statement. In most case locating the base depends on voluntary compliance. This is particularly tru of income and sales tax bases, where voluntarily supplied information is th government's major source of information. For property taxes, this burde falls more heavily on the public agency. Where voluntary compliance is o great importance, it is vital that government agencies educate the public abou what is included within the base and provide assistance on how to report thi information to meet the requirements of the law. Public education is necessar to make voluntary compliance work effectively.

The base can be quite easy to locate, or it can be almost impossible. Althoug voluntary compliance is still a major source of income tax collections, thi compliance has declined in recent years. Where the base is difficult to locat through governmental action, voluntary compliance will decline even more This is especially true if taxpayers perceive that others are not disclosin information.

The government depends on employers reporting employees' wages an benefits for income taxes. Income earned from the sale of stocks or bonds ca be determined through the sales transactions themselves. Interest earne through investments can be discovered through the records of lending insti tutions unless such investments occur outside the jurisdiction of state o federal governments, in which case such tracking can be extremely difficul Voluntary compliance becomes the predominant way to determine incom earned. A sales tax base is determined through transactions of some sort. If government can locate transactions itself, the base can be established. Busines licenses and registrations can identify vendors who are likely to sell product to be taxed. The case of a retail sales tax depends on vendors, who record th sales transactions themselves. The use tax largely depends on citizens report ing the item where it is intended to be used. Where no registration takes plac the discovery of the transaction is extremely difficult. If, for example, a perso bought a car in Nevada for use in Utah, the base can be determined for ta purposes at the time that person registers the car in Utah to obtain licens plates. If, however, that person were purchasing a television or a piece o furniture that did not require registration in Utah, it would be very difficu for state revenue officials to locate the furniture to tax it. Where states hav reciprocal assistance agreements, some of these transactions can be traced.

States determine sales tax liability and thereby determine the base in thre different ways.[1] In several states, the tax liability rests with the vendor—th business selling retail products to consumers. This is perceived to be a ta liability associated with the privilege of doing retail sales activity in the stat The liability computation is then determined based on the price of th products sold by that vendor. The unique feature of this approach is tha vendors may not have to "shift" the costs of the tax to their customers visibly, even though the value of retail sales determines liability. A second way to determine tax liability is by specifying that the consumer is the actual payer of the tax. In this case, the tax liability rests with the consumer, and it is based on the selling price of the item purchased by that consumer. The vendors merely serve as "agents of the state" in collecting these taxes from their customers. Finally, a hybrid approach is used in several states whereby the tax liability rests with the vendor, but that vendor must shift the liability associated with that tax to customers.

Property tax represents the greatest diversity in base identification. Real property (land and permanent improvements to the land) is relatively easy to locate and identify, being practically impossible to move or to hide. The use of land surveys, air surveys, land records, and computerized mapping makes locating such property almost certain. Some tangible personal property such as cars and airplanes can also be located easily, largely through licensing and registration processes. Still, if someone lives in one area and registers personal property in another area to avoid payment of revenue, state and local governments can find it difficult to systematically locate such property (such as jewelry, guns, coins, or collector's items). Other types of tangible personal property, such as furniture, appliances, and the like, that are easily moved and that do not require registration are much more difficult to locate. Abuses can occur simply because people may believe no one else is voluntarily declaring such property and will therefore not notify the government of its existence. Finally, intangible personal property such as stocks and bonds are almost impossible to locate without voluntary compliance. This greatly increases the administrative cost associated with locating such property. The result has been the elimination of most intangible and tangible personal property from the property tax base. This has represented a tremendous shift in tax base at the local level, where such tangible personal property used to be the major focus of the property tax.

Business activity taxes have bases that are by and large easily identifiable. Corporate income and excise taxes are handled in much the same manner as personal income and consumption taxes. Employee taxes based on employee wages are located at the same time as payroll or income taxes. Where difficulties in locating the base occur, it is largely the same problem as that associated with personal taxes. With an inventory tax, for example, inventory can be moved or sold to avoid location for tax purposes. For this reason, many inventory taxes have been eliminated.

Revenues derived from other levels of government have bases established by the granting agency. In many instances, this is determined by formula, as described in Chapter 5; in other situations, it is determined on a case-by-case, project-specific basis.

Quid pro quo payments are easily identifiable because the revenue base represents the good, service, or privilege provided. Such a good or service must be identified, made exclusive, and chargeable before it can be used as a revenue source. The same can be said of such things as penalty payments and gifts. The very identification of a legal infraction or gift defines the base itself.

◆ PLACING A VALUE ON THE BASE

Placing a value on revenue bases varies dramatically in its difficulty and therefore, its cost. As discussed in Chapter 4, monetary values are assigned to some public transactions. This is true of revenue bases. A person's income, property, or purchases all have dollar values. Setting the value for a tax on the purchase of a privately sold good or service is quite simple—the tax equals the price of the private good. In other cases, for example, setting the cost of a building inspection permit, the value is much more subjective.

Income for purposes of federal and state taxation is never clearly defined in the tax code; rather its definition is assumed through the series of reductions in tax liability that are built into that tax structure. The value of the income is not actual "gross income" but, rather, income that is subject to the tax itself. It would be much easier administratively for governments to simply establish gross income as defined in some standard way as the value base.

By doing this, however, the federal government would eliminate the use of the tax code to stimulate certain kinds of behavior (e.g., building more homes) and make the tax less equitable by not allowing certain kinds of exemptions and deductions. By creating this myriad set of reductions in the definition of actual income, the tax system has created a valuing structure that has greatly increased compliance costs (through increased time and effort in calculating income value) and administrative costs (through increased need for verification and audits to determine accuracy of income tax forms). We will discuss this compliance issue in some detail later in the chapter.

Consumption taxes are usually easy to value because they are determined by the price of the item being consumed ad valorem or through simply counting the number of units included in the transaction itself. In this case the private market determines the value and the government accepts this value in its determinations for tax purposes. If an identical toaster sells for $30 at Store X and $25 at Store Y, the actual tax base value would be different, depending on where the individual buys the toaster. With units as the measure, however, whether an individual bought 10 gallons of gas at a gas service station or at a local convenience store would make no difference because the value is determined by the units themselves rather than the individual cost of those units.

Valuing the wealth holdings of individuals and businesses is perhaps the most difficult area of tax administration. This is because not many of these holdings are bought and sold each year and, therefore, their value must be determined by surrogate measures. In other words, some measure of approximate wealth value must be used, which leads to distortions and conflicts between presumed market value of that holding and the value of that holding for tax purposes. In addition, if these holdings are vast and if the market values of various types of holdings are changing rapidly, the difficulty in placing a value on such holdings becomes greater.

Real property values are the most common example of this difficulty. In most cases one of three methods is used: (1) market value, (2) replacement value, or (3) capitalized value. In some cases a combination of these three is developed. Under a market value approach, property is assigned a value that equal to or a proportion of the appraised value of that property. (This is also referred to as fractional assessment.) The appraised value is determined by locating properties with similar characteristics (e.g., location, square footage, number of rooms, structural design, and so forth) that have been sold on the private market recently. This surrogate measure is then applied to determine the value of the property base for tax purposes. This approach works reasonably well where some substantial number of property sales transactions are taking place and where property is homogeneous. It is less suitable to property that has little turnover or where property characteristics are very unique.

Replacement cost is a popular approach to valuing property where the market approach is unsuitable. Under such a system the property is valued by the best estimates of what it would cost to replace that property minus any depreciation that would have occurred because of the age of the property itself. Depreciation reflects the decreased value of the property that occurs because of age and use. This system depends heavily on obtaining current and accurate construction or building costs and a defensible depreciation rate.

Capitalized value is determined by the estimated income that a particular property produces. This method is most appropriate for commercial and rental properties. The formula to determine value is based on the actual or estimated income production and a "discount" rate or annualized rate of return. This rate is usually associated with what the property owner might expect to see as a rate of return on the property as an investment. This can be some market interest rate, such as a commercial lending rate, or it can be based on another type of measure. The formula would operate as follows:

yearly return/rate of return = capitalized value

$90,000/.06 = \$1,500,000$

Clearly determining the annualized rate of return is crucial to this method. A shift of 1% can radically change the value of property. In the example just cited, if the discount rate had been 5%, the property value would have increased to \$1,800,000.

It is almost prohibitively expensive to assess or to revalue all property every year. The worst type of assessment is often referred to as "hello stranger," where reassessment is done only when property is sold. This approach leads to enormous inequities among like-valued properties. Therefore, most assessors use one of two approaches to update their information on property value when sales information is not available. The first is referred to as segmented or cyclical assessment. In this case a certain portion, say 20%, of properties are reassessed each year. At the end of five years, in this case, every property has been revalued for tax purposes. A second approach is a periodic annual mass reassessment—every certain number of years, all properties are revalued at one time. Which approach is used depends on costs and the nature of the property market. Although annual assessment may be the most equitable, it is also the most expensive. A rapid turnover of property in the community may necessitate annualized assessment of some sort. Where property is relatively stable and sales are low, a segmented or cyclical approach may be acceptable. Because few communities can afford the costs associated with annual assessment, most use current sales along with a segmented or cyclical evaluation system. Anything short of annualized assessment creates disparities among similar properties. These disparities are likely to be more severe in very active property markets where land and buildings are rapidly appreciating.

Property can be revalued without assessment by increasing or decreasing all properties in particular categories (e.g., residential, commercial, agricultural) by a particular amount. This may place the properties as a group closer to market values, but it can further aggravate disparities among those properties. If, for example, two properties were of equal market value, say $50,000 but house A were appraised at $20,000 and house B at $40,000, clear disparities would exist. The average underassessment would be 60% of market value, but the range of disparity would be $20,000. If you wanted to eliminate the extent of underassessment, you could raise the assessed value of each house 40%, but this would also increase the disparity. House A would now have an assessed value of $28,000, only 56% of market value, whereas House B would be assessed at $56,000, 112% of market value. The range of disparity would be increased $8,000—from $20,000 to $28,000.

The approach used to assess property and the timing at which assessment occur both play an important role in determining horizontal equity as it relates to property taxes. The most serious weakness of property tax administration is the disparity of assessed values for properties of equal value. One way in which assessors can determine the equity of their property valuation is through calculating a coefficient of dispersion. This method "provides an estimate of how accurately the assessor apportioned the property tax burden among owners of different properties according to their 'true' value; a lower coefficient indicates a more consistent assessment."[2]

Under this approach, a sample of properties within a community is selected for study. The assessed value and actual market value are determined for these properties. A ratio of the assessment value to market value is computed for each property, and an average ratio is calculated. An average deviation from the mean is determined, and from this information a coefficient of dispersion can be calculated. The lower the coefficient, the less disparity exists among properties. The higher the coefficient, the less equitable are the assessment results.

◆ APPLYING A REVENUE RATE

Once the base has been measured, computing revenue liability appears quite simple. The revenue value is multiplied by the nominal rate, producing the revenue liability.

Revenue Base x Face Rate = Revenue Liability

As discussed earlier, the base for income taxes includes taxable income after tax liability has been applied. Actual revenue liability, however, is not finally determined at this point because some credits can exist.

The revenue or tax rates vary with the amount of the base. Under the federal tax code, for example, there several rates for adjusted income, ranging from 5% to greater than 30% for adjusted income above that amount. In some states, the rate is flat, meaning all citizens have the same rate applied against income value, whereas other states have varying rates.

Sales tax rates are generally a fixed flat percentage of sales value or fixed amount per sales unit. At the state level, for example, the retail sales tax rate usually ranges from 3% to 7% of the sales value, that is, purchase price. Excise taxes, such as those on gasoline or cigarettes, are a fixed amount multiplied against the number of units sold (e.g., 5 cents a gallon or 20 cents per package of cigarettes). In these cases, the actual rate will vary with the value of the product sold. For example, the local convenience store gasoline sells for $1.20 a gallon. At the full service station a block away, however, that same gallon of gas sells for $1.25. In each case a tax of 20 cents per gallon is applied. Taxes as a percentage of total cost to the individual purchasing the gasoline at the convenience store are higher than for the individual purchasing gasoline at the full-service station. The actual percentage paid in taxes is higher as the unit price of the product declines.

$1.20 per gallon plus 20 cents = $1.40 per gallon (6.00% effective tax rate)
$1.25 per gallon plus 20 cents = $1.45 per gallon (6.25% effective tax rate)

For user fees, flat rates, varying rates, and per unit rates are used. Varying rates are appropriate where there are significant peak demands for services, where variable costs increase, and where demand is reducing a finite resource.

The Washington, D.C., metropolitan area public transportation system is an example of how such rates are applied. Bus and subway systems have enormous fixed costs. These are costs that exist no matter how much their services are used. The bus has to be used, the driver paid, and fuel consumed whether 1 person or 30 people ride. Also, the demand for the bus and subway system is greatest during rush hour, when peak usage can require an enormous number of buses and trains. The transportation system must be built to meet this peak demand even though the system may reach this peak usage only a few hours a day. During nonrush-hour periods, the system has much less demand and that demand can be price elastic. This means that if the price of the bus ticket or subway fare is too high, people may choose not to use that means of transportation. The situation is quite different for rush-hour commuters, who find that the price would need to increase substantially before they would want to buy a car, drive it in rush-hour traffic into downtown Washington, D.C., and then pay $9 or $10 per day to park the car in a garage. In other words, commuters are a more captive audience for the transit system than are noncommuters. The Washington area transit system incorporates these factors into pricing its product. Rush-hour subway and bus rates are much higher than nonrush-hour rates. Rates during rush hour are based on distance traveled. The farther an individual commutes, the more the bus fare. During nonrush-hour, there is a reduced flat-rate fare to use the subway, no matter how far you want to travel on the system. This encourages noncom-

muters to use the subway system or bus system as a means of transportation
Finally, this approach spreads out demand and helps increase revenues.

Property tax rates are determined differently than either income or sales
taxes. Local and state governments first determine their total anticipated
expenditures during the coming year. They then estimate the revenues they
will collect from all sources, excluding the property tax. The difference between these two minus any delinquencies that are anticipated represents the
revenue yield that will be required from the property tax to balance their
budgets. This revenue amount is then divided by the total assessed valuation
of the taxing jurisdiction, and the resulting number represents the tax rate for
that government. An example best illustrates this approach.

If a local government anticipates spending $500,000 in the coming year and
expects revenues of $100,000 from nonproperty tax sources, the remaining
$400,000 will have to come from property tax revenue. If you assume 4% of
these taxes will be uncollectible, you must increase your revenue projection
to include that delinquency—in this case, $17,000. If the actual assessed value
of property for this local government is $20 million, the rate would be
determined as follows:

amount to be levied/assessed valuation = tax rate
417,000/20,000,000 = 0.02085

If a property owner's house were assessed at $100,000, the tax liability would
be computed as follows:

$100,000 x 0.02085 = $2085

The tax liability is $2085 for that calendar year.

◆ COLLECTION OF REVENUE

The process of collecting revenue is a fairly mechanical one. Residents,
businesses, and vendors complete collection forms periodically and forward
these forms along with payment of income and sales taxes to the respective
government agencies. The vendor must initially collect retail sales tax funds
from customers at the point of sale. The sales tax on items such as cars and
boats is often collected by the government at the point where the vehicle is
registered and receives operating tags or stickers. Income tax collection and
sales tax collection often depend substantially on voluntary compliance.

Income tax collections depend heavily on withholding from wage payments. Federal and state governments require employers to withhold from
employee paychecks a percentage of their income that is equivalent to the
amount of taxes they will be required to pay at the end of the year. Employers
then remit these collections to the government, usually on a quarterly basis.
At the time the final income tax payment becomes due, the employee then
submits only income tax payments not covered by the amount withheld

Withholding not only eases the administrative cost of collecting revenue but also greatly improves compliance by taxpayers. Under federal tax law, self-employed individuals making more than certain amounts must submit payment of an equivalent amount for withholding on a quarterly basis to ensure collection and to improve federal cash management.

Property tax collections are handled differently. Assessors prepare and mail tax bills to property owners at some point during the year. These bills represent tax liability from several taxing jurisdictions and must then be paid at some date in the future. In many cases, payment can be made in two installments. Where mortgages are held by lending institutions, these institutions may pay the property tax bill and set up separate escrow accounts with their clients to cover the anticipated costs of these taxes. Where state and local laws permit, county assessors can provide incentives for early payment or prepayment of property tax. This not only speeds up collection but also can increase funds available for investment. Where late payment occurs, penalties and interest charges are assessed both to cover the costs associated with not having the property tax receipts available to the government and to create adequate incentive for prompt payment.

User charges are billed or collected at the point where a good or service is provided. As with vendor collection of sales tax revenue, collections of user fees occur periodically throughout the year, depending on demand, and must be processed on a daily basis in many instances. This differs substantially from income and property taxes, which are usually collected only during certain times of the year. Collection of sales taxes by states occurs monthly or quarterly, depending on the volume of sales tax generated.

Agencies responsible for collecting revenue are responsible for reviewing the accuracy of the payments. This review is based on the tax return forms submitted by the vendor or taxpayer. Collection and processing can be continuous, as with user fees, or it can be cyclical, as with income, sales, and property taxes.

The steps in processing revenue receipts will vary by revenue source but often contain the following:

1. Obtaining revenue receipts from mail or over the counter

2. Opening and logging the revenue forms and the receipts (checks, money orders, and cash)

3. Reviewing and cross-checking return form information and tax receipt amount (where errors have occurred, either those submitting the revenue must be notified to submit additional revenue or the agency must process an overpayment or refund)

4. Making deposits of cash to bank accounts (in some cases attaching copies of checks to revenue return forms before the depositing of the checks)

5. Verifying bank account balance with deposit slips

6. Processing revenue return information for computerization

7. Verifying computer entry

8. Systematically monitoring and auditing selected returns for substantive accuracy.[3]

◆ COMPLIANCE

Monitoring compliance is a key element of revenue administration. Al though many revenue sources involve voluntary participation by taxpayer and customers, compliance can be predicated by how likely it is that error and omissions will be caught by the agency processing payment. Some form of audit is the most commonly used method to determine whether or no collections are what they should be. Revenue audits provide several ver beneficial administrative advantages. In addition to helping ensure increase voluntary compliance, they also provide an opportunity for the agency t review its own procedures and operations to determine how efficient it revenue administration process is. Audits also help uncover policy and pro cedural problems with the revenue system that otherwise would be difficul to locate. For example, if a number of audits of individual tax returns sho taxpayers making the same mistake in computing their tax liability, th problem might be corrected by revising the form or clarifying instructions thus reducing the likelihood of the mistake occurring in the future.

The Examination Division of the Internal Revenue Service is responsibl for "the selection and examination of all types of federal tax returns."[4] Ta returns selected for audit can be based on a random sample of tax returns o can include tax returns that have certain characteristics (e.g., particular in come levels or claimed deductions). The great increase in computer capabili ties at the federal, state, and local levels has greatly increased the sophisticatio and capabilities of the selection process. This sophistication has allowed stat and federal governments to focus their efforts on tax returns that have th greatest likelihood of undercollection. The IRS field office notifies taxpayer that they are subject to an audit. The taxpayer is also told the areas of the ta return that will be included in the audit, who is responsible for conductin the audit, and a particular time when he or she will be expected to meet an discuss the audit with a local field auditor or examiner.

Auditors focus on those areas of the tax return that have the most likel computation errors or those that are most susceptible to abuse, such a itemized deductions, tax credits, and personal exemptions. For businesse areas such as depreciation, tax credits, and net worth computations are likel audit targets. The auditor's expertise in understanding tax law and regulation is critical to the success of the audit process. The IRS has specialized audi capabilities that focus on international enforcement. This is a particula concern where multinational corporations and various overseas tax shelter can exist. States can often "piggyback" on federal audits to obtain informatio on such taxpayers. The federal government also has specialized auditors fo estate and gift taxes.

◆ THE APPEALS PROCESS

Considerable time in revenue administration can be spent dealing wit appeals or complaints from taxpayers. Appeals usually occur after an aud process has discovered an underpayment of some sort in sales and incom axes. The federal or state government has collected the tax liability voluntarily submitted by the taxpayer or vendor, but through the audit process these governments have concluded that additional revenue is due from those individuals or businesses. The appeals for property tax are made between notification to the taxpayer of the base value of property and the taxpayer's payment. When tax bills are mailed, property owners discover that their property has been reassessed and is now valued at a higher dollar amount than they believe is fair or equitable.

Appeals of federal personal and corporate income-based taxes are handled through IRS district offices and service centers throughout the country. The appeals process is relatively complex and includes a number of due-process steps. Taxpayers can appeal to the IRS district director through a letter or through a formal written request. An appeal conference can then be held, where the taxpayer can present a case to the IRS staff responsible for hearing such requests. Such a conference can be denied by the IRS when IRS staff believe the appeal is based on political, religious, or philosophical grounds rather than on the substantive or technical interpretation of the laws or regulations themselves.

If the issue cannot be resolved through such a conference, the appeal must move to the federal court system, including the Tax Court and in some cases the U.S. Claims Court or Federal District Court. The U.S. Circuit Court of Appeals can also be involved in an appeal from a lower court decision.[5]

State income tax appeals can be handled in various ways. Most common are three-step appeals. The first appeal is to the state tax commissioner. If the appeal is denied, a taxpayer can appeal to an administrative appeals board. A final appeal would be through the state court system unless it also represents a federal claim. In Nebraska, citizens must go to the state court system if the state Tax Commission denies their appeals because no special administrative appeals board exists. Oregon has a special tax court at the state level that hears appeals should redress not be provided through the Director of Revenue. Should the appeal be denied, the taxpayer can then appeal to the State Supreme Court.[6] Illinois has established a board of appeals comprising three members appointed by its Department of Revenue Director.[7] The board can waive penalties and interest for "on reasonable cause" and can also reduce tax liability based on the "likelihood of collection." If two of the three board members support some form of tax relief, the board makes this recommendation to the Director of the Department of Revenue. The Director must then approve the recommendation, and the board then can issue an order granting the relief.

ENFORCEMENT ◆

Enforcing the collection of earned income is a problem for both tax and nontax revenues. Enforcement costs for certain revenues run higher than for others. This depends on the level of voluntary compliance, the structure of the appeal process, and the difficulty in locating taxpayers, either those who have incurred revenue liability or end users of goods and services.

Enforcement of revenue collections assumes that those who have incurred the liability have failed to pay for that liability when it was due. The initial step is to notify the business or individual that payment has not been received and to indicate the costs associated with not paying off the liability as soon as possible. Enforcement of tax collections, as with many tax and revenue sources is through use of charges in excess of tax liability, usually in the form of late interest payments or added penalties. At the federal level, this set of civil penalties is complex and depends on the infraction incurred. One category is referred to as interest of deficiencies and is based on prevailing interest rates and is sufficiently high to eliminate the incentive not to pay when the tax is due. Penalties for filing a late personal tax return are substantial, starting at 3 percentage points above the federal short-term rate of 5% a month and increasing to a maximum of 25% or more. A minimum penalty is also assessed that recoups the initial cost of the IRS to locate taxpayers who have not filed.[8]

Additional penalties can be assessed where it is assumed that the late payment was due to conscious negligence. Other penalties exist for such things as placing a higher value on property than market value. This is also referred to as underpayment of estimates. An example would be a university professor who donated his old textbooks to the university and asked for a tax deduction for this contribution far in excess of their actual value. Where fraud has been proved, a penalty of 50% is assessed on the amount of tax owed to the government. An additional 50% penalty is assessed on the interest charged against the tax amount that was not paid if that tax amount was fraud related.[9]

Where collections of deficiencies in tax payments are not forthcoming, many avenues exist to obtain those funds. Garnishment of wages, placement of liens, seizing of personal property, and freezing of bank account assets are all avenues that can be pursued. Although this may be action of last resort, it is necessary in a limited number of cases. The costs associated with these actions may never be recouped; however, without enforcement of this nature, the number of taxpayers who might try to avoid paying their tax liabilities could increase.

Collection of state income tax revenue follows the federal pattern. Apparently the largest problem facing income tax delinquencies at the federal and state level are small businesses rather than individuals. This is likely to be a problem across tax areas (e.g., sales, income, payroll, and property). The key to collecting revenue owed in these cases is to move quickly. The longer the account remains delinquent, the more likely that it will not be collected. All states have some combination of penalties and interest charged on late or delinquent income tax payments. They vary in the number of contracts made, or the amount of time allowed for collection. The key to successful collection of delinquent taxes is to make the cost of not complying so high that anyone able to pay will. Failure to do this leads to evasion and increasing default.

Massachusetts provides an excellent example of how a state enforcement program can be developed.[10] The Massachusetts Revenue Enforcement and Protection Program (REAP) incorporates a number of administrative and procedural elements to increase collections of delinquent taxes. Among the most important are stringent new penalties for noncompliance, including

- Computer-assisted cross-checks for possible tax violators
- Use of state's licensing power to cancel licenses of tax evaders
- Scrutiny of government vendors to determine tax compliance

Illinois spells out in great detail the steps in the enforcement process for those who have a tax liability.[11] Their "Taxpayer Bill of Rights" notes that Illinois has the authority to "levy against, or seize" real estate and personal property "in order to pay past-due tax, penalty and interest." Such property can be sold within 20 days. Illinois can also file liens against real estate or personal property and can levy against wages, requiring the tax-delinquent individual's employer to "deduct up to 15%" of the individual's wages to pay past-due taxes.[12]

Amnesty programs are being heavily used to increase compliance. Since the early 1980s, more than 30 states have used some form of tax amnesty. Pennsylvania and Delaware are the latest to use this approach. Although these programs appear to provide some short-term increases in revenue collection, research also indicates that it may have little impact on improving tax collections over the long term.[13]

Property tax enforcement is tied to state and local statutes. In many instances, the process is more cumbersome and drawn out than for federal or state delinquent tax collections. Due-process procedures can take several years before properties can be foreclosed on and sold for back taxes. Even so, taxpayers often have until the actual point of sale to pay.

As with sales and income taxes, penalties and interest can be charged on delinquent property taxes. In many instances these charges are below market interest rates, thus providing little incentive for tax invaders to pay promptly.[14] After an extended period of time, tax liens can be placed on the property. Foreclosure on the property can follow. In most cases, the assets of the taxpayer other than the property itself are not targets for collection. Rather, local enforcement and collection efforts focus on the property itself. Where the property is worth little, no incentive exists for the owner to pay back taxes. This creates serious problems for the locality because of the extended amount of time that such foreclosures take. Where property is not being maintained and cared for, local governments can do little to improve it until they gain legal control of that property. This was a serious problem in New York City, where many uneconomic renter-occupied properties were being abandoned by their owners. In this case, a "fast track" foreclosure process was developed so the city could take over and maintain the properties.

Enforcement for user fee revenue is the same as would be true for any business selling goods and services. Such services are treated as enterprise funds and should be accounted for when earned. Should payment be delayed, interest charges are place on the balance. These charges are often equivalent to private finance charges. If no payments are forthcoming, collection efforts are increased through direct contact. Some public agencies have contracted with collection agencies to bring chronic bad debt accounts up to date. One step that is always available to public entities is to eliminate access to the service for nonpayment. This is sometimes difficult to do for moral or political reasons. For example, a public electric utility considering shutting off low-income person's electricity in winter might incur the wrath of citizen and politicians alike. Level payment plans and credit counseling are likely to be much more successful and politically acceptable than cutting off servic indiscriminately. Similarly, stopping refuse pickup to a residence where the property owner refuses to pay will not solve the public health problem. Other avenues, such as filing liens against the property or garnishing income, while continuing to pick up the garbage, are much more acceptable alternatives.

At some point, certain receivable accounts that are not paid will need to b written off as uncollectible. Although this is not a pleasant alternative, an organization faces some uncollectible debts.

◆ **ORGANIZATION FOR REVENUE ADMINISTRATION**

Several different issues confront public organizations when they are devel oping an effective organizational structure for handling revenue administra tion. Among the most important are specialization, decentralization, an coordination.

Public agencies such as state governments, which administer more than on major revenue system, must decide how much coordination should exis among the staff assigned to administer different revenues. Agencies must als decide how specialized these staffs should become in handling managemer issues. Specialization can occur in two ways: by function and by revenu source. Function refers to actions that cut across substantive revenue area For example, processing checks is a function that is basically the same whethe the checks are coming from income tax payments, sales tax payments, or use fee charges. This is quite different from organizing around a specific tax sourc such as sales or income. In many instances, some combination of both wi occur.

Many states have combined administrative structures to handle sales an income taxes. This is often referred to as having a functional organization. Other states combine some activities and separate others. For example, i some states auditing functions are separated, whereas collection and process ing are combined. Finally, in a few states, separate administrative structure are created to handle these two major tax sources.

According to Due and Mikesell, functional integration of administrativ structures has several things to recommend it, including the following:

- Reducing taxpayer compliance costs
- Increasing efficiencies and reducing cost to the state
- Increasing trends toward functional integration[16]

There are also some negatives to functional integration. It can confuse taxpay ers and lead to an increasing importance and focus on one revenue source a the cost of reducing administrative efforts placed on the other. If sales an

ncome tax administration are integrated, one might receive more audit
esources or collection enforcement attention than the other. If they are
dministered separately, this is less likely.

Another problem associated with functional integration has to do with
evels of staff specialization. Tax laws and regulations become increasingly
omplex as attempts are made to make them more equitable or reduce
oopholes and abuses, and the administrative expertise needed to manage the
•peration of that tax increases. This complexity means that greater and greater
legrees of specialization will be required to explain, monitor, and enforce the
ollection of the tax revenue. Functional integration moves in the other
lirection, toward less and less specialization. As mentioned earlier, this has
ed some states to integrate some functions (e.g., secretarial, clerical, collec-
ion, data processing) and separate others (e.g., taxpayer education, auditing,
ompliance monitoring, and enforcement).

Another issue facing public agencies is how much to centralize or decen-
ralize their revenue organizations. In general, agencies have decentralized
hose functions that require direct contact with the taxpayer, constituent, or
ustomer. These areas (education, auditing, enforcement) are also likely to be
he areas of greatest specialization. On the other hand, responsibilities asso-
iated with infrequent direct contact (collection, data processing, clerical) are
he most likely to centralized; for example, much of IRS compliance, auditing,
axpayer service, and criminal enforcement functions are handled in its
listrict offices, whereas other staff functions (such as personnel, public affairs,
nd planning and research) are predominantly handled through a central
•ffice.

Perhaps the element most likely to change to the nature of revenue admini-
tration is technology. The rapid growth in information technology has made
he identification, collection, and enforcement of revenue much easier than
vas true even five years before. Use of computer technology to aid property
ax assessment or to identify those who are not paying outstanding tax
iabilities is now readily available. *Forbes* magazine noted that the IRS now uses
uch things as relational data bases and expert systems to target potential
onfilers. In 1993 alone, IRS agents accessed more than 130,000 cash trans-
.ctions affecting more than two million taxpayers, more than three times the
umber of such searches that had occurred just the year before.[17] Coordina-
ion that is now possible between local, state, and federal authorities because
•f technology should greatly aid the administration of revenue systems.

CONCLUSION ◆

Revenue administration is a complex subject, involving a number of differ-
nt functions and activities and depending heavily on the revenue source
tructure itself. Some revenue sources and structures are difficult to adminis-
er because of the unique nature of the revenue or how it is applied. Others
re much easier to administer and have low costs relative to revenue collected.

Administration of any revenue source must be concerned about an accurate location and definition of its base, precise valuing of that base, development of an efficient way to process revenue returns, a way to ensure accurate and timely collections, and a way to provide accurate information and assistance to those who pay revenues to public agencies. These tasks are difficult and require continuous effort, but they are the key to successful revenue management.

DISCUSSION QUESTIONS

1. At what point should states and communities look at the "inefficiencies" of locally based property tax assessment compared with the political benefits of keeping the decision about property value at the local level?

2. How can states do a better job of coordinating the collection of various revenues?

3. What are the benefits and drawbacks for states to totally integrate income tax systems with the national government?

4. What relationship exists for public and nonprofit agencies between revenue administration and cash management practices?

◆ NOTES

1. John F. Due and John L. Mikesell (1983). *Sales taxation: State and local structure and administration.* Baltimore: Johns Hopkins University Press, pp. 24-25.

2. J. Richard Aronson and Eli Schwartz (Eds.). (1987). *Management policies in local government finance* (3rd ed.). Washington, DC: International City Management Association, p. 222.

3. Clara Penniman (1980). *State income taxation.* Baltimore: Johns Hopkins University Press, 131; and Due and Mikesell, pp. 161-166.

4. Internal Revenue Service (1981). *Internal Revenue Service Manual.* Washington, DC: Internal Revenue Service, p. 1118.4.

5. William L. Raby and Victor H. Tidwell (1985). *Introduction to federal taxation.* Englewood Cliffs, NJ: Prentice-Hall, pp. 18-5, 18-7.

6. Penniman, pp. 94-95.

7. Illinois Department of Revenue (1995). Taxpayers' Rights WWW site: http://http.bsd.uchicago.edu/~idor/loboa.htm.

8. John Walker (1995). U.S. Tax Code On-Line WWW site: http://www.fourmilab.ch/ustax/ustax.html.

9. Internal Revenue Service (1981). *Internal Revenue Service Manual.* Washington, DC: Internal Revenue Service, p. 1118.4

10. Ira Jackson (1986, December). Tax administration. In Steve Gould (Ed.), *Reforming state tax systems* (pp. 333-346). Washington, DC: National Conference of State Legislators.

11. Illinois Department of Revenue.

12. Illinois Department of Revenue.

13. Pennsylvania Department of Revenue (1995). Tax amnesty WWW site: http://www.epix.net/homepage/parev/docs/regtext.htm.

14. Aronson and Schwartz, p. 224.

15. Due and Mikesell, p. 108.

16. Ibid.

17. Janet Novak (1994, April 11). You know who you are, and so do we. *Forbes, 153*(8), 88.

SUGGESTED READINGS ◆

ıhn H. Bowman (Ed.). (1995). *Taxation of business property.* Westport, CT: Praeger.
ıhn F. Due and John L. Mikesell (1983). *Sales taxation: State and local structure and administration.* Baltimore: Johns Hopkins University Press.
lara Penniman (1980). *State income taxation.* Baltimore: Johns Hopkins University Press.

Forecasting
and Estimating

Forecasts and estimates are efforts to provide admittedly inaccurate quan titative assessments of unknown values. As such, they are prediction concerned with either future, current, or past time periods. Forecasts deal wit the future whereas estimates deal with current or past periods. Forecasts o revenues and expenditures for the next fiscal year are unknowable because th actual events have not yet occurred. In a similar fashion, a current or pas quantity of something might not be known simply because it is not ye counted or measured or because it is not feasible or possible to measure i precisely. Widely publicized statistics concerning economic conditions ar estimates; examples include the Gross Domestic Product, unemployment, an Consumer Price Index figures. Many other quantitative figures used by publi organizations are estimates and forecasts because decision makers want to us the latest available information to make choices.

Forecasting in public finance administration is most visible as revenue an expenditure forecasts during the budget process. If used properly, forecast can provide the realistic options available to a public organization as policy makers strive to relate total revenues and total expenditures by making specifi decisions. Other future-oriented techniques that use forecasting include pen sion administration, capital budgeting, economic development administra tion, cost analysis, cash management, and investing. Estimating is not widel recognized as being a conceptually distinct and useful way of developin imprecise quantification of things in the past or present periods. Estimatin is particularly useful in cases where actually counting something is extremel expensive (e.g., unemployment or Gross Domestic Product) and where i would be so time-consuming as to reduce the value of the information. I both cases, estimates are like forecasts in providing imprecise information fo choices. In addition to the many cases where estimates are used to produc forecasts, estimating is used particularly within fiscal years to estimate reve nues and expenditures and, thereby, to decide whether to make adjustment n expenditure and cash management plans. Estimates of current conditions re used to adjust plans based on forecasts.

Estimating and forecasting are analytically and technically similar; they nswer the question "How much?" Their primary difference is whether the quantity is past or current and potentially knowable or in the future and not knowable. The primary advantage of estimating over forecasting is that it is possible to acquire more information to check an estimate. That is to say, if estimate information produces an unexpected result, more information for he same time period can be gathered. More same-time period information or forecasts requires waiting.

Forecasting and estimating contrast with cost analysis techniques discussed n the following chapter. Although forecasting and estimating often support ost analysis, cost analysis is used less frequently and in a more focused fashion o deal with specific questions or issues. Estimating and forecasting are used o support routine public finance administration processes. Forecasting and stimating are more pervasive, simpler, and closer to private-sector modes of nalysis than cost analysis.

THE PURPOSE AND THE PROBLEM ◆

Estimating and forecasting have the same basic purpose of providing the best possible quantification of some unknown value. The quantity that is developed is used to make decisions. If revenue forecasts show an increase or decrease, decision makers are likely to make an adjustment in revenue or expenditure plans. The same is true in all areas where estimates and forecasts re used. Predictions are used to seize opportunities, to avoid problems, and o hold firm when things appear to be proceeding smoothly.

The general problem is that all predictions are inaccurate to some degree. The specific problem in any set of circumstances is the degree of inaccuracy. n situations where forecasting is used for policy analysis, the precise degree f accuracy is less a concern than is the contribution that forecasts can make o clarify the implications of various choices. Sometimes, a greater degree of ccuracy is desired and expected than is possible. Many predictions can be generally or grossly accurate, but precisely correct predictions are desired. For xample, accuracy rates of 90% and 99% sound very good until you think hrough the consequences of such rates. Assuming no other inaccuracies, deviations of 1% and 10% on the revenue side of a budget are very different vents. An error of 1% less revenue than predicted requires an adjustment of only 1% on the expenditure side, using reserves, borrowing, or some combination to deal with that error. A revenue forecast that was 10% higher than actual revenues would cause a major problem requiring drastic actions for most public organizations. Accuracy cannot be guaranteed because events cannot be guaranteed. Predictions always err. Also, the political consequences f errors include criticism for being in error at all and for producing particular problems. Two kinds of defenses exist for dealing with prediction errors: echnical and political.

Public organizations and officials defend themselves technically from prediction errors in three general ways. First, they pursue the most reasonably accurate prediction techniques available for matters of major consequence. For example, making great efforts to forecast a main revenue source makes sense but not for minor revenue sources. Part of this defense against inaccuracy is to avoid expecting greater accuracy than is probable. A historical record of accuracy for forecasts that compares forecasts to results or precise information to estimates is useful for developing an understanding of the likely range of accuracy. Of course, the degree of accuracy pursued depends on the importance of the item being estimated or forecast. If an organization receives or spends 80% of its budget in one category, that category is where the greatest possible accuracy should be sought. The underlying assumptions are that errors in smaller items are offsetting, some high and some low, and are collectively less in error than individually, whereas errors in large items are less likely to be offsetting and more likely to cause difficulty.

Second, public organizations build error protection countermeasures into their actual predictions. An initial method is to introduce a systematic bias into the procedures that adjusts an estimate or forecast in the direction that is least likely to prove troublesome. For example, biases toward the low side in revenue forecasting and the high side in expenditure forecasting are not likely to cause major problems, as they do not produce a budgetary imbalance requiring remedial action. Also, these biases run counter to the generalized tendency toward optimism assumed by most public program proponents. There are many ways to introduce a bias into forecasts. On the revenue side it is best to do so in an explicit fashion to avoid creating an excessive bias. If the historical average error on a forecast has been 2%, you might do the forecast and then make a 3% or 4% downward adjustment in it. On the expenditure side, a conservative bias can be found in relatively high forecasts of prices and numbers of things budgeted for. Also, where opinion is used as a basis for forecasts, opinions slightly weighted in the direction of more safety guard against the most adverse outcomes.

Third, public organizations build contingent defenses against the consequences of prediction errors. These are planned measures for unplanned events that allow them to cope with unexpected occurrences. Generally these defenses are against being in situations where an organization would have less money than was predicted. These include maintaining asset reserves, sometimes in the form of "rainy day" funds; imposing a variety of controls on expenditures, which make it possible to make expenditure adjustments that effectively make expenditures flexible; and making provisions for access to borrowing and credit. These measures are meant to be used to close a gap between erroneously predicted revenues and expenditures, usually within a fiscal year. Sometimes, political officials find monies set aside for contingencies too irresistible and choose to spend them.

If an organization systematically defends itself technically against errors, it can build large reserves as well as avoid other problems. When the size of financial reserves become a problem, reserves can be partially dissipated by explicitly budgeting them as a revenue source and reducing reliance on other revenue sources in a self-conscious and orderly fashion.

Political concerns often motivate optimism, which runs counter to the technical recommendations made here. Typically, proponents of public programs prefer high revenue estimates to make additional program funding possible and low expenditure estimates for programs they support to make gaining support for them easier. Conversely, opponents prefer the opposite kind of forecasts. The only purpose of slight biases in forecasting advocated here is to create error in the directions that are easiest to handle. Such intentional biases can be adjusted up or down, depending on the accuracy rates experienced, the sufficiency of revenue supplements, and the means of adjusting expenditures.

Political defenses against prediction errors hinge on the basic premise that predictions are not being systematically biased for political advantage. Because predictions can be gauged against reality, systematic bias becomes very apparent. The two political defenses are being unbiased and open. Being unbiased means striving for reasonable levels of technical accuracy in predictions, even though proponents or opponents of proposals and levels of revenues and expenditures will argue that bias exists because predictions do not conform to their views. Life is too frequently unfair, but eventually a record of unbiased predictions can be shown. Being open means being completely candid that predictions inevitably are in error and about all details of how predictions are made. Openness increases credibility of predictions. Frequently, the reasons for errors, such as sudden changes in economic conditions, major new revenue sources, or new programs, can be determined after the fact. When errors are predicted and prediction techniques openly explained, then people interested in the errors are more likely to listen to explanations. Also, if predictors show that they have nothing to hide, people are more likely to believe that the predictors have nothing to hide.

Florida, Louisiana, Indiana, Kansas, and several other states use an extreme version of openness called *consensus forecasting* for budgetary forecasts. Consensus forecasting is not a technique as much as it is an institutional arrangement: Representatives of the executive and the legislative branches work together to agree to budget forecasts; the forecasts are finally made only when the participants agree on them. In some cases, the consensus process also involves representatives of the business and academic communities.[1]

ESTIMATING AND ◆
FORECASTING TECHNIQUES

Many specific techniques produce predictions. The techniques vary little between estimates and forecasts, except that estimates have no future time dimension. All techniques can be assigned to one of four groups, depending on the basis used to make the forecast or estimate. In many actual cases, two or more of the four different types can be used together to produce a forecast. The four technique groups are based on opinion, sampling, time series, and associations.[2] Despite some mathematical complications involved in applying some of these techniques, understanding them and their uses does not require competence in advanced statistics. The explanations are framed as simply as possible, and statistical concepts and equations are minimized.

Opinion Techniques

Opinion techniques rely fundamentally on one or more persons' opinion of current or future phenomena or events. Opinion techniques are denigrated by the term "guess" and justified by the term "expert opinion." Public organizations often use these techniques.

The obvious problem with opinion techniques is the degree of accuracy. Accuracy depends on the source of opinion. Opinions of experts are reasonably expected to be more accurate than those of nonexperts. Where the estimate or forecast is repetitive, experts' opinions can be assessed for their historical degree of accuracy. Generally, public finance administration forecasting is repetitive, and, therefore, the accuracy of various techniques can be calculated. Opinion-based techniques rely on assumptions, directions of changes, relationships, or figures that do not have a substantial, systematic evidential basis as much as they rest on the judgment or intuition of the person or persons rendering the opinion. Developing an opinion can involve using available information in some explicit fashion, such as reasoning by analogy or providing a scenario, or implicitly processing information and opinion without an explicit rationale at all.

The most common opinion techniques include raw opinions of an individual with dubious expertise, expert opinion, multiple expert opinions, and iterative or processed opinions of experts. The raw opinion of a person not recognized as an expert can be used when no expert is available for whatever reason. This occurs in unique situations or where the estimate or forecast is of so little importance that any prediction will suffice. The opinion of one expert is particularly suited for situations where there is only one expert or where one expert can be expected to produce a sufficiently accurate prediction. Where the degree of accuracy of a prediction is important enough, a group of experts can be used. Of course, this takes more time and effort. Also, once one has a set of expert opinions, how to use them must be determined. In other words, do we use the set to achieve a measure of central tendency (e.g., average or median) or to predict a range, or should the set be interpreted in some other manner? With multiple expert opinions, you have to find a way to interpret them. With a singular expert opinion, you tend to accept the opinion in the form given. Finally, expert opinions can be processed or iterated. When this occurs, expert opinions are gathered and fed back to the experts, who then produce revised opinions. As the process develops, the experts come to consensus opinions. This is generally called the *Delphi technique.*

Sampling Techniques

Sampling techniques involve observing some portion of a group of phenomena and extrapolating from that portion to create an impression of the group as a whole. The general underlying assumptions of sampling techniques are that an adequate sample of a group can be observed and that there is a known r a reasonably assumed relationship between the sample group and the whole group being sampled. Sampling techniques are estimating techniques, which re very similar to opinion polling techniques, though most things sampled or public finance administration are less volatile than opinions.

Sampling techniques can be divided into those used for estimating and those for forecasting. The key difference is that there is a known or a reasonble expectation that sampling concerning future things is likely to be less ccurate than sampling concerning current things. The future is generally uzzier and likely to be contingent on some "as of now" unforeseen events or onditions.

For estimates of current things, standard statistically appropriate sampling nd extrapolating techniques can be used. Basically, starting with an assumpion or two concerning the total number of phenomena to be estimated and heir probable distribution, we calculate an adequate sample size and error nargin to estimate the unknown value of the whole group of the phenomena n a reasonably accurate fashion. Generally, random samples and normal distributions are assumed in discussions of statistical extrapolations. Stratiied and clustered samples are more common in practice, and nonnormal distributions are not uncommon. Despite such deviations, a reasonably done ample and statistical extrapolation produces useful results. To the extent that greater accuracy is desired, a larger sample has to be taken or some additional nformation or assumptions introduced into the statistical extrapolation. The ey is that false precision is not very helpful in estimating. Larger samples decrease the error range by reducing the probability that the sample differs rom the overall group. Of course, it helps to use appropriate sampling echniques because the techniques are more frequently a source of error than re statistical computations. Additional assumptions or information can be used to provide a correction for some known deviation. For example, in using pinion polling data for voting, some pollsters weigh each opinion by the haracteristics of the individual based on the historical voting probability of eople with those characteristics. Another correction that can be used is for eap years, which are 1/365 longer than other years.

Three typical sampling problems involve forecasting, technical ability, and ystematic bias. First, forecasting based on estimates is tricky, especially if the orecasting basis is weak. For example, forecasting people's behavior based on heir current opinions or projections is not likely to produce highly accurate orecasts, whereas forecasts based on firmer plans are still not very certain. The key in using sampling to forecast is contrary evidence; contrary evidence est indicates the limits of forecasting based on estimates. For example, initial ampling data from a later period that are not consistent with an estimate-ased forecast should be taken as a sign that the initial forecast is incorrect. olitical polling is instructive because it appears that who wins particular lections depends partially on which day an election is actually held, as first ne and then another candidate is ahead in the polls. Second, unfortunately, stimators' technical abilities do not compare with their self-estimation in nany cases. Technical errors in using sampling and statistical techniques are ot uncommon. Also, where there is limited evidence to support assumptions f the total number and the distributional characteristics of a group of phenomena, a possibility exists that results will be inaccurate to a greater than expected degree because the assumptions are incorrect. Finally, in using sampling, you have to be constantly alert to see if the sample observations have any systematic bias. This is done by repeatedly asking the question, "Is there any reason to believe that the observed phenomena may differ from the total group of the phenomena?"

A peculiar sort of sampling creates a test case experiment and samples the tested group. Such a test case uses a sample group with a known or assumed relationship to the general group of phenomena. An experimental treatment is applied to the sample group that is observed for the expected effect. Then an extrapolation is made to the general group. Such test cases are tricky to do and not always possible.

Sampling is primarily used for estimating, particularly in auditing, though estimates are used frequently to calculate forecasts. Few efforts in public finance administration involve forecasting based on samples, though samples are used in general and specific economic forecasting (e.g., purchasing agent predictions and corporate hiring, investment, and research and development plans).

Time-Series Techniques

Time-series techniques predict based on the past temporal patterns of the thing being predicted. The basic assumption is that the future is like the past, which is a good and useful assumption if you have sufficient past information to estimate the present or forecast the future. Generally, time series techniques are oriented toward forecasting rather than estimating, although it is possible to use past information to predict a current or past quantity.

Time-series techniques start simply and become increasingly complicated by inclusion of additional time factors that are computed using various statistical methods. The additional time factors in the last sentence refer to changes in values of the thing forecast over different time periods (e.g., does the thing vary over particular time cycles such as months?).

The simplest time-series forecast is that a quantity of something in the next future period will be the same or close to the same as it is in the present or the last past time period. This assumes that little of consequence changes over the two time periods.

Another common time-series technique called *trendline forecasting* forecasts future values of a thing by using the current value plus the rate and direction of change between the current period and the previous period or periods. Rendered into an equation for the graphically inclined, this means

Next Period Forecast = Current Period Value + or - depending on the direction of change (Current Period Value x the Rate of Change between the current and the past period)

This method can use multiple past periods to calculate a rate of change value. The idea behind trendline forecasting is that something continues to change on the same line that it has changed in the past. If one uses only one

ast, one current, and any number of future periods, one gets a perfectly
raight line if the values are placed on a graph. Interestingly, current-period
gures are either estimated or forecast to some degree to provide figures for
endline forecasting. One glaring weakness of trendline forecasting is that it
iscounts the possibility of the trendline changing direction or altering its rate
f change to a great degree. In other words, trendline forecasts do not have
ny chance of forecasting turning points.

Moving averages is a technique whereby values from some number of past
me periods, and perhaps the current time period, are averaged to produce a
orecast value. The "moving" part of the term means that the number of values
sed to produce the forecast does not change but that those values progress
or every forecast—the oldest past time period value is dropped and the most
ecent past or current time period value is added to the numbers averaged.
his technique is particularly useful where there is not a steady pattern of
nange over time. An example of a moving averages forecast is a forecast that
nyone's weight tomorrow is equal to the average of today's and yesterday's
eight figures.

Time-series techniques become increasingly complex as additional ef-
orts are made to increase the accuracy of forecasts. The more advanced
echniques can be grouped into those relying on exponential smoothing,
ecomposition, and both autocorrelation and adaptation. *Exponential smooth-
ng* gives more weight to more recent observations than earlier ones. This can
e done in a variety of ways.[3] *Decomposition* involves taking changes over time
nto account as separate elements to make forecasting calculations (e.g.,
ends over time, cycles over time, seasonal variations, and random fluctua-
ons). The difference between exponential smoothing and decomposition
echniques is that the former deals with all variation on a holistic basis (i.e.,
eighted averages over time are computed with heavier weights for those
earest to the current period whereas the latter deals with each time variation
ement on an individual basis).[4] The more complicated time-series tech-
iques use mathematical models that rely on measurements of autocorrela-
on and adaptation. *Autocorrelation* refers to the degree to which a variable
lates to itself during different time periods. For example, revenues during
ne month of January during different years may show a high degree of
utocorrelation, that is, they are much alike. Using statistical manipulations,
ne can use autocorrelation data to build advanced forecasting models. *Ad-
ptation* means that a model changes its values when there is a change in the
me-series data for a variable.[5]

The complexity of advanced time-series techniques should not obscure the fact
nat they are concerned with forecasting a single variable over time. The complex-
y is possible because variations over time are surrogates for other factors.
his simplifies the conceptual situation but allows for complex computations.

Associational Techniques

Associational techniques are fundamentally more complex than any of the
nree previously discussed groups of predicting techniques. Associational
echniques are also called explanatory or causal techniques. Basically, these

techniques predict a value for one or more variables based on one or more other variables. The three previously discussed sets of techniques deal explicitly with only one variable, even though they all implicitly take some other factors into account in some fashion. Associational techniques rely on one or more assumptions regarding the relationships of variables, often based on historical evidence. Actual figures used in associational predictions are cross sectional or time series in character. Cross-sectional refers to data from the same time period as the variable or variables to be predicted. Time-series data comes from different time periods (i.e., data from one or more time periods is used to predict variable values in one or more later time periods).

Associational techniques relevant to making predictions in public finance administration include deterministic equations, leading indicators, correlation, simple regression, multiple regression, econometric models, and input output models. The most simple associational technique uses *deterministic equations*. This forecasting technique is not discussed by general forecasting specialists but is recognized in literature discussing public finance administration predictions.[6] One or more equations are posited based on known or assumed relationships between two or more variables that generally take the form A x B = C. Although such equations appear to have limited utility in dealing with complex situations, the technique is widely used where the predicted relationship is reasonable and where the method of deriving the predictor value or values is reasonably accurate.

Dog license revenues provide a basis for demonstrating a deterministic equation and displaying the difference between cross-sectional and time-series data. Dog license revenue is a function of the license fee and the number of dogs licensed: Dogs x Fee = Revenue. With a known fee, the predictor variable is the number of dogs licensed, which is assumed to be equal to the number of dogs for this example. A cross-sectional predictor can be derived based on some opinion or estimate technique for predicting the number of dogs in the jurisdiction. Also, if the jurisdiction is small enough, one might actually be able to count the dogs. Another cross-sectional basis might be another deterministic equation based on the amount of dog food sold relative to the number of dogs. Time-series data could use past patterns of dogs to predict the current number of dogs (e.g., trendline pattern based on an average rate of change) or some data from one or more preceding periods (e.g., number of dogs sold by pet shops).

Another relatively simple technique involves leading indicators. A *leading indicator* predicts changes in something before the actual change. Leading indicators appear particularly useful in predicting turning points, but in practice the technique has not been impressively accurate. More often than not, leading indicators relevant in the public sector are more useful for flagging something for further examination rather than being useful for making predictions. One major exception is using leading economic indicators to forecast general economic conditions, even though the accuracy is not particularly noteworthy even there.[7]

A third relatively simple type of associational technique is correlation. Very simply, a *correlation* is a measure of the strength of a relationship between two variables with respect to the degree to which they vary. In other words, measure of correlation measure how much variables vary together. A perfect correlation measurement would be an instance where variables vary in a mirror image of one another. Practically, this approach requires an extremely high correlation between two variables and a relatively high accuracy in the predictor variable. The ultimate degree of accuracy is determined by both the strength of the correlation that predicts the amount of variation in the predicted variable and the degree of accuracy of the prediction of the predictor variable. If a correlation predicts 90% of the variation in the predicted variable and if the accuracy of the predicted value of the predictor variable is 90%, then the resultant correlation-based prediction appears likely to be approximately 81% correct, .9 x .9 = .81, which is not exactly perfection. Correlation techniques are very similar in technical detail to regression-based techniques and rely on some of the same statistical calculations. Correlation approaches are not often used in the public sector.

The remaining techniques are based on *regression equations,* which differ from the previously discussed associational techniques in that prediction error is statistically included in the prediction. The first three associational techniques discussed assume a fit between a description of a relationship and one or more predictor variables without considering any expected degree of error in making a prediction. Error ranges can be calculated, but that is not an intrinsic part of the prediction calculations.

Regression equations and correlation are related. Correlation statistics are meant to show the degree of relationship between two variables, whereas regression equations are meant to predict the value of one variable based on one or more other variables. In making such predictions, we use previously recorded values of variables to create an equation that describes the relationship between the variables. A simple regression equation usually involves two variables and a linear relationship—a straight line can be used to graphically represent the relationship. The basic form of a simple, linear regression equation is

$$Y = a + bX + \text{error estimate}$$

where Y is the predicted variable, a is the value of X where Y equals zero, b is the rate of change in Y relative to X, X is the predictor variable, and the error estimate is a statistical estimate of the range of error for the particular equation.

This and all other regression equations can be used to predict values of Y by inserting values for X and doing the relevant computations. Regression equations describe predictions that minimize deviations from past observations and thereby deal with error by minimizing expected errors. Also, the error estimate, which is not always displayed, is a measurement of the past degree of randomness of the observed data.[8]

Simple regression equations look exactly like what a forecaster needs to make accurate predictions, but several factors limit their utility. First, we need many observations or measurements of the variables to develop reasonably accurate regression equations, usually over many time periods. Second, we have to assume that the relationship has not changed over time. A shift in an associational relationship over time reduces the accuracy and thereby the utility of regression equations in forecasting. Third, we have to make a number of assumptions about the relationships between variables to create a regression equation. If the assumptions err, the equation will not be accurate. Finally, we have to estimate or forecast a current value for the predictor variable, which is another source of error.[9]

Multiple regression extends simple regression by adding a second or perhaps more predictor variables to the equation. A multiple regression equation looks like a simple one for more variables. Here is an example of a multiple regression equation:

$$Y = a + bX + cZ + \text{error estimate}$$

The term cZ distinguishes this equation from the simple deterministic equation above. It includes Z, a second predictor variable, and as Z varies, Y varies at the rate of some value c. Multiple regression is used because more predictors can produce more accurate predictions and reduce the error estimate. All the difficulties inherent in simple regression apply to multiple regression, however, along with a few others relating to whether statistical assumptions are correct. Multiple regression looks particularly good at first glance but suffers from being extremely complex to implement because of the level of sophistication and the sheer level of statistical operations required.[10]

The next step in increasing complexity is the use of *econometric models* which were created to attempt to replicate in equations the measurable relations of variables in an economy. Literally, they were first used to mathematically model a whole national economy. Econometric models involve "simultaneous multiple regression equations."[11] Literally, this means that predictions are made based on two or more multiple regression equations that involve interdependent variables. *Interdependent variables* vary in relationship to one another. Simultaneous equations are used to include variable interdependence into the prediction model. Examples of interdependent variables used in econometric models are measures of the level of economic activity, inflation, and unemployment, which are used to make economic forecasts or to forecast other variables based on economic conditions (e.g., revenue). The conceptual and computational complexity of econometric models result from the interdependency of variables. As constructing an econometric model is extremely costly and requires a high level of expertise, few public organizations construct their own. Instead, econometric model predictions can be purchased from consulting agencies that have their own econometric models or consulting agencies can create small secondary econometric models that use economic predictions from their own primary model.[12]

Econometric models are used most often for general economic forecasting, which can then provide input for other forecasting techniques. Also, econometric models are used to forecast revenues related closely to economic conditions (e.g., sales and income taxes). Econometric models are probably more useful for analysis than prediction in most cases. Their primary forecasting advantage is their greater capacity to identify turning points.[13]

Finally, *input-output models* are a special kind of econometric model that attempt to predict demands for different industries. In effect, they predict how changes in demands on one or more industries will affect demands made on other industries. Here, "industries" really means segment of an economy. In addition to simultaneous multiple regression equations concerning economic conditions in general terms, input-output models require similar simultaneous equations that relate industries to one another with respect to input and output.[14] Such models appear to be useful only for governmental policy-making purposes for various industries, particularly for taxation and economic development policies.

MONITORING ◆

Monitoring of predictions means relating later information to predictions to assess their accuracy. The basic idea is to use more or better information to confirm the accuracy of a prediction or to show the degree to which a prediction appears to be inaccurate. The degree of accuracy depends on the expectations of those concerned with the matters predicted. Although a degree of accuracy can be computed mathematically, the significance of any degree of inaccuracy is a matter of judgment. Information used to monitor predictions is usually later in time than predictions and involves actual measurements. Also, one monitors things that are important. If monitoring provides evidence that a prediction is reasonably accurate, proceeding with plans based on that prediction makes sense. If monitoring provides evidence that a prediction is not reasonably accurate, new predictions can be made and plans recast.

Actual methods of monitoring predictions depend on the availability of data and information. Actual data are best, because anything less than actual data can be erroneous. For example, a forecast monitored by a later estimate that shows a large discrepancy can be partially attributable to some degree of error in both predictions. Forecasts are likely to show a greater degree of error than estimates. Regardless, whenever monitoring shows a prediction to be in error to a significant degree, the prediction should be scrutinized for its accuracy.

Technically, the forms of monitoring are mathematical or judgmental.[15] In *mathematical monitoring,* measured deviations from predictions are compared with anticipated degrees of error. When the deviations are greatly or systematically outside the anticipated range of random fluctuation, significant prediction error has occurred. A variety of mathematical techniques can serve this purpose. *Judgmental monitoring* relies on looking at more or later information to see whether the prediction exceeds what is an acceptable level of deviation from a prediction in the judgment of the observer. A predetermined accuracy level is best because wishful thinking can be avoided.

In any event, the key issue for all prediction monitoring in public finance administration, whether faced explicitly, is what effect monitoring information will have on an organization. If there is no likely effect of monitoring,

then why bother? If the monitoring information shows predictions to b
reasonably accurate, continuation of a plan is indicated. If the monitorin
information is not reasonably accurate, then plans and planned actions hav
to be changed. Degrees of reasonable accuracy are closely associated wit
defenses against inaccuracy. A higher level of defense against inaccuracy i
predictions reduces the likelihood of seriously inaccurate predictions. In som
situations, the degree of error in a prediction falls within the cumulative leve
of prepared defenses and can be handled easily. In other words, contingenc
plans are sufficient to deal with the level of error. In some situations, howeve
the degree of error in a prediction is so great that greater adjustments ar
required than those prepared by the organization. Such errors require majo
changes.

Except for not predicting well, not defending against prediction errors, an
not monitoring, lacking a predetermined level of degrees of prediction inac
curacy is probably the most common prediction problem. Predetermine
trigger points allow organizations to deal with their best grasp of reality rathe
than wishing, which probably will not make it so.

◆ MERITS OF THE DIFFERENT TECHNIQUES

All the techniques discussed can be used to predict in various public financ
administration areas. Each particular technique has advantages in differin
circumstances. The key factors are the future time horizon, data situatior
costs, time requirements, ease of use, and accuracy. Each of the four group
of techniques discussed generally vary on these factors.

Opinion Techniques

Opinion-based predictive techniques are not limited to any particula
future time horizon, which is an advantage. The data used for opinion tech
niques do not have to meet any standards of qualification, which is a
advantage. The cost of opinion techniques is usually low. Opinion prediction
can be produced when there is little lead time. The prediction is one or mor
individual's opinion, which is intelligible to most people. The accuracy c
opinion predictions is very poor in routine or repetitive situations in com
parison with all other technique groups but can be superior where the tim
horizon is extended and where the other techniques are not applicable.[1]
Opinion techniques are the techniques of first and last resort. They are th
easiest to use and, therefore, the first techniques generally used. Also, becaus
they can be used under any circumstances, they are the last used when th
other techniques cannot be used appropriately. An appropriate test for quan
titative prediction techniques is whether they can be used well enough in com
parison with an opinion technique to be worth the additional cost and effor

The problems associated with opinion-based techniques are generally re
lated to accuracy in routine, repetitive situations where human predictor
show the same human tendencies to err. The three general categories of erro

ccording to Wheelwright and Makridakis, are an overemphasis on searching or supporting evidence rather than contrary evidence, overconfidence generated by increasing amounts of evidence based on the ill-founded belief that greater amounts of information produce proportionally greater accuracy, and overconformity among groups.[17] In addition to recognizing and guarding against these error-producing tendencies, predictors can systematically review various biases and limitations inherent in particular opinion prediction techniques to avoid unnecessary inaccuracy.[18]

Sampling Techniques

Sampling techniques are limited to the current and past periods. Sampling depends on data availability, data accuracy, and data that conform to assumed patterns. Based on assumptions about the actual phenomena quantified and the data used, the costs of sampling techniques vary with the method of sampling and the size of a sample. It takes approximately the same number of samples to predict unemployment or prices within a state as it does for all of the states together as a whole, with approximately the same level of expected accuracy. The methods of securing samples vary in cost from self-reporting samples, where individuals or organizations fill out questionnaires, to on-site observations, where people are paid to take samples. In only a few specific applications (e.g., tax auditing or accounting system-oriented auditing) is it possible to use preexisting data collection systems to make estimates because most data systems are not organized in a manner conducive to making estimates. Generally, sample-based estimation takes place only when the anticipated value of having the prediction exceeds the costs involved. The general exception is federally collected data, which are oriented toward serving various constituencies by having the federal government collect and process data. The federal government does not expect much value to itself as an entity for these efforts. Sampling techniques typically are not extremely time-consuming but do require from a week to a few months to complete when started from scratch. Sampling techniques are relatively easy to use and are generally intelligible to people with a modicum of statistical understanding. Many other people have a sense of what a poll or sample prediction means. Accuracy of sampling techniques is relatively high, ranging from 80% to 99% accuracy.[19] Of course, greater accuracy costs more and is possible only because complete accuracy is theoretically possible by actually counting or measuring the predicted phenomena.

Time-Series Techniques

Time-series techniques vary from simple to very complex. The future time horizon of time-series predictions is limited in comparison with opinion techniques and depends on the number and length of past time periods and the past stability of the data. In other words, time-series predictions are generally limited to the next few time periods because for each additional time period projected into the future there is an additional possibility that the predicted variable will undergo some fundamental change. The greater the stability of a variable in the past, the further into the future we can predict. The data situation for time-series predictions involves requirements for some past period data that are comparable with one another and for which special cases are known. Special cases means that data anomalies caused by unique circumstances are explained. For example, if the data for a given period are partially a result of a one-time event, that anomaly can be considered in making a time-series prediction.

The costs of time-series techniques vary, depending on the degree of technical sophistication of specific techniques. As many sophisticated techniques are included with microcomputer software packages and as microcomputers become widely available, the additional costs of predictions will be primarily for the expertise and the data rather than the computations. The data requirement always involves some cost, and expertise involves costs whether purchased from a consulting firm or provided by someone in the organization who takes the time to learn how to use a particular forecasting technology. The simpler techniques are inexpensive and not time-consuming. The requirements for the more advanced techniques are a function of manipulating data in more complicated patterns. Still, if the data required exist, even the most complicated techniques can be used in a month or two. If there are no usable data, you have to collect data through some number of time periods to make predictions. Also, the more advanced techniques generally require data from more time periods.

Time-series predictions range from very simple to more complicated techniques, but they are relatively easy to use because they intuitively make sense. The time basis of predictions makes them more real than other techniques for many people because users can see a connection between the past, current, and future time periods. The accuracy of time-series techniques is superior to any other group of forecasting techniques if data are available and if they are used to forecast one to a few time periods into the future. The moderately complex or difficult techniques are more accurate than the more complex ones. Specifically, exponential smoothing and decomposition are the most accurate forecasting techniques.[20]

Associational Techniques

Associational techniques vary from the simple to the complex. The key difference is between the very simple deterministic equations approach and the regression-based techniques. Deterministic equations are so simple that their merit depends as much or more on the merits of the method used to derive the predictor variable or variables as on the relationship between the predictor variable or variables and the predicted variable. Also, the two other simple associational techniques of leading indicators and correlation are not much used in the public finance administration or generally for predictions.

The only other real area of concern in associational techniques is regression-based techniques, which range from the simple two-variable equation model to the mind-numbing models that attempt to mimic national econonies. The future time horizon of regression techniques is from one to several but less than 10 time periods. With regression techniques, it is possible to predict a few more time periods into the future than with time-series techniques but fewer than with opinion techniques. Regression techniques require more data in that they require data for two to many variables and require more time periods of data than time-series techniques generally. The larger number of variables is defined by the particular techniques, which associate more than one variable. The larger number of time periods of observation is a function of the sampling requirement that we have a sufficiently large sample to avoid invalidating the statistical assumptions made. Regression equations are a form of inferential statistics that are based on probability theory that requires minimum sample sizes to make a reasonable attempt to infer statistically. In simple terms, regression equations require a minimum of 30 to 50 observations to have a chance of producing valid forecasts. With that number of observations required, regression techniques have to use monthly or shorter observation periods because yearly observations tend to change over time in some fundamental way. Also, waiting 30 years for data to accumulate requires excessive patience.

Another data concern is that cross-sectionally related data require that some other method be used to derive the value of the predictor variable or variables to plug into the regression equation or equations. Regression techniques are the most costly and time-consuming because of the intrinsic difficulties of finding relationships that can be used to predict values of variables and the technical difficulties of creating, maintaining, and using regression equations. They do not eat just anything. Numerous consulting firms provide a whole range of services in dealing with econometric equations. Often forgotten in our era's "golly, gee whiz" attitude toward "scientific" things is that data do not jump into equations but are manipulated by people into equations based on assumptions. The work involved is done by human beings and is extremely difficult. Therefore, regression equations are not always correct. Also, regression equations are not easy to use because most people do not understand how the equations work in either a theoretical or practical sense. People tend to avoid what they do not understand.

A crucial facet of the uneasiness in using regression forecasts is that users are often unaware of the statistically probable level of error that can be computed for any regression prediction. The error range is important in predictions. The accuracy of regression techniques is more often assumed than proven. Just because the techniques are more complex and difficult, it does not follow that they are more accurate. In most cases, time-series techniques are superior in accuracy, primarily because a variable predicts itself better than any other variable does. Also, all the costs and difficulties associated with regression techniques increase as more complex techniques are used to increase the predictive accuracy. Finally, the accuracy is a function of the accuracy of the predictor variables, which are forecast or estimated themselves. Despite these shortcomings, however, these techniques are thought to be more useful for identifying turning points than any other techniques and more serviceable for general economic forecasting. Regression techniques are often used more to analyze things rather than to forecast them.[21]

◆ GENERAL AND OCCASIONAL USES

A wide variety of public finance administration situations call for prediction techniques. In a few areas, prediction techniques are generally used, an in a number of areas, they are used occasionally. Generally, forecasting is use in the areas of pensions, fiscal forecasting of revenues and expenditures, an cash management, which are respectively relatively long, medium, and shor in their time frames. Though prediction techniques can be used in almost an area, they are used only occasionally in several public finance administratio areas. First, there are a number of occasional uses where the time frame involved are long. These include capital budgeting, multiyear revenue an expenditure forecasting, and economic development analysis. Second, ther are a number of technical areas where prediction takes place in a time fram depending on the particulars of the situation. These areas include cost analy sis, investments, and risk management. Here, a discussion of pension an fiscal year prediction can show practical applications.

Pensions

Predictions for pensions paid by public organizations are forecast on th basis of expert opinions and deterministic equations. The particular type c pension discussed here, defined benefit, is one of two types, which are distin guished in a later chapter. Also, monitoring long-range pension forecasts i particularly useful because monitoring allows opportunities to correct fore casts, which are assumed to have some degree of inaccuracy to start witl Basically, it all starts with an equation that states the preferred situation fo pensions—that pension assets are predicted to be equal to pension liabilitie

Pension Assets = Pension Liabilities

Then, both pension assets and pension liabilities are predicted using tw separate sets of equations to determine whether the two sides of the basi equation are equal, and if not, in what direction and to what degree th equation is in imbalance. First, pension liability equations are used to comput the dollar value of pension liabilities, or how much the public organizatio will have to pay. These equations use opinions or assumptions about th number of people who will be eligible for what pension benefits, which ca depend on the period for which the individuals will draw pension benefit The equations are for the number of people, the pension benefits, and th length of time for some benefits. An extremely abbreviated version of thes equations might look like the following:

Pension Liabilities = Liability for Benefit One + Liability for Benefit Two and so on
Liability for Benefit One = Number of People Eligible x Value of Benefit
Number of People Eligible = Potential Number of People Eligible x Rate
    at Which Potential People Become Eligible

Value of Benefits = Terms of Pension (Lump Sum Payment of a Set Amount,
  a Variable Rate Amount Based on Future Values for a Fixed Period,
  or a Variable Rate Amount Based on Future Values for an Indefinite Period)

Examples include a $10,000 death benefit to heirs, a payment of 70% of an
employee's last-year salary paid on a monthly basis for 20 years, or 70% of the
average of an employee's last three years of salary paid for the rest of that
person's life.

Obviously, some of these require much more complicated equations than
do others. Although some values to be inserted into the equations can be
forecast using other techniques, opinion forecasts predominate because any
forecast over an extended period of time, say 20 to 40 years, is an opinion.

The second set of equations concerns the assets. Pension assets are a
function of pension revenues (i.e., money set aside for pensions, and yields
from investing pension revenues over time). A simplified version of those
equations might look like the following:

Pension Assets = Revenues for Each Time Period +
  Investment Yield for Revenues for Each Time Period
Revenues for a Time Period = Number of Employees x Revenue Base x
  Contribution Rate or Rates (e.g., 20 employees x salary x 13%, 6% from
  employees and 7% from employer)
Investment Yield = Revenues for a Time Period x Interest Rate x Investment Period

The values in these equations are either known or opinions.

Pension forecasts are almost certain to be in error to a substantial degree.
The key to using long-range forecasting is to monitor forecasts and re-forecast
as more data become available and to act on more current data. Long-range
forecasting produces both a greater probability of error and greater opportunities to adjust for error.

Fiscal Year Forecasting

Revenue and expenditure forecasting focuses on fiscal years, which in most
cases are one calendar year in length. Revenue forecasting varies in technique
by the size and characteristics of the revenue source, the forecasting sophistication of those responsible, and the fiscal situation.[22] Expenditure forecasting
varies primarily by type of expenditure.

Revenue forecasting begins with a division of forecasting efforts to particular revenue sources. The individual revenue sources are forecast separately.
Three common technique patterns appear. First, small revenue sources (e.g.,
dog licenses), unpredictable sources (e.g., death taxes and grants), and those
forecast by operating agencies (e.g., reimbursements for services) are generally forecast on an opinion basis, though simple time-series techniques can be
appropriate. Opinion techniques are used where a low level of technical
forecasting sophistication exists or little evidence supports the belief that a
more technically sophisticated technique is worth the extra effort.

Second, a curious combination of an associational technique and time series-based opinions is found when forecasting relatively large revenue sources in organizations with a modicum of forecasting sophistication. Basically, deterministic equations using base, rate, and delinquency rates are set up, and values derived from a review of historical patterns and current economic conditions and revenue forecaster's interpretation of those patterns are plugged into the equations in some way. An example is

Base x Rate = Revenue Liability
Revenue Liability - (Revenue Liability x Delinquency Rate) = Yield

Although this looks primitive, it is probably the most common approach in revenue forecasting.[23]

Third, revenues are forecast on the basis of regression equations, predominantly econometric models, in organizations with extremely sophisticated forecasting capacity, such as federal, state, and larger local governments. Generally, the forecasting of revenues is derived from a more general econometric model that is created to forecast economic conditions and modified to produce revenue forecasts. In some cases, the forecasts are made by taking econometric models used to forecast revenue bases and using those values in deterministic equations. Some states purchase econometric forecasts because they are available.

At this point, the astute reader will have said, "What happened to time-series techniques?" Although a complete answer to that question is not possible, we can point out that there is not a high level of forecasting sophistication available in the public sector, that periodic changes in circumstances (e.g., wars, policies, rates, and economic conditions) render time-series forecasts more difficult and less accurate, and that the authors may not be aware of innumerable hotbeds of public-sector time-series forecasting.

Expenditures are generally forecast by type and are less based on economic conditions than revenue forecasts are, except for mostly federal tax expenditure, entitlement, and income-support-oriented programs. As with revenue forecasting, the same three common patterns of expenditure forecasting appear. First, opinion methods are used for forecasting small and unpredictable expenditure categories. Second, deterministic equations using opinions based on recent history are used for many expenditure categories. Opinions about expenditures include relative shifts in the number of expenditure items and their costs, which are affected by perceptions of factors, such as political forces, policy shifts, unresolved bargaining, technological changes, workload predictability, and general as well as specific price changes. Third, where expenditures are a function of economic conditions (e.g., tax expenditures, agricultural subsidies, and unemployment compensation), econometric models can be used. Econometric models are not as commonly used in forecasting expenditures as revenues. As before, time-series techniques are notable primarily by their absence.

CONCLUSION ◆

Financial prediction is necessary in many areas of public finance admini-tration. As with many technical areas, understanding the fundamental situation is more important than following all the technical details. We predict to orm plans, expect prediction errors, build defenses against inaccuracy, and 1onitor predictions. The key to understanding public finance predictions is .nderstanding the fundamental situation and the information and assump-ions used in producing a prediction. Failure to do so can put you in a situation nmortalized by Steven Cherney: "He who relies on a crystal ball may eat rushed glass." Mr. Cherney did not note anything about seasonings.

DISCUSSION QUESTIONS

1. What are all the various ways that you could forecast the federal government's surplus or deficit for future years?

2. How do the various ways compare in their uses and accuracy?

3. Individually assign values to the accuracy of a forecast, the use of monitoring for forecasts, and contingent defenses for dealing with forecasting errors. Discuss the relative weights of the assigned values. What does this exercise predict about individuals' use of forecasting, monitoring, and contingent defenses? Who would you have deal with forecasting, monitoring, and making provisions for gasoline on a long trip? Would a gasoline policy manual help?

NOTES ◆

1. Tony Hutchinson (1991, March). The good, the bad and the uncertain in revenue rojections. *State Legislatures*, pp. 22-24.

2. The following treatment of techniques relies heavily on two sources: Steven C. Wheel-right and Spyros Makridakis (1985). *Forecasting methods for management* (4th ed.). New York: hn Wiley; and David M. Georgoff and Robert G. Murdick (1986, January/February). Manager's aide to forecasting. *Harvard Business Review*, 64(1), 110-120.

3. Wheelwright and Makridakis, pp. 62-66.

4. Wheelwright and Makridakis, p. 83.

5. Wheelwright and Makridakis, pp. 111-115 and 137-138.

6. Wheelwright and Makridakis, pp. 42-43. The authors focus on forecasting techniques that se "randomness" to forecast ranges of forecasting errors.

7. Wheelwright and Makridakis, pp. 200-201.

8. Wheelwright and Makridakis, pp. 162-163.

9. Wheelwright and Makridakis, pp. 144-145, 152-157, 162-163, 169.

10. Wheelwright and Makridakis, pp. 170-179, 190.

11. Wheelwright and Makridakis, p. 193.

12. Wheelwright and Makridakis, pp. 194-196.

13. Wheelwright and Makridakis, pp. 198-200.

14. See Henri Theil (Ed.). (1966). *Applied economic forecasting, volume 4: Studies in mathe-atical and managerial economics*. Amsterdam: North-Holland, pp. 168-255.

15. Wheelwright and Makridakis, p. 214.

16. Wheelwright and Makridakis, p. 346.

17. Wheelwright and Makridakis, pp. 319-329.

18. Wheelwright and Makridakis, pp. 321-347.

19. Wheelwright and Makridakis, pp. 241-244.

20. Wheelwright and Makridakis, pp. 263-277.

21. Wheelwright and Makridakis.

22. Two examples of analysis of fiscal stress and revenue forecasting are Irene S. Rubin (198?, Winter). Estimated and actual revenues: Exploring the gap. *Public Budgeting & Finance, 7*(4 83-94; and Susan A. MacManus and Barbara P. Grothe (1986, April 13-16). *Revenue forecastin techniques and reactions to fiscal stress: Select U.S. counties.* Prepared for delivery at the America Society for Public Administration Annual Meeting, Anaheim, California.

23. Larry D. Schroeder (1984). Multiyear fiscal forecasting in San Antonio. In Carol W. Lew and A. Grayson Walker III (Eds.). *Casebook in public budgeting and financial managemer* (p. 272). Englewood Cliffs, NJ: Prentice-Hall.

◆ SUGGESTED READINGS

Howard A. Frank (1993). *Budgetary forecasting in local government: New tools and technique* Westport, CT: Quorum Books.

David M. Georgoff and Robert G. Murdick (1986, January/February). Manager's guide t forecasting. *Harvard Business Review, 64*(1), 110-120.

Spyros Makridakis and Steven C. Wheelwright (1987). *The handbook of forecasting: A manager guide* (2nd ed.). New York: John Wiley.

Robert Rodgers and Philip Joyce (1996). The effect of underforecasting on the accuracy c revenue forecast by state governments. *Public Administration Review, 56,* 48-56.

Steven C. Wheelwright and Spyros Makridakis (1989). *Forecasting methods for management* (5 ed.). New York: John Wiley.

Cost Analysis

ost analysis refers to a group of related analytical techniques for taking costs and benefits into account as a means of making informed decisions. Cost analysis contributes to assessing the costs and benefits of decisions. As indicated in Chapter 4, costs are negative whereas benefits are positive. *Costs* include all reductions in value—when something is bought, its cost is the money price paid. Costs can, however, include any reduction in positively valued things or increases in negatively valued things, for example, increased pollution. In contrast, *benefits* include all increases in value; when something is sold, its benefit is the money price collected. Benefits can, however, include any increase in positively valued things or decreases in negatively valued things, for example, decreased pollution. Cost analysis techniques focus attention on the specifics of choices in a systematic way. Cost analysis provides tools that we can use to process information for decisions. Cost analysis cannot be used as a substitute for decision making. Decision makers are well served by cost analysis when it provides information for a decision and ill served when cost analysis techniques are used inappropriately to determine a "correct" decision because it was reached "scientifically." Decision-making concerns appropriately guide the use of tools rather than tools guiding decision-making concerns. In other words, the tools should assist decision makers rather than replace them with technical calculations.

Cost analysis differs between the public and private sectors. A private firm considering a business decision analyzes only its own costs and benefits. In contrast, a public organization's use of cost analysis necessarily involves looking at the impact of decisions on its public. The administrative and compliance costs of taxes are good examples. The compliance costs of taxes—what it costs individuals and businesses to comply with tax laws—are important because the public organization is acting on behalf of the public. Private firms look only at their own costs and benefits and not at costs imposed on others or at benefits solely gained by others.

Cost analysis is applied economics. As such, cost analysis allows us to apply powerful economic concepts in explicit, formal analysis instead of relying on informal judgments of costs and benefits. The cost and benefit logic of decision making introduced in Chapter 4 is formalized here to a greater degree. That process of decision making involves answering the following questions:

1. What are the options?
2. What are the consequences of the various options?
3. What are the costs and benefits of the consequences?
4. Which option has the most favorable configuration of costs and benefits?

Cost analysis techniques vary in the degree to which this logic is formalized.

The economic concepts used in cost analysis include opportunity cost incrementalism, marginalism, and incentives. *Opportunity cost* simply means the opportunities given up by making any choice. This concept is helpful in framing alternatives and weighing true costs. The classic application in the public sector is where large amounts of money have been spent on one alternative. In that case, as in any other, the difference between any two alternatives is any future use of resources. Past expenditures are no longer opportunity costs. The real choices are currently available alternatives. Without using the notion of opportunity cost, public officials tend to take past expenditures into account in making decisions.

Incrementalism, here, means analyzing the differences between alternatives rather than analyzing everything about them. For example, if two highway plans for a state differ only in one particular highway, all that is worth analyzing when judging between the two plans is how they deal with that one highway.

Marginalism refers to marginal values, which are values of additional units of products. At some point, the supply of products involves increasing costs each additional unit costs more than the preceding one, and the value of additional units of any product decreases. Marginalism considers the relativity of many values and makes it possible to relate values to one another and to avoid absolutist "all or nothing" decisions. Traffic safety is a useful area for showing how marginalism is used in analysis. Absolute prohibition of automobiles would greatly reduce traffic deaths. Other values are marginally more important to society, however. Traffic safety is approached in a variety of ways when the marginal costs are exceeded by the marginal benefits (e.g., highway design and regulation, vehicle design and regulation, and driver regulation).

Incentives refer to the observable phenomena of behavior being affected by things. By observing how people behave, we may be able to design better policy alternatives or those reflecting demonstrated preferences.

Cost analysis relates to other topics in this text. Cost analysis, along with Chapter 4, "Money and Values: Monetary Values," is an explicit presentation of an economic perspective. This perspective and the techniques can be applied to the subject matter of most other chapters. Cost analysis is closely related to capital budgeting, financial issues associated with personnel, and purchasing because cost analysis is used for future-oriented decisions. Also cost analysis is technically related to the previous chapter on forecasting and

stimating. Finally, accounting efforts are important in developing or provid-
ng information for cost analysis.

Cost analysis techniques are often not confined specifically to the bounds
f finance administration. These techniques are used to contribute to policy
nd operational decisions. Operational decisions, those concerning operating
hoices, are often analyzed because they are less complex. Policy decisions—
rhat to do—are often more complex because they encompass a wider range
f concerns. Operational questions include type of machinery, personnel,
pplies, or technique. Policy questions include regulations, revenue levels,
ervices, and facilities. Analyzing operational decisions occurs after relevant
olicy questions have been settled.

The high cost of cost analysis presents barriers to its use. Some conditions
re favorable for its use. First, it is helpful if the people making decisions are
nterested in receiving information on realistically possible choices. Often,
ost analysis is done as a means of influencing decision makers or the public
.e., used as political ammunition), which has limited utility. Second, cost
nalysis helps most when the value of better decisions is large. Practically, this
neans large amounts of money are involved, on a one-time basis as in capital
udgeting, or in large numbers of recurring events, such as the costs of filling
otholes. Third, cost analysis techniques are best applied where they are most
ppropriate:

1. Retrospective, past, rather than prospective, future, analysis
2. Alternatives with similarities, such as choice of road projects, rather than yes-no
   decisions
3. Operational rather than policy issues
4. Estimates and forecasts of demonstrated accuracy
5. Costs and benefits that can be valued monetarily

enerally, these conditions tend to favor the less complicated cost-analysis
echniques.

The three most common forms of cost analysis are simple cost, cost-
ffectiveness, and cost-benefit analysis. All three are interrelated. First, simple
ost analysis is the least inclusive. It involves only formal analysis of costs. The
arious costs of each alternative are computed, and the sum of the costs for
ach alternative is compared. The benefits resulting from each alternative are
ssumed to be the same, self-evident, or judged informally. Second, cost-ef-
ctiveness analysis involves taking the sum of the costs of each alternative and
ividing those costs into a prediction of the beneficial effect for each alterna-
ve. The resulting figure is a unit cost, the cost per unit of the effect. Third,
ost-benefit analysis involves relating the sum of the costs and the sum of the
enefits of each alternative. Cost-benefit analysis differs from cost-effective-
ess analysis because it deals with multiple beneficial effects and monetary
aluation of those benefits. Examples may show the distinct aspects of each:
. simple cost analysis of two trucks for garbage collection results in a single
ost figure for each truck. Cost-effective analysis produces a unit cost figure
or each truck for some common measure of a beneficial effect (e.g., per ton

of garbage collected or per number of garbage collection stops). Finally cost-benefit analysis would produce a single figure for each alternative that would allow them to be compared, usually a net benefit figure showing the difference between the value of predicted benefits and costs for each truck.

The three different forms of cost analysis can be shown in different equations. First, the starting point for any cost analysis is private-sector cost analysis, which can also include predicted private benefits. Private-sector cost analysis uses only values as they affect the private entity, person, or business. In doing private-sector cost analysis, costs include increases in spending and liabilities and decreases in income and assets; benefits are exactly opposite increases in income and assets and decreases in spending and liabilities. The public-sector equivalent of private-sector cost analysis is estimating and forecasting expenditures and revenues. In the public sector, however, public organizations deal with externalities, which are effects on individuals or interactions to which they are not direct parties. That is to say, public organizations are responsible for considering effects on their publics. Simple cost analysis involves predicting costs to an organization and costs to its public.

Predicted Costs to Organization + Predicted Costs to Relevant Public
= Simple Cost of an Alternative

Cost-effectiveness analysis uses exactly the same concepts and procedures to establish the simple cost of each alternative. In addition, the effect (assumed benefit) is predicted and divided into the simple cost.

$$\frac{\text{Simple Cost}}{\text{Number of Predicted Effects}} = \text{Unit Cost}$$

Cost-benefit analysis uses the same procedures for simple cost and additionally predicts the number and value of benefits to provide a sum of benefits. The equation relating costs and benefits normally shows net benefits.

Benefits - Costs = Net Benefits (or Net Costs)

Cost analysis is an area that generates much debate on issues about its theoretical bases, technical limitations, and criticisms. Some see cost analysis as useful in making all public decisions; others see it as completely valueless. A discussion of issues follows the presentation of the techniques. Each set of techniques is discussed and exemplified with a detailed example. In our opinion, cost analysis is best thought of as a variety of tools that can be used to supply part of the information for decisions.

Cost analysis techniques are often used by opponents and proponents of particular points of view to influence the course of decision making. Used in such a manner, cost analysis techniques are incorporated into a larger advocacy effort. Such uses of cost analysis can purposely distort the actual cost analysis to "prove" that one alternative is unequivocally correct. Such cost

nalysis is a proper target of suspicion because cost analysis does not definitely
prove anything.

SIMPLE COST ANALYSIS ◆

Simple cost analysis isolates cost for analysis rather than relating costs to
benefits. Simple does not equate with easy, however. Simple cost analysis
involves answering the question, "How much does each alternative cost?"
Although expenditure predictions are the most obvious place to seek cost information, costs include impacts on the revenues, assets, and liabilities of public
organizations and impacts on their publics. The distinctive feature of cost
analysis in the public sector is inclusion of impacts on the public. Interesting
examples are requirements at the federal level and in 35 states for cost
predictions of legislation imposing significant costs on other governments.[1]

Simple cost analysis is used to make operational decisions within fiscal years
and to make policy decisions extending over a number of years. In doing so,
costs are determined precisely in a formal manner. The process of simple cost
analysis includes the following steps:

1. Determining alternatives
2. Finding cost factors
3. Quantifying cost factors
4. Valuing cost factors
5. Calculating the sum of cost factor monetary values
6. Making the decision

Determining Alternatives

This step is often overlooked. Selecting alternatives to examine can be the
most important action taken. Excluding any realistic alternative can produce
different results. Also, selecting one reasonable and one or more unreasonable
alternatives could "prove" that the reasonable alternative is a better choice.
Determining alternatives to analyze is worth carefully considering at the
beginning of the process rather than at the end.[2]

Finding Cost Factors

Finding cost factors involves examining alternatives to see what cost differences exist. This requires focusing on the specific differences between the
alternatives. Costs can be divided into those affecting an organization and
those affecting its public. The costs to a public organization tend to be more
easily discovered, partly because direct expenditures are the most obvious
costs. Reductions in costs are treated as negative costs. For example, a cost
analysis of free parking includes decreases in revenues as a cost and a decrease
in expenditures to collect and to enforce parking fees as a negative cost.
Negative costs for a public organization are included in a simple cost analysis

when they reflect clear, direct expenditures. Costs to the relevant public are often less clear-cut. The way to develop a list of cost factors is to start with a list of factors based on common sense and to refine the list with the assistance of technical knowledge. For example, a five-mile road appears relatively easy to analyze. Two cost areas not immediately apparent, however, are intersections, which are different from regular roadways, and signs and other equipment along the road and at intersections of the road. Both of those areas exemplify the sort of detail available through a technical understanding of an area. Assistance from substantive technical experts is extremely useful.

Finding cost factors for the public is more difficult. Many cost factors are obvious. For example, road construction inconveniences are an obvious area to review. The obvious factors are listed by analyzing the differences between alternatives. Other relevant sources of information should also be considered. People who may be affected by the alternatives should be questioned, including both organizational members and members of relevant publics. Relevant sources of information include proponents and opponents of alternatives, those making competing claims for products, and those criticizing alternatives. People directly involved are frequently overlooked. Asking affected members of a public organization and the public for comments is useful because it can validate previously listed cost factors as well as uncover additional ones. In any event, comprehensiveness is the watchword at this stage in the process. Later, some factors can be excluded from the analysis but only after an attempt to be comprehensive has been made. It is better to include factors tentatively before finally excluding them because they are not sufficiently important rather than excluding them as much as possible. A broad focus is preferable.

Categories used to develop list cost factors can be helpful. The most common cost categories are real and pecuniary, external, tangible and intangible, direct and indirect, operating and overhead, and fixed and variable.

All costs can be classified as real or pecuniary. *Pecuniary costs* are costs incurred by one portion of a collectivity because of a gain by another portion of a collectivity. A tax payment is a loss to a member of the public and a gain to the taxing organization. No real cost is present because only a transfer within the collectivity has taken place. Within a collectivity, there is no opportunity cost, though there is separately for the individuals and the organizations involved. A *real cost* is one that makes a net impact on the collectivity rather than reflecting a transfer of money or value within the collectivity. This varies by organization. For example, a shift between insurance premium costs for men and women would be a pecuniary cost for a state, if no net change occurred, but it would be a cost to any nonprofit organization devoted exclusively to the economic well-being of women or men. Pecuniary costs often appear as changes in income to some group. The question is whether the income comes from another portion of the collectivity. The income of businesses along a road that are affected by a road project is pecuniary to the extent that some other businesses in the same jurisdiction are affected. For example, some people shift their restaurant patronage from Pete's to Joe's during road construction and even more from Joe's to Pete's afterward. As long as the shifting

ccurs within a jurisdiction, it is pecuniary. A shift across jurisdictional
oundaries is a real cost to one of the jurisdictions involved.

External costs are costs imposed on those outside of a collectivity and,
herefore, are not included in a cost analysis. Pollution costs outside a terri-
orial jurisdiction are external costs. Again, this is a matter of perspective.
ollution is regulated at the national level partially to force state and local
overnments to take external costs into account. External costs are one reason
or using larger jurisdictions to deal with policy issues.

Tangible costs represent physical factors whereas *intangible* costs do not.
ain, the enjoyment of scenery, and social harmony are intangibles. The
ategory of intangibles is helpful in stretching to find less obvious but not
ecessarily less important cost factors.

Three closely related pairs of cost concepts are direct and indirect, operating
nd overhead, variable and fixed. *Direct costs* represent immediate conse-
uences of choosing an alternative, whereas *indirect costs* represent conse-
uences that develop further in the future. A highway has the direct costs of
onstruction and can have indirect costs of lowering property values adjacent
o it. *Operating costs* are incurred in carrying out an activity, whereas *overhead
osts* are generally necessary to support and maintain an organization. The
perating costs of a highway agency would include construction and mainte-
ance costs, whereas the cost of telephone service or office space is an
verhead cost. *Variable costs* change, depending on levels or units of goods or
ervice provision, whereas *fixed costs* do not change. The variable costs of a
ighway agency are those associated with how much construction and repair
ctivity it engages in, whereas the fixed costs, which include debt payments,
ome salaries, and other overhead expenses, do not change relative to the
ariable costs.

Quantifying Cost Factors

Each cost factor on a comprehensive list is quantified or eliminated from
onsideration as being insufficiently important to quantify. Quantification
nvolves predicting (estimating or forecasting) the number of units of the cost
actor involved. Some factors are eliminated from consideration either beause they are too few in number or too low in value to be worth calculating
r are listed as unquantifiable cost factors that are handled judgmentally.

Quantification takes a variety of forms. The key is developing reasonably
recise numbers using appropriate methods. For physical facilities, the factors
an be quantified in physical measurements (e.g., square feet and cubic yards).
ost factors that reflect completely discretionary expenditures (e.g., capital
acilities and nonentitlement services) are usually relatively easier to quantify
han those that depend on predictions of human behavior. Quantification of
uman behavior is probably best handled through historical extrapolation.
his helps avoid unrealistic assumptions of rational behavior. Despite over-
helming evidence of real hazards, people fail to wear seat belts, continue to
moke cigarettes, and argue with professors. If something is imprecisely
uantifiable, a predicted range is preferable to a single prediction with three

digits to the right of the decimal point (e.g., 2,000-20,000 compared with 10,000.001).

Valuing Cost Factors

Attributing values to cost factors depends on their characteristics. Three situations involving valuing cost factors exist: monetary, monetized non-monetary, and nonmonetized nonmonetary costs. Monetary costs are ordinarily valued in monetary terms. All other values are ordinarily nonmonetary (i.e., not bought and sold). Nonmonetary costs can be divided into those that are valued in money terms and those that are not.

Nonmonetized nonmonetary costs cannot be valued in terms of money. They are simply listed as valuable. A classic example is the eradication of species.[3] Even though something may not be monetarily valued, it should be retained as a consideration where it appears relevant.

Valuing monetary costs and monetized nonmonetary costs are handled differently. Monetary costs are predicted by using existing markets or transaction prices.

Valuing monetized nonmonetary costs is more challenging. There are three ways: exercising judgment, asking people, and using analogous monetary cost equivalencies (i.e., similar things that are priced). Judgment involves rendering an opinion of a value. In some cases, people are interviewed or surveyed to report their values for various things. The most generally used technique of valuation is reasoning by analogy. Someone determines what things are similar to the cost factor. Then, the analogous items are priced. In such cases, the items can have a direct price or the value is inferred from behavior. Examples include time, life itself, and scenic beauty. The price of time for people is established in various labor markets. In estimating the value of people's time, a price based on prevailing wage rates is used. The value of life can be inferred from behavioral information, such as the wage differential between more and less life-threatening occupations. In valuing life, analysts attempt to use the value that people appear to place on their own lives. The value of scenic views can be inferred from the costs incurred to gain access to the view. In many cases, only some partially equivalent phenomenon can be found. For example, it may be possible to value a life but not the pain associated with an illness.

Values used in cost analysis are necessarily judgmental in character. Even if inaccuracies exist, consistency in the use of the same values for competing alternatives and impartial selection of values are of greater concern. Some degree of inaccuracy is impossible to avoid, but changing values or selecting values to favor particular alternatives undercuts the possibility of useful results.

A vitally important value of great consequence in cost analysis where costs occur over time is the *discount rate*. A discount rate is used to measure the difference in values of a thing at different points in time. Discount rates are very closely related to interest rates because they both represent differential time preferences. People prefer present values to future values; interest rates reflect how much more money people prefer to have in the future to forgo the use of their money in the present. A discount rate is used to calculate discount factors. A *discount factor* is a numerical value that indicates the fractional value that a future value has at the present time. If the discount rate is 10% per year, the value of a dollar a year from now is $.90 and two years from now $.81. The discount factors are .9 and .81.

Interest rates for debt are one market measure for computing a discount factor. When costs occur over time, particularly when two or more alternatives have different patterns of costs over time, discount factors can be used to compute a *net present value* for each alternative, that is, what the current value is of each alternative.

We can view a discount factor in a number of ways. Some say that a discount factor is a statement of the relative time preference of society for incurring costs. In practice, this means estimating the relative values of current costs and costs at periods in the future. Thus, a discount factor is a measure of a societal preference for current relative to future consumption. Another way of looking at a discount factor is in opportunity costs, that is, alternative uses for the resources. This can be determined by looking at investment markets for determining the rates of return on investments or on relevant debt instruments. A discount factor is used to calculate the present value of quantifiable values that decline in value over time. The term signifying discounted future values is *net present value*.

Selecting discount rates to compute discount factors can be theoretically discussed from many relevant angles based on such factors as the accuracy of the price system, human behavior relative to particular situations, and whether nonrenewable resources are involved.[4] Practically, the choice is generally made within the range of corporate and public debt rates. Public debt rates are advanced as showing the "real" cost of money to public organizations because that is what they pay for using money. This is criticized as being too low because of preferential income tax treatment and artificially low levels of risk. The other major alternative set of rates is corporate debt rates, which are not taxed preferentially or artificially protected from risk. Further arguments can be advanced on behalf of both sides of this issue. As a matter of convenience, it may be more appropriate to use a corporate rate when analyzing a service enterprise and a public debt rate for a traditional governmental service.[5] Historically, the most frequent abuse of cost analysis has been through inappropriately low discount rates.[6] The impact of discount factors in cost analysis can be seen in Table 8.1, which shows the current value of $100,000 received 20 years in the future, the net present value. The table shows the results of different discount rates that are translated into discount factors using the formula at the bottom. For example, the discount factor for 1% for 20 years is .81954. These discount factors reflect the cumulative effect of annually compounded interest rates. Table 8.1 clearly shows the impact of selecting different discount rates on future values; the current value decreases as the discount rate increases. The practical significance has its greatest impact where the alternatives are to implement a project or not and where the costs of different alternatives are distributed differently over time. Consistent use of market-based discount rates helps avoid using a discount rate that will excessively favor one or more alternatives.

TABLE 8.1   Interest Rates and Values Over Time

Interest Rates (%)	Net Present Value of $100,000 20 Years in the Future (rounded to the nearest dollar)
1	81,954
2	67,297
3	55,369
4	45,639
5	37,689
6	31,180
7	25,842
8	21,455
9	17,843
10	14,864
11	12,403
12	10,367

Calculational Formulas:

$100,000 x Discount Factor = Net Present Value

Discount Factor = 1 divided by $(1 + i)^t$

where i = interest rate and t = number of compounding periods.

The apparent difficulty of calculating discount factors was overcome historically by using books of tables to look them up. Now, most computer spreadsheet software programs have some equivalent calculation routine, and those that do not can be used to calculate discount factors relatively easily using the definitional formula at the bottom of Table 8.1.

Calculating the Sum of Cost Factor Monetary Values

Calculating the total monetary cost of any alternative is a mechanical process that can be done in different sequential orders. Nonmonetized nonmonetary costs are listed separately. Monetarily valued costs are computed to produce a single total monetary cost for each alternative, which can be compared with every other alternative. Unless done carefully step by step, errors can easily creep into such calculations.

A discussion of the process may be helpful. First, the monetary value of each cost factor is calculated for each time period, one cost factor for one time period after another. All cost factors for each time period have to be calculated. Regardless of order, we have to compute the monetary value of all cost factors for all time periods. Each monetary cost factor for each time period is calculated by multiplying the numerical quantity (the number of units) by the monetary value of each unit. Second, the monetary values of cost factors for each time period are added together for a time period total. Third, if appro-

riate, the monetary cost for each time period is discounted. The nominal or
ace value of the total monetary cost of each time period is multiplied by a
iscount factor. Fourth, a single total monetary cost figure for each alternative
s calculated. All of the monetary costs (discounted or not) for all the time
eriods are added together to produce a total, which is also the net present
alue if all the values are in one time period or if the costs are discounted.

A simple example may help make the calculation process clearer. The
xample is an alternative with two cost factors, one that is current and,
nerefore, not discounted and one that occurs over a three-year period.

ost Factor 1:
   Estimated Current Cost:
   Estimated Current Cost = Quantity x Value = 100 x $100 = $10,000
ost Factor 2: Three Years
   Year 1 Estimated Current Cost = Quantity x Value =
   100 x $100 = $10,000
ear 2 Predicted Cost = Quantity x Value =
   100 x $100 = $10,000
ear 3 Predicted Cost = Quantity x Value =
   100 x $100 = $10,000

Time Period	Monetary Values Before Discounting		Discount Factor	Discounted Value
stimated Current and Year 1 Costs	$20,000		None	$20,000
ear 2 Predicted Costs	$10,000	x	.9091	= $ 9,091
ear 3 Predicted Costs	$10,000	x	.8264	= $ 8,264
otal Net Present Value (sum of discounted values)				$37,355

Note: The discount factors for the second and third years of costs assume an
nterest rate of 10% per year and discounting periods of one and two years
espectively. The current year is not discounted, and all future years are
iscounted on an N - 1 basis. That is to say, 1 is subtracted from the year to
etermine the number of years to discount a value. A current year value is not
iscounted, a second next-year value is discounted for one year, and a third-
ear value is discounted for two years. If we were to analyze tremendous
mounts of money with certain interest rates and precise values, it might be
easonable to discount on a monthly or even a daily basis. For most cases,
early discounting is most appropriate because the estimation accuracy does
ot support greater precision in discounting assumptions.)

Making the Decision

Making a decision based on simple cost analysis is not always easy. Where
nere are no other significant differences, the cost difference between two or

more alternatives can be used. Several differences cloud decisions, howeve:
First, nonmonetized costs can vary between alternatives. These costs shoul
be considered in choosing among alternatives. Second, other concerns tha
are not costs per se may be important. Distributional impacts among group:
especially the poor and rich, concern many people. Such concerns or value
can provide a partial basis for making decisions. Third, different positiv
results from alternatives can be considered, even if not quantified. Fourtl
costs alone may not be a sufficient basis for making a decision when th
difference between two or more alternatives is less than the probable erro:
For example, if a cost prediction is accurate within 10% of true costs, then tw
alternatives less than 10% apart may not be sufficiently different. In case
where cost differences are relatively minor, other considerations are relativel
more important. Finally, when choosing between an alternative and nothin
broader issues and choices can be implicit considerations, including all othe
programming options and leaving money in private hands.

Making a decision based on simple cost analysis is not mechanical. It doe
not remove all other considerations. Simple cost analysis is a mode of devel
oping information for decision making rather than a substitute for it. Unfor
tunately, some people expect the numbers to replace thinking.

Simple Cost Analysis Example

The following example is a simple one used to minimize difficulties. Th
area for cost analysis is garbage collection.

1. Determine Alternatives

    Presently garbage is collected by the illustrious firm of Dirty Harry and Son
    A reforming official (whose motto is, After the garbage that I have taken, I reall
    know garbage) says that garbage collection could be done better by the loc:
    government. The two obvious alternatives are private-sector and public-sectc
    production of the service.

2. Find Cost Factors

    Alternative 1: Private

    A list of cost factors determined through a review of collection operations an
    a survey of some customers includes the following:

    No public expenditures

    Garbage collection fees in three categories:

    A. Commercial
    B. Residential curbside collection
    C. Residential back door collection

    Spilled garbage

    Alternative 2: Public production (residential curbside)

Predicted public expenditures (assumed to be predicted as discussed in previous chapter)

Loss of option: residential back door collection

No spilled garbage

> (Note: Loss of a garbage collection license fee is not included as it is a pecuniary cost. Any unemployment cost due to the closing of a private company is assumed to be external.)

3. Quantify Cost Factors
   Alternative 1: Private

Number of customers:
  30 commercial
 100 residential curbside
 100 residential backdoor
Spilled garbage: 5 times a month

   Alternative 2: Public

Predicted public expenditures
Loss of option: 100 residential backdoor collections

4. Value Cost Factors
   Alternative 1: Private

Commercial rate: $100 per month
Residential, curbside: $8 per month
Residential, backdoor: $12 per month
Spilled garbage: intangible

   Alternative 2: Public

Predicted public expenditure
Loss of option: monetary value difficult to determine

> Although 100 customers pay $4 per month more for residential backdoor collection (price difference between residential backdoor collection and curbside collection), estimating the monetary value of that option is difficult practically because the customers would keep their $4. The real value of the option is any value beyond the $4 previously paid by the customers.

5. Calculate sum of cost factor monetary values and list nonmonetized factors
   Alternative 1: Private

  Commercial customers: 12 (months) x 30 x 100 = $36,000
  Residential curbside: 12 x 100 x 8 = $9,600
  Residential backdoor: 12 x 100 x 12 = $14,400
Total Costs: $60,000
  Spilled garbage:—60 times a year—intangible

Alternative 2: Public

Predicted public expenditures per year = $56,000
Total Costs: $56,000
   Loss of residential backdoor collection option—monetary value difficult to determine

6. Decide

The choice of using the local government to collect garbage or allowing the private sector to continue this function in this example can be reduced to a comparison of two sets of information. The comparison is between (1) the spilled garbage associated with private garbage collection at greater costs and (2) the lesser dollar cost associated with public garbage collection and the loss of the residential backdoor collection option that is a real loss because people presently voluntarily choose it. As presented here, the analysis is not clear-cut. The difference between the two alternatives is that Alternative 1 costs $4,000 more and provides the option of residential backdoor collection to customers, whereas Alternative 2 involves 60 fewer garbage spills a year. In such cases, individuals may have a personal preference for one factor or another. In this analysis, the possible factors to prefer are less spilled garbage, $4,000, residential backdoor collection option, the certainty of the current situation, the uncertainty of monetary costs of the proposed alternative, and the nonmonetary political values associated with private- and public-sector provision and production of services. The cost analysis in this example leaves us with a decision that is still a matter of judgment but one that is illuminated by analysis.

◆ COST-EFFECTIVENESS ANALYSIS

Cost-effectiveness analysis extends simple cost analysis by relating the costs of an alternative to its results. The term *cost-effectiveness* may be misleading because the conceptualization is of analyzing alternatives by relating their costs to their presumed beneficial effect. The result of a cost-effectiveness analysis is a unit cost, an average cost for each unit of a benefit produced. This reflects a concern for what is commonly referred to as "efficiency."

Sometimes, cost-effectiveness analysis is described as involving an analysis of a maximum effect for a fixed cost or a minimum cost for a fixed effect. Both of these are versions of cost-effectiveness analysis with an additional constraint. Cost-effectiveness analysis conducted at the same approximate scale without a minimum or maximum constraint produces the same result: a unit cost for each alternative. Where the alternative is not to do something, the unit cost is zero for zero units.

Cost-effectiveness analysis is particularly suited to situations where there are two or more similar alternatives, where an operational decision is involved and where a single benefit is presumed. In a situation where the decision is whether to do something, cost-effectiveness analysis adds little to simple cost analysis. In policy areas, unit costs can be misleadingly precise because of less than completely reliable predictions of quantities and values. Cost-effectiveness analysis generally requires a singular benefit effect for the sake of computation. Where the benefits are multiple, we must specify some relationship (e.g., all are

alued equally) to produce a single figure to compute a single unit cost figure
or each alternative. Where there are multiple consequences without a speci-
ed relationship, cost-effectiveness analysis is not possible.

The process of conducting a cost-effectiveness analysis is similar to a simple
ost analysis, but it requires additional operations. The following list of the
rocess steps shows the simple cost analysis steps in an ordinary fashion and
dditional cost-effectiveness analysis activities within parentheses.

1. Determine alternatives (make sure they are all suitable for cost-effectiveness
   analysis)
2. Find cost factors (and effect or effects)
3. Quantify cost factors (and effect or effects)
4. Value cost factors
5. Calculate the sum of cost factor monetary values (and unit cost)
6. Make the decision

Determining Alternatives

Determining alternatives may have occurred before any concern for formal
nalysis when two or more parties have joined a dispute about which of two
r more alternatives is preferable.[7] In such cases, analysts are usually limited
 the disputed alternatives. Participants in such political situations can be so
cked into alternatives that any other alternative will be rejected regardless
f technical merit. Yet it is preferable to consider alternatives other than the
isputed choices. In cases where consideration of further alternatives is pos-
ble, such an analysis should definitely be undertaken.

Political characteristics of an alternative may make it unacceptable to the
erson or persons ultimately responsible for the choice. Such concerns can be
 obvious as the City of Detroit considering buying foreign-made automo-
iles, the State of Missouri considering funding for an airport for the St. Louis
rea in Illinois, or the U.S. government purchasing military equipment from
 company owned by a hostile foreign government, such as Libya. In other
ises, the political concerns are more subtle and can occur because no one is
upporting an alternative. In such cases, the best way to determine whether
mething is politically acceptable is to ask the person or persons responsible
r the choice of alternatives. Developing a previously unconsidered alterna-
ve can prove useful when the alternative is politically acceptable. Calm consid-
ration of matters sometimes produces alternatives not obvious to political
isputants, who tend to lock themselves into positions. Sometimes, additional
ternatives can be effective compromises or meet everyone's concerns.

Technical characteristics of alternatives can make cost-effectiveness analysis
appropriate for three reasons. First, in cases where a significant portion of
e costs of an alternative cannot be monetized, alternatives considered using
ost-effectiveness analysis are harder to compare. It may be more appropriate
 stay with simple cost analysis in such cases. Otherwise, you may get stuck
alfway between the two approaches and not treat values in an appropriately
onsistent fashion. Second, cost-effectiveness analysis should be avoided when

the quantity of the effect is so difficult to predict that it makes any ratio figure suspect. The choice in such a case is to use a range of quantity and ratio figures or to use simple cost analysis. Where one alternative cannot be analyzed we using cost-effectiveness analysis, then the choices are to shift to using simple cost analysis, to discard any alternatives not suitable for cost-effectiveness analysis, or to treat an alternative or alternatives with due respect concerning accuracy. Third, cost-effectiveness analysis should be avoided when there are multiple positive effects that cannot be equated or valued relative to one another. One effect is the norm for cost-effectiveness analysis; two or more effects can be used if you have some way of using a single measuring scale. A single measuring scale can be used where all effects are counted equally, and measured by some relative scale where one effect is equal to some number of another effect, or are measured on some objective scale, for example, weight in pounds. If you cannot create a single effect scale, your choices are (1) to discard the unmeasurable multiple effect alternative from cost-effectiveness analysis and to use cost-effectiveness analysis on the remaining alternatives (2) to handle some portion of the effects intuitively, or (3) to shift to using either simple cost analysis or cost-benefit analysis to treat the benefits more consistently.

Finding Cost Factors
(and Effect or Effects)

The cost factors are treated the same way as they are in simple cost analysis. Finding the effect or effects of an alternative is generally fairly easy. The result for which the alternatives are being considered are the purpose of ever considering alternatives. This is similar to finding the cost factors.

Quantifying Cost Factors
(and Effect or Effects)

Quantifying effects is probably the most difficult aspect of cost-effectiveness analysis. The difficulties are not always obvious. The obvious problems are those generally associated with analysis. Many apparently one-effect situations are really multiple-effects situations when scrutinized. Street sweeping and highway use are examples. The objective of street sweeping is to clean streets. The cleanliness of streets can be measured by either visual inspection or by examining what is cleaned from streets. Overly simplified, there are both paper debris, which is affected by air currents, and heavy debris, which is not affected by air currents because of its weight and volume. Street-sweeping machines blow paper debris out of their path and sweep up heavier debris. The single objective of street sweeping breaks down when quantification is required, and, at that point, some choice about primary emphasis or creative counting has to be made. The street-sweeping objective can be counted by visual measurement, by the weight or volume of material picked up, or by an index that uses both. Obviously, a scale including both material picked up and visual measurement requires some value relationship between the two. Prob bly, one or the other method of quantification will serve in any particular situation.

Highways provide another example of ambiguity in quantification. Highways are used to move vehicles. Different kinds of vehicles carry different things, however. Commercial vehicles include trucks, buses, vans, and cars carrying material and people from one point to another. Varying size service vehicles carry people and perhaps equipment and supplies; big trucks carry large quantities of cargo over relatively long distances; small trucks make deliveries within a limited area; and short- and long-haul buses carry varying numbers of people. Cars are the most common vehicle and could, by themselves, be the primary focus. Cars are used in the same manner as buses, however—to carry people. Also, the same number of cars can carry substantially different numbers of passengers. Counting cars on a highway at one point misses the variable distance traveled on that highway by different cars. Ultimately, one normal cost-effectiveness effect measurement for highways is passenger-miles, which excludes cargo.

Both examples are relatively simple ones to show that complexity is likely to exist in any cost-effectiveness analysis situation and that it is possible to use one objective even if some aspects of a situation have to be ignored in the formal computation. Such decisions can be reported with the formal analysis.

Also, in quantifying a single effect in cost-effectiveness analysis, we tend to cycle back to the first two questions in the logic of cost analysis—what is the issue and what are the options. In the two cases discussed here, what really is desired from street sweeping and highways is clarified in the quantification process. Also, alternatives to street sweeping and highways become more available after this kind of analysis. For example, a vacuum machine of some kind is an alternative to deal with loose papers on streets, and rail transportation and dedicated bus lanes on highways are alternatives to new highways for moving people.

Estimating the quantity of an effect is best done with accurate historical data compiled by a neutral party. Suppliers of products and proponents of policies are usually suspect as data providers. Traffic counts and street cleanliness studies are two examples of possible data sets. If no data are available that directly relate to the effect at issue, the choices are to collect some or to use some tangentially related data to form reasonable assumptions. Data collection is certainly more expensive.

Tangentially related data are any pieces of information that appear to have some sort of relationship with the subject matter under discussion. Examples might include complaints about dirty streets for street sweeping or shopper counts at shopping centers for highways. Tangentially related data are hard to characterize except to say that they appear to have some relationship to the desired effect.

After obtaining data concerning the desired effect, some relationship between the alternative and the desired effect must be predicted. Assumptions and data are used to predict. For example, in a homeless shelter study, an average count of 100 people at a soup kitchen can be used to calculate an average number of homeless in a community. It can be predicted, based on experiences elsewhere, however, that only some portion of the homeless use public shelters. That information is probably best predicted using need-to-usage ratios, whether based on data from other communities, from local experience, or from a judgment on local conditions. Assuming that anything will proceed exactly as we desire is fruitless. Ordinary optimism found in these matters can be countered for the sake of accuracy by looking for deviations from preferred behavior.

Valuing Cost Factors

Cost factors are valued, and effects are not. Effects are valued indirectly in relation to costs as indicated in the following discussion of calculations.

Calculating Sum of Cost Factor
Monetary Values (and Unit Cost)

Calculation of the sum of cost factors and the resulting unit cost figure may or may not be discounted to a present value. When a differential distribution of costs exists over time, discounting to net present value takes place. If the effects of alternatives are unevenly distributed in time, their number can be discounted in a manner similar to monetary discounting. If the alternatives are similar in time patterns, such discounting is superfluous. This seems odd until any positive effect is viewed in the dimension of time. Then, current effects are more valued than future ones. For practical reasons, a financial market interest rate is the most appropriate rate of discount.

The costs can be summed for one time period when there is an even pattern of costs over time. If not, costs over time are computed by time period and discounted to a net present value. Effects are not discounted if they are evenly distributed over time, are in the current period, or are similar across alternatives. Once a sum of costs and effects is determined, the number of effects is divided into the costs. The result is a unit cost figure.

Making the Decision

A decision can be made in three different ways. First, when the choice is between alternatives of a similar character that do not have significant issues or concerns outside of the quantified factors, the obvious choice is the alternative with the best unit cost. If the reasonably expected margin of error is larger than the difference between alternatives, then the alternative chosen is only somewhat likely to be marginally better than other alternatives. In other words, if the difference in unit costs is not greater than the error margin, either choice can be superior.

Second, when one alternative is under consideration, the unit cost figure becomes a cost price tag for each outcome. For example, street sweeping may have a unit cost of $10 per mile. Then, the unit cost figure is intuitively compared with all other possibilities, including not collecting money for producing the effect as well as possible alternative effects. In such cases, the costs are discounted. The choice is a matter of judgment.

Third, where costs or effects are not included in the calculation of the unit ɔst figure, such costs or effects must be considered intuitively by decision ɨakers, along with unit cost figures. In effect, these additional factors are ʻeighed in relationship to one another and the difference between unit cost gures. This situation does not indicate that cost-effectiveness analysis has ɨiled but that other factors can be weighed relative to unit cost figures. It is a ɨistake to assume that precise figures are important. Two precise unit cost gures diminish in importance as they approach each other. This occurs when ɩe alternatives' monetary values are not significantly different, when the ɨargin of error is relatively large relative to the difference between alterna-ves' monetary values, and when there are significant nonmonetized values. ɔost-effective analysis is an aid to decision making, not a substitute for it. It not appropriate to discard useful information if it cannot be blended into unit cost figure. Overly simplified decisions are more the mark of simple ɩther than good decisions.

Cost-Effectiveness Example

The example used here cannot be an extension of the previous example ɛcause the effect in that example was fixed. In any situation where the ɩutcome or cost is fixed, examining the unfixed or variable elements is ɩfficient for decision-making purposes.

A relatively simple cost-effectiveness example involves selecting one of two ifferent pieces of similar equipment, two garbage trucks.

1. Determine alternatives

   The two alternatives are similar-capacity garbage collection trucks. Deter-mining the alternatives for choice of garbage trucks may be more complicated than presented here, but for the sake of this example any complications are assumed away. Such details might include truck capacity, left-side or right-side driving controls, and traditional sitting down or standing up driving arrange-ments. These are only a few of the many additional complications that can be considered. Note, however, that each additional feature requires preparation of at least one additional alternative. One more alternative occurs when one more option is considered (e.g., adding or subtracting one feature to another alter-native). Doubling the number of alternatives occurs when each of the existing alternatives is considered with and without an added feature. As a practical matter, only so many alternatives are worth the effort of analysis. Those alter-natives are frequently selected through use of informed judgment from people responsible for operations or policy development.

2. Find cost and effect factors

   Finding the cost factors means directly comparing the alternatives to discover the differences. The two trucks differ only in price and personnel requirements. One truck has an expected useful life of three years and the other five years. A year of service is the unit chosen to be the effect in this example. The cost and effect factors are listed below.

Alternative 1:

Cost Factors:
  Price
  Purchasing costs
  Personnel requirements - one
  Fuel
  Buyback payment (negative cost)
Effect: Three years of service

Alternative 2:

Cost Factors:
  Price
  Purchasing costs
  Personnel requirements - two
  Fuel
  Buyback payment (negative cost)
Effect: Five years of service

3. Quantify cost and effect factors
    The quantification of effects has already occurred. The quantities for eac
cost factor are given or predicted.

Alternative 1:

Price: $20,000
Purchasing cost: $300
Personnel cost: One 40-hour-per-week employee
Fuel: 2,400 gallons a year
Buyback payment: $3,000

Alternative 2:

Price: $30,000
Purchasing cost: $300
Personnel costs: Two 30-hour-per-week employees
Fuel: 2,000 gallons a year
Buyback payment: $2,000

    It may be helpful to explain a few of these factors. Purchasing costs woul
not be included in a simple cost analysis because there is no difference betwee
the two alternatives. When alternatives differ in effect, however, all costs hav
to be included to properly determine a cost-effect ratio. In the present case, on
alternative has purchasing costs of $100 per effect and the other has $60 pe
effect. Other possible factors (e.g., maintenance costs) are not included for th
sake of simplicity. The fuel varies because the truck using two people idles les
while garbage is collected. All the other quantities are assumed values. Mostl
the quantification includes values.

4. Value cost factors
    Valuing remaining cost factors for the two alternatives is simple, as they a
market priced already.

Alternative 1:

Personnel: One employee, 40 hours a week: $15,000
Fuel: $1.00 per gallon

Alternative 2:

Personnel: One employee, 30 hours a week: $10,000
Fuel: $1.00 per gallon

5. Calculate unit costs
   The calculations require discounting because of the unevenness of the two alternatives' time periods. The discount rate assumed for this example is 10%. The discount rate chosen is especially important when the alternatives differ in length of time, as in our present example.

Alternative 1:

Current (nondiscounted) Costs:
   Price: $20,000
   Purchasing Costs: $300
Year One:
  Operations:
   Personnel: $15,000
   Fuel: 2,400 x $1.00 = $2,400
Total Current Costs: $37,700

  Future Costs (to be discounted):
Year Two:
  Operations:
   Personnel: $15,000
   Fuel: $2,400
  Year Two Total: $17,400
Year Three:
   Operations: $17,400 (same as year two)
   Buyback Payment: $3,000 (negative cost)
   Year Three Total: $14,400 ($17,400 - $3,000)

Summary of Alternative 1 Costs Discounted at 10%

Time Period	Raw Dollars	Discount Factor	Net Present Value
Current	37,000	None	37,700.00
Year Two	17,400	0.9091	15,818.34
Year Three	14,400	0.8264	11,900.16
Total Net Present Value:	$65,418.50		

Total Net Present Value Divided by Effect = Unit Cost
$65,418.50 divided by 3 years of service = $21,806.17
Unit Cost: $21,806.17

Alternative 2:

Current Costs:
Price: $30,000
Purchasing Costs: $300
Year One:
Operating Costs:
Personnel: Two 30-hour-per-week employees x $10,000 = $20,000
Fuel: 2,000 x $1.00 per gallon = $2,000
Total Current Costs: $52,300
Future Costs (to be discounted):
Year Two:
Operations:
Personnel: One 40-hour-per-week employee = $20,000
Fuel: $2,000
Total Year Two Costs: $22,000
Total Year Three and Year Four Costs: $22,000 each (same operations
costs as Year Two and no other costs)
Year Five:
Operations: $22,000 (same as Year Two)
Buyback Payment: $2,000
Total Year Five Costs: $20,000

Summary of Alternative 2 Costs Discounted at 10%

Time Period	Raw Dollars	Discount Factor	Net Present Value
Current	52,300	None	52,300.00
Year Two	22,000	0.9091	20,000.20
Year Three	22,000	0.8264	18,180.80
Year Four	22,000	0.7513	16,528.60
Year Five	20,000	0.6830	13,660.00
Total Net Present Value: $120,669.60			
Discounted Value Divided by Effect = Unit Cost			
$120,669.60 divided by 5 years of service = $24,133.92			

6. Decide
Deciding, in the present example, means choosing the alternative with the
lowest unit cost, which is Alternative 1. Note that the choice of alternatives is
not intuitively obvious from the earlier presentation of relevant information or
values. That is why cost-effectiveness analysis can be useful—cost-effectiveness
analysis can help provide less than obvious answers to some questions.

COST-BENEFIT ANALYSIS ◆

Cost-benefit analysis is the most difficult, least used, and most discussed cost analysis technique. Its difficulty stems from the valuation of benefits in monetary terms. Relative to costs, benefits are harder to predict because they extend over a longer period of time and because benefits are unlike market-valued items. Cost-benefit analysis is not often used in practical situations because of its time consumption, technical difficulties, and expense. Cost-benefit analysis is widely discussed because it follows the logic of economic decision making to the greatest degree, and economists find it interesting.

Cost-benefit analysis extends beyond cost-effectiveness analysis in that effects of an alternative are valued. For each alternative, a sum total of monetarily valued benefits is calculated. Anything that cannot be monetarily valued tends to remain at the side of the analysis. The total costs and total benefits of each alternative are mathematically related to one another to produce a single cost-benefit relationship number that can be used to compare the monetary values of all the analyzed alternatives. As before, any nonmonetized costs or benefits must be handled intuitively; in effect, they are off to the side to be reviewed in connection with the final figures.

The process of cost-benefit analysis parallels simple cost analysis and cost-effectiveness analysis in that benefits are handled in the same way as costs. Benefits, however, are extremely tricky. Benefits, unlike costs, range from an even dispersion over time to a future-weighted pattern of benefits. Costs tend to be disproportionately current, near-term, or even over time rather than increasing in the future. Capital projects are classic examples of high near-term costs and high future-term benefits because capital projects are built on predictions of future demands or requirements for services. As usage of a capital project increases, so does the value of its benefits. As noted in the previous chapter, the further into the future we predict, the greater are the chances of unpredictable occurrences that can alter a situation. As predictions of benefits are extended over time, their accuracy decreases, especially by proponents or opponents of a particular alternative. Contributing to this difficulty is the dependence of benefit predictions on future human behavior. For example, the rate at which people use tennis courts at public parks varies greatly over a period of years, but a cost-benefit analysis must use some prediction.

Benefits are listed, quantified, and valued in a manner similar to costs. Benefits are identified from the perspective of expected beneficiaries (i.e., how they value benefits). Benefits initially listed can be numerous and interrelated. Interrelated benefits require careful treatment to ensure that one benefit is not counted more than once. For example, a water project that provides water for irrigation should use increased land values or increased returns on the land from irrigating crops. Double counting occurs if both increased land values and increased returns from the land are counted as benefits. Triple counting occurs if we place a value on the water in addition to the other two values. In listing benefits, double counting can be avoided by reviewing each additional benefit to determine whether it is independent or dependent. Independent benefits are different from all other benefits and dependent benefits are another version of something already listed because they depend on the already-listed benefits. In quantifying benefits, the insignificant benefits are set aside, possibly with a listing of those near the dividing line to show that demarcation. Then, quantification is a matter of predicting. Ordinarily, except for guesses that are presented as matters of expert opinion, a time frame and a quantitative basis are required. The time frame is the period of time for which the predictions are made. The overall time period is usually in years, with predictions being made for specific year periods. The time frame chosen is based on historical evidence, judgment, or both. The quantitative basis for prediction is historical evidence, assumptions, or both. Generally, the pattern of predictions is some historical pattern that is assumed to be changed by the alternative under consideration. Although this seems at first to be trivial, the assumption of changed behavior is almost always relevant because that typically is a major reason for choosing an alternative. In benefit quantification, the more prediction is based on historical experiences or evidence, the greater are the chances that it will be accurate. The greater the reliance on assumptions without historical evidence, the greater is the need to predict conservatively. Also, the further into the future benefits are predicted, the more uncertain they become. Even more so than with costs, a range of benefits predictions is appropriate. Once the time frame and assumptions have been made, any prediction method can be used.

Picking values for benefits can be more difficult than predicting benefit quantities. If a benefit is a marketable item, valuing is relatively easy. Public activities are typically undertaken because the benefits are not marketable, however. Typical benefits include such things as persons' lives or time saved and personal enrichment from cultural experiences or natural beauty. Theoretically, to the extent possible, values are derived on a market base. Time saved can be valued in relation to some wage rate, even though some people involved cannot sell their time, some time is in such small increments as to make it unmarketable, or some time can be used simultaneously for other purposes. All these reasons justify using some fraction of an actual wage figure.

Values posited for lives saved tend to cause many people problems. Lives have to be valued for use in cost-benefit analysis. Lives can be valued for the sake of analysis in a variety of ways. Two approaches rely on markets. First, human lives are valued by what persons require in extra wages to engage in risky occupations. Wage differentials and increased risk of death are used to compute the market value that people engaging in those occupations appear to put on their own lives. Another approach simply predicts a person's earnings over a lifetime. These, and other, approaches have technical problems. If human lives are not valued, however, cost-benefit analysis is not possible when human lives are involved.[8]

Personal enrichment from a cultural experience or natural beauty can be valued in two parts. First, what a person may pay for the personal enrichment can be predicted from market information. For example, what people pay for an analogous experience or scenic view is an appropriate market basis. Housing cost differentials for scenic views, the cost of traveling to scenic views, and

he cost of admission to cultural experiences are three examples of market
bases for valuing benefits. Adjustments may be necessary on various grounds,
but the market starting point is useful in distancing analysis from arbitrariness
or at least setting some limits from concrete experiences. Second, some
benefits that accrue to individuals can be valued by the community at large
(i.e., the community, which does not receive the benefits, values individuals
receiving the benefit). Following Richard Musgrave, such benefits are generally called *merit goods*. In such cases, the value of a benefit can include an
prediction of the amount the community at large is willing to pay or contribute toward the provision of a benefit. Many charitable activities and cultural
facilities are inexplicable without considering the benefit preferences of those
who support them. Overall, valuing benefits requires caution. Widely varying
values can be obtained easily. Using standard methods for determining values
for competing alternatives is preferred.

The calculations used for computing a grand total of benefits for an
alternative are essentially the same as for costs. The predicted number of each
benefit for each time period is multiplied by the appropriate value or range
of values. The benefit values for each time period are added to produce a
benefit value total for each time period. The benefit value total for each time
period is discounted, and all of the discounted time period values are added
together to produce a total net present value for the benefits. The discount
factor is the same for the costs and benefits in each time period.

The final calculations in cost-benefit analysis result in a single number
showing a relationship between the costs and the benefits of each alternative.
The single number can be used to rank all of the alternatives under consideration. Such a number can be computed in a variety of ways. The preferred
computation is simply subtracting costs from benefits to produce a net benefit
or cost figure. A second method is computing a cost-benefit ratio. This
computation can be manipulated by definition of costs and benefits and,
thereby, provides a figure that is precise in appearance only. A third method
uses computational procedures designed to determine the rate of investment
return on the costs. The most common example is the internal rate of return.
Such measures have the same difficulties associated with the ratio approach,
as well as involving extremely complex computations. Such measures are
designed to help distinguish between alternatives with slight time differences
in the patterns of costs and benefits. Such differences themselves are probably
well within the margin of reasonable error in cost-benefit analysis.

Cost-Benefit Example

The issue area in this example is garbage collection, with the focus on
whether to have a unified system of backdoor collection or a unified system
of curbside collection. A variable rate system for different collection service is
an alternative that is not considered. The first step of the process has been
completed. Public organizations typically tend to avoid systems allowing for
options. As usual, all alternatives have not been carefully considered prior to
formal analysis. The example, as in many actual cases, starts after the alternatives have been selected (step 1).

2. Find cost and benefit factors

Costs:

Alternative 1, Backyard: time of personnel, fuel, pet mace, and liability insurance

Alternative 2, Curbside: time of residents, more garbage cans, and more garbage can racks to move them

The obvious cost factors are fuel and the time of residents and personnel. The other factors may be less obvious. First, more garbage cans may be required because of the wear and tear from being blown into the streets. Second, some people will purchase or build racks to move their garbage cans. Third, the garbage collectors are fearful of dogs in yards and, therefore, will require some support to enter backyard areas; pet mace is one solution. Fourth, pet mace will not succeed in all cases, so it is wise to increase liability insurance to cope with injured garbage collectors and dogs.

Benefits: Difference in benefits only; the garbage will be collected using either alternative.

Alternative 1, Backyard: less cost to residents as specified in costs of other alternative, and other benefits, which include convenience to residents, fewer forgotten garbage collections, and fewer incidents of spilled garbage

Alternative 2, Curbside: less public cost relative to the other alternative

The first alternative provides advantages to residents in time, garbage can and garbage can rack costs, convenience, and missed garbage collections and advantages generally related to spilled garbage. With curbside garbage collection, garbage will not be picked up when a resident forgets to put it at the curbside. Also, trash at the curb will be blown over by the wind or knocked over by dogs. In either event, there will be loose garbage in the street. The second alternative is only attractive because it costs the service provider less than the other alternative. Note that on an expenditure basis alone, the second alternative is the obvious choice but that consideration of costs and benefits to residents makes the first alternative a competitive one. The benefits of each alternative include the avoidance of costs of the other alternative. Also, the specific benefits of the first alternative could have been counted as costs of the second alternative however, they cannot appropriately be counted in both places.

3. Quantify cost and benefit factors

Costs:

Alternative 1, Backyard:

Time: 40 seconds per residence to collect garbage from backyards
200 x 40 x 52 = 416,000 seconds = 115.56 hour
Fuel: 20% increase, 2,000 x 0.2 = 400 gallons per year
Pet mace: one dozen cans per year
Liability insurance: monetary value, not quantified

Alternative 2, Curbside:

Time: Average time of residents to curb and back to residence is 80 seconds for 200 residents per week for 52 weeks a year
80 x 200 x 52 = 832,000 seconds = 231.11 hour

Cans used for backyard pickup are replaced on average once every three years rather than every five years for those used for curbside pickup. An average of two garbage cans per residence is assumed. Under a five-year replacement cycle, one-fifth of the cans are replaced every year: 400 cans divided by 5 equals 80 per year. Under a three-year replacement cycle, 400 divided by 3 equals 133.3 cans per year. The difference between the two is 53.3 cans per year.

A prediction of the presence of garbage can racks at 10 percent of residences is picked right out of thin air: 200 x 0.1 = 20 garbage can racks.

Benefits:

Alternative 1, Backyard:
Less cost to residents as aggregated in cost computations for other alternative
Convenience factor: 200 residences x 52 weeks = 10,400
Fewer forgotten garbage collections, one per residence per year = 200
Fewer incidents of spilled garbage: 10 incidents a week x 52 = 520
Alternative 2, Curbside:
Less cost to service provider as measured by costs in other alternative

4. Predict cost and benefit values

Costs:

Alternative 1, Backyard:
Personnel: $8.40 per hour, includes fringe benefits, indirect payments, and overhead expenditures
Fuel: $1.00 per gallon
Liability insurance quotation: $2,000
Alternative 2, Curbside:
Time of residents: Median wage rate = $6.00
Garbage cans: Modal price of garbage cans sold by local stores: $8.00
Garbage can rack: Modal price of can racks sold by local stores: $17.00

Benefits:

Alternative 1, Backyard:
Convenience: $1.00 per week
Forgotten garbage collections: $8.00 (see earlier example)
Trash in street: intangible
Alternative 2: No predicted values for benefits

5. Calculate cost and benefit values

Costs:

Alternative 1, Backyard:
Time of personnel: $8.40 x 115.56 = $970.70
Fuel: $1.00 x 400 = $400.0
Pet mace: one dozen = $50.00

Liability insurance: quotation = $2,000.00
Total: $3,420.70

Alternative 2, Curbside:
Time of residents: $6.00 x 231.11 = $1,386.66
Garbage cans: $8.00 x 53.3 = $426.40
Garbage can racks: $17.00 x 20 = $340.00
Total: $2,153.06

Benefits:

Alternative 1, Backyard:
Avoid curbside costs of $2,153.06 to residents
Convenience: $1.00 x 10,400 = $10,400
Avoid forgotten trash collections: $8.00 x 200 = $1,600
Avoid trash in streets: 420 intangible incidents
Total: $14,153.06 and 520 fewer incidents of trash in streets
Alternative 2, Curbside:
Avoid costs to service provider of $3,420.70

Compute Net Benefits (or Net Costs):
Benefits - Costs = Net Benefits (or Net Costs) Alternative 1, Backyard:
$14,153.06 - $3,420.70 = $10,732.36 and 520 fewer spilled garbage incidents
Alternative 2, Curbside: $3,420.70 - $2,153.06 = $1,267.64

6. Decide

On the surface, the decision is very easy. The backyard garbage collection alternative has a net benefit more than five times larger than the curbside alternative and an intangible benefit of 520 fewer spilled garbage incidents—advantages in money and cleanliness. Observe how some of the assumptions might come under attack, however. First, the overwhelming difference dollar-wise between the two alternatives stems from the specific benefits to residents, mostly the convenience factor. Although the assumption appears reasonable because one-half of the residents were paying $4.00 more for backyard collection before and not all of that is accounted for in the other costs and benefits, someone is likely to say that it does not represent an accurate assessment of the situation. This argument could also be applied to forgotten trash collections.

Second, the time of residents may be dismissed because they cannot sell 80 seconds a week whereas the service provider will darn well have to pay personnel and other cost factors in hard, cold cash, reluctantly parted with by the residents. If the first and second arguments were accepted, the second alternative would be preferred on a monetary basis alone, though that would have to be balanced against the intangible benefit of the first alternative.

Another way to approach the analysis of benefits is to use the value placed on backyard collection when it was commercially collected, which was $4.00 more per week for 100 residents. That value, $20,800 per year, was what some residents paid; that is to say, that is a market prediction of the value of backyard garbage collection for a year. If that figure is used in place of the specific predicted benefits, the backyard garbage collection alternative is the obviously preferred alternative on a monetary basis. The advantage of this approach is the market basis of the value of the benefits to residents.

In this example, policymakers could use the analysis performed to make the decision, could simply ignore the analysis, or could disagree with the analysis. The initial analysis of benefits is more likely to be ignored or disagreed with than the second, market-based analysis of benefits. In any event, good analysis does not guarantee good decisions.

ISSUES IN COST ANALYSIS ◆

Cost analysis, particularly cost-benefit analysis, involves a variety of controversies. Unlike most other public finance administration techniques, widespread doubt exists about the utility of cost analysis. Critics say that cost analysis is not useful because it does not provide good answers and is not necessary. Some say cost analysis is inaccurate at best and frequently flimflam. Also, critics say that analysts ignore or overlook important considerations.

The issue of utility can be divided between the need for answers provided by cost analysis and the accuracy of those answers, which are both related and fundamental. The argument against cost analysis is simple: The benefits do not outweigh or justify the cost. In other words, the information provided by cost analysis does not alter public organization decisions. In this view, information that is otherwise available leads to the same decision. Whether this criticism is true depends on the appropriateness of the analysis. Cost analysis' appropriateness varies with circumstances. Appropriate circumstances tend to overlap those that enhance the technical feasibility and decision-maker openness. If decision makers are not interested in the results or the results are not likely to be technically sound, then cost analysis is not appropriate.[9] Thus, simple cost analysis is generally more appropriate because it is more often technically feasible. Cost-effectiveness analysis is next in appropriateness, followed by cost-benefit analysis. Too often cost-benefit analysis is used in inappropriate circumstances as a device to influence public opinion. Although economists use cost-benefit analysis to look at ill-defined, long-term policy issues, they do so with an appreciation of the technical limitations of such analysis. Others who proceed into this nebulous, shadowy world of graphs and equations often fail to appreciate technical limitations. Economists tend to look to cost-benefit analysis as a form of rational decision making without always appreciating the value and passion bases of politics, whereas abusers of cost-benefit analysis attempt to shape values and excite passions for their preferred position.

Underlying the utility issue is the question of accuracy.[10] The basic argument is that cost analysis results are not based on reality but instead result from analysts' feverish imaginations. In too many cases, this criticism is true. Accuracy and inaccuracy are functions of objectivity and technical limitations. Objectivity, in the sense of honestly attempting to find the truth of the matter in cost analysis, is necessary for accuracy and is not always present. Examples of partisanship on issues abound where people attempt to shade the truth slightly in the language of cost analysis or completely falsify cost analysis results. This is the primary problem of accuracy that can be easily resolved by not relying on partisans as cost analysts. Technical limitations on accuracy are not as easily resolved but can be dealt with by recognizing them and not relying on the results of the analysis to be precise. The degree of technical inaccuracy can be predicted by reviews of previous work in the same area with actual figures (i.e., actual costs, effects, and benefits). An Environmental Protection Agency review of their own and industry cost figures for controlling pollution in specific industries found that the analysis was typically off by 50%. In one case, predicted and actual costs varied by 400%.[11]

Any of the cost analysis forms can be used to provide falsely precise results (i.e., results to the dollar, penny, tenth, or hundredth). The accuracy appears perfect when one merely looks at the numerical results. As Thomas Lynch aptly states it, "Numbers have a way of seeming so final and clear."[12] E. H Mishan's version of the accuracy problem of precision is frequently cited by economists under the general heading of a recipe for Horse and Rabbit Stew which calls for one horse and one rabbit. According to Mishan, what can be dealt with precisely in cost analysis is represented by the rabbit, whereas the horse represents the less certainly handled aspects.[13] The whole accuracy problem depends on how closely predictions of future events parallel the actual future and how closely posited values relate to how people actually value things. The key factors are the assumptions on which the results are calculated Assumptions include the numbers of different cost and benefit events, their values, the discount rate, and any significant nonmonetized values. Generally cost analysis that is relatively simpler has fewer problems with accuracy. Costs are easier to predict and value than benefits and are fewer in number and nearer in time. Values necessarily are determined by analysts' judgment Discount rates are very important because they have a large impact on cost analysis results, particularly cost-benefit analysis. Also, inappropriate quantification of nonmonetary values or ignoring significant nonmonetary values can distort results.

Given knowledge of how cost analysis works, we can do several things to enhance the accuracy of results. First, a fair choice of realistic alternatives is helpful. Too often, the results of analysis are predetermined by the choice of alternatives or their formulation. Unless the analysis is applied to appropriate alternatives, accuracy is not possible. Second, the analyst or user of cost analysis can be sure that all assumptions are spelled out. The assumptions determine the results and are the place where nonspecialists have the most reasonable opportunity to judge accuracy. Third, efforts to show the sensitivity of particular cost analysis efforts to variations in assumptions help. A set of high, medium, and low assumptions can show the plausible range of cost analysis results. Variations in discount rate assumptions are particularly useful. Fourth, nonmonetized and insignificant costs and values can be reported to allow decision makers to decide how important they are. Fifth, any indication of partisanship should indicate that the cost analysis results are suspect Therefore, analysts outside the controversy are to be preferred. Sixth, explicit presentation of all steps in cost analysis is preferable to presentation of final figures. The details of the analysis are probably more useful than the final figures. Finally, users of cost analysis should recognize that cost analysis is not

erfectly accurate and that it can be used only relative to its accuracy. Practially, that means that cost analysis provides some indication of the cost,
ost-effectiveness, or benefit-cost relationship of some alternatives. Cost analysis
better than nothing and can best be used to divide alternatives into those
rith a cost analysis prognosis that is positive, indeterminate, or negative. In
ther words, cost analysis serves best for eliminating extremely poor choices
om consideration, showing that others are a matter of judgment, and
idicating that others appear to be relatively favorable. Given the degree of
recision possible with cost analysis, following the numerical results blindly
not appropriate when the differences between alternatives are indetermi-
ate or slight. Cost analysis is not a substitute for judgment.

Another issue is that cost analysis leaves something out. A frequently cited
spect is equity, though the same is said to apply to risk, uncertainty, and
ecuniary effects. Some argue that cost analysis, particularly cost-benefit
nalysis, is remiss in not considering who pays for and who benefits from
articular policies. The concern of such critics is whether the various alterna-
ves tend to equalize the distribution of costs and benefits in society. The
oncern for equality is nonmonetary and, therefore, cannot be included as an
itrinsic part of cost analysis, though it is possible to predict relative distribu-
onal impacts of costs and benefits. Analysis of distribution is simply a
ifferent sort of analysis, which can be done coincidentally with cost analysis.
uch analysis is particularly useful when it appears that the less well-off have
o bear a disproportionate share of the costs of an alternative. Cost analysis in
self is simply not a kind of analysis appreciated by individuals principally
oncerned with equity. Equity is not costs or benefits.

Some people fault cost analysis for being unable to deal with risk and
ncertainty. Risk refers to a known probability of an event occurring; uncer-
ainty refers to unpredictable events. Uncertainty is a given that all forms of
nalysis deal with by assuming that uncertain events will not occur, whether
ositive ones such as technological breakthroughs or negative ones such as
isasters. When uncertain events occur, the validity of any analysis is then
uspect and possibly subject to revision. Risk is easily dealt with in cost
nalysis. One merely multiplies the probability of an event occurring (the risk)
y the value of the event (cost or benefit) to predict an expected value. If the
robability and value figures are correct, the analysts will be correct about risk
n average. For example, if a person dies in road construction for every 100
iles of construction, then each mile of road construction carries with it a
.01 probability of a death. A 10-mile road construction project would have
n expected value of 0.1 lives lost. Also, risk, cost, and benefits forecasts can
e adjusted to reflect relevant data collection efforts. An analyst might not be
recisely correct on any project and still be correct on average.

Pecuniary effects in cost analysis refer to effects of alternatives that do not
nvolve increased costs or benefits but do involve shifts of money or resources
mong those within the scope of the analysis. For example, payments to public
rganizations from constituents or vice versa are neither costs nor benefits if
ne scope of the cost analysis includes the public organization and the con-
tituents. The same is true of resources among constituents. Pecuniary effects
re sometimes taken into account, even when they should not be a matter of

concern. Groups who benefit from pecuniary effects claim them as benefits and groups who suffer claim them as costs. The key is the scope of analysis. Also, public policymakers fail to maintain a sufficient scope of analysis when they see revenue increases as benefits. Physical facilities often affect the distribution of private business activities. For example, a new state park with swimming, fishing, and picnicking facilities is likely to increase the business of the nearby stores that cater to these pastimes at the expense of stores farther away. Pecuniary effects are real and important to those affected, but they do not figure into cost analysis directly. The logic of cost analysis is to analyze the situation for the whole scope of those involved with attention to particular beneficiaries or sufferers. The question is what the costs and benefits are for the public entity and its constituents. Without such a holistic viewpoint, cost analysis is not for a public organization but for private gains or losses.

◆ CONCLUSION

Cost analysis can be used to develop and organize information about choices. Its use can range from being applied to simple alternatives with few technical complexities for predicting costs to extremely complicated series of alternatives with many technical issues for assessing cost and benefit relationships. Probably the best course of action is using cost analysis to inform decisions rather than mechanically taking the precise numerical results as definitive of the true value of the particular alternatives. Cost analysis provides tools that can be used well, if applied appropriately and fairly and interpreted sensibly. People who expect too much from cost analysis get it.

DISCUSSION QUESTIONS

1. Use cost analysis to analyze the practice of a state prison to leave certain guard positions without guards some of the time to save money. Posit all relevant values and numbers and apply the techniques discussed here for a one-year time period. Would it make much difference to you if you lived near or in the prison or not? Would that change your analysis?

2. What are the ways in which cost analysis can be a malleable tool in the hands of analysts or others with a predetermined agenda? How can you try to use cost analysis in a more objective manner?

3. What are the differences in applying cost analysis to operating decisions, the construction of facilities, and social programs?

4. Outline how to proceed on a cost analysis of a federal social policy that provides for the adoption of a million children. One policy uses tax preferences, another uses changes in the legal system, and another uses direct service provision.

1. Catherine H. Lovell and Hanria R. Egan (1983, Autumn). Fiscal notes and mandate requirements in the fifty states. *Public Budgeting & Finance, 3*(3), 3-18; and Roy Meyers and Mary Ann Curtin (1983, Autumn). State and local cost estimates. *Public Budgeting & Finance, 3*(3), 16-118.

2. Irving K. Fox and Orris C. Herfindahl (1964, May). Efficiency in the use of natural resources: Attainment of efficiency in satisfying demands for water resources. *American Economic Review, 54*(2), 199-202.

3. This is an area of controversy played out most often at the federal level in courts and the halls of Congress. The U.S. Congress passed the Endangered Species Act in 1973 to protect endangered species from being further endangered by federally funded projects. The most famous series of conflicts in the area was over the fate of the snail darter fish and the $100 million plus Tellico Dam on the Little Tennessee River. In that case, the federal courts up to and including the U.S. Supreme Court protected the tiny fishes from the Tennessee Valley Authority, the Carter administration as represented by the Attorney General, and various acts of the Congress in pursuit of completing the dam. Finally, after a protracted conflict, the Congress exempted the Tellico Dam from the provisions of the Endangered Species Act. Fortunately, from the perspective of the snail darter adherents, more of the little fishes were discovered in additional places in sufficient numbers to survive despite the consequences of the dam. Other species may not be so lucky. For accounts of this case, see the *New York Times,* August 1, 1976, p. 30; March 11, 1977, p. 31; November 15, 1977, p. 30; April 7, 1978, p. A11; April 19, 1978, p. A19; June 4, 1978, sec. 6, p. 39; June 14, 1978, p. A24; June 16, 1978, pp. A11, A12, A13; January 24, 1979, p. A21; September 26, 1979, p. 17; October 7, 1979, sec. 4, p. E9; November 8, 1980, p. 6; December 6, 1981, sec. 1, p. 57.

4. Discount rates are discussed in almost all accounts of cost analysis and specific angles are analyzed in specific places. A comprehensive discussion can be found in Raymond F. Mikesell (1977). *The rate of discount for evaluating public projects.* Washington, DC: American Enterprise Institute for Public Policy Research, pp. 1-40.

5. Mikesell, pp. 42-43.

6. Abuse of discount rates has been most commonplace on water-related projects. See Mikesell, pp. 3-5; Fox and Herfindahl, pp. 199-207; Cost-benefit trips up the corps (1979, February 19). *Business Week,* pp. 96-97.

7. Two politically opposite versions of this can be found in James C. Miller III and Bruce Yandle (1979). *Benefit-cost analyses of social regulation.* Washington, DC: American Enterprise Institute for Public Policy Research; and Michael Wines (1982, January 16). Reagan's reforms are full of sound and fury but what do they signify. *National Journal,* pp. 92-98.

8. E. J. Mishan (1976). *Cost-benefit analysis* (2nd ed.). New York: Praeger, pp. 298-320.

9. Thomas Lynch (1995). *Public budgeting in America* (4th ed.). Englewood Cliffs, NJ: Prentice-Hall, pp. 167-173.

10. Peter Self (1975). *Econocrats and the policy process: The politics and philosophy of cost-benefit analysis.* London: Macmillan. Self provides an informed and informative criticism of cost analysis. Also, Steven Rhoads argues cogently that most critics of cost analysis who question accuracy are often on shaky ground, even though there are many solid grounds on which to base criticisms. See Steven Rhoads (1985). *The economist's view of the world: Government, markets, and public policy.* Cambridge: Cambridge University Press, pp. 124-139, 140-222.

11. Stanton Miller (1980, December). Cost-benefit analysis. *Environmental Science and Technology,* pp. 1415-1417. Other related discussions of specific reviews are found in Fox and Herfindahl, pp. 199-200 and Otto Eckstein (1961). *Water resource development.* Cambridge, MA: Harvard University Press. pp. 98-104, 115-117, 273-277.

12. Lynch, p. 140.

13. Self, pp. 87-90; and Mishan, pp. 160-163.

◆ SUGGESTED READINGS

Establishing the cost of services (1990, May). *MIS Report, 22*(5). Washington, DC: Management Information Service, International City Management Association.

Edward M. Gramlich (1981). *Benefit-cost analysis of government programs.* Englewood Cliffs, NJ: Prentice-Hall.

Robert H. Haveman and Julius Margolis (Eds.). (1970). Analytical problems in policy analysis. Part Three of *Public expenditure and policy analysis.* Chicago: Markham.

Joseph T. Kelley (1984). *Costing government services: A guide for decision-making.* Washington, DC: Resource Center of the Government Finance Officers Association.

A. R. Prest and R. Turvey (1965, December). Cost-benefit analysis: A survey. *The Economic Journal, 75*(300), 683-735.

9

Expenditure Administration

Expenditure administration deals with spending money just as revenue administration focuses on the collection of money. This chapter covers the "proper" handling of money rather than the specifics for which money is spent. Spending money in the public sector is subject to an extended process with a variety of controls. The controls are procedures to secure approval of spending and to prove that spending conforms to those approvals. The controls result from public distrust. There are two reasons for distrust. First, the public believes that public organizations are using "their" money. Second, public officials are not seen as having the same motives as individuals and businesses to handle resources carefully. Unlike the private sector, a loss or mistake does not directly affect the personal financial position of any public official. Because of public distrust as well as a regard for prudential handling of resources, public officials go to great lengths to ensure that expenditures are made properly.

The desires to spend and to control spending are distinct. Those interested in particular things, including agency operating officials, push for spending on those things. Those interested in controlling spending are members of the public who are concerned that public expenditures are minimized and that monies are handled carefully. Pressures to spend lead governing officials to authorize expenditures for various things, and pressures to control spending lead governing officials to set up procedures for spending. Public officials emphasize the two desires in varying degrees. Expenditure authorizations go to operating personnel. Control procedures result in an extended expenditure process. The control procedures are generally overseen by central finance offices. Within operating agencies, control procedures are carried out by top agency officials and by financially oriented staff members. Except for a few people who primarily control expenditures, higher-level officials are more oriented toward controlling spending and lower-level officials are more oriented toward spending. For the most part, the desire to spend is exercised with various procedures being followed to ensure that spending takes place in an appropriate manner.

The expenditure process entails sequential actions taken by officials with different responsibilities. The expenditure process reflects the conflicting desires in its five parts. First, policymakers decide on general expenditure procedures and specific expenditures. Second, central finance officials and line officials communicate expenditure authority from policymakers to operating officials. Third, operating officials spend money. Fourth, officials charged with controlling spending review expenditures. Finally, treasury officials pay for expenditures; they put the check in the mail. In actual situations these activities overlap.

◆ DECIDING ON EXPENDITURES

Deciding on expenditures is primarily a matter of choosing the ends and means to achieve those ends, which is the goal setting and budgeting part of the public policy process that extends from the governing bodies to actual operational decisions. Ends served by public organizations vary widely; means are more commonly similar to categories and forms of expenditures made to pursue those ends. Three other important aspects of expenditure decisions include the degree of permanence, the formality, and any limits placed on the decisions.

Public expenditures can be categorized in a variety of ways. Typically budgeteers focus on categories of expenditures. The typical categories of expenditure by public organizations, usually in some combination, are organizational unit, objects of expenditures, functions, accounts, program or project designation, performance activities, and zero-base budget packages. The typical forms of expenditures by public organizations include purchases, transfer payments, debt payments, tort liabilities payments, tax expenditures, and credit activities.[1]

Relatively permanent expenditure authority is important because it indicates a politically protected status for particular expenditures. Expenditure authority is found in policy documents. Policy documents can be divided into those that provide authority to act (i.e., enabling authority or authorization) and those that provide authority to spend (i.e., appropriations). Enabling authority is found in standing rules or laws, which are relatively permanent. Appropriations are ordinarily applicable to a particular period in time, usually a year.

Some expenditure authority is relatively permanent. Contract authority, debt authority, and entitlements are found in enabling legislation. *Contract authority* allows an agency to enter into contracts for goods and services. *Debt authority* allows an agency to borrow money. *Entitlements* require payment be made to individuals or organizations that meet eligibility criteria. Entitlements provide continuing or standing expenditure authority, which is also called permanent appropriations, that continues or stands until the law authorizing the expenditures is changed. Contract authority and debt authority do not provide such authority, but the end result is the same.

Earmarked revenues are similar to permanent expenditure authority in that enabling rules or laws commit a public organization to spend certain revenues in a particular way. Often, earmarking is used to help justify an unpopular revenue measure by linking it to a popular expenditure area.[2]

Entitlements and earmarked revenues can be changed only by changing a standing rule or law, which is politically difficult. The reason for entitlements and earmarking is to make expenditures relatively permanent. At the federal and state levels, entitlements, earmarked revenues, and debt payments commonly exceed half of a government's expenditures.

Appropriations are the most commonly recognized form of expenditure authority. Appropriations are made in budgets. Most of the time, budgets provide only expenditure authority for the time period of the budget, but the federal government does use multiyear appropriations for weapons and construction projects and, occasionally, appropriations without any time limit, which are referred to as no-year funds. Budgeted appropriations are relatively stable over time; although made yearly, budgets authorize the same things each year with relatively modest changes.

Finally, governing officials of a public organization may decide to make an expenditure, and then make that expenditure. This is typical of a smaller public organization that does not use a budget.

Formal decisions are broad and general. As one moves from policy to operational levels, expenditure authority is communicated less formally. Those using resources prefer informal communication of expenditure authority for two reasons. First, formalities consume time and resources. Second, documentary records constrain. Central officials try to increase control through general rules and requirements for information, whereas operating officials seek autonomy by arguing that their situation is unique, that recording requirements are burdensome and pointless, and that they know what to do.

Operating officials who make expenditures demarcate the formalities of deciding on and communicating expenditure authority and the informality of using resources. They make the deals, place orders, hire people, enter into contracts, and otherwise spend money. At this point, expenditure administration often becomes the more informal activity of managing. Management is generally positive: This is what we are attempting to do through standard operating procedures, review of work, and specific directions. Expenditure controls are negative: You are not allowed to use public organization resources in certain ways. Expenditure controls are oriented toward preventing fraud, waste, and abuse (use of organizational resources for personal advantage).

Limits placed on expenditures control them. Expenditure limits are substantive—what money can be spent on—and procedural—how money can be spent.

Policy decisions express *substantive limits* by specifying expenditure categories. Substantive expenditure limitations are usually stated positively; money shall or may be spent thus. The implication is that no money shall be spent except as provided.

Procedural limits are typically expressed in negative terms. A familiar example is found in the U.S. Constitution, Article I, Section 9: "No money shall be drawn from the treasury but in consequence of appropriations made by law."

Procedural limits generally follow the form of "No money shall be spent except that 'X' is done." There are many "Xs." Procedural limits cover the manner in which expenditure authority is granted or decided on and how it can be communicated, spent, reviewed, and paid. Procedural limits allow expenditures to be closely controlled. Procedural limitations can also be embedded in other finance functions, such as purchasing bid requirements.

Expenditures violating a substantive or procedural limit are the formal responsibility of persons who make them. Although correcting a mistake, getting approval after the fact, or just hiding a mistake are possible, responsibility can be a burden. A finance officer said to one offending official, "I reject your voucher and recommend that you return the desktop copier or pay for it with your own personal funds."[3] At the federal level, officials can be charged with a felony for violating limits under the Anti-Deficiency Act.[4]

◆ COMMUNICATING EXPENDITURE AUTHORITY

Expenditure authority is originally created by policymakers in a formal statement. Authority to spend is communicated to operating officials, frequently in a manner specified by standing rules or laws. Expenditure authority is incompletely specified in formal documents. Policymakers provide flexibility to persons making operating decisions.

Communicating expenditure authority starts at the top. Usual participants include the executive and a finance office or treasury. Typically, the chief executive communicates expenditure authority to the top operating officials who, in turn, communicate expenditure authority to their subordinates, and so on until everyone with expenditure authority is told exactly what that authority is. Relevant finance offices are apprised of the amounts of money made available to various units and officials.

On the surface, communicating expenditure authority appears simple. Participants find the process exciting, however, because more is specified in the communication process and less expenditure authority may be communicated than appropriated. Policymakers decide the broad outlines. Subsequent communicators of expenditure authority add limits and directions to those specified by the governing officials. These occur through six processes that communicate expenditure authority: allocation, apportionment, allotment, special approvals, transfers, and reprogramming. These processes are widely but not universally used. The following discussion focuses on appropriated expenditures.

Allocation, Apportionment, and Allotment

Allocation, apportionment, and allotment are similar processes and are often confused with one another because of their similar names. All occur before or at the beginning of a fiscal year.

Allocation is the least common and results in a lump sum of expenditure authority being divided into expenditure categories. For example, an admintrator who has been appropriated a certain amount may decide to spend articular amounts on personnel or equipment. This is similar to appropria- ons made by policymakers; when administrators do it, it is called allocation. llocations can be communicated to subordinates, who are constrained by 1e allocations.

Allotment and apportionment differ from allocation in that some expen- iture authority is held and some transferred to someone else. The retained xpenditure authority is later released relative to circumstances. Where both re used, apportionment precedes allotment.

Apportionment is particularly concerned with time periods. Apportionment a distribution of expenditure authority by central officials among major rganizational units for particular time periods by expenditure categories. Its evelopment occurred to stop federal agencies from spending all of their ppropriations early in a fiscal year and then asking for more.[5] Apportion- 1ent follows appropriations. Policymakers provide appropriations to organ- :ational units.

Agency X Appropriations, Fiscal Year 1997	
ersonnel	$2,000,000
ontractual Services	$ 800,000
upplies	$ 100,000
quipment	$ 100,000
	$3,000,000

fter appropriations are made, apportionment rules are communicated to gencies. These typically include what portion of agency appropriations is -ithheld to form a central contingency reserve (5% is common), how much an be spent during particular periods (three months, which is called a uarter, as in quarter of a year, is the common period used), and in what ategories money is to be apportioned (usually, expenditure categories used re those in appropriations or budget proposal documents). Agencies apply or apportionment of appropriated funds; that is, they request that executive fficials approve reduced amounts of expenditure authority within time eriods and expenditure categories for their organizational units. After ap- ortionment is requested by agencies, executive officials approve and com- 1unicate their approval to operating agencies and any central finance units. . sample apportionment of funds for Agency X follows.

Agency X Approved Apportionment, Fiscal Year 1997	
.ppropriations	$3,000,000
.eserve for Contingencies	$ 150,000
.pportioned	$2,850,000

| Expenditure | Quarters of Year | | | | |
Category	1st	2nd	3rd	4th	Total
Personnel	$475,000	$475,000	$475,000	$475,000	$1,900,000
Contractual Services	$400,000	$100,000	$200,000	$60,000	$760,000
Supplies	$30,000	$20,000	$15,000	$30,000	$95,000
Equipment	$15,000	$15,000	$40,000	$25,000	$95,000
Total	$920,000	$610,000	$730,000	$590,000	$2,850,000

Several points can be made about this example. First, every expenditur
category here shows a 5% reduction from the previous table of appropriation
for FY 1997. Usually, the overall figure is reduced and spread unequally amon
the expenditure categories. Second, expenditures are distributed uneven&
over the quarters to reflect certain expenditures being necessary in differen
time periods. Third, money not spent in a time period can be spent in a late
time period within the fiscal year. Finally, this apportionment is weighte
toward the earlier periods favoring the agency because it has money availabl
for expenditure. Agencies attempt to make their favored expenditures at th
earliest possible moment and to put politically popular expenditures in th
later quarters, whereas central officials try to delay expenditures to creat
more control and flexibility for themselves. If emergencies arise, agencies ma
request reapportionment.

Allotment, the most common, is the process of communicating expenditur
authority from administrative superiors to their subordinates. Administrativ
superiors take whatever expenditure authority is communicated to them an
communicate most of it to their subordinates, usually without any additiona
time period or expenditure category restrictions. Other limitations or instruc
tions can be communicated with allotments.

Money withheld can be distributed to operating agencies as appropriate
late in the third and fourth quarters, can become savings on expenditures, o
can be used in an area of an organization for which it was not initiall
intended. The release of contingency reserves to agencies toward the end c
the fourth quarter leads to the much decried year-end spending by agencie
Critics tend to forget that the money thus spent was appropriated and woul
have been spent earlier if agencies could do so. Contingency reserves create
by allotment and apportionment are a source of organizational influence fo
those who control them because they can reward positive behavior wit
additional expenditure authority.

A brief recap of the three processes may make it easier to keep ther
separate. Allocation involves dividing expenditure authority by expenditur
categories. Apportionment involves dividing expenditure authority by tim
periods and possibly expenditure categories. Allotment involves dividin
expenditure authority by administrative superiors to their subordinates.

Special Approvals

Operational units may be required to obtain special approvals to spend. Special approvals can be routine or a response to special circumstances, such as budget difficulties or abusive use of particular expenditures. Special approvals typically apply to specific categories, such as travel, training, personnel, equipment, or large amounts of money. Travel and training are controlled for public relations reasons, whereas personnel, equipment, and large expenditures are controlled to deal with budget shortfall situations (e.g., a hiring freeze).

Transfers and Reprogramming

Transfers and reprogramming describe changes from expenditure plans. *Transfers* refer to the movement of expenditure authority between expenditure categories. In the case of Agency X, a transfer might be made from Personnel to Equipment. *Reprogramming* refers to changing plans on spending money within an expenditure category. For example, Agency X might change its plan to hire an accountant in favor of hiring an MBA graduate. Transfers occur between accounts, and reprogramming occurs within accounts. They epitomize control and flexibility in budget execution.[6]

Both processes begin when operating officials detect possible changes from expenditure plans and decide that a change is desirable. An expenditure plan can be in the form of appropriations, a budget proposal, or an operating budget. Often, broad appropriation categories are used to grant expenditure authority. Still, policymakers expect that operating officials follow the detailed budget proposals presented in support of appropriations requests. Deviating from detailed proposals is generally considered a violation of an informal budget agreement.

After a prospective change is identified, operating officials may make transfers or reprogramming decisions under their own authority, after approval by superior administrative officials, or after approval by the chief executive or policy-making body. In larger organizations, administrators may have some authority to transfer or reprogram. Typically, such authority is subject to limitation by category, by percentage, or by dollar amount of expenditure authority. Even then, they communicate any transfer or reprogramming decisions to their superiors. The importance of communicating such changes is that they negate previous spending decisions. In smaller organizations, all changes may require approval by the policy-making body.

SPENDING ◆

In the private sector, money or a commitment to pay is exchanged for some good or service. In the public sector, all decision making and communication of expenditure authority are essential to the expenditure process. Actual expenditures take place only after operating officials determine that they are authorized to act, have the money or resources to spend, and have decided precisely how to proceed, that is, who to hire or what to buy. Public-sector organizations spend in three ways: when they make commitments, when they incur obligations, and when they consume resources.

Actual spending often begins with a *commitment to spend*, which indicates an intention to spend money in a particular way. Commitments can be communicated internally or externally and can be recorded in an accounting system as encumbrances. Examples of commitments include deciding to spend money in particular ways, awarding contracts, hiring someone, notifying individuals that they are eligible for an entitlement payment, and approving a credit application or a tax expenditure claim. Some commitments are irrevocable—for example, entitlement payments, credit approvals, and tax expenditures—because they are based on standing laws.

Commitments made to vendors are frequently accompanied by a contingency statement concerning the consummation of a commitment. Typical contingency conditions include cancellation of agreement provisions, future choice, and budgetary constraints. Cancellation provisions are usually unconditional. Future choice provisions set up a commitment to a vendor wherein the public organization can obtain some amount of a good or service at some point or during a fiscal year. Budgetary constraints occur when an agency does not have expenditure authority to consummate commitments. Even legally binding commitments can be rescinded when vendors believe it is advantageous to assist a public organization in budget difficulties rather than risk losing future business opportunities.

Obligations are incurred when a public organization acts to create a legally binding responsibility to pay someone for something. A contract entered into without any contingency condition is an obligation. Also, obligations occur when a commitment is consummated by a good or service being accepted by a public organization, for example, an employee works or services are rendered.

Spending also occurs when *resources are used* and are no longer available. This view of expenditure is not widely used. The two most important cases are where costs occur before obligations and in the federal budget process. When stockpiles of resources are drawn on or when employees accumulate benefits, such as sick leave, costs are incurred that require future payments. Measurements of such costs are important to monitor future obligations. If not formally accounted for, such costs can create huge hidden financial responsibilities that people in the future will have to deal with. In the federal budget process, budget proposals take the form of estimates of expenditures as costs for the future fiscal year, even though Congress appropriates through obligation authority. Although the cost notion of expenditure is not widely employed in the public sector, it can be useful. Expenditure controls on resource consumption are organizational controls even more than controls over obligations.

REVIEWING ◆
EXPENDITURE DECISIONS

Spending is further complicated by reviews. Reviews take place before, during, and after spending. They primarily determine that spending conforms to all procedural and substantive limitations and requirements placed on expenditures. Routine reviews include accounting reports, disbursement reviews, pre-audits, and post-audits. Also, operating officials make special reviews and strive to meet all requirements placed on them.

All the routine reviews are discussed in other places. Accounting reports were discussed in Chapter 3, "Public-Sector Accounting." Disbursement review is discussed in the next section. Pre-audits and post-audits are discussed in Chapter 17, "Auditing."

Special review efforts include budget reviews, campaigns to reduce expenditures, and investigations of expenditures. Budget reviews, the questioning of operating officials by superior or governing officials about budget proposals, often simultaneously review past expenditures. A question about proposed budgets is frequently, "How has an operating unit used its expenditure authority in the immediate past and current fiscal year?" Although not as detailed as other procedures, budget reviews can expose various kinds of difficulties.

Campaigns to reduce expenditures involve restricting particular expenditures to assist an organization in constrained budgetary circumstances. In such cases, the expenditures targeted are usually those most susceptible to being abused. For example, academic departments with constricted budgets may limit long-distance telephone calls, photocopying, and supplies. Such campaigns are often associated with special records on the use of restricted resources, which are periodically reviewed.

Investigations of expenditures take place after problems appear. Allegations are made that something has been handled improperly. They come from many sources, including members of the public, governing officials, vendors, and operating officials. For example, the federal government uses "Fraud, Waste and Abuse Hotlines," which are toll-free telephone numbers for anonymous calls involving allegations of fraud, waste, and abuse. The first hot line appeared after whistleblower legislation to protect operating officials who reported problems was found not to be working well enough. The most general one is operated by the Government Accounting Office, 1-800-424-5454. The most prominent investigations are those undertaken by law enforcement agencies to ferret out fraud. Efforts to deal with abuse and waste appear to be far more common. Public officials often focus on potential problems and apply special efforts to reduce difficulties. Both the Carter and Reagan administrations instituted formal efforts to curb fraud, waste, and abuse, for example, Medicaid Fraud Control Units Act (1977), Inspector General Act (1978), and Federal Manager's Financial Integrity Act (1982).

◆ PAYING

Paying money is usually called disbursement or disbursing. Money take different forms and so does disbursement. A treasury office or officials mak most payments, whereas operating officials make a few. Also, treasuries review expenditures.

Payments by persons in operating positions are limited so they can b controlled. Such payments include (1) payments out of petty cash, (2) pay ments made by a person in an operating position and reimbursed to tha person on submission of the appropriate information and forms to th treasury, (3) payments made from a separate account held by an operatin agency not controlled by a treasury, (4) payments made by transfers of budge authority through adjustments in accounting records, and (5) payments mad through the treasury from an unrestricted account. Petty cash payments ar restricted in amount because of their potential for misuse. Petty cash pay ments avoid the cost of processing small payments through a treasury pay ment system. Still, petty cash expenditures are documented by receipts.

Expenditures made by persons in operating units and reimbursed by pay ment from a treasury are for expenditures where treasury payment would b extremely difficult. Many goods and services have to be purchased by cas payments. Travel and food expenses are two categories that overlap here. Also emergency situations occur.

Payments from a separate account held by an operating unit refer t situations wherein an operating unit has physical and fiscal control of money Such money is not controlled in any way by a treasury. Money in separat accounts generally comes from grants or agency-collected charges.

Payments can be made by adjusting accounting records within or betwee agencies. One unit provides a good or service for another unit, and paymer is made by taking expenditure authority from one unit as an expenditure an recording it as revenue to the other unit in the accounting records. No mone changes hands.

Finally, a borderline case of operating unit payment of expenditures occur when an operating unit controls an unrestricted treasury account, an accour containing unappropriated monies subject only to agency control. Such mc nies come from grants or other monies generated by the operating unit.

Most public organizations make payments from a central treasury. Trea surers and the treasury office are usually separate from other units to ensur that they focus on the proper handling of public monies. This generall includes cash management and investment of public funds, which are dis cussed in Chapters 11 and 12 respectively. Treasury officials also review expenditures. They review documents directing them to pay monies to deter mine that those requesting payments have expenditure authority in a prope category and that procedures have been followed.

The process of treasury payment begins with an expenditure decision in a operating unit. To make a treasury payment, some document is generate showing that a public organization is obligated to pay someone. That docu ment, usually a voucher, includes a designation of the basis of the expenditur authority. In larger public organizations with more sophisticated accounting systems, the designation is an expenditure account number; in smaller units, it is a claim by a particular person for a particular organizational unit or project. In any event, a voucher identifies the person and organizational unit requesting the payment, the expenditure category involved, the amount, what the payment is for, and to whom the payment is to be made (name and address). Voucher review by a treasury involves checking to see that there is expenditure authority in the expenditure category, that the person submitting a claim is entitled to do so, that an obligation has been incurred, and that all applicable procedures have been followed. Sometimes treasuries check that the person being paid is authorized to receive payment. Some of these items may be reviewed by a purchasing or accounting department before a treasury makes payment.

Expenditure review by treasuries sounds like nit-picking. It is. Such nit-picking, however, safeguards public organization monies. Review of expenditure authority by authorized person by category prevents overspending. Treasuries stand as the last line of defense. The process of treasury review is sometimes called treasury certification, as a treasury certifies (makes certain) that a payment is correct.

After treasury review, a treasury pays. It makes payments and accounts for them. Frequently, the act of paying is preceded within the treasury by an internal review of the payment. One person prepares the payment, and another reviews it.

Accounting records take three forms. First, treasuries list payments in their own accounts. Second, accounting records for the organizational units responsible for spending show payments as realized expenditures. Third, treasuries account for money payments to monitor how much money they have in their accounts; they prefer not to run out.

Payments for expenditures take several forms. They include cash payments, internal accounting entries, checks, electronic fund transfers, and warrants. As noted, cash is used primarily for small payments or for reimbursed items that do not add up to large amounts. Cash is not a favored form of payment because of difficulties in tracking it. Internal accounting entries have been discussed earlier.

Checks are familiar. A financial institution holds money in identifiable accounts. To pay someone, someone else writes directions on a piece of paper called a check, which directs a financial institution to give a specific amount of money to a person or organization named on the check or to the bearer of the check, and delivers the check to the person or organization being paid. Checks are "demand" instruments, which means that a check is paid when it is presented. The consequence is that sufficient resources must be kept in a checking account to cover or pay for all outstanding checks, that is, demands on the account.

Electronic fund transfers are an electronic version of checks, which use the extra step of specifying the account into which money is to be paid and accomplish payment over electronic wires. Electronic fund transfers are used where there is an ongoing relationship between a public organization and a payee because they require the preliminary work of acquiring financial institution and account numbers along with permission of the person being paid to make payments by wire. In the future, electronic fund transfers may become the ordinary payment method because they leave a beautiful paper trail at a relatively low cost for the organization paying while being quicker, more convenient, and safer for the payee.

Warrants are a form of payment used by state and local governments when required to do so by state law. Warrants are written payment documents that resemble checks in most features. They were used initially where there were no financial institutions. One public official issued a claim on the public treasury, called a warrant, and the person holding the warrant presented it to the treasurer for payment. If the treasurer had the money, the warrant was paid in cash. If not, the treasurer made a list of warrants in the order that they were presented and made payment on warrants in that order as money became available. Later, as financial institutions became available, banks took over the treasurer role of paying.

Warrants have one important characteristic: They are not demand instruments. Governments do issue warrants when they do not have money to make payments, and those paid by warrant have no legal recourse to secure money from governments because warrants constitute legal payments. Governments pay warrants when they choose. Usually, warrants are treated as checks. When a warrant-issuing government gets into a cash flow problem, it can cheerfully issue warrants. The State of California did this in the mid-1980s and early 1990s, when it paid its employees with warrants that were not covered by funds on deposit to pay the warrant holders. This causes implicit financing. Warrants are also used as an explicit short-term financing device, where a government enters into an agreement with a financial institution so that the institution pays money to warrant holders and charges interest to the government for holding warrants until money is paid for them. A third warrant financing situation occurs when debt-financed construction projects cannot be financed by bonds until the construction is completed; this control measure ensures the completion of construction projects. When that occurs, construction firms can be paid for their work with warrants, regardless of whether they will be redeemed by a financial institution. In some cases, people possess expensive warrant wallpaper because they thought warrants were checks and the governments that issued the warrants did not have money to pay the persons holding the warrants.

◆ CONCLUSION

Expenditure administration is an area of public finance administration of highly detailed activity, which is generally ignored by the public. When there is difficulty, the public clamors for more controls. Many controls are already in place. Public organizations already have plenty to do in deciding on communicating, using, reviewing, and paying for expenditures.

DISCUSSION QUESTIONS

1. Are different individuals suited for controlling and making expenditures?
2. Can reviews create problems? What kinds of problems? How big are the problems? Are they bigger than the problems of not having reviews?
3. A city discovered that when a formalized purchasing system (formal tracking of permission to make purchases and actual purchases) was installed expenditures dropped dramatically, 20% in one month. Later, city council members decided to have the system dropped. What are the possible reasons for the drop in expenditures? Why would city council members decide to eliminate a purchasing system?

NOTES ◆

1. Lance LeLoup (1986). *Budgetary politics* (3rd ed.). Brunswick, OH: King's Court Communications, pp. 46-59, 232-237; and Allen Schick (1986, Spring).Controlling nonconventional expenditure: Tax expenditures and loans. *Public Budgeting & Finance, 6*(1), 3-19.

2. J. Richard Aronson and John L. Hilley (1986). *Financing state and local governments* (4th l.). Washington, DC: The Brookings Institute, pp. 188-194.

3. City won't pay for copier purchased by parks chief. (1986, May 11). *Omaha World-Herald,* 7B.

4. Thomas Lynch (1985). *Public budgeting in America* (2nd ed.). Englewood Cliffs, NJ: rentice-Hall, pp. 85, 204.

5. Louis Fisher (1975). *Presidential spending power.* Princeton, NJ: Princeton University Press, 28.

6. LeLoup, pp. 221-229, discusses these and other discretionary processes available at the deral level. The same issues are addressed in Bernard T. Pitsvada (1983, Summer). Flexibility federal budget execution. *Public Budgeting and Finance, 3*(2), 83-101; Frank D. Draper and ernard T. Pitsvada (1981, Fall). Limitations in federal budget execution. *The Government ccountants Journal, 30*(3), 15-25. Control by limitations and flexibility are both necessarily part expenditure administration.

10

Purchasing

When we talk of the importance of public organizations in society, we often assume that they directly produce and distribute their vast array of goods or services. Actually, most government activities are supported by purchases made from the private and nonprofit sectors. Nonprofits also purchase a significant share of goods and services from the private sector. Privatization of public activities has become a key component of both governmental and nonprofit agencies. MacManus notes it is the dominant form of contracting for state governments.[1] Rarely does the nonprofit sector actually produce its own goods, and many public services are supported by private business. Examples bombard us every day: Community-based housing development corporations contract with home builders and developers to construct low- and moderate-income housing. States contract for Medicaid managed care providers to serve low-income families. Local governments contract everything from fire protection to hospitals.

Purchasing raises three types of concerns for public organizations. One concern is deciding what to buy. In other words, an agency determines its needs and plans for expenditures on the products and services it requires to accomplish its plans. A second area of concern is the specific processes and procedures for purchasing these goods and services, or how to buy. The process of buying these goods or services is also referred to as procurement. These procedures are important whether an agency is buying paper clips or space shuttles. Moreover, public agencies come under considerable scrutiny in how efficiently and fairly they operate purchasing systems because individuals see their money being used by public organizations. You only have to hear about "sweetheart" contracts or construction "kickbacks" to understand the ingrained skepticism that exists among members of the public concerning public procurement. Third and finally, the agency must be concerned with finding the good or service it requires at the lowest possible cost. Costing out products is a particularly important part of purchasing.

WHAT TO BUY ◆

Perhaps the first item to consider when deciding what to buy is the plan that the organization has adopted for the year, the budget. This document, as described in Chapter 2, can specify what goals and objectives are to be accomplished in the fiscal year, what specific functions are to be carried out, what departments or divisions will be responsible for those activities, and what objects of expenditure will be needed to accomplish those purposes. If a state decides that highways are important, the budget can delineate several decisions, depending on the level of specificity recorded in the budget and the linkages that exist with the capital improvements program, as discussed in Chapter 13. For example, who will pay for this highway work? Is new construction or rehabilitation of existing highways the major objective, or is it a combination of both? What department of state government will be responsible for overseeing this work? Does the funding for this work come from taxes, earmarked user fees, intergovernmental transfers, or some other source? Will the work be done by state employees or will it be contracted out to other public or private agencies? If the work is to be done by state employees, the state will need to hire workers, buy equipment, and buy supplies. The state can also choose to subcontract for some of the work and have state employees do only a portion. The budget is a planning tool indicating the policies of the organization in extracting resources and providing goods and services. Clearly goods and services that are purchased outside the agency must be planned in some detail through the budget process.

Once these questions have been answered, the agency should have some understanding of what goods it will need to purchase directly and what services it will need to procure from others. The organization also determines how much of a particular good or service it needs. It is not enough to know that the state needs to reconstruct a highway; it also needs to determine how many linear feet of construction will be required, which provides the basis for determining how much labor and materials will be required to accomplish the reconstruction of this highway over a particular period of time.

A key element of communicating what an organization needs are written specifications. Specifications are often mentioned only in conjunction with bidding procedures, but an agency really should have clear descriptions of what is to be bought even if only buying from a friendly neighborhood hardware store. Simply stated, specifications for a product tell the person purchasing and the vendor from whom the agency is purchasing exactly what is needed. This provides direction to the vendor, reduces confusion, and provides some assurance to the agency that what is bought meets their particular needs.

One ongoing difficulty facing public organizations is the increasing complexity of products being purchased and the growth of purchasing services. In both cases, specifications are difficult to develop. Mechling makes the distinction between "commodities" and "noncommodities," noting that the former represents "simple, well-known, off-the-shelf goods and services" whereas the latter includes "complex, novel, and/or customized goods and services."[2] Noncommodities require more innovation in defining how specifications are developed and prepared. Still, without written specifications, an agency becomes dependent on vendors to determine what is needed, and the chances increase that products will not meet the agencys' needs. The potential for sloppy purchasing decisions without adequate concern for effectiveness or efficiency will increase.

◆ HOW TO BUY

Even before a public agency decides what to buy, it develops policies and procedures to ensure that those products or services can be obtained in the most efficient and effective manner possible. According to Kelman, the process by which public organizations purchase goods and services derives from a lack of trust the public has in government. For this reason, public procurement processes are encased in elaborate rules.[3] What factors should be included in such a procurement policy? Several aspects have been identified by the American Bar Association in its Model Procurement Code.[4]

- Clarity
- Consistency
- Provision for public confidence
- Fair and equitable treatment of vendors
- Increased economy and maximizing of purchase values
- Fostering of competition
- Safeguards to ensure quality and integrity

In all cases, the goal of a purchasing system for any public organization is to obtain the most appropriate and highest quality good or service possible for the least cost. Although everyone may agree with this noble goal, the road to reaching it can be rocky.

◆ MANAGING PURCHASING

The administrative structure of purchasing varies dramatically among public agencies. At one end of the spectrum, highly decentralized systems operate where purchasing decisions are made by department heads or even individual employees within an organization. Centralized purchasing, on the other end of the spectrum, is very common in larger organizations and does not allow much discretion to lower-level managers or employees.

Decentralized Purchasing

Fire Chief Ed Nossle of Rustic Village decides that his department is in dire need of a new dalmatian to ride on the fire truck. Old Shep, the fire station mascot for more than 15 years, is so old he keeps falling off the truck on sharp turns. Chief Nossle knows that Fred Purina down on Saw Mill Road has sold dalmatians for years and that Fred has always supported the department by purchasing tickets for the fire department's annual raffle. Chief Nossle calls up Fred and offers to buy a dalmatian. Fred tells the Chief he just happens to have a new litter and would be happy to sell one of his new puppies for $200. The Chief agrees, and Fred delivers the puppy the next day. Only later does Mayor Harrison learn of the purchase, when the bill from Fred shows up on the agenda of the monthly village board meeting.

Rustic Village clearly operates a decentralized purchasing system. Such a system may lack several characteristics besides focused responsibility for procurement policies and procedures.

1. It is unlikely that any standardized, written guidelines for purchasing exist within the organization.
2. Purchasing decisions may or may not be linked to either the budget or the financial accounting system.
3. Internal controls for purchases of goods and services may be lacking.

All these characteristics may have existed in Rustic Village. Problems are created when purchasing is decentralized with few standards or internal controls. This is not to say that allocating procurement decisions to lower levels within the organization is always bad. There are advantages to such a system in some instances. For example, if a department is highly specialized and requires materials or services that are unique to its activities, allowing that department to make its own procurement decisions makes a great deal of sense. Still, even in an instance such as this, standard procedures and policies should be in place that ensure that the procurement process results in cost-efficient purchases.

Centralized Purchasing

A generally preferred method of organizing public purchasing efforts is centralization of procurement decisions. Such a centralized system includes

1. A person or department responsible for purchasing within a public or nonprofit agency. This can be a department that reports directly to the chief executive officer or it can be a division within an existing administrative department, such as a state department of administrative services.
2. Assignment of most procurement responsibilities, such as the development of regulations, monitoring of purchasing activities, and approval of purchasing decisions, to a single individual within that agency.
3. Creation of a policy board or group to assist in drafting procurement policies and oversight functions related to their implementation.
4. A preference for formal procurement methods, which includes competitive sealed bidding for most purchases of goods and services.

Centralized purchasing responsibility has several distinct advantages. allows more control over the expenditure of funds by the organization. Chie Nossle and 10 other department heads buying items without prior approva and without standards or procedures leaves the mayor, the village board, an a chief administrator with very little control over where the village's money i going and no way of determining whether they spent too much.

Focusing control of the procurement process allows the agency to bette ensure that purchases are not only cost-efficient but also that no imprope actions are taking place. If a football coach gets a free set of golf clubs fror the local sporting goods store and that same store receives that football coach business for all school athletic equipment, serious questions can arise abou the legality and ethics of such a transaction.

If one individual or department is responsible for the bulk of the procure ment that occurs in an organization, it is much easier to weed out duplicatio and purchase items in bulk to reduce overall costs. If 10 separate department purchase lightbulbs from several different vendors, it is unlikely that the pric they pay is as low as if they had purchased them jointly.

Competitive purchasing is a common facet of centralized purchasing Although Chief Nossle and Fred Purina were good friends and the Chief knev Fred sold dalmatians, a procedure that included written specifications for th type of dog required and some form of competitive purchasing would hav probably resulted in a better price. Using competitive purchasing assumes tha costs will be reduced and that services and product quality will be increased

Combination systems are also possible. For example, department heads car be given discretion in purchasing items if certain procedures are followed. Th village could have required Chief Nossle to contact a minimum of three do breeders and provided them with clear written specifications. If Fred's dalma tian puppy fit the specifications and the $200 was a competitive price, th Chief could have been authorized to purchase the pooch without a highl formalized system. In this example, processes are centralized, but decision are decentralized.

Six Purchasing Functions

In a centralized system, the purchasing agent or purchasing department i responsible for the overall operation of procurement in the organization Aronson and Schwartz list six purchasing functions this individual or depart ment must perform.[5] First, a purchasing agent must be familiar with the sources of supply. Although this can be quite simple when the agency is dealing with very standard goods or services, it becomes more difficult when those goods and services are unique.

A second function of a purchasing agent is to understand pricing and market characteristics that shape procurement decisions. By understanding prices of particular products, a public agency is in a position to take advantage of cost-saving opportunities that present themselves. If the Fire Chief does not understand the market for dalmatians, he is at a competitive disadvantage with vendors who want to sell him one. The organization risks paying too much buying at the wrong time, or buying the wrong thing without this understanding

A third function of purchasing agents is to know what statutes or other legal constraints apply to their organization. Laws often place severe restrictions on public purchasing. Local governments often find requirements imposed locally or by their state that mandate that they purchase goods or services from within the state or locality. If this is the case, obtaining the lowest and best price for a particular item can be very difficult. Also, public organizations are often restricted in the procedures they use to purchase products and services.

Fourth, purchasing agents must be responsible for reviewing and implementing the policies and procedures that are used in procuring goods and services. The best policies in the world will have little effect if no one is implementing them.

Fifth, handling interactions with vendors and contractors is a function performed by purchasing agents whose importance cannot be overlooked. The kind of relationship an agency develops with these individuals often dictates how responsive they are to that organization's needs. This applies not only to the prices of particular items but also to service as well. Are vendors willing to "go the extra mile" to assist the agency? Although it is hard to put a dollar figure on such service, it is often critical to operational success. This makes it possible for a purchasing agent to know whom to depend on and whom to watch more carefully. Such knowledge evolves over time only after an agent becomes familiar with vendors.

Finally, purchasing agents represent an organization in the bidding process. This process includes requests for proposals, taking bids, evaluating bids, negotiating the prices, and relaying the results of that process to the bidders themselves.

Purchasing Nontraditional Services

Increasingly, governmental and nonprofit agencies are in the position of purchasing services that do not provide for highly routinized approaches to procurement. Among the most common are purchases of services. Services, according to Fearon and Bales, include advertising, auditing, architectural, legal, security, and general consulting services. A survey of both private and public managers indicated that more than half the total dollars used to purchase items were spent on services, with only 32% spent to purchase services handled by purchasing departments for governments. The department most likely to purchase services outside of a purchasing department was finance. These findings indicate that nontraditional purchases are much less likely to be centralized than are more traditional items. Where this is the case, purchasing policies and procedures need to be communicated to line and staff departments who make such purchasing decisions.[6]

ELEMENTS OF ◆
THE PURCHASING SYSTEM

Successful governmental and nonprofit purchasing systems have several key elements, which should be clearly explained in written policies and procedures adopted by the policy body of the organization. Among the most important elements are the following:

- Defined responsibilities of the various aspects of purchasing within the organization
- Methods for procuring goods and services
- Written specifications
- Requirements for vendors and contractors
- Ethical standards for behavior
- Internal controls
- Inventory management

Specifications

As discussed previously, written specifications are particularly important in purchasing. Neuman and Carren argue that such technical specifications are one of the most important and certainly one of the most difficult aspects of procurement. This is true for several reasons. First, specifications indicate to the vendor what parameters the agency expects to be met in the vendor's response. The National Academy of Public Administration has noted that most problems with vendors occur "because of ambiguous, ill-defined and poorly written contracts that did not include important details, parameters, and specifications."[7] Specifications that are too narrow or detailed can result in higher cost proposals or possibly no response at all. In one community, a request for proposal (RFP) was sent to various contractors for the construction of a major arterial street. When the date for the bids arrived, no responses were received. City officials were puzzled by this and called various contractors to ask why they had not bid. The response was that the specifications called for a particular grade of material and a particular process of construction that were only feasible on major interstate highway construction. A relatively small city street project was simply not economically feasible to the contractors based on the specifications provided in the RFP.

Not only can specifications be too narrow, they can also be too broad and ambiguous. This leads to responses that have no consistency or standardization, which can increase costs because of the confusion and opportunities for expansion in the minds of the vendors and contractors. If a public agency advertises for bids on a computer system and does not specify what needs the agency has and what criteria will be used to evaluate proposals, the agency could end up with proposals for anything ranging from a Notebook computer to a Supercomputer. Blending enough details in specifications to allow standardized responses and enough flexibility and responsiveness to allow competitive responses is a difficult task.

Another factor that makes writing specifications difficult is determining the form those specifications should take. Among the most common are comparable or equivalencies to brand names (Scott brand paper towels or comparable), specific products or materials (Ford Escort), particular design characteristics, and particular operation characterizations and performance criteria (water pipe

1ust be able to withstand so many pounds of pressure for a particular period
f time). Neuman and Carren point out that performance is probably most
ften the preferred form of specification. This is true for several reasons.[8]
erformance-based criteria allow the vendor or contractor some flexibility in
esigning the bid response. There are nine ways to skin a cat. If an agency
equires that its cat be skinned in only one way, the agency can increase its
osts and reduce the competitive responses to the request. Besides, somebody
1ay develop a tenth way that is both cost-efficient and productive, even if not
leasant for the cat.

Still, performance-based specifications are not always the best approach to
se. If a state is concerned about the quality of materials that are used in a
articular construction project, quality standards can be specified as well as
erformance of the construction standards. It is not unusual for public
gencies to require that a particular grade of building materials or a particular
/pe of design be used in their construction specifications.

As mentioned previously, one of the most important aspects of good
pecifications is standardization. This promotes understanding by those re-
ponding to the procurement request and, more important, allows the agency
> compare responses more effectively. Nothing is more frustrating in a
rocurement process than to try to evaluate preferences among a series of
esponses when there is no comparability. If an agency allows vendors to
espond using their own criteria or their own terminology, selecting the lowest
nd best response is almost impossible. In some cases, procurement needs do
ot allow for total standardization. This is particularly true when negotiated
ids or noncompetitive negotiation are used, but standard specifications
lould be used when possible.

Finally, developing specifications can be difficult because of limited expe-
ence by a public agency or because of its unique needs. It is particularly
nportant that public managers search out other organizations that have had
milar projects or programs and adapt their experiences. This not only saves
onsiderable time and effort but also helps eliminate problems associated with
nanticipated situations that others have faced in the past.

Purchasing Methods

There are four basic methods of purchasing goods and services and choos-
1g among particular vendors: (1) competitive bidding, (2) competitive sealed
roposals, (3) negotiated bids, and (4) noncompetitive negotiations. Each can
e appropriate, depending on the cost of the item being purchased, the timing
f the purchase, and the unique characteristics of the product or service.
1acManus noted that a survey by the National Association of State Purchas-
1g Officials shows that "most states have specific written criteria outlining
idding requirements and procedures," including publicly opened sealed
ids, bidding lists, written criteria for suspending or debarring bidders, writ-
:n procedures for handling sole source providers, and emergency proce-
ures.[9] Many local jurisdictions have similar policies.

Competitive Bidding

Soliciting competitive sealed bids is the most appropriate type of procure ment method for large purchases where there are numerous potential suppli ers. MacManus notes the National Institute of Governmental Purchasin definition as "the process of publicizing government needs (public notice inviting bids, conducting public bid openings, and awarding a contract to th lowest responsive and responsible bidder."[10] She also notes that this proces is supported (but not always correctly) because it is perceived to promot many purchasing goals (openness, efficiency, fairness, and competition). Mos purchases or contracts for capital improvements and equipment are handle in this manner. Many public organizations are required by law to do competi tive bidding for purchases greater than a certain dollar cost. This dollar cos differs among organizations, but because it is written into statute, the amoun often is not adjusted as the actual cost of items increases. The federal govern ment requires competitive bids of its grant-in-aid recipient for purchases o more than $10,000 and recommends it for purchases below this amoun Many state and local governments have limits ranging from $1,000 to mor than $25,000.

Competitive sealed bids have several characteristics. First, the announcemen of the future purchase is formally advertised. Nonprofit organization and stat and local government announcements are often placed in a newspaper o general circulation. The federal and some state governments advertise i publications such as *Commerce Business Daily* or other special-interest publi cations that vendors and contractors are likely to read. Local governments an nonprofit organizations often advertise in newspapers with the greatest loca circulation. Notice of the purchase can also be mailed directly to thos suppliers who are known or who are likely to be interested. If the organizatio has a preapproval process for contractors, those who are preapproved ar often mailed solicitations directly. This formal advertising is often referred t as a Request for Proposal or RFP.

RFPs contain considerable information about the items to be purchase and the purchasing process. They include specifications for the product o service desired, the due date for responding, and the general legal require ments to be met by both the vendor and the organization. Any bondin requirements are also specified in the RFP. Any schedule for holding a prebi conference to answer questions about the RFP is provided along with an nouncements of bid awards.

To guard against spurious or frivolous responses, most RFPs require bi bonds. These bonds specify that if the vendor is awarded the contract and doe not execute the agreement within a certain specified time, the dollar amoun of the bond is forfeited to the public agency. These bonds are usually 5% t 10% of the contract amount and provide sufficient incentive to the contracto to perform the contract.

Competitive bids also often require performance bonds. Performance bond provide financial assurance to the public agency that the contractor/vendo will perform to the standards specified in the contract and RFP. If the contrac or fails to do so, the performance bond is forfeited to the agency. Performance bonds for large contracts are usually for 100% of the project cost.

A third type of bond, a payment bond, can also be required with the bid proposal. This bond assumes that subcontractors, suppliers, and other third-party participants with the vendor or contractor will be paid for their work or supplies.

Although each of these bonding requirements is important as both incentive to the supplier and protection to the agency, they can reduce the number of potential bidders. This is particularly true for smaller purchases and for minority contractors. Public organizations should look for other alternatives when the bonding requirements are so strict that they reduce competition. It is also important to realize that the costs of these bonds are passed along in the price of the project or product.

To ensure fairness and reduce the chances of collusion or tampering, all bids competitively solicited are sealed and not opened until the bid opening ceremony. Often, sealed bids are received at a specific location until the close of business on a particular day. The time and place are specified in the RFP. Once a bid is submitted, it is usually stamped by the public agency with the date and time of receipt and then initialed by the person who received the bid. This person is often present at the bid opening to ensure that the bids have remained sealed and have not been tampered with. An additional internal control is to require that two persons log receipt of the bids and be present at the bid opening.

To protect a public agency from accepting a bid that exceeds the funds allocated for the activity or product or what the market would pay for that good or service, internal bid estimates can also be developed and announced at the bid opening. If the lowest competitive bid exceeds that internal bid estimate, an agency can legally reject all bids. In some instances, bid rejection is legally required. Such a position is often found in RFPs written in terms such as "reserving the right to reject any and all bids."

To protect the bid process and not place the agency in the position of having to reject all bids, options for varying levels of service or quality of goods can be specified in the RFP. These options result in greater and lesser expenditures, so some portion of the bid can be accepted. In other instances, the agency is allowed to negotiate down the cost of the good or service after the bids have been accepted by reducing the scope of that good or service in the RFP. This is more commonly a characteristic of competitive proposals. If such options are not included and all bids are too high, a new RFP must be developed and the entire process repeated.

Competitive Sealed Proposals

Competitive sealed proposals have many of the same characteristics as competitive bids; however, they allow more flexibility in defining the specifications for the good or service. Formal advertising may not be required, and the solicitation of proposals can be made to a select group of vendors rather than through a general call for bidders. According to the American Bar

Association, "The competitive sealed proposal method is available for use when competitive bidding is either nor practicable or not advantageous."[11] For example, if the number of available vendors is limited or the type of good or service is limited, proposals may provide the best opportunity for the public agency to keep costs low and yet be sure it is receiving a competitive proposal. Judgment plays a more important part in sealed proposals, and more comparisons can be drawn between different vendors' products and services. Also, with competitive sealed proposals, more room for negotiation exists after the bids have been opened. This is not true for competitive sealed bids.

Negotiated Bids

Negotiated bids are more flexible in structure and operation than either competitive sealed bids or proposals. As with competitive sealed proposals, negotiated bids are often solicited from a sample of qualified vendors or service providers. They may or may not be formally advertised. The major distinction between competitive and negotiated bids is that although bid responses can be confidential, they are subject to adjustment and change before final acceptance and legal approval. Negotiated bids are commonly used for procuring professional services, such as hiring an accounting firm and selecting a consultant for planning or engineering.

Even though negotiated bids entail considerable flexibility, they do not eliminate the need for clear specifications or internal bid estimates. The lack of clear specifications can allow a contractor to set the parameters for the product or activity, which can result in an organization purchasing something that does not meet its needs, costs too much, or both. Often, if an agreement cannot be reached with the vendor for what appears to be the lowest negotiated bid, the public agency can then open negotiations with the next lowest bidder. This is not possible with either competitive sealed bids or competitive sealed proposals.

Noncompetitive Negotiations

This type of procurement is properly undertaken when only one source exists for the particular good or service and competitive bidding would be fruitless, or when an agency has attempted competitive solicitation with unsatisfactory results. Sole source bidding is unusual in most public agencies but is often seen in very large agencies, such as the Department of Defense, or in very small communities. Sole source bidding does have some practical uses. For example, federal agencies contract with certain public interest groups to provide technical assistance to their membership, and such contracts are based on noncompetitive negotiation simply because no other group has access to that membership to the level and extent that the interest group does. The federal government also negotiates noncompetitive contracts in some cases because of the size of the project or the unique skills or capabilities required. Rural local governments carry out noncompetitive negotiations because qualified bidders are simply not available.

A noncompetitive bidding process can be justified because of unique needs or because of emergency situations that simply do not allow bidding or rebidding particular items. If a state government has requested bids on a construction project aimed at eliminating hazardous waste and all bids received do not satisfy the requirements specified in the RFP in one way or another, that state can go to some form of sole source contract to resolve the emergency health situation. It is important to keep in mind that agencies may not use sole source bidding because they are lazy or for some other personal reason. Sole source bidding is also an opportunity for collusion or other illegal activity. Any policy on nonnegotiated bids should be very clear concerning its use and potential abuse.

Noting earlier comments concerning "noncommodities," the key issue facing public and nonprofit agencies is balancing the approaches to bidding that are used and the items and services being purchased. As Kelman noted, "More of what government now buys is complex and hence ill-suited to the kind of complex specifications in contractual language that the original system used as a way to achieve good substantive performance by vendors."[12]

GENERAL REQUIREMENTS ◆
AND CONDITIONS

No matter which approach is used, it is important that the public agency develop a consistent set of policies and procedures for all vendors. Although relationships with vendors and contractors vary, depending on the type and availability of the good or service required, the organization should stress general requirements in its purchasing policies, particularly those tied to competitive or negotiated bids. These requirements should be clearly specified in the Request for Proposals and in the pre-bid conference. These policies also should be reflected in the general requirements and conditions to vendors.

Conformity and uniformity of bid and proposal responses are extremely important to allow comparisons among bidders. Lack of conformity is or should be sufficient reason to reject bid proposals. It is important in public organizations that vendors do not try to unduly influence policy leaders by end runs around the procurement process. This can be particularly troublesome in smaller agencies, where certain policy board members are interested in the purchase of a particular item or where clear procurement policies do not exist. It is not unusual in small local governments to have the local merchants call a council member to argue the merits of their product. This lobbying, if allowed to exist, can seriously erode the purchasing process.

It is often important for vendors to know, first, that a public agency has the right to reject any and all bids, and second, that if budgetary constraints occur, the agreement can be canceled after a bid has been accepted and the contract signed.

Bid and proposal requests can specify that the vendor or contractor hold the public agency harmless from any liability that might occur, especially as the result of any patent or copyright infringement. This is important where new technology is involved or where some new capital equipment is part of the proposal.

When possible, agencies should require the contractor to guarantee the prices stated in the bid response for a reasonable period of time. In many instances, this is the period of time between the acceptance of the bid and the signing of a contract. For products where price fluctuations are very common, this time period may have to be short. To ask for price guarantees for an inordinate time period with no price adjustment can preclude vendors from bidding.

Finally, bidders should clearly understand that they are responsible for the accuracy and completeness of their responses. This saves any misunderstanding about what was not expected in the bid response. Correspondingly, the agency is also bound not to change the rules in the middle of the game. Some contractors are notorious for submitting bids that are neither responsive nor responsible. Responsive means that a bid is consistent with the specifications. It is not unusual for a bidder unable to meet the specifications to submit a bid that describes a completely different product or service and then make the case that the specifications were either too restrictive or misdirected, even taking this argument directly to the policy board. Managers must convince the policymakers that their specifications accurately reflected the needs of the organization and that the bid submitted violated the requirements of responsiveness. A responsible bid is one made by someone who clearly has the capability and competence to meet the specifications and requirements of the proposed project or activity. It is the duty of the agency to verify this capability by checking references, evaluating previous work products, and discussing the vendor's capabilities with other public agencies that are familiar with those capabilities.

◆ EVALUATING COSTS IN PURCHASING

A key concern of any purchasing process is cost. Those things that help reduce costs or avoid cost increases in the future while retaining quality of service are paramount issues for public agencies. Several factors play a role in purchasing cost.

Inventory Management Costs

Quantity costs. For many products or services purchased by public agencies, costs can be reduced by ordering in substantial quantity. The unit costs are reduced as the total volume of the purchase increases. Such purchases reduce the transaction costs to the vendor and can greatly reduce inventory costs. Purchasing in great quantities, however, also can lead the agency to increase its holding costs, which are discussed later.

Ordering costs. Often overlooked are costs associated with ordering goods. Each time a particular item is ordered, costs increase. Personnel must place the order, specifications may have to be developed or revised, and paperwork associated with the order must be processed. Costs will also be incurred by eceiving the good. These costs must be compared with the cost savings associated with bulk purchases and with the potential costs associated with storing the good over an extended period of time.

Holding costs. Holding costs focus on inventory management and are very similar to cash management, discussed in Chapter 11. The agency's goal is to reduce costs and promote efficiencies by purchasing in sufficient quantities to receive the best price possible, keeping inventories at their optimum levels to serve the needs of the organization, and minimizing carrying costs.

Some goods lend themselves more readily to an inventory system than others. For example, it may make a great deal of sense to carry an inventory of janitorial supplies that are heavily used. It may make less sense to purchase a large number of a more specialized item that is not replaced often. Holding costs are incurred by an organization when an item sitting in inventory deteriorates over time, becomes obsolete, takes up needed storage space, or increases the organization's insurance costs. This demonstrates the trade-off facing an inventory manager. Keeping a particular item in stock can reduce the cost of ordering that item and reduce the delays that might exist if the agency had to purchase it separately, but it can also be costly to keep such an item in stock for an extended period of time.

How does an agency organize its inventory policies to take advantage of cost savings at the point of ordering a good and yet not end up paying excessive holding costs resulting from unused inventory? The agency should choose those goods that are the most important in cost savings versus holding costs for analysis and then analyze the use of these particular products. This can be easily accomplished by using some type of cost accounting system, as described in Chapter 3. If such an accounting system does not exist, some type of management information system could be developed that would allow the purchasing agent to track usage in some manner. This can be accomplished most easily where supplies are centralized. If the janitorial personnel are responsible for replacing all burned-out lightbulbs, some tracking of their use could be accomplished by having those individuals keep track over a period of time. It makes no sense to stock up on cases of 10W-40 motor oil if you find that this particular type of motor oil is not used very frequently or the vehicles that use such oil are about to be replaced.

Outage costs. Another piece of information that is critical for inventory managers is the costs that occur when particular items are out of stock and must be ordered from private vendors. Two major issues should be considered: the availability of the item and the cost associated with single purchases. If the item is likely to be unavailable for at least some period of time, this can create varying degrees of difficulty for the agency. If a particularly critical piece of equipment breaks down because of a faulty part and the manager knows in advance that the part will take several weeks to replace, it may be advisable to have that part on hand, even if the chances of it being needed are quite small. In effect, the organization is insuring itself against unacceptable delays or problems that could arise because of particular types of equipment failure. Backup generators in hospitals are another example of this strategy.

An inventory manager must determine when inventory items should be restocked by number of items in stock or date for seasonal items. This estimate must be based on current demand and estimates of replacement requirements. An agency should not buy any more than is required based on these factors unless the agency anticipates price increases in the product that would exceed its costs of holding the goods over an extended period of time. The agency should also not purchase items in bulk that can become obsolete before they are even put into use.

Lease Arrangements
Versus Purchase Costs

Leasing has a long history, with one author noting that it began as early as 1400 BC with the use of charter ships being leased to merchants on the western coast of the Mediterranean sea. Although leasing has existed in both public and private agencies for many years, its attractiveness to public and nonprofit organizations has grown steadily throughout the past decade.

This increased interest is largely the result of cost savings available through leasing particular products for their use rather than outright purchase of those items. A cost analysis of options for leasing, lease with the option to purchase or outright purchase is particularly important when looking at equipment that will depreciate over time. This might include an agency's vehicle fleet, office equipment, computer and other data processing equipment, and similar types of items. A number of advantages tied to cost have been made to support lease options. Leasing lets you take advantage of the time value of money but spreads costs that don't have to be committed to buying an item that reduces your purchasing power. Leasing reduces pressure on the operating budget by spreading costs over an extended period. Leasing adds flexibility by reducing the commitment to the purchase of an item that may not meet the organization's needs in the future.

One factor that should be considered is how long the agency plans to keep the item. Those items that will be kept only for a short period of time might be good candidates for a lease arrangement, especially if the items depreciate rapidly. Cars are good examples. If a state decides to buy a fleet of cars for its highway department and also plans to replace those cars in two, three, or four years, the total cost associated with purchase and maintenance might be higher than the cost of simply leasing those cars over the same period of time.

A second factor to be considered is how the equipment or goods will be paid for. If the public agency uses funds from its operating budget to pay for the cars, the costs will be substantially less than if it were to pay for the cars by issuing bonds. Under the first arrangement, no debt or debt administration costs are involved, and the actual cost would be less. Under the latter arrangement, debt and debt administration costs would make the actual cost higher. The benefit of such an arrangement is that the actual cost of the automobiles would be spread out over several years rather than incurred in one specific year. Lease arrangements can be quite attractive compared with purchasing the cars by issuing debt.

A third factor to consider in deciding whether to lease equipment is the obsolescence of that equipment over time. This is of particular concern when high technology equipment, such as computers, is involved. In such a rapidly hanging field, equipment can become obsolete within one or two years. Most computer experts advise that businesses replace their data processing equipment every three years. If this is the case, it might be better for the agency to lease the equipment rather than purchase it outright, depending on any resale value the items might have.

Finally, the agency should look at the possibility of buy-back options and the resale value of items before they are purchased. With a buy-back option, the vendor agrees to buy back the item on a particular date at a predetermined price. This agreement can make the outright purchase more attractive than a lease arrangement by providing a guaranteed market for the product. Also, if the agency can be relatively sure of the resale value of the product at the time the agency is planning to sell it for replacement purposes, the benefits of purchase versus lease arrangements can be determined. If the product has an inconsistent depreciation record and resale price is anything but certain, however, either a lease arrangement or guaranteed buy-back option may be the best alternative.

Types of Leases

Vogt and Cole identified several forms or types of leases. A "true lease" is where the agency gains the use of an item but does not gain ownership.[13] Under this lease arrangement, the time frame of the lease is always less than the useful life of the item being leased. A "conditional-sales lease or lease-purchase agreement" has the characteristics of a installment sale. Ownership is acquired in the item at the time of the agreement, with the date at which ownership transfers subject to the terms of that agreement. The lease payments are similar to installment loan payments in this instance.

"Tax exempt lease" represents a conditional-sales lease where the state or local government is the lessee and a private entity is the owner of the property. In this type of lease, any interest generated from the lease payments is exempt from federal and in some cases state or local income taxes, and this makes it an attractive arrangement for a private lessor. In many cases state and local governments can use this approach to lower the overall cost of capital items or property that it acquires. According to Vogt and Cole, many tax-exempt or lease-purchase agreements require that the government can cancel the lease without penalty if funding is not appropriated to cover the costs of this lease. This is referred to as "nonappropriation" and is included to avoid the classification of such leases as long-term debt under many state statutes.

"Capital and operating leases" are established in accordance with Governmental Accounting Standards Board (GASB) and Financial Accounting Standards Board (FASB) requirements. One key element for accounting standards is the lease time frame. Generally, a lease is categorized as a "capital" lease if the term of the lease is equal to or more than 75% of the item's useful life. If is less than 75%, it is considered an "operating" lease. A "finance lease" has lending institution or investor as the lessor, and the governmental or nonprofit agency leases the item and over time acquires use of that property. The agency must pay for any operating or maintenance costs. It is a form of true lease.

"Sale-leaseback leases" represent an increasingly common transaction for some governmental and nonprofit agencies. In this form of lease, the agency sells property to an investor (often a lending institution) who immediately leases that facility back to the agency. It is structured as a true lease. The reason for creating such an arrangement is to transfer tax benefits to the private investor. "Leveraged leases" are also a form of true lease, in which a financial institution or investor lends the agency from 50% to 80% of the money needed to purchase a leased item. The lender then has the leased property and the lease payments as collateral on the loan but not to the general credit of the agency. If the agency is a private entity, it could deduct the full depreciated value of the property even though the agency has invested considerably less than that amount in the item. This is an attractive lease approach for private businesses but is less useful to government and nonprofit agencies that cannot depreciate fixed assets for tax purposes.

A "net lease" requires the organization that owns the property or equipment being leased to be responsible for operation and maintenance costs. A "gross lease" expects the agency leasing the item to cover these costs. A "net-net lease" is one where the owner of the property covers all costs of operation and also "guarantees" the agency leasing the property that the property will have some minimal value at the end of the lease period.

"Certificates of Participation leases" represent a tax exempt syndication of "shares" of the lease, usually through private placement. This has become popular with local governments in recent years. Finally, "rental agreements" can be considered a type of lease but usually involve paying for the use of someone else's property for a shorter time period than most lease agreements.

Life Cycle Costing

Life cycle costing (LCC) has gained considerable attention over the past several years. According to Coe,[14] this approach looks at the total costs of use or ownership (e.g., ownership costs) of a particular item or system rather than just the initial costs of purchases. This can be done by actually observing the costs of the product over time, asking the vendor to supply information on such costs, including all operating and maintenance costs; or by using information that has been collected from other agencies and organizations on what these costs may be. A similar approach, Total Cost of Ownership (TCO) includes costs from the very beginning of the idea of purchasing a good or service to the very end of the useful life of that product or service.[15]

According to Seldon, life cycle costing was originally developed by the U.S. Defense Department in the early 1960s, and the primary motivation was to save money on "operating and support costs." Another motivation, according to Seldon, was to encourage long-range planning and to avoid the "false economies" of focusing solely on the lowest purchase price.[16] He also notes that it has several uses, including long-range planning and budgeting, program comparisons, improved decision-making concerning replacement of aging equipment, ongoing program control, and improved selection of competing vendors.

Life cycle costing has several steps. The first is to determine the useful life and costs of owning the item during that period of time. The second step is to determine what the product will be worth once it has reached the end of that useful life—in other words, its salvage value. The third step is to place these future costs and salvage value in present-day terms by discounting these costs to net present value. Once this information is available, the agency can calculate the life cycle costs by "adding to the acquisition cost the discounted ownership costs less the discounted salvage value cost."[17] Other costs that might be included in life cycle analysis are such things as personnel and training costs associated with the purchase of product or service and potential liability costs associated with the risk or exposure to loss created by this product or service.

This approach to costing is invaluable to public agencies that are trying to evaluate their actual purchase costs. It can be cheaper in the short run to buy a less expensive product, but life cycle costing can show that the costs over the life of that product can be much higher when such things as downtime, maintenance costs, and other such costs are considered. Such an approach can lead to more informed decisions by managers and save substantial resources. There is a downside, however. Life cycle costing can be expensive to implement because of the additional staff time and the potential need for outside technical and legal help that may be required to carry it out. The General Accounting Office (GAO), for example, found considerably higher administrative costs associated with use of life cycle costing for the purchase of transit vehicles for the Urban Mass Transit Authority.

PURCHASING POOLS ◆

One area that has gained increasing interest in recent years, particularly among local governments and nonprofit agencies, is the use of cooperative agreements among agencies to buy goods in greater quantities. Such cooperative or pool purchasing has several distinct advantages. First, it allows agencies to save by buying goods in sufficient quantities to receive preferential prices from vendors. Such price breaks vary by product but can be as high as 60% or more. Second, pool purchasing can offer the agency better quality control because the quality of specifications and the oversight given to vendors is better than each agency is capable of doing on its own. Third, the organization can find a broader selection of vendors willing to bid on the goods because of the size of the purchase. This in turn provides a broader selection of products and, in all likelihood, better quality and lower costs.

Even with these benefits, pool purchasing also has major drawbacks. First, it requires participating organizations to give up some flexibility. Second, it can require changes in operations. This is because most cooperative purchasing arrangements require the purchases to be done at one particular time agreeable to all the participants in the pool. This may not be as convenient to some agencies as would be the case if they alone selected the timing of the purchases. Third, pool purchasing also can remove control from an agency and locate it somewhere else. It represents one more step beyond centralized purchasing and can cause even more resistance among department heads who are used to controlling the purchasing themselves.

Finally, cooperative purchase agreements can increase the carrying costs for the pool organizations. In other words, when the agency purchased items in small quantities, need for storage space was minimal. When items are purchased in large amounts, however, those items will have to be stored somewhere for an extended period of time. They must be stored so they do not deteriorate, which can require special facilities. This can also increase the insurance costs of the organizations. Somebody has to coordinate, manage, and transport inventory items. Clearly, considerable thought should be given to the costs of such enterprises. Pool inventory costs vary dramatically by the type of product stored, the length of storage anticipated, the access to transportation to obtain the items from their central storage point, and the staffing needed to manage the inventory of that product.

The steps in a cooperative purchasing system are not all that different from those used in any purchasing system. Each organization prepares a listing of the products that will be needed, when those products will be needed, and how many units of the product will be required over a particular period of time. A centralized department or agency is selected to manage the purchasing process, and contractual agreements are developed among all the members of the pool. Once this has been completed, bid proposals should be prepared, bids solicited, bids awarded, goods inspected and tested to determine compliance with bid specifications, and finally, goods should be distributed to participating agencies. In some cases this last step can be delayed if a centralized inventory or warehousing system is created as part of the cooperative effort.

◆ ETHICS AND CONFLICT OF INTEREST IN PURCHASING

Ethical conduct and conflicts of interest are recurring problems in public purchasing. Some conflicts are unintentional and in many instances go unreported. Other cases are flagrant and conscious acts to deceive the public. Even the appearance of impropriety can damage a public agency's credibility with its constituents and lead to greater mistrust by the public. The media is constantly ferreting out stories of some public official who has used a position for personal gain, whether it is allegations made by Robert Caro about Lyndon Johnson's relationship with a major capital construction firm, or a revelation about construction kickbacks on a local street project.[18] Such stories erode public confidence and demonstrate lack of internal control over purchasing and procurement practices. The American Bar Association (ABA) lists such areas of ethical conduct that should be addressed by public organizations in their purchasing systems.

The first of these is employee conflict of interest. The ABA lists three categories of conflict of interest: (1) where the employee or an immediate member of the family has financial interest in some procurement activity; (2) where any business or organization in which the employee, or any member of

ie employee's immediate family, has a financial interest or would benefit
:om the procurement; or (3) where the employee knows he or she or an
nmediate member of his or her family has negotiated with any person or
usiness involved in the procurement in some way.

A second area, disclosure, is considered an important element of ethical
onduct in public organizations. If any financial benefit is to be received by
ny employee from any procurement made by the organization, this benefit
hould be disclosed to the proper authority in the organization. Failure to
isclose such a benefit could result in sanctions.

Third, gratuities and kickbacks are another ongoing problem. Any gratuity
eceived that in any way can be connected to the procurement or contract of
n agency with outside vendors should be considered unethical. The football
oach example mentioned earlier illustrates such a gratuity. Kickbacks are
efined as "any payment, gratuity, or offer of employment . . . made by or on
ehalf of a subcontractor under a contract to a prime contractor or higher-tier
ibcontractor or any person associated therewith, as an inducement for the
ward of a subcontract or order."[19]

A fourth area of concern is contingency fees. Such fees are used to hire an
idividual or firm to solicit contracts, with that firm or individual receiving
fee that is contingent on obtaining that contract. For example, ABC Con-
:ruction Company hires Sally Average to solicit contracts for them with the
nderstanding that Sally will receive 10% of the value of every contract she
icceeds in bringing in. The incentives under such a plan can lead Sally to
arry out unethical activities to secure those contracts. For this reason, con-
ngency fees are considered an injurious practice. Contractors who use such
gents to obtain agency contracts can undermine the ethical conduct of public
mployees, therefore public agencies often outlaw such contingency-fee-
ased agents.

A fifth area of concern is highlighted in federal government experiences.
ormer government employees often lobby on behalf of private interests for
avorable treatment, and this points to the difficulties in restricting public
mployees from going to work for private companies with whom they have
orked. Still, this should be a concern for governments. Two avenues can
ddress this problem. Employees who are involved in the procurement of a
endor can be restricted from leaving to work with that vendor. This can be
iore easily done by disqualifying that vendor from future contracts than by
estricting the employee after he or she leaves government service. Another
pproach, one historically followed by the federal government, is to restrict
ie ability of a former employee to do business with that department or agency
'ith whom he or she worked for a specified period of time. Such restrictions
re clearly based on the idea that such practice is unethical. Court cases
ivolving former presidential aides Lyn Nofziger and Michael Deaver show
iat ethics laws can be enforced.

A final area discussed by the ABA is the use of confidential information. It
unethical for a public employee to use confidential information for personal
ain or to benefit anyone else. Horror stories about local officials buying
iture right-of-way for streets and highways that they know will be located in
particular area have been all too common in recent years.

Ethical conduct in the purchasing of goods and services should not only b represented in a formal written policy but also should represent an over arching goal of the public organization, and the management should work t instill in all employees the importance of such conduct.

◆ CONCLUSION

Purchasing is a complex and demanding task. It is a key focus for publi financial managers who are concerned about effective delivery of service t their constituents. How purchasing systems are organized, the processes o deciding what to buy, and how to buy it play a major role in how effective a organization will be.

Purchasing should be closely tied to the budget plan for an organization. I should, in most instances, be centralized in one department. Finally, purchas ing should be based on written policies and procedures covering all aspects o the purchasing process from selecting goods and services to inventory man agement and disposal.

DISCUSSION QUESTIONS

1. How can public and nonprofit managers best protect the interests o their organizations when purchasing items dependent on technolog that rapidly become obsolete?

2. It is not uncommon for nonprofit organizations to recruit policy boar members who are professionals in areas such as law, accounting, bank ing, and so forth. How do such organizations ensure that they will no violate conflict of interest or ethics laws when it comes to purchasin such services?

3. How do public and nonprofit organizations begin to incorporate im pact analysis, performance management, and benchmarking concept into the purchasing processes?

4. Review the local newspaper over a two-week period and analyze th number of stories that focus on purchasing issues affecting governmen tal or nonprofit organizations. What are the issues raised in thes stories? What tone do they have? Do they reflect positively or negativel on the organizations identified?

◆ NOTES

1. Susan A. MacManus (1992). *Doing business with government.* New York: Paragon Hous

2. Jerry Mechling (1994, August). Reinventing technology procurement. *Governing Mage zine, 7*(11), 76.

3. Kelman, Steven (1990). *Procurement and public management.* Washington, DC: AEI Pres

4. American Bar Association (1986, April). *The model procurement code for state and loc governments* (3rd ed.). Washington, DC: American Bar Association, p. 1.

5. J. Richard Aronson and Eli Schwartz (Eds.). (1987). *Management policies in local government finance* (3rd ed.). Washington, DC: International City Management Association, pp. 37-40.

6. Harold E. Fearon and William A. Bales (1995). *Purchasing of nontraditional goods and services.* Tempe, AZ: Center for Advanced Purchasing Studies.

7. National Academy of Public Administration (1989). *Privatization: The challenge to public management,* 34.

8. Dave Neuman and Paul M. Carren (1976, January). Public purchasing: Principles and recommended practices. *Management Controls, 23,* 12.

9. MacManus, p. 73.

10. MacManus, p. 42.

11. American Bar Association, pp. 21-22.

12. Kelman, p. 89.

13. See John Vogt and Lisa A. Cole (1983). *A guide to municipal leasing.* Chicago: Municipal Finance Officers, for many of the comments included in this section.

14. Charles K. Coe (1981, September/October). Life cycle costing by state governments. *Public Administration Review, 41*(5), 564-568.

15. Lisa M. Ellram (1994). *Total cost modeling in purchasing.* Tempe, AZ: Center for Advanced Purchasing Studies.

16. M. Robert Seldon (1979). *Life cycle costing.* Boulder, CO: Westview Press, p. 3.

17. Seldon, p. 566.

18. Robert Caro (1983). *The years of Lyndon Johnson: The path to power.* New York: Knopf.

19. American Bar Association, p. 70.

SUGGESTED READINGS ◆

American Bar Association (1986). *The model procurement code for state and local governments* (3rd ed.). Washington, DC: American Bar Association.

David Neuman and Paul M. Carren (1976, January/February). Public purchasing: Principles and recommended practices. *Management Controls, 23,* 8-13.

11

Cash Management

C ash management means regulating the flow of money into and out of a public organization to benefit its financial position. The purposes of cash management include bringing political and financial advantages to a public organization. The political advantage is public appreciation of a capable organization paying and collecting monies in an appropriate fashion. Traditionally, the overriding focus of cash management has been on the financial advantages, which have principally been seen as the investment income possible. Managing cash flow makes money available for short-term investment. Investment return can be calculated or measured in a variety of ways, the following being one of the easiest to use:

Investment Return = approximately $.03
    (precisely .0278) per day per interest rate point per $1,000 invested
$.03 x 2 days x 10% x $10,000 = $6.00

Less noticeable, but no less real in the final analysis, are decreased costs made possible by cash management. Possible decreased costs are decreased prices of purchases, decreased costs of borrowing, lower financial service costs, and fewer costs in handling money. Purchases can be made less costly by timing them relative to necessity and cash availability, by avoiding interest charges for late payments, and by taking discounts for early payment. Borrowing costs can be reduced by reducing the amount and time period. Reduced financial service costs are possible by thoroughly reviewing them and either reducing the services obtained or securing more competitive pricing of financial services. Finally, costs in handling money can be minimized. Each of these advantages is discussed in more detail later.

Investment income makes a bigger budget splash than any of the decreased cost advantages of cash management because investment appears as a source of revenue and because costs are buried in the details of an organization's financial systems. Nonetheless, cost savings contribute to positive cash balances and are more valuable than investment income in many cases. Also, investing cash balances can become habitual and cause a political backlash when balances are high. During the Proposition 13 tax revolt in California, the state treasury held more than five billion dollars. Also, looking at cash balances for investing can lead officials to forget that a public organization and its constituents should be seen as a totality. Cash can be managed in two parts. First, a pattern of cash flows (i.e., movement of money into and out of an organization) is created, either haphazardly or as a matter of design. Ideally, the pattern represents a designed comprehensive cash management system with rules of procedure. In some cases, an organization may have to operate separate cash management systems for separate accounting funds because of restrictions applicable to specific funds. Second, an organization operates a designed cash management system.

SYSTEM DESIGN ◆

The time value of money, the key to financial analysis of cash management, can be described best by the expression, "There is no such thing as idle cash."[1] Someone is always using cash. Cash not used by a public organization is being used by someone else. When a public organization holds checks from others or has money in a noninterest-bearing checking account, then some financial institution is using the money. Actually, until the 1970s, it was common to find public organizations blithely using noninterest-bearing checking accounts with balances in excess of a million dollars. The investment return on a million dollars is $10,000 per year for each point of an interest rate.

Over the past two decades, the availability of diverse financial services and investment vehicles has contributed to an environment in which public organizations can benefit from the time value of money. The financial purpose of a cash management system is to maximize the positive time value of money and minimize the negative time value of borrowed money under the constraint of the costs involved in seeking these ends. Two limitations on securing positive time value exist. First, a public organization should not look to secure positive time value at the expense of its constituents. Collecting from and disbursing to constituents themselves should not be manipulated principally to make investments. Second, we should not be so blinded by the positive time value of money that we fail to see whether costs involved in achieving an investment yield exceed the value of that yield. For example, failure to make timely payment of bills can result in interest charges or late penalties. The cost of such charges or penalties can exceed the value of investing the same amount of money.

Analyzing Cash Flow

System design begins with discovering the existing patterns of cash flows into and out of an organization based on accounting records by creating models that represent cash flows on an estimated base from past information. To track revenue flows, we examine revenues for source or measure, amounts, and dates. Also, we can review associated factors that affect revenue flows (e.g., billing date, payment date, and economic factors). The revenue flow is the first place to analyze: All other balances and flows depend on revenues. After reviewing revenue flows, we can construct a model (i.e., a pattern, of revenue flows by time periods showing how much revenue of various kind was received when). A revenue flow model shows revenue flows into a public organization on a daily, weekly, or monthly basis. Larger organizations use smaller time scales because larger amounts of money are involved. We can simply use a prior year example, if it is representative of earlier years and stable, but that is risky; two or more years are preferable. A pattern of revenue flows usually shows regular and irregular sharp peaks and low valleys. Most public organizations receive large portions of their tax and interorganizational transfer revenues on a yearly, semiannual, quarterly, or monthly basis. The regular peaks are usually monthly or quarterly revenue collections; the irregular peaks are the yearly and semiannual revenues; and the valleys are composed of revenues that flow more steadily, mostly quid pro quo payments. Even where peaks and valleys are regular, explainable differences occur (e.g., sales taxes higher around the Christmas season). Some revenue sources are simply erratic (e.g., gift and death taxes).

The second aspect to model is expenditures or disbursements. Disbursements are tracked by amount and date. Also, we can review related factors such as terms of payment, payment cycles, and expenditure type. A model based on prior years of information shows a pattern of irregular and regular peaks and valleys. The regular peaks are employee payment dates and regular vendor payment dates. The irregular peaks reflect unusual events less often and mostly are yearly or semiannual payments, which include interorganizational transfers, debt, capital expenditures, yearly billed services, and unusual events.

The third aspect to model are the balances held by a public organization. Even though they are frequently referred to as cash balances, technically balances are the sum of liquid assets, including both cash and short-term investments. Revenue and expenditure flows, along with previously held liquid assets, determine the levels of the balances. Liquid assets are increased by revenues and decreased by disbursements. In modeling balances, we track the two parts and the total. First, cash is cash in hand or in checking accounts. Second, short-term investments have an investment period of less than a year and many can be sold in a short period of time to other investors. The two amounts can be tracked for one or more years to create a model of balances and their two component parts.

The total balance at any point shows how much money is available to make payments and invest. Both parts can be evaluated by whether their relative shares of the total are appropriate. For cash on hand, the question is whether cash on hand suffices to make payments. Not enough cash means costs occur. Too much cash means not enough is invested. These questions can be answered after a simple or complex analysis of the components of balances. The simple analysis involves looking at the amounts and making a judgment about whether a pattern looks reasonable. If cash management has not been done systematically, relatively large amounts of cash on hand are probable. Money in an interest-bearing account can be counted as invested. A more complex analysis of the balances includes costing out all features of the cash flow patterns: financial services, investment returns, and decreased costs. More complex analysis is justified as amounts of money, time periods, and apparent deviations from a favorable pattern increase. Ten to 15 million dollars in noninterest-bearing accounts for a year is an ample clue that the balances might be handled better.

Improving Cash Flow

Ways to improve cash flows and balances can be explored after the existing pattern of cash flows and balances has been analyzed. Improving cash flows usually involves speeding up revenues, slowing down cash expenditures, and maximizing the use of balances, principally through investments after decreased cost opportunities have been maximized.

Revenues

Revenues can be accelerated in a variety of ways to get money into financial accounts for use or investment. First, the date or dates on which payments are due to a public organization can be moved up. Obviously, this practice has limits; next year's taxes cannot be collected this year. Changes can involve going to an increased number of payment dates to acquire some of the revenue earlier, but the costs of handling more payments have to be considered. Another possibility is to move a payment date from the 15th to the 1st of a month. One point to remember in changing cash flows is that advantages for one party are costs to another party. Aside from cash management efforts, moving payment dates has tended to be used as a quick fix in budget crises where a solution to expenditures exceeding balances is to move revenues from one period to an earlier period; the equivalent expenditure adjustment is to move expenditures from a current period to a later one.

Second, it may be possible to move up the date of billing or notification of payments. Earlier billing or notification generates some earlier payments.

Third, incentives for early payment and disincentives for late payment improve revenue flows. Many public utilities offer a small discount for prompt payment that also reduces rates of nonpayment. On the other side, late payment penalties as well as interest charges discourage late payments. Penalties and interest charges have to be sufficiently high to make payments to a public organization more attractive than other uses of the same money. Other methods principally used by public utilities are reports to credit bureaus and the use of collection agencies.

Fourth, early collection can be accomplished in a variety of ways. Two examples are on-the-spot acceptance of money and electronic fund transfers. A grant recipient accepting $10 million in person to save 3 days in the mail can earn more than $8,000 in interest income at 10%. Incurring costs to secure large payments is worthwhile. Generally, a messenger or agent collects the money as a check and takes it to a financial institution for deposit in a special account, and the deposit is then transmitted to the organization's main financial institution. In some cases, payments of grants or shared revenues are made by electronic fund transfer. Some states accept electronic fund transfers for tax payments; two require certain payments in that fashion. Indiana requires large corporate taxpayers—those remitting more than $10,000 monthly— to pay this way. Washington requires large companies to do so for motor vehicle fuel taxes.[2] Electronic fund transfers are the preferred method of speeding up payments because they are relatively cheap and produce a record of the transaction by an independent organization.

Fifth, faster processing of revenue money is useful. It was no joke when a high-ranking official in the U.S. General Services Administration was fired for holding a $50,000 check for six months. Three methods of faster processing are a lockbox system, streamlined processing, and systematic depositing. Deposit of money in the form of checks, currency, or credit card charges, which are likely to increase in use, into a public organization's accounts more quickly increases balances.

A lockbox system uses another organization to process payments. The payments are made directly or through the mails to a lockbox organization which rapidly deposits the payments to an account of the public organization, makes a record of payments and deposits, and forwards such records and any other appropriate paperwork to the public organization involved. A lockbox system usually involves a financial institution that can make deposits on its own premises. Of course, lockbox systems involve costs, as other organizations do not ordinarily provide services for free. Lockbox systems are appropriate where other organizations can process deposits cheaply and where mailing time can be reduced. For example, some utilities use stores and financial institutions to collect direct payments of utility bills.

Streamlining the process of payments as handled by a public organization means that payments are moved quickly into a public organization's accounts in the course of revenue administration. In practice, this means identifying payments as soon as possible and eliminating all but absolutely necessary activities between physical possession of money and deposit. Payment envelopes supplied by public organizations and external indications of whether an income tax return envelope involves a payment or a request for a refund are two examples of identifying payments. The necessary steps between physical possession and deposit are usually opening envelopes; recording payments; associating payments with other paperwork, which are usually forms for computing tax liability before separating payments and forms; endorsing payments for deposit; filling out deposit forms; and physically transporting deposits to a financial institution. As several of these steps are interrelated, it is possible to pursue them at the same time with appropriate technologies. For example, a computerized record of a payment can be used to associate a payment with tax liability forms and to fill out deposit forms, as well as merely record the payment. How sophisticated and expensive a processing system should be depends on the amount of money being processed. Less sophisticated technologies, such as payment envelopes and electric letter openers, can be as helpful as the more sophisticated ones and generally cost less. Large volume is a prerequisite of automating revenue administration for cash management purposes. Also, automation provides a better record of actual flows and a database for projecting future revenue totals and revenue flows.

Determining when making a deposit is worthwhile requires comparing the ain from a deposit and its costs. Two kinds of deposit situations occur, regular nd irregular. First, regular deposits are typically made daily, weekly, or on ome other periodic basis. Where revenue flows are regular, deposit periods an be set easily. Sometimes, periodic deposits are used only to facilitate ayments. Second, irregular deposits can be made when a sufficiently large mount is on hand so that the gain from making a deposit exceeds the cost of oing so. The value of deposits can be computed using the simple formula iven at the beginning of this chapter. Although this appears obvious, care in iis area can lead to great benefits. For example, the City of Seattle gained $1.8 iillion yearly by making its regular daily deposit in the mid-afternoon rather 1an the morning; this earned them an extra day's interest on every deposit.[3]

Expenditures

Expenditures are regulated to increase balances and to reduce costs. First, xpenditure controls, including apportionment, allotment, and special ap- roval, can be used to track and to brake unnecessarily early payments. Three articularly useful expenditure controls for this purpose are oversight of eimbursement payments, apportionment, and prohibition of unseasonable urchases. Where one public organization is reimbursing another, review of roper documentation and periodic field audits of records can be appropriate. 1 some cases, state and local officials have claimed reimbursements some- ʻhat earlier than appropriate from federal agencies because of differing ccounting practices. For that reason, some federal agencies have become articularly sensitive to monitoring reimbursements and advance cash claims. t the same time, state and local officials are correct when they argue that their overnments have to finance federally supported activities when they have to ʻait for reimbursements or disbursements. Cash management is a zero-sum ame; one party's gain is always another party's loss.

Apportionment is wonderful for cash management; it increases the amount nd the certainty of balances. Prohibition or avoidance of unseasonal expen- itures also helps. Unseasonal expenditures occur when something purchased annot be used because of the time of the year (e.g., air conditioners in winter ionths). Avoidance of unseasonal expenditures is facilitated by a centralized urchasing process, special clearances, and apportionment. In some cases, owever, unseasonal purchases can be preferable if a vendor is willing to rovide price discounts. In such cases, it is best to compute and compare the ost of the alternatives.

A second method of slowing expenditures is delaying discretionary pay- 1ents to later dates (e.g., grant payments, gifts, or shared revenues). The same ffect can be achieved by changing the terms of grant program payments from dvances to reimbursements or generally tinkering with the payment eligibil- y rules to slow the rate of payments. This can have practical or political ffects.

A third method is to use periodic payment dates which can also reduce rocessing costs. Two prime areas involve vendors and employees. For vendor ayments, having predesignated payment dates once a week or once or twice a month avoids the need to make payments on other days. When this type of policy is followed, vendors appreciate notification so that they can meet price paperwork deadlines to be paid. In dealing with vendors and periodic payment dates, two costly practices to avoid are delaying payments excessively and failing to take early payment discounts. Delaying payments discourages vendors from selling to a public organization, which can increase expenditure costs by lessening the number of suppliers or by encouraging vendors to impose late payment charges, whether explicitly in contracts or implicitly in the price of the products. Putting off vendors initially appears to be very fruitful until their ability to set prices is observed.

Early payment discounts can reduce costs. The benefits of early payment discounts depend on the effective rate of return, which is a function of the face rate and the time periods involved, the amounts of money involved, and the cost of speeding up payments. Generally, the effective rate of return on early payment discounts exceeds any other use of money. For example, a 1% discount for payment within 10 days of billing, which speeds up the payment date by 20 days, provides an effective rate of return of 18% per annum. A computational formula is

Effective Rate per Annum = Face Value of Rate x 360 day year/
    Days payment is earlier

For example,

Effective Rate = 2% x 360/10 days = .02 x 36 = .72 or 72%

An increase in the period of time that a payment is made early decreases the effective rate. Higher rates of return for discounts can be less valuable than the costs of processing early payments. Two areas matter here—the dollar value of the early payment and the actual processing costs of early payments. The first area, the dollar value of early payment, depends on the effective rate calculated previously, and the dollar amount of the bill.

Effective Rate x Amount = Value of Early Payment

Another area of concern is the cost of processing early payments. In many local governments, no payments can be made until after the actual bill has been presented to the governing body and received its approval. The costs of early processing include identifying discount opportunities and running them through an expenditure control and disbursement system as individual items, which is more costly than treating them as routine items. The calculations of dollar values in both areas can be compared to determine when early payments are appropriate.

Employee payment periods should be standard and as long as feasible. Personnel concerns matter. Certain employee groups can be paid on a monthly basis without problems. Other employee groups have problems with anything beyond a two-week payment cycle because of a lesser ability to manage personal finances. The longer time between payment dates, the longer money is available to a public organization. The standardization of payment periods into one or two primary payment cycles is useful in increasing the predictability of payment amounts, increasing the time availability of money, and, perhaps, reducing payroll processing costs.

A fourth expenditure flow device is *playing the float.* The float refers to the time between when a payment is issued and when money is paid out of an issuer's financial account. The basic play is to make payments that exceed the amount of money in an account with the expectation that the issuer can correctly predict when money is required in accounts to make payments. Money held from accounts is invested.

This practice has diminished in recent years as the float period has diminished and financial accounts from which payments are made became interest-bearing. The float period for payments consists of three time periods: in the mails, in the hands of payees, and in the hands of one financial institution that seeks payment from the financial institution on which the payment is drawn. The last was the longest until financial institutions began using automatic clearinghouse and electronic fund transfers, which reduce the time involved from more than a week to overnight. A generally increased awareness of the time value of money has diminished the time vendors and other payees hold payments. Payments are in the mail for only a few days, despite the many jokes about the postal system. Also, the advent of interest-bearing checking accounts diminished the value of playing the float because there was less financial incentive to move money in and out of payment accounts. The primary use of the float notion now is to make payments at the end of a week to maximize the time of the float by forcing payees and financial institutions to hold payments over weekends.

Handling Money

Handling money involves keeping money available to make payments and investing the rest of the balances. The costs of financial services, discussed in the next section, affect this.

Generally, money available to make payments can be conceptually divided into two parts: the predicted current-period expenditures and a reserve amount to deal with unplanned events. Also, money can be borrowed to make payments when balances and ordinary revenues are overtaken by expenditures or when a short-term loan costs less than the loss of income from an investment. The reserve amount depends on the size and stability of a cash flow, the value of investment opportunity, and the costs of moving money between investments and financial accounts. Generally, the costs of moving money can be compared with the predicted value of investment returns.

Although we discuss investing systematically in the following chapter, a few brief comments on investing cash flows highlight cash management concerns. First, if there are no legal restrictions, public money should be deposited in interest-bearing accounts. Formerly, a financial institution would provide "free" services to the public organization in return for noninterest-bearing deposits. Second, safe handling of cash flow monies requires that they be handled with an aversion to risk taking, which means following the maxim "Do not gamble with public funds."[4] Cash flow money pays bills, and predicting investment market swings is gambling when you are engaging in short-term investments. In the City of San Jose, the former employees responsible for cash management invested large amounts of money in multiple-year bonds with the expectation that the market would move favorably and make the city lots of money. The market swung the other way and cost the city $60 million. The time periods of investments for cash flow purposes should be no longer than the approximate time period the money is available for investment. With so many investment possibilities, even considering extensive legal restrictions, matching time periods is not difficult. Third, state-managed investment pools are ideal for smaller local subdivisions, where they are available. Fourth, larger amounts and longer periods of investments usually provide higher rates of return. Fifth, investment income must be distributed properly to each accounting fund from which money has been invested. The easy way involves an investment fund to account for investments for which a periodic, usually daily, rate of return is calculated. The amount of return for other funds is the amount in the investment fund multiplied by the rate of return for every period.

In handling money, three things to remember are real effects, transaction costs, and the advantages of pooling. *Real effects* means that the effects of transactions are traced through to their conclusion. A common practice in some local governments is to make "no-cost" loans between funds. One fund "loans" money to another fund for a period of time and is repaid the same amount. The real effect is not a no-cost loan. The real effect includes a shifting of value between funds, the time value of money, and a net gain or loss for the local government. One fund receives a benefit at the expense of another, which can be technically illegal and in violation of a basic principle of fund accounting. Also, depending on other factors, the government can have a net gain or loss. Large no-cost loans lead to net losses in cases where the government could have borrowed the money for one fund at a lower rate than it could obtain as an investment rate.

Transaction costs are the costs incurred in handling money, whether depositing money, investing it, or making payments. The amount of transaction costs affects the pattern of handling money. Increased transaction costs can offset or exceed money handling meant to create advantages. Two rules of thumb help in this area. First, the larger the transaction, the less important the transaction cost. Second, the larger the number of transactions, the larger the transaction costs.

The advantages of pooling are related to costs, selection of financial service providers, and availability of favorable rates. *Pooling* means bringing as many common transactions together as possible. Pooling provides advantages in checking accounts, investments, and debt by lowering the transaction costs to the public organization and service providers, which makes it possible for service providers to provide better rates to the public organization involved.

Financial Services

In many cases, the costs of financial services provide the key to deciding the precise pattern of handling money. Though financial services could include services for every topic in this text, financial services relevant to cash management are performed primarily by financial institutions, which maintain accounts for customers.[5] Such institutions frequently provide advice in this area. Services are associated with checking, short-term investment, and short-term debt accounts. For example, checking accounts involve deposits, which can include revenue collection or messenger services; payments, which can include wire transfers; and records for such accounts. Also, related data-processing services include payroll processing, accounting, and account reconciliation. Financial institutions can even provide an overall cash management service. The precise character of such services varies greatly.

At one time, financial institutions frequently provided services in return for public organizations depositing money in an account. That practice has faded as financial services became deregulated and as public organizations figured out that they were better off doing their own investing.

The only way to know the true costs of financial services is to measure all the costs and compare the available alternatives. This can be as simple as comparing the rate of returns on checking accounts. In many cases, a simple choice can mislead us because financial institutions provide a variety of other services, some of which can be priced relative to checking account services. For many rural local governments with only one financial institution in their territorial jurisdiction, a simple choice can be the only choice because the chance of using a nonlocal financial institution is zero. Other public organizations can choose from two or more financial institutions. Also, even the small, rural local governments may be able to obtain one or more financial services on a competitive basis (e.g., long-term debt).

Financial services can be seen as purchasing situations, which are preferably handled on a bid or pricing basis. Aside from situations with political biases, which include states spreading their deposits into a large number of depositories and local governments staying with local institutions, financial services can be handled on a purchasing basis. Services can be bundled together or separated for a competitive or negotiated bid process, or prices can be obtained and the best choices made based on cost analysis. Generally, minimizing the number of financial institutions used as depositories or for services cuts operating costs. More institutions, unless there is a monetary advantage, increase the costs of handling money for keeping track of and moving money. The exception is a financial service that can be purchased on a stand-alone basis (e.g., debt or investment accounts, or where there is a possibility of exposing the public organization to a loss from the failure of one or more financial institutions). Deposit insurance issued by federal and state agencies covers deposits to a certain amount in federally and state-chartered regulated institutions. Deposits beyond insured limits are at risk unless some further form of security exists.

Security can be found in the practice of *collateralization.* It can be a lega requirement imposed on financial institutions or on governments, or set u as a prudent measure by a public organization to protect its assets. Collater alization means a financial institution puts up collateral for a deposit highe than any insured level by giving the legal right of ownership of the collatera to another party under certain conditions. Collateral is usually in the form c federal government-issued securities. If collateralized deposits cannot b made available to a public organization, the organization has the legal righ to take possession of the collateral. Collateralization has costs but is preferabl to exposing a public organization to the risk of losing money. Collateralizatio: failed many public organizations in the 1980s, when they did not undertak all of the legally required steps to secure the collateral.

One area of concern in choosing among competing financial service op tions is legal restrictions. Principally, such legal restrictions have been prom ulgated by states upon themselves and, even more so, their legal subdivisions The more common legal restrictions include what a legal depository of publi funds is, what a legal investment is, collateralization of deposits, unusua payment devices or procedures, and debt. Generally, banks are legal deposi tories of public funds. In some places, credit unions, savings and loan institu tions, investment banks, and insurance companies are not legal depositorie for state and local governments. If an organization is not a legal depository, person responsible for depositing money in that organization is liable for an resulting loss. Even where they are not legal depositories, however, it may b possible to purchase financial services from such institutions. Even so, th legal depository restriction limits the number of financial institutions avail able to some state and local governments. Some states have relaxed depositor laws in reaction to deregulation of financial services.

What investments are legally available affects cash management for han dling money and possible investment returns. The tendency in state law appears to be toward safe or local investments, both of which tend to provid less in the way of yields. State have relaxed laws in this area to some degree t account for new forms of investments.

Unusual payment devices or procedures requiring unique treatment o public organization payments increase the costs of checking services. Suc: costs can be minimized by a legal agreement whereby a government agrees t avoid conditions requiring such practices or to pay extra when those practice become necessary. For example, rather than treating warrants discussed in th expenditure administration chapter as warrants and charging extra for th extra processing, warrants can be treated as checks with a government main taining an agreed-on adequate balance in the account, making adequate credi arrangements, or making some other provisions to deal with cases wher warrants are not treated as checks (e.g., a service charge for every warran exceeding the available deposit balance and any credit balance).

Laws affecting debt are discussed in a following chapter. The principal lega cash management issues with debt are what debt can be used for, what form it can be issued in, and what can be done with the proceeds. Debt may not b legally authorized to assist in cash flow. Debt can be restricted to being issue in certain forms and not others. Finally, subject to federal income tax laws an elevant state laws, state and local debt proceeds may or may not be favorable nvestments.

Laws prohibit or restrict many financial services. Although this can be rustrating, policymakers have reasons for the high level of legal regulation of governmental use of financial services. The motive is to protect the public rom risky financial practices that have caused problems in the past.

Reviewing a cash management system periodically maintains its utility. Also, a system can be reviewed when changes in laws, flows, or financial practices occur.

SYSTEM OPERATIONS ◆

The primary activities in operating a system of cash management are orecasting, monitoring, regulating flows of money into and out of the organization, and investing. Ordinarily, public organizations forecast how much money they expect to have at the end of a fiscal period. Starting at the beginning of a fiscal year and considering budgetary figures along with relevant historical data and system characteristics, a cash manager forecasts the flows and balances rom revenues, expenditures, and the beginning balances for the fiscal year for monthly, weekly, or shorter time periods. Large amounts of money increase he value of forecasting precision and shorter time periods.

The majority of revenue and expenditure flows are generally predictable. Unless information to the contrary exists, revenue and expenditures for each ime period can be assumed to be evenly distributed. A cash flow forecast hows balances and flows at the beginning and end of time periods. Though upported by much more detail, a cash flow forecast looks like this:

Beginning of Year Balance: $10,000

First-Month Flows:
Revenues: + $30,000
Expenditures: - $10,000 =
Balance after one month: $30,000 (This balance is the ending balance for the first month and the beginning balance for the second month.)

Second-Month Flows:
Revenues: + $5,000
Expenditures: - $15,000 =
Balance after two months: $20,000

The pattern is completed for the entire fiscal year. The resulting balance figures are the general focus thereafter.

The balance minus a minimum reserve amount is the amount generally available for investment. The period of investments depends on how long how much money is available. Investment planning mostly involves comparing alternatives by calculating investment yields and costs. Also, the strong of spirit can forecast patterns of yields on investments into the future or rely on someone else's forecasts. The advent of interest-bearing checking accounts reduced the monetary advantages of investing, however, because checking accounts provide a low-cost yield with little to no risk. The real value of any other investment is the rate difference between it and the checking account rate multiplied by the amount of time and money involved minus the transaction costs. For example, a $10,000 investment for 90 days at a rate of 2% higher than a checking account rate yields approximately $50 more than the return available from keeping the money in a checking account before any transaction costs are taken into account.

During the fiscal year, those responsible for cash management monitor flow and balance forecasts, available investment alternatives, and related events to regulate a cash management system if necessary. Ordinarily, forecasts of flows and balances deviate to some degree from the forecast. If the deviations are minor, forecasts can be considered correct for practical purposes, and no or small regulatory actions are taken. If the forecasts are off significantly, taking action becomes necessary. If revenues have increased or expenditures have decreased, higher balances are invested. If lower revenues or higher expenditures occur, likely adjustments include reducing short-term investments, clamping down on expenditures, or borrowing for a short period. Planned investments can be abandoned in favor of previously inferior alternatives. Real events provide the earliest indicators of the need to change from a plan. Obvious examples of real events include the downturn of a major industry or a significant natural disaster. Depending on the public organization, different less catastrophic events are predictable precursors of cash flow changes. For example, organizations using sizable amounts of energy to operate find their cash flows change with temperature patterns. Also, monitoring helps to expose possibilities for improving a cash management system.

If the monitoring shows no major deviations in flows, balances, investment alternatives, or predictive events, cash managers continue praying. If monitoring reveals significant changes from the forecast, cash managers make choices to regulate flows. Generally, regulation is aided by larger contingency reserves, investment hedging by investing a portion of an entity's money in short-term investments that can be easily sold without a loss, and credit arrangements with financial institutions. These provisions as fundamental parts of a comprehensive cash management system make its regulation simpler and more advantageous. Each provision also has costs, however.

In regulating cash flows, altering basic features is tempting. The most common change is not paying vendors, though not paying employees and moving up the collection dates of revenue measures are not unheard of. Such changes are generally counterproductive and inappropriate from a technical viewpoint and generally reflect budget and political problems affecting cash flows. Cash management systems can be changed for political or budgetary reasons or for technical reasons. The regulatory phase of cash management is not the time to tinker with a system, though the existence of the need for regulation can provide some insight into possible system changes.

Operating a cash management system requires that everyone does what they are supposed to do. Despite many laws and regulations on the subject, the General Accounting Office regularly finds federal officials making pay-

1ents too late or too early, holding checks, failing to charge interest on late
ayments, and failing to pursue collection of money owed.

CONCLUSION ◆

Cash management can range in utility from helping to meet payment
eadlines to providing a little more revenue, to providing a little more in the
·ay of services, and to being a significant source of revenue for a public
rganization. Its use depends on the amounts of cash available to manage. The
mallest public organization can collect and pay money in a timely fashion.
1edium-sized public organizations can benefit from following a principles
pproach, that is, acting on the basic principle that no cash is truly idle and
ccelerating revenues and braking expenditures within prudent boundaries.
arge organizations can use a systematic approach and secure advantages by
irtue of the sheer volume of cash movements in their cash management
/stem. Cash management is another form of managing public organizations'
:sources.

DISCUSSION QUESTIONS

1. How much money should a public organization keep around? What
   other things affect how much money to keep around?

2. To what degree is attention to cash management likely to be sympto-
   matic of an organization's attention to financial management concerns?
   Of all the areas studied so far in your readings, is any other area more
   likely to reflect generally on financial management of an organization?

3. Under what conditions or circumstances would it be better for a whole
   organization to have a detailed cash management plan or to establish
   principles and have subunits develop more detailed plans?

4. What trade-offs exist when a governmental or nonprofit agency pursues
   an aggressive cash management program?

5. Contact two nonprofit agencies, one that largely depends on grants and
   donations and one that is largely funded through user fees. Compare
   and contrast their cash management practices. What major differences
   did you find? How did their revenue sources affect these practices?

6. Interview managers in two different local governments in your area. Ask
   them how they contract for banking services (e.g., sole source, competitive bid) and whether they use minimum compensating balances or
   direct fees to pay for these services. Compare and contrast the responses
   you receive with good purchasing and cash management practice.

7. What key factors should be considered in determining how sophisticated
   an organization should be in pursuing cash management programs?

◆ NOTES

1. This phrase was brought to the authors' attention by William Giovanni, a colleague and a astute practitioner of public finance administration.

2. Barry R. Burr (1988, January 4). Indiana requires electronic tax payments. *City and State* 5(1), 4.

3. Rodd Zolkos, (1987, September). Treasurer, Lloyd Hara, Seattle: Creating a model for th nation. *City and State, 4*(9), 19.

4. This phrase was brought to the authors' attention by William Giovanni.

5. Two sources that discuss all kinds of financial services with fundamentally differer approaches, including those also pertaining to the subject matter of other chapters, have bee published by the Governmental Finance Officers Association. Girard Miller (1984). *Selectir financial services for government,* (Chicago: Government Finance Offices of the United States an Canada), takes an overall approach to selection (e.g., pricing and formal agreements); an *Government Finance, 13*(1) speaks to particular services, such as external audits and depositorie

◆ SUGGESTED READINGS

Choose any one of the following, as most treatments of cash management ar local government-oriented and highly repetitive with respect to one anothe. All cover investment to some degree.

Haskin and Sells Government Services Group (1977). *Implementing effective cash management local government: A practical guide.* Chicago: Municipal Finance Officers Association.

Nathaniel B. Guild, Michael Clowes, William Deane, Peter F. Rousmaniere, and David A. Shepar Jr. (1981). *The public money manager's handbook.* Chicago: Crain Books.

Philip Rosenberg, C. Wayne Stallings, and Charles K. Coe (1987). *A treasury managemei handbook for small cities and other governmental units.* Chicago: Municipal Finance Office Association.

Investment Administration

The news stories in the 1990s sent shock waves through the public sector. Orange County, California, lost more than $1.7 billion because of speculative investments. Odessa College of Texas lost more than $28 million because of risky investment strategies. These stories highlight the importance and risks associated with public investment decisions. Public organizations at all levels have found that investing otherwise idle dollars can provide additional resources at a time when existing revenue sources fail to meet increasing demands for services.

Investing refers to using money to make money. Investment policies and practices by public agencies have become increasingly sophisticated and complex at the same time that the awareness of the importance of such practices has grown. Only a few years ago it was common for many state and local agencies to ignore investment strategies. Even federal agency personnel were lackadaisical about investment activities. This is no longer true. Almost all public official understand the importance of investment earnings to their organization's overall fiscal health.

This chapter explores investment as an important issue facing public mangers, factors affecting investment decisions, the types of investment instruments that are currently available, and the various administrative issues facing public agencies involved in investment of resources.

Failing to invest idle funds takes away the opportunity to increase the holdings of any public agency. Money has time value. It is worth more today than it will be tomorrow. For this reason, individuals and organizations pay a premium for the use of money. In normal times, the longer individuals use an agency's money, the more they will be willing to pay. This payment usually comes in the form of interest. When a public agency "invests" funds in an investment of some sort, it places money (often referred to as principal) at the disposal of others with the understanding that at some point in the future they will have those funds returned with a premium, interest. The public agency is responsible for getting the largest investment return that it can, while protecting the principal that is invested.

Most investment decisions are made in one of two situations: short-term and long-term. Short-term investing is concerned with investing idle cash that will be needed some time during the current fiscal year. This type of investment is most commonly associated with cash management where incoming revenue during a particular period exceeds outgoing expenditures. An example is a state government that collects sales tax revenues from vendors on a quarterly basis and finds that expenditures do not require using those dollars until the second month of that quarter. In this case, cash is available for investment for at least one month and perhaps longer. Another example is the investment of bond proceeds before the expenditure of those dollars.

Long-term investing deals with investment periods longer than a year. Long-term investments help reduce the burdens on future citizens by generating investment income for future use. Examples of this type of investment are trust and agency funds, endowment funds, sinking funds, and risk pool funds. These funds contain dollars that are held in guardianship by the public agency for some specified period until they are allocated back to those who are to benefit from that guardianship. The most common are pension plans into which an organization and its employees place money. Those dollars earn interest, which is used to pay pensions when employees retire or become eligible to withdraw those dollars. In these cases, the investment periods are much longer than under a traditional cash management situation.

Other examples of long-term investments are risk pool, sinking, and endowment funds. *Risk pool funds*, monies to pay for losses and liabilities from a combination of public agencies, are invested to gain interest while providing protection of principal. *Sinking funds* are funds set aside for a specific future use, especially capital expenditures. Examples are money set aside for the future purchase of a piece of equipment or repayment of a bond. While an organization is waiting to spend the money, it invests these funds. Finally, many public organizations receive endowments from private parties interested in supporting a particular activity of that organization. The endowment is not, in most cases, used to promote this activity directly; instead, the money is put in an endowment fund and invested, and the return earned on those investments is spent on the activities themselves. University foundations function in this way. Interest earned from endowments helps pay for faculty salaries or capital construction projects.

◆ FACTORS AFFECTING INVESTMENT POLICY

Investment decisions in the public sector are determined by legal, political, and financial factors. Each is important and cannot be ignored when developing investment policies and procedures.

Legal Factors

As with many decisions affecting public finances, agencies must first understand the legal constraints they face. Nowhere is this more true than in

ivestments. Federal, state, local, and nonprofit financial managers are re-
:ricted. The prime concern of policy officials is the safety of public invest-
1ents. Historically, this concern is based on the source of public dollars, the
ixpayer. There is a strong legal tradition that restricts the use of public funds
) investments that provide the greatest protection. Such restrictions are often
iirected toward types of depositories and investments that are considered
.sk-free, such as guaranteed certificates of deposit, and away from those that
ave higher degrees of risk. Even in cases where risks can be greatly reduced
1rough diverse investments, legal restrictions prohibit certain types of invest-
1ents to governmental investments. In other instances, restrictions are greater
)r states, and least on nonprofit organizations and federal government.
»espite increased flexibility, financial managers find that the federal and state
overnments' ability to obtain high rates of return is limited because of
onstitutional and statutory restrictions.

State and local governments can also face geographical restrictions on
'here they can invest their money. The Advisory Commission on Intergov-
rnmental Relations found some instances where cities had to invest their idle
ash in local lending institutions. It is not unusual to find laws that restrict
)cal government investments to state or locally related investments. In other
istances, restrictions may be based on a percentage of total investments.[1] A
:ate, for example, may be required to invest a certain percentage of its
ivestment dollars in state or local projects or securities. In other instances,
ollars may have to be invested in U.S.-based businesses. In previous years,
:ates, localities, and the governing boards of many universities have passed
1easures that restrict investments in firms doing business with South Africa.
uch restrictions make it more difficult for a public agency to receive the best
ite of return. Finally, state or local laws may require that investments be
)llateralized. This means that an investment must be guaranteed by another
:curity, often federal government securities. *Securities* refers to investments
1at are represented by a piece of paper signifying ownership; the piece of
aper "secures" ownership of an investment. Although this reduces some risk,
often leads to lower yields. This is common in states that require banks
suing certificates of deposit to public agencies to secure those deposits with
:deral securities.

Political Factors

Even if legal restrictions do not constrain a public agency, political factors
ften do. Many legal limitations are based on political concerns rather than
:onomic realities. Before the end of apartheid, divestitures in investments
:lated to South Africa were very visible. Although experts debate the exact
nancial impact of such a policy, most agree that it reduces investment
1come.

Local governments and nonprofit organizations face these and other po-
tical realities every day. When they consider investing short-term idle cash,
reat pressure exists to invest those dollars locally rather than in financial
istitutions outside the community. Those who argue for investment strate-
ies based on maximizing investment income with the least risk conflict with

those who argue for investment decisions based on social or political grounds. Recent attempts in many states to set aside a portion of pension investment for "social" purposes, such as state-based economic development or venture capital projects, have raised strong objections from financial managers, who fear reduced income and increased risk, and from pension fund beneficiaries. Such policies can also run counter to legal or historical views that see public dollars as resources that are held "in trust" by government for the employee (e.g., pension funds). In this view, investments should be selected to serve the prime beneficiaries, in this case, the employees. Investing for maximum return greatly restricts the use of certain investment vehicles that might otherwise be used to help stimulate local economies. Still, Michigan, Alabama, and others have moved in this direction. Such actions are more likely with general investments and less likely with pension funds, where employee groups can be expected to raise objections.

Financial Factors

Financial factors greatly affect investment decisions. The wide array of investment options and the highly technical nature of financial markets require increased sophistication by public agencies. The trend is toward more sophisticated investment techniques because of two factors. First, the investment markets have grown more complex. Choices exist today that were unheard of only a few years ago. Second, each basic investment type or instrument includes a wide variety of options that can change the character of the investment. All options must be reviewed for each investment instrument. As instruments become more plentiful and the complexity of those instruments increases, the ability to make proper decisions becomes more complex. At some point, an agency must decide whether its desire to increase investment income is worth the additional costs of hiring or contracting for the expertise necessary to keep abreast of changing investment instruments and markets.

◆ INVESTMENT CONCERNS

Investment decisions hinge on four concerns; risk, liquidity, yield, and size. They do not usually hinge on the flip of a coin or a roll of the dice. All four are interrelated and have many facets. Time is important as well. What follows is a brief description of each concern and the role it plays.

Risk

Investment risk refers to the anticipated possibility of loss. Miller lists three types of risk: (1) default risk, (2) market risk, and (3) liquidity risk.[2] Default risk refers to the possibility of a public agency losing all or a portion of its investment principal. "The risk of default is the probability that the issuer will be unable or unwilling to redeem an investment."[3]

TABLE 12.1 Hedging Strategies

Strategy	Process	Purpose
1. Long hedge	buy futures	lock in future yields to protect against falling yields of existing instruments
2. Short hedge	sell futures	lock in current yields against the chance of a rise in rates of funds to be borrowed later
3. Arbitrage	buy cash contract; sell or short a futures contract	increase yields
4. Spread	buy one futures contract; sell a different but related contract	increase yields

Market risk refers to the possibility of a loss resulting from choosing a relatively poor investment from among all available ones. The loss is the difference between a good choice and a bad one. The Orange County case discussed earlier provides an extreme case of market risk loss. Market risk occurs because of an inability to predict future market changes accurately. Incorrect predictions result in market losses, whereas correct ones result in investment managers being praised. Market loss occurs because of the choice of the time period or the type of investment. Market loss is guarded against by spreading investments among various choices, in other words, by diversification and hedging. The term *diversification* refers to using different types of investments, whereas the term *hedging* particularly refers to the investment strategy of using different time period investment options as well as any two options with opposite investment expectations. Hedging is like betting on both entrants in a two-horse race; there is no chance of large winnings or large losses.

Gerald Miller devised a short table explaining the use of hedging strategies (see Table 12.1).[4]

Derivatives have become closely associated with hedging strategies and market risk. Although they are presented as high-risk investments, they can actually reduce risk if handled properly. Derivatives are "government securities whose value is based on another security or index."[5] A governmental or nonprofit entity will invest in a "futures" fund of some type that will ensure a certain rate of return linked to the value of some underlying asset security or hard asset such as a stock. If that underlying asset increases in value, the rate of return increases as well. The danger occurs when investment managers use these securities to increase interest rate yields relative to market value of existing federal securities. Investing in futures funds that represent relatively stable assets, such as collateralized mortgage obligations, may have limited market risk. Investing in futures funds associated with more volatile assets increases risk substantially.

Finally, losses can occur because the dollars invested cannot be collected immediately even though those dollars are safe. This becomes a particular concern for short-term cash needs of public organizations. The need to turn longer-term investments into cash to meet a particular need can cause a loss of investment income because of early withdrawal penalties or actual principal loss when assets must be converted to cash (e.g., real estate or money borrowed until investments can be liquidated).

Investment instruments range greatly in default risk. U.S. government securities are assumed to be totally safe because they are backed by the full faith and credit of the federal government. The assumption is that if the federal government is unable to back up any of its securities, the loss to the public investors is the least of their problems because the federal government will have collapsed.

Other securities are considered riskier because those protecting investors' principal and interest are less able to do so. For example, if a corporation declares bankruptcy, investors lose at least some of their principal and interest. You can reduce some of the risk by investing only in corporations that appear very strong, but the risk is still higher than in government bonds, where bankruptcy is still unusual.

Finally, some individual investments have high degrees of risk. Investing in a new small business is an example of high risk because most fail within a few years.

Liquidity

Liquidity refers to how easily a security converts to cash. Investments range from high liquidity to low liquidity. For example, NOW accounts (Negotiable Order of Withdrawal) are very liquid types of investments, whereas investments in real estate and other commercial enterprises have low liquidity because it takes some time to convert an investment into cash.

Long-term debt investments have been made more liquid through the creation of secondary markets. A "secondary market" is a market for investors to buy and sell debt investments. If a public agency purchases a bond and wants to have the principal and some interest on that investment before the bond is scheduled to be repaid, the agency can sell it to someone else.

Investments are made with liquidation in mind, so that money becomes available when needed, and some of the investments can be liquidated, if necessary. Short-term investments are set for the time periods money is available, invested in instruments with secondary markets, or both, which usually means debt investments. Long-term investments are partially invested for appropriate time periods, usually bonds, and partially invested in relatively easily liquidated instruments, usually bonds and stocks. Short-term investments are much more time sensitive.

Yield

Yield indicates what return the investor receives over and above the amount of principal invested. This is also referred to as "rate of return" and "interest." Yield varies with other factors discussed in this section. In most cases, as risk increases, so does yield, and as liquidity increases, yield decreases. In other words, those investing are paid a higher amount if they are willing to assume greater risk that their principal will be lost and if they are willing to give up access to their principal for an extended period of time. This latter case is referred to as a "positive yield curve." Yield curves can be negative. This occurs when investors assume that long-term investments will produce lower returns than current short-term investments. Though relatively rare, situations can arise when demand for short-term investments is extremely high.[6]

Size

In most instances, rates of return will be directly affected by the size of the investment. The larger the investment, the fewer the number of transactions required, so savings can be made by both the investor and the seller of the investment. This allows the seller to pass along a portion of those savings to the investor in the form of a higher rate of return. In some cases, investment instruments may not be available below a certain dollar size because of transaction costs. Overnight investments, for example, may have to exceed $1 million.

We can see the high degree of interrelationship among these four factors. Public agencies must carefully weigh each to determine how to receive the highest yield with the lowest risks. Public agencies may have investments with a range of yields and risks. A diversified combination of investments is referred to as a *portfolio*. A portfolio should include a number of investments so that high yield and low overall risk can be maintained. As a general rule, risk is lowered and liquidity increased with short-term investments, whereas yield is increased with longer-term investments. Public investors must decide how important yield is relative to immediate access to their money.

INVESTMENT INSTRUMENTS ◆

The range of investments available to public agencies is enormous. Each has its own particular advantages and disadvantages. Investments can be divided into two groups, debt and equity. Equity approaches to investment focus on returns from ownership of an asset, whereas debt (sometimes referred to as fixed-income investments) is associated with future payment of loans by borrowers.[7] Debt investments are those where the basis is the legal ownership of promises of future payments by some entity that has borrowed money. Money is loaned or debt instruments purchased so that future payments can be obtained. Equity investments are those where the basis is the legal ownership of something. Equity investments are made to generate income or to sell at a later point in time when the investment has a higher price. Common debt investments are

- U.S. Treasury issues
- U.S. government agency securities
- U.S. government-sponsored corporate bonds

- Municipal bonds
- Bank and other financial institution debt
- Corporate securities
- Real estate mortgages
- Foreign government securities

Common equity investments include

- Common stock
- Preferred stock
- Mutual funds
- Convertible bonds
- Real estate investment
- Venture capital funds

We first focus on the myriad of debt investments available to public agencie and then turn our attention to the equity investments. It is important to not that the position of public agencies investing in debt of other public entitie puts those agencies in a position quite different from the one they face as a issuer of debt. When investing in debt instruments, the public agency acts a an owner of someone else's debt.

Debt Investments

Treasury Issues

The U.S. Treasury issues bills, notes, and bonds. A Treasury bill is a deb certificate issued by the U.S. Treasury for a certain period, with payment of specified amount at the end of the period. *T-bills,* as they are commonl referred to, represent short-term debt for periods from 13 to 52 weeks. Th minimum amount of debt that can be purchased is $10,000, with additiona amounts available in $5,000 increments.

Treasury notes and bonds are for longer periods. Notes represent obliga tions between 1 year and 10 years. Bonds represent obligations of 10 years t 30 years. Like T-bills, they are fully backed by the federal government.

Treasury bills, notes, and bonds are sold at auction on a weekly basis. T-bill are auctioned based on a "discount" value of the security. In other words, thos wanting to bid for a T-bill offer an amount for the purchase of the bill. Th difference between the purchase price and the face value of the bill represent the interest earned on the bill. For example, if a public agency bid is $97,05 for a $100,000 T-bill, the effective annual interest rate for a 91-day bill is 12%. For notes and bonds, bids are made in the form of specific rates of retur rather than for a discount value.

Public agencies can buy treasury issues through intermediaries such a banks or other financial institutions, or they can bid for them directly throug a U.S. Treasury auction. Interestingly, if the agency does not want to put in a individual bid, it can request what is known as a noncompetitive bid, which

ontractually commits the agency to pay the average price of competitive bids
or those securities. This is particularly useful for agencies that are buying
ecurities in small denominations or lack the expertise to bid competitively.
t should be noted that all Treasury securities have an active secondary market.
'his makes them more liquid, which increases their value to some extent.

Federal Agency Securities

Federal agency securities are issued by the Federal Financing Bank (FFB)
or various federal agencies, including the Import-Export Bank, the Farmer's
Iome Administration, the Small Business Administration, and the Govern-
1ent National Mortgage Association (referred to as Ginnie Mae). A great deal
f federal debt is issued through the FFB. These securities can be purchased
hrough intermediaries such as brokers, security dealers, fiscal agents, finan-
ial institutions, or through some type of financial syndicate that handles
1em. These debt securities vary in maturity but in all cases are guaranteed by
he federal government.

U.S. Government Corporation Securities

The federal government sponsored the creation of a multitude of corpora-
ions with quasi-public purposes. These corporations, although owing their
xistence to federal legislation, act independently of the federal government,
nd, in most instances, the debt they issue to finance their activities is not
ormally guaranteed by the federal government. Among the most common of
hese corporations are the Farm Credit System, the Federal Home Loan
Aortgage Corporation (Freddie Mac), the Federal National Mortgage Asso-
iation (Fannie Mae), and the U.S. Postal Service. Debts issued by these
orporations are of varying maturity and have an active secondary market.
'ields tend to be slightly higher for these securities because of the higher risk
ssociated with them.

Municipal Bonds

Municipal bonds are long-term debt issued to finance a wide range of
ublic works and other public-purpose activities at the state and local level,
vhich are discussed at length in Chapter 14. Most of these bonds are exempt
rom federal income taxation, as are federal securities, and carry a lower yield
han do taxable bonds. These securities tend to be less attractive to public
nvestors because they have no use for the tax advantages the bonds provide,
vhereas the tax advantages cause others to pay more for such investments than
hey otherwise would.

Financial Institution Debt

This category contains some of the most attractive short-term securities
ised by public agencies. Negotiable Order of Withdrawal accounts (known as
JOW accounts) may be the most common. These represent interest-bearing

checking accounts held by agencies. Perhaps the most popular are Certificates of Deposit (CDs). These debt instruments are issued by banks and other financial institutions in varying denominations with short-term fixed maturity dates. CDs can be negotiable or nonnegotiable. Negotiable CDs can be sold on a secondary market, whereas nonnegotiable CDs cannot. Nonnegotiable CDs are less attractive, unless they provide a higher rate of return to compensate for their lack of liquidity. CDs are popular because they provide competitive rates of return, they can be purchased through local financial institutions, and they are highly flexible and very safe. CDs offer flexibility in two ways. First, they can be issued for different lengths of time. Second, they can be issued for different dollar amounts. CDs also offer a high degree of safety. Amounts of less than $100,000 are guaranteed by the federal government if issued by a federally insured financial institution.

Repurchase agreements (REPOs) represent a financial tool that is often misunderstood. As described by the Government Finance Officers Association, a REPO consists of two simultaneous transactions. First, an investor purchases securities (collateral) from a bank or dealer. At the same time, the selling bank or dealer contractually agrees to repurchase the collateral security at the same price (plus interest) at some mutually agreed future date.[9]

REPOs are very attractive short-term investments because they provide considerable flexibility for short time periods and competitive rates of return. Risk should not be a major concern if the securities backing the REPO are verified and represent U.S. government guaranteed investments. Losses can occur with this type of investment, however, if the securities purchased are based on collateral that is less than the agreement calls for or, in the worst case, nonexistent. The recent loss incurred by municipalities in Iowa was caused by repurchase agreements where the collateral was not secured. Repurchase agreements are not legal or are highly regulated in several states because of their risk and questions about the ownership of the securities themselves.

Corporate Securities

Such diverse businesses as utilities, railroads, and major commercial businesses issue long-term debt in the form of corporate bonds to finance activities. The debt can be guaranteed through some form of collateral or simply by the good name of the company. Obviously the risk level for such debt varies dramatically, depending on the collateral pledged and the financial standing of the business. Because of this, corporate bonds pay a higher yield than do T-bonds.

Another form of corporate security is often called commercial paper and refers to short-term debt issued by corporations to cover cash flow or temporary operating shortfalls. This debt is attractive because of its flexibility, yield, and liquidity. Risk, as with corporate bonds, varies by the collateral and financial health of the issuing business. There is no secondary market for commercial paper, though some businesses will repurchase their own paper before maturity. This greatly increases the liquidity of the debt. As with

nunicipal and corporate bonds, commercial paper can be rated by one of the
nvestors services.

Real Estate Mortgages

Real estate mortgages have either a fixed interest rate over a long period of
me or variable interest rates over some extended period. Those who believe
nat interest rates may decline over the long term invest in fixed-rate real estate
nortgages. This is particularly true if those mortgages are guaranteed by the
ederal government, as is the case with those sold by the Government National
Mortgage Association.[10] Other nonguaranteed mortgages or mortgage funds
re also possible investment vehicles and can represent a more liquid invest-
nent than was true in the past because of the highly active secondary market
or such securities.

Foreign Government Securities

One of the highest risk forms of debt investment is in foreign government
ecurities. Of course, those from governments that appear stable and that
rovide attractive flexibility and yields might be considered. As many major
U.S. banks learned, debt issued by foreign countries can be a high-risk opera-
on, however, which many public agencies find legally and politically unac-
eptable

Equity Investments

Common Stock

By investing in publicly traded common stock, a public agency becomes a
artial owner of a corporation. This means that any profits earned by the
orporation are either paid to stockholders as dividends or reinvested in the
orporation, which tends to increase the value of the corporation's stock. The
ssumption often is that the stock will increase in value and be sold at some
uture time for a capital gain. It is also possible that no profit will be earned
nd that the stock will decrease in value. In this case, the public investor will
ave a net loss from the initial investment. The attractiveness of stocks or
onds depends on expectations concerning future inflation.[11] The key is to
uy at low prices and sell at high prices.

Preferred Stock

Preferred stock operates in a manner similar to common stock except that
ividends are fixed and have priority over common stock dividends. This
rovides some additional security to the public investor; however, it is likely
o earn less than common stock.

Convertible Bonds and
Convertible Preferred Stock

There are bonds and preferred stock that can be converted to common stock at some predetermined time and at a particular price. This option is attractive to investors because it adds flexibility and yield potential over and above that of common stock and yet provides additional security by having a preferential position over common stock should the corporation be faced with selling of assets.[12]

Real Estate

More and more public agencies are placing a portion of their long-term investment portfolio into real estate holdings. These represent income producing investments and tend to be highly speculative. Mississippi and California have recently moved in this direction. Many public investors believe this is a sound investment to hedge against inflationary pressures and to provide stable investments over the long run. The negatives include lack of liquidity and flexibility. Also, as with any equity investment, the danger exists of losing principal. Considerable expertise is required to ensure against major losses in this area.

Venture Capital Funds

One of the most recent investment strategies among state and local governments involves using long-term investment resources to help stimulate state or local economic development activity. One way to accomplish this is through equity investments in venture capital funds. These funds provide equity capital to start-up businesses with high profit potential. They also have a high potential for failure, and, therefore, the investor is counting on enough successes at a high level of profit to more than offset the losses from business failures. Risk is high for this type of investment; potential returns are also high. Liquidity is limited, and investment is based on issues other than strict economic return in most instances.

Money Market and Mutual Funds

In money market funds, you buy shares, known as *equity*, in a fund organized into a diverse portfolio. This is a less direct way to invest than by purchasing the investment directly from the agency or corporation. The underlying individual securities are usually highly varied, and investors depend on fund managers to diversify the fund in such a way as to provide strong rate of return while spreading the risk of securities so no major losses occur. Money market funds provide flexibility and liquidity with reasonable rates of return. The quality of mutual funds varies dramatically, however, and therefore, the rate of return and risk vary. Some mutual funds are high-risk ind focus on stocks; others are invested in guaranteed securities such as nunicipal bonds or government securities.[13]

States and localities may be limited in the types of investment instruments hey may use. Despite the stories like that of Orange County, most government igencies are conservative investors. A recent survey by Mattson, Hackbart, and Ramsey found that few states are allowed to invest in commercial paper (9), iff-shore deposits (16), or Eurodollar certificates of deposit.[14] When we look it actual investments by states, the overwhelming percentage of their portfoios are in debt investments: treasury bills, repurchase agreements, certificates if deposit, and U.S. Agency securities.[15] State statutes and preservation of :apital and liquidity are the driving investment forces for both states and ocalities.

Nonprofit agencies may have many fewer restrictions on investment approaches. For this reason, policy board oversight can be even more critical in ensuring fiduciary concerns are addressed.

INVESTMENT ADMINISTRATION ◆

Investment administration deals with the procedures necessary to implement he investment policies of the public organization. To achieve effective implenentation, the policies of the organization must be clearly articulated. These policies should specify the investment decisions, how decisions are made for he timing and location of the investments, and any other legal or adminis- rative requirements that should be included in any investment activity.

Goals, Objectives, and Strategies

Many investment goals, such as the "prudent man rule" standard discussed n Chapter 16 or the desire to maximize rates of return, may seem self-evident, iut this is not always true. For example, a public agency may find that "social nvestments" contradict the goal of maximizing rates of return because such eturns may be in areas that do not service social purposes.[16]

Many strategies depend on the goals and objectives of the organization. In he example of maximizing rate of return, numerous issues must be addressed, ncluding such things as

- The impact of inflation on appreciation
- Short-term versus long-term investments
- The relationship of liquidity needs to long-term investment rates of return
- Safety or risk of investment
- Form of investment

To some extent, strategies are based on expectations about the future. For xample, expected inflation rates (high rates lead to equity decisions, whereas ow inflation leads to debt investment decisions), but in other cases these trategies are based on legal constraints and policy goals.

Who Should Be Involved—
Internal Versus External Management

Many public agencies by law have separate boards or commissions to oversee investment decisions, particularly those affecting public-sector pension plans. Even where such boards exist, responsibility to implement investment policies rests with either top management and the staff specifically assigned to overseeing the investment process or outside investment brokers or managers hired specifically to oversee policy implementation.

According to Guild, there are advantages and disadvantages to both of the approaches to managing the investment portfolio of public organizations. Internal managers allow more direct control by the policymakers and closer communications.[17] Conversely, internal management can also lead to greater politicization of the investment process. In addition, insufficient staff expertise or organizational myopia can lead to reduced diversification of investments and increased risk. Finally, competent internal management can be very costly for small organizations.

External management allows a public organization to select the most competent and experienced investment expertise, and for small organizations it offers the opportunity to retain such expertise at a reduced cost. Hiring external management does not abrogate the responsibilities of the agency to oversee the implementation of their investment program. The reduced control that occurs with contracting out such a service can create problems for this reason.

Guidelines for Implementation Decisions

In implementing any investment program, the first step is to ensure adherence to legal requirements affecting investment decisions. This includes any limits on the distribution of investment monies among the various instruments that might be available. If legal limits exist on certain investments or if such investments are limited based on policy objectives (e.g., no more than 10% of investments can be placed in corporate bonds), this should be clearly enunciated in the written policy. Another limit is some specification of the quality of investment instruments. If, for example, a public agency wants to ensure that no corporate bonds below a certain grade are purchased, this should be expressed in writing. Other guidelines are maturity requirements, corporate stock to be given priority or to be divested, yield requirements, and the like. Virgil Moon, Finance Director of Cobb County, Georgia, highlighted several implementation rules:

- Stay away from investments you do not understand
- If you cannot describe the investment to your policy officials, stay away from it
- Avoid high-risk situations in credit, liquidity, or market risk
- Suitability of investments is as much the manager's responsibility as it is their financial consultant.[18]

Finally, internal controls protect the integrity of the investment process.

CONCLUSION ◆

This chapter has pointed to the wide variety of investment situations and actors facing public agencies. Both debt and equity investments can play a major role in increasing the financial position of governments and nonprofit organizations. The days when public dollars sat idle have largely disappeared and been replaced by aggressive investment programs at the state and local levels. When possible, public managers can improve their understanding of this rapidly changing field. They provide the direction and support to see that public funds are not only protected but also used to the full advantage of their organization. Sound investment strategies help achieve this objective.

DISCUSSION QUESTIONS

1. What constitutes good investment practice? What criteria should be used? What questions should be asked in designing an investment program?
2. What kinds of risks are the most important to governmental organizations? Do they vary among different types of governmental agencies? Are they different from those that exist for nonprofits? Why?
3. Interview finance managers in three different governmental or nonprofit agencies. Ask them if they have written investment policies and procedures. How do they differ?
4. Compare issues faced by managers purchasing investment services from those that exist for other types of services (e.g. bond underwriters, attorneys). What are the major differences? Similarities?

NOTES ◆

1. U.S. Advisory Commission on Intergovernmental Relations (1977). *Understanding state and local cash management.* Washington, DC: U.S. Government Printing Office.
2. Girard Miller (1986). *Investing public funds.* Washington, DC: Government Finance Officers Association, p. 41.
3. Girard Miller, p. 41.
4. Gerald Miller (1991). Investment managers and innovation. In *Government Financial Management Theory*, p. 155. New York: Marcel Dekker.
5. Rhett D. Harrell (1995, June). The soul of a cash management machine. *Governing Magazine*, p. 72
6. Miller, p. 119.
7. Miller, pp. 185-186.
8. Nathaniel B. Guild (Ed.). (1981). *The public money manager's handbook.* Chicago: Crain Books, pp. 191-194.
9. Municipal Finance Officers Association (1981). *A public investor's guide to money market instruments.* Washington, DC: Municipal Finance Officers Association, p. 43.
10. Miller, pp. 98-99.
11. Miller, pp. 308-310.
12. Miller, pp. 308-310.
13. Municipal Finance Officers Association, pp. 59-64.

14. Kyle Mattson, Merl Hackbart, and James R. Ramsey (1990, Winter). State and corporat cash management: A comparison. *Public Budgeting & Finance, 10*(4), 21-22.

15. Mattson, Hackbart, and Ramsey, pp. 21-22.

16. Guild, p. 195.

17. Guild, pp. 185-186.

◆   **SUGGESTED READINGS**

Girard Miller (1986). *Investing public funds.* Washington, DC: Government Finance Office Association.

Municipal Finance Officers Association (1981). *A public investor's guide to money market instru ments.* Washington, DC: Municipal Finance Officers Association.

John E. Peterson (1979). *State and local government pension fund investment.* Washington, DC Government Finance Research Center, Municipal Finance Officers Association.

Capital Budgeting

Capital budgeting refers to the efforts by public agencies to develop a financial plan of action directed at the funding of land, improvements, facilities, and equipment for use in the immediate, intermediate, and long-term future. According to Forrester, it is closely tied with many objectives of budgeting and financial management, including debt administration, assessing financial condition, and supporting economic development.[1] Budgeting for capital items is most often associated with longevity, high cost, and major impact. Items that have a useful life extending beyond a single year are considered to have longevity and are candidates for capital budgeting. Such items become fixed assets. Also, high-cost physical items that make a substantial impact on an annual budget if funded in any one year are candidates for capital budgeting. Finally, items expected to have a significant impact that are not easily changed are often included within a capital budget. Examples of capital items are all around us. Land, public buildings, large and expensive equipment, and public improvements, such as streets and sewers, are all items that should be included in a capital budget.

Costly items with a short useful life and low-cost items with a long useful life are often excluded from capital budgets. Thomassen noted that in states, for example, "human" and "intellectual" capital, research and development, training and education, and loans are all excluded from the capital and budgeting process.[2] Personnel costs can be quite large but do not represent permanent or semipermanent fixed assets to the organization. Correspondingly, typewriters or personal computers are not "consumed" within the first year of purchase; however, their cost can be readily absorbed into the annual operating budget rather than added to the capital budget.

The effort to carry out capital budgeting varies. Some extra effort can be exerted within the context of a regular operating budget. At the other extreme is a capital budgeting process, apart from the regular budget process, that produces a separate multiyear capital budget as a part of a larger process usually referred to as a Capital Improvement Program (CIP). The differences are the number of years involved, whether there is a separate budget, whether there is a separate budgeting process, and whether capital budgeting is done explicitly in the context of a broader planning effort.

Many factors affect a decision about implementing a separate capital budgeting process. Is it seen by the public as a useful tool in assessing the government's role in the economy? This would be particularly important at the state and national level, because large governmental organizations can use capital acquisition and development as a way to increase or decrease capital formation.[3] Capital items should be able to be identified physically, and they should be measurable. Only then can the item or items be separated physically as part of the budget process. Capital budgets allow more balance between revenue and expenditure flows from year to year. This is particularly important for small nonprofits and governments because large expenditures can cause severe fluctuations in annualized budgets. The capital budget should allow better predictive power concerning the need to add or replace capital items over time. The abilities to depreciate fixed assets and develop replacement schedules are often linked with capital budgeting processes for this reason. Finally, capital budgeting should allow better decision processes in assessing opportunity costs and considering varying choices that public and nonprofit policy boards face.

A capital budgeting program carried out within a single year usually is incorporated within a regular budget. Capital items are separated in parts of the budget document itself. Among the most common are "special analyses" sections and special justifications or clearances for expenditure items (e.g., computers, telephone systems, and so forth).

Multiyear capital budgeting is often included in the regular budget presented to policy officials, but annual costs are listed separately from expenditures planned over an extended period of time. Annual budgets include only the expenditures for capital items.

The most commonly discussed capital budgeting process, the one discussed in this chapter, is one in which there is a separate capital budget document. This budget is usually multiyear and reflects the policy of the governmental body or statutory requirements. This document can be partial or comprehensive. An example of a partial capital budget is one required by law, which includes only one type of capital item (e.g., a six-year road plan). A separate process for creating a capital budget allows multiyear planning to take place outside the annual pressures in the yearly operating budget adoption process. The results of the capital budgeting process are then incorporated into the operating budget process by reflecting and adjusting the capital expenditures in each fiscal budget year.

When this separate process occurs within the context of a broader planning effort, the approach often resembles a Capital Improvement Program (CIP) which is a "multiyear planning instrument used by governments to identify needed capital projects and to coordinate financing and timing improvements in a way that maximizes the return to the public."[4] A CIP includes a capital budget. For our purposes, a capital budget is a budget document, separate from the operating budget, that incorporates the revenues and expenditures for capital projects during one or more particular years. The CIP includes a longer time frame for projects and facilities than those associated with a

ngle-year capital budget. Capital budgeting is also a broad concept and refers
o "a process of generating investment proposals, estimating costs and benefits,
electing criteria for the choice among projects and using these criteria to make
ecisions."[5] Capital budgeting may or may not result in a separate capital
udget; for our purposes, however, the terms will be used interchangeably.

THE USES OF CAPITAL BUDGETING ◆

Capital budgeting is an important tool for most public agencies. It is used
xtensively by state and local governments, as well as by the nonprofit sector.
ccording to Thomassen, about 40 states have capital budgets of some type.[6]
imilarly, Forrester found that more than 70% of local governments with a
opulation greater than 75,000 that responded to a 1992 survey had a legally
equired capital budget.[7]

Although the federal government does not currently have a capital budget,
does incorporate most elements of the capital budgeting process. For
xample, the Office of Management and Budget keeps track of capital invest-
ient programs within the federal budget. Still, that listing may include only
art of the immense amount of fixed capital assets existing within the national
overnment. There is no direct accounting for fixed assets within the federal
udget or accounting systems.

Those advocating a capital budgeting process at the national level mention
our potential purposes most often.[8] First, it provides a planning process for
nvesting federal resources in capital assets.

Second, it provides some focus to the enormous inventory of existing assets
nd the benefits created by those assets. By having a separate plan for acquiring
apital assets, federal officials are more likely to focus attention on these items
s identifiable and separate from those associated with the operating budget.

Third, a capital budget helps clarify the difference between debt that is
ncurred to purchase capital assets and debt that is incurred to pay for current
perations. One criticism leveled at the lack of a national capital budget is that
ny deficit accumulated at the federal level is misleading if accumulated fixed
apital assets are not included also. Others argue that many of the capital assets
wned by the federal government (e.g., antiballistic missiles) are not likely
ver to be converted to more liquid assets and, therefore, have little to do with
e balance of assets and liabilities of the national government.

Fourth, a final proposed use of capital budgeting at the national level is to
elp develop some relationship between the repayment of debt and the useful
fe of the capital asset itself. This issue, which relates to the intergenerational
quity of payment for the capital asset, is discussed in more detail later.

Many uses ascribed to the adoption of a federal capital budgeting process
re also true for other public organizations. In addition, other uses have been
lentified. Creating a capital budgeting process for planning for the acquisi-
on and development of future capital assets provides continuity when
irnover of policy leaders and administrative staff occurs.[9] It also provides a
iethod whereby very dissimilar projects can be compared and contrasted by
ieir need, costs, and benefits. Capital budgeting can also provide a framework

by which policy officials can make decisions among competing projects and facilities, which otherwise might be carried out in a haphazard and uncoordinated way. Finally, capital budgeting provides a way to "smooth out" lumps in budget years that might otherwise occur through the periodic expenditure of large sums of money for capital assets. It provides a useful vehicle for relating an organization's needs and the finances available to meet those needs.

◆ ELEMENTS

Three major elements exist within a capital budget process: (1) planning, (2) cost analysis, and (3) financing. Each requires a certain amount of research capability, staffing (either external or internal), organizational capacity, and expertise. Each of these elements is discussed in detail in the following sections.

Planning

Effective capital budgeting requires a comprehensive planning effort. This effort includes a number of elements: (1) an inventory of existing capital assets, (2) a review of constituent demands for goods and services in the future, and (3) a review of replacement needs of existing capital assets.

Surprisingly, most public and nonprofit agencies lack a comprehensive inventory of their capital assets. Depending on the size and holdings of the public agency, such a list can be relatively easy to produce or can represent an enormous undertaking. Such an inventory can include some of the following elements: the type of facility or equipment asset; the date the asset was acquired; the initial cost of the asset; any improvements that have been made; the existing condition of the asset; the level of utilization of that land, facility, or equipment; its depreciated value; replacement cost; and the anticipated end of its useful life or replacement date. This inventory can be used as the first step in a risk management program as well as a capital budgeting program.

Perhaps one of the most difficult parts of a capital budget planning effort is to develop a clearly defined needs analysis to help the organization determine future demands for capital assets. Information on current and future needs guides where public resources should be directed in acquiring capital assets. Such analysis requires the incorporation of existing replacement needs, a review of shifting external changes, and any anticipated internal changes that affect the need or demand for such capital assets.

An analysis is used most commonly for major capital improvement projects such as buildings, streets, sewers, and large equipment. In some cases, the approach is similar to the environmental scan elements of strategic planning. The agency should consider factors, both internally and externally, that affect the needs associated with capital acquisition. Several factors are incorporated into such analysis. Shifts in population size and location provide indication of where new and different demands for services are likely to occur and where new facilities may be required. This is very common with public school systems, where changes in the number of elementary school children and corresponding changes in the number of high school students may require acquiring some new buildings and closing others. School districts may also find that overall existing facilities are adequate but are located in areas of declining populations. Another example is a community where the population is shifting to undeveloped areas that decides to purchase land for development of future facilities for recreation, a fire or police station, and so forth. Changes in facility use can also occur. The advent of the Americans With Disabilities Act (ADA) requires retrofitting existing buildings for disabled access and to ensure that new structures meet accessibility standards. Similarly, states must consider the impact of increasing speed limits on the useful life of highways. Other changes in legal requirements can necessitate capital expenditures in the future.

Demographic and cultural changes of the existing constituent base and changes in legal requirements can portend increasing demands for services. Changes in federal and state laws affecting health care benefits for the poor and elderly have increased demands for facilities and services, particularly at the state level.

Planning includes a systematic review of the replacement needs of existing facilities and equipment. Most facilities and equipment have an expected useful life span, which may range from a few years to as many as 40 years. Replacement periods can be based on either wear and tear and usage or on technological obsolescence. Streets, sewers, and front-end loaders are examples of the former, whereas computers, telecommunications equipment, and other electronics equipment exemplify the latter.

Technological obsolescence does not mean that facilities or equipment do not work or require increased maintenance. It simply means that more recent advances in technology have made the facilities or equipment less useful than new facilities or equipment to meet current and future demands. This is a very different situation from one in which equipment, because of wear and tear, has increasing downtime when it is unavailable or where the maintenance and replacement part costs begin to exceed the actual depreciated value of the equipment itself. Streets that are constantly under repair or buildings with major structural and mechanical problems are recommended strongly as candidates for replacement.

Replacement schedules should be developed when facilities and equipment are acquired. This allows a public agency to plan years in advance of the actual need for the replacement. This information can also be placed on a capital budgeting calendar so that replacement decisions can be contrasted with decisions for acquisition of new capital assets.

These replacement schedules should be based on useful life, with a clear understanding of the trade-offs between replacement relative to repair or maintenance and between replacement and modernization. Replacement schedules—which are forecasts, after all—should be adjusted yearly to account for factors that have changed since that schedule was developed. For example, street replacement may be based on assumptions about level of usage. If the usage or wear and tear is greater than originally thought, the replacement schedule should be adjusted to reflect such a change.

Cost Analysis—
Evaluating Expenditure Decisions

Perhaps the most difficult decision faced by policymakers and administrators is choosing which capital assets to acquire or replace. Most public organizations have limited resources and face legal as well as political restrictions on their ability to raise revenue. For these reasons, a limited number of capital items can be acquired during any one time period. Priorities must be set to fund those that are considered the most important. Importance can be determined by some form of economic analysis or by other concerns (political need, fairness, or visibility). Assuming, however, that some form of systematic analysis is useful, most finance professionals suggest using a systematic method to evaluate the importance of various capital acquisitions. These methods involve numerous criteria—quantitative, qualitative, and political. The key is to match available revenue sources with a wide-ranging set of expenditure options and to match expenditure options to revenue availability. Criteria can be developed that are simple or complex. Among the most common are the following:

- Costs of any particular project, facility, or equipment relative to competing projects, facilities, or equipment
- Costs relative to benefits for competing projects, facilities, or equipment
- Relationship of the capital asset to the specific goals and objectives of the organization
- Financial impact of the project on defined beneficiaries
- Capital costs relative to operating and maintenance costs
- Spin-off benefits of the capital asset to other public and private activities
- Effect on improved efficiency of organizational activities
- Political costs and benefits of the project
- Legal mandate of a project or activity mandated by law
- Chances for external funding
- Relationship to future needs and demands

Although this list is not exhaustive, it does provide a wide range of criteria to consider when developing an evaluation system. The major focus in deciding which capital assets to fund lies in the area of cost.

As discussed in detail in Chapter 8, cost-effectiveness and cost-benefit analysis can be used to compare capital expenditure items. Not all capital expenditures are associated with their cost relative to their benefits, however. Many decisions are made on other bases. State and local governments would be unlikely to spend the level of resources they currently do on such things as hazardous waste disposal sites if it were not required by the federal government. Other decisions are made on the grounds of equity rather than cost. Providing mass transit facilities in low-use areas may make little economic sense. If these areas are also populated by low-income citizens, however, eliminating such facilities simply because they are not economical is often rejected by public agencies responsible for such facilities on the basis of equity nother example pertains to disabled access to public facilities. Retrofitting ublic buildings or transportation equipment and facilities to allow for disbled access is not the most cost-effective way to ensure particular outcomes; owever, it does serve social and political objectives or meet legal requirements that make such expenditures necessary.

There are many different ways to evaluate capital expenditures. Various actors can be weighted in level of importance and then ranked according to quantitative system.[10] Opinion surveys can be used along with qualitative nalysis to determine level of support for various projects. This is especially elpful if a project or facility is potentially controversial among elected fficials or citizens affected.

Financing

No matter how various projects are ranked, rated, or prioritized, the funding of capital items is contingent on adequate revenue. Revenue sources hould suffice to encompass both the capital expenditure and the operating r maintenance costs associated with that expenditure. It makes little sense to urchase a piece of equipment if an organization cannot afford to maintain r repair it.

Two major modes of financing capital projects are pay-as-you-go and ay-as-you-use. The most conservative financing approach is pay-as-you-go. his simply means that the expenditure of funds for a capital item does not ccur until the money is in hand. Debt is not incurred to fund all or a part of ie capital item. On the other hand, pay-as-you-use proponents argue that nancing should occur as the capital asset is used. Incurring debt to fund such n item is logical because the debt can be paid throughout the item's useful fe.

Both approaches may be appropriate, depending on the particular situation acing the organization. Both have inherent strengths and weaknesses. Pay-asou-go ensures that an organization does not borrow money to finance capital ssets. Interest charges are a measure of opportunity cost. Public organizaons must choose between more expenditures to have more capital facilities nd equipment, which means more revenues, and fewer expenditures, fewer apital items, and fewer revenues. Unfortunately, fewer expenditures and evenues and more capital items is not possible. If concern exists about orrowing money and incurring debt to obtain capital facilities, the pay-asou-go approach may be the more acceptable action.

The disadvantage of pay-as-you-go can be substantial. Many capital items rould never be acquired or replaced because funding is simply not available rithin existing resources of an organization. In this sense, pay-as-you-go iscriminates against larger expenditures. In small organizations or where the apital item is expensive, the pay-as-you-go approach can create much greater uctuations in the budget expenditures from year to year and can also create uctuations in the revenue load of the organization's supporters. This is not particular problem for the national government, which has such an enormous budget that any one capital expenditure is unlikely to have a substantial npact. In a small town, however, building a new fire station or paving a street can have a substantial impact. In addition, the concept of intergenerationa equity is violated with a pay-as-you-go approach. This means that those wh benefit from the item are not necessarily the ones who finance the asset. Fo example, if taxpayers in a community use money that had been saved over period of years to build a recreational center, the beneficiaries of the cente may not be the same as those who put their tax dollars toward building i Some may move away or die. Then, they will have helped pay for a facility tha they never had a chance to use. This is considered inequitable. Pay-as-you-us financing is beneficial for a number of reasons. First, it helps spread the cost of the capital asset over a number of years, thus making acquisition o replacement more feasible in many cases. It avoids great fluctuations i expenditures and revenues. Second, it provides for intergenerational equit by allowing those paying taxes or user fees for a particular capital expenditur to have access to that item.

There are dangers associated with the pay-as-you-use approach. The great est concern is that financing of capital items might exceed the useful life o that asset. In other words, a public agency should not finance a piece o equipment for 10 years if it is likely that the equipment will need to be replace in 5 years. Such borrowing can place the agency in a financially precariou situation, where it is using current revenues to pay for capital assets that n longer exist.

Several options exist for public agencies that do not wish to rely exclusivel on either pay-as-you-go or pay-as-you-use. One approach would be to use substantial down payment for a capital expenditure and to finance the re mainder through borrowing. In this way the amount financed through deb can be reduced, yet intergenerational equity can be partially protected. similar approach is to shorten the maturity date of the debt that is issued t finance a capital acquisition so that debt costs are minimized and items ar funded before the end of their useful lives.

Another option is to set up a sinking fund that can cover costs associate with replacing a capital item. Money is put into the fund yearly. This is simila to debt in extended funding and is used extensively in replacing equipmen and other short- or intermediate-lived capital items. The money can b invested in interest-bearing accounts, and the principal and interest ca accumulate at the rate such that at the time a capital asset must be replaced the funding necessary to pay for that replacement is readily available. It i extremely important that when such funds are created, they are maintaine separate and distinct from other funds. It is often tempting to raid these fund to help cover the costs of other operating items within the budget or to dea with other concerns, such as revenue shortfalls.

Under certain circumstances, leasing provides an attractive alternative t either financing approach. This is a variant of pay-as-you-use, because own ership is not involved. When a capital asset is likely to have a very short usefu life, as is the case with certain kinds of equipment (automobiles and comput ers and so forth), or where the financing costs (both for incurring debt an for servicing and maintenance) will be clearly lower, leasing is an alternativ to acquisition. In many instances, a public agency can obtain title to the capita asset at the end of a lease at a minimal cost. The disadvantage to this, howeve s that the asset may have reached the end of its useful life at the end of this period.

Administration of the capital budgeting process is often shared among operating, planning, and finance officials. Each group has an important role to play. Operating departments within public organizations funnel requests for capital items to their financial officials. Those responsible for planning within the public organization review trends and developments as they affect the need for various capital projects, facilities, and equipment and submit this information along with the various requests that are made. The finance officials must provide a critical review of each request, provide evaluative criteria for ranking the relative importance of each, and determine a financing system to fund the most important items.[11]

In most instances, a 5- to-10-year capital improvement plan is submitted to the policy board of an agency for its review and approval. This multiyear plan includes all major capital construction and acquisition projects scheduled during that time. The capital budget includes the revenue and expenditure amounts for capital items that are to be constructed or acquired during the coming year. In most instances, a capital improvement plan is revised and approved each year along with a capital budget.

A major problem of capital budgeting is that some perceive it as a static process. Once a five-year capital budget plan is adopted, some in the agency assume that they do not have to deal with it again for another five years. In fact, the capital budgeting process is a dynamic one. As an organization's financial situation changes and as environmental factors change, it is important that the capital budget plan reflects these changes. At a minimum, the plan must be updated annually to reflect shifting priorities and concerns.

Another problem is that many public agencies treat the capital budgeting process as a paper exercise and often ignore it during the annual budget process. This is often the case for local government officials when state or federal law mandates some type of capital budgeting process but elected officials are not convinced of its appropriateness and do not participate in the development of the capital budget themselves. This is especially evident when the later years of a capital budget are populated with the same proposals as in the initial year, none of them either chosen or dropped. The key can be to link some form of strategic planning to the agency's budget process, including the capital budgeting process.

Capital budgeting has an important role in most public organizations. It provides a systematic method of planning future capital expenditures and allocating the financing resources necessary to fund them. The process of planning for capital construction and acquisition incorporates many elements discussed in other chapters: cost analysis, debt administration, cash management, risk management, and accounting. Planning requires both policy analysis and qualitative analysis. It also helps provide a clear direction for the organization.

Although it is not necessary to incorporate a capital budget in the capital budgeting process, the two are closely intertwined. Control, management, and planning all play important roles as they do throughout all financial management areas. Most large communities and large states operate with some form of capital budget and budgeting process. Many nonprofits do as well. Its importance to financial management is likely to increase in the future as resource constraints and demands for services continue. Capital budgeting provides one of the most important ways to organize and prioritize expenditures to meet the future.

DISCUSSION QUESTIONS

1. Study a local governmental or nonprofit organization that has a capital budgeting process. How often does the organization update its budget? How closely is the budget followed in making capital investment decisions? What criteria are used in placing items on the budget and in setting priorities for those items?

2. What linkages exist between accounting, debt administration, cost analysis, and capital budgeting processes? Are they different among different types of governments or nonprofit agencies? Why?

3. What factors would you include when prioritizing items for a capital budget? What makes this different for public agencies compared with private ones?

◆ NOTES

1. John Forrester (1993, Summer). Municipal capital budgeting: Blueprints for change *Public Budgeting & Finance, 13*(2), 85-101.

2. Henry Thomassen (1990, Winter). Capital budgeting for a state. *Public Budgeting & Finance, 10*(4), 72-86.

3. Thomassen, p. 79.

4. Girard Miller (1984). *Capital budgeting: Blueprints for change.* Washington, DC: Government Finance Officers Association, p. ix.

5. Stephanie Goldman (1987, Autumn). AABPA Symposium: Capital budgets—Expanded use in federal sector. *Public Budgeting & Finance, 7*(3), 5.

6. Thomassen, p. 79.

7. Forrester, p. 90.

8. General Accounting Office (1986, July). *Budget issues: Capital budgeting in the states* Washington, DC: U.S. Government Printing Office, pp. 4-5.

9. Miller, p. ix.

10. Miller, p. 125.

11. Alan Walter Steiss. *Capital facilities and debt administration*, Volume I. Washington, DC The National Training and Development Service, VI. 7-6.

Public Debt Administration

Public debt administration frequently appears confusing at first. One reason is a mystique associated with extremely large amounts of money. Total debt of all public organizations is approximately $6 trillion to $7 trillion, which does not include any future obligations for social security or unfunded pensions. State and local governments typically borrow from $1 billion to $200 billion each year. Another reason for confusion is unique terminology, which stems from euphemistic expressions for the acts of borrowing and loaning money; a large-scale investment industry with various diverse participants, roles, and relationships; different public borrowers; different debt purposes; and highly technical legal doctrines. The key relationships are who borrows what from whom and who owes what to whom. Everything else relates somehow to a debt relationship.

Debt is a liability, an obligation. A debt relationship can be summarized as A owing money to B. It starts with some party, A, borrowing money from another party, B. In addition to the money borrowed—the principal—A must make an additional payment to use B's money for a period of time—the interest. Debt, in effect, is an act of renting money for a period of time. Any confusing debt situation can be clarified by working from the base of who owes whom, what is owed, and when it is owed. Everything involved with debt starts there. Although a public organization that owes money seldom shifts a debt obligation to another party, the entities that are entitled to repayment of debt frequently can and do transfer the legal right to repayment.

Some confusion about debt can be alleviated by identifying various terms used for common debt transactions. First, terms used to describe the act of borrowing money are to *acquire debt,* to *incur debt,* to *issue debt,* to *float debt,* to *sell debt,* and to *enter into debt.* In many cases, another word is added to or substituted for "debt," further obscuring the borrowing relationship (e.g., "to sell bills, notes, or bonds" or "to sell a debt issue"). The terms *bill, note,* and *bond* refer to specific debt contracts: a promise to pay specific amounts of money at one or more future points in time. A *debt issue* refers to the total amount borrowed when a group of debt contracts is sold together at one point in time.

This terminology comes from the investment industry and a reluctance by public officials to be clear about borrowing money. Related terms, *debt issuer* and *debtor,* refer to the entity that borrows money and owes money relating to specific debt contracts. Second, the act of loaning money is called *purchasing debt* or *buying debt* or some substitute term for *debt* that signifies one or more specific debt contracts. In effect, those lending money buy future money payments. Third, once a debt relationship has been established, the initial lender is said to own a debt contract. An owner of debt contracts is also referred to as a *debt holder* or *creditor.* Fourth, transfer of the ownership of debt, usually specific debt contracts, is also spoken of as buying and selling debt. Such transfer of ownership of debt contracts is both similar to and different from the original debt relationship. Similarities include the terms *buy* and *sell* and the maintenance of a debtor-creditor relationship. Differences include the nonparticipation of the original borrower, the initial lender's exit from the situation, and the introduction of one or more third parties to a debt relationship. Secondary buying and selling of debt contracts does not change the fundamental debt relationship; only the particular entities that are due repayment are different.

In addition to entities that invest in public debt and those that are in debt, investment market participants play a host of specialized roles. Specialized roles refers to activities by persons or organizations that work with buyers and sellers of debt. Two common ones are bond counsel and underwriter. A bond counsel is a lawyer or law firm specializing in the law of municipal debt. An underwriter is a business that buys and sells debt; usually underwriters buy all of a debt issue directly from the debt issuer and sell various numbers of specific debt contracts to investors.

Different borrowers and purposes are used to group and differentiate debt. Public borrowers are divided into the two classes of federal and municipal, each of which can be further subdivided into groups. Federal borrowers include the U.S. Treasury, other federal agencies, and federally sponsored corporations. Municipal borrowers are state and local governments and other entities acting under their authority, which also generally includes nonprofit organizations. Further specificity of borrowers includes particular organizational unit or type, such as housing agency or utility.

Different purposes of debt are identified by different terms. A debt can be identified by either the use of money or the source of monies for repayment. A revenue bond is a good example. The term *revenue* signifies that money has been loaned for a revenue-producing project and that the debt will be repaid from the revenues generated by the project (e.g., utility revenue bonds).

Legal technicalities of public debt result from an enduring interest in regulating public debt among the federal and state governments. The federal government directly regulates federal debt and debt markets and has a regulatory impact on other public debt through federal income tax provisions. State governments regulate their own and their subdivisions' debt for authorizations, purposes, limits, and processes. Both federal and state courts become involved when lawsuits arise between parties in a debt relationship. Two primary areas of legal technicalities are state provisions to safeguard citizens rom improper debt and federal efforts to use income tax provisions to favor ɔarticular behavior or to gather revenue.

Three things to discuss before getting into the main body of the chapter are ɔublic debt administration as one of three liability areas, public debt admini-tration as related to investment, and the order of the chapter. Public debt ɪdministration is one of three areas in public finance administration that ɔocus on liabilities; the other two are risk management and personnel benefits, ɾnostly pensions. Risk management involves contingent losses and liabilities. ᵖersonnel benefits involve payments due to persons as a result of an employ-ment relationship with a public organization. The three areas share common ɪspects, the most important being the future impact of liabilities. Because of ɪhe size of future impacts arising from these three liability areas, careful ɔlanning is appropriate.

Public debt administration is closely related to investment. The investment ːhapter (Chapter 12) discussed investment markets from the perspective of ɪn investor; the public debt market is one part of the overall debt market and s discussed here from the opposite side of transactions—owing money. Chapter 12 introduced investment markets and their functioning, specific ɪebt terms, and features of public debt.

The order of topics in this chapter is purposes of public debt, the federal ːovernment and debt, public debt characteristics, public debt markets, and ɪhe public debt process. First, the purposes of debt relate to all public debtors. ᵖecond, the federal government has a unique relationship to all debt and ːspecially public debt. Third, public debt characteristics are described in ɪetail. Fourth, the overall debt market, often called the credit market, is ɪescribed as the place where money is borrowed. Finally, the public debt ɔrocess is discussed.

PURPOSES ◆

Four common purposes of public debt are (1) managing the national ːconomy, (2) making expenditures that exceed revenues over a long-term ɔeriod, (3) making expenditures that exceed revenues over a short-term ɔeriod, and (4) financing specific large expenditures over a period of time, ɪsually capital expenditures. These purposes are used by different public ɔrganizations in varying amounts. Two are predominantly federal and two ɪnvolve other public organizations issuing municipal debt.

The two purposes where the federal government predominates are manag-ing the national economy and making expenditures that exceed revenues over ɪ long period. Only the federal government is in a position to manage the ːconomy or consistently borrow large amounts of money. Federal debt in its various guises exceeds two thirds to three quarters of all public debt. Federal ɪebt is entered into by relatively few agencies and is held by many investors.

The purpose of managing the national economy is singularly a federal ːovernment purpose. The role of federal debt in the area of monetary policy is theoretically simple but practically complex. The federal government sells or buys debt to increase or decrease the amount of money in circulation money available for other investments, prices, and interest rates, all of which affect other facets of the national economy. Economic management operates partially through supply and demand of federal debt at different prices. The federal government has the unparalleled legal privilege of creating money to make any payment. Its only constraints are the practical consequences of its actions. For example, one reason that the federal government borrows money to pay for deficit spending is that the alternative of making money by writing checks causes price inflation.

The two primary debt purposes of municipal borrowers are short-term excesses of expenditures over revenues and specific large-scale expenditures. The federal government does not borrow for short-term expenditure excesses because its expenditure excesses are long-term. Short-term expenditure excesses are only temporary. For example, if a local government spends more than it has on hand and uses short-term borrowing, it pays the money borrowed back in less than a year. The federal government continues always in a long-term expenditure excess position.

Municipal borrowers borrow for short periods because of erratic revenues and occasionally larger than normal expenditures as a part of normal cash management. The amount can be viewed in two ways: either less than one tenth of municipal debt owed at any one point in time or between one fifth and one third of municipal debt borrowed in a given year. The first view is more fundamentally sound; amounts owed are more relevant than amounts borrowed.

Borrowing for specific large-scale expenditures primarily funds capital expenditures, more for facilities than equipment. Also, to a limited extent long-term debt can be used for pensions and tort liability claims. Generally long-term borrowing occurs for large expenditures that are impossible or inappropriate to pay for from current revenues. This purpose accounts for more than 90% of municipal debt owed at any given time.

◆ THE FEDERAL GOVERNMENT AND DEBT

The federal government's relationship to debt in the United States is difficult to deal with and approximately similar to a 900-pound gorilla sipping tea at a tea party; the gorilla is impossible to ignore but dealing quickly and adequately with all the subtleties involved is not possible. Federal involvement with debt is probably immeasurable. First, and most obvious, the federal government owes more money than the total owed by all other public entities in the United States. A related nonobvious measure of its involvement with public debt is that the federal government is also the single largest owner of its debt; one tenth to one third of federal debt is held by federal agencies and sponsored corporations. Second, for debt of all kinds, the federal government specifically regulates investment markets.

Third, many federal government policy efforts are implemented through treatment of debt by providing or withdrawing specific advantages to particur debt situations. Specific advantages include special rates, tax treatment, nd guarantees.

Fourth, the federal government attempts to manage the national economy enerally through monetary and fiscal policies. Monetary policy concerns the ze of the money supply, particularly its rate of growth; fiscal policy concerns ne size and composition of revenues and expenditures and resulting budget-ry surpluses and deficits. Federal debt facilitates increasing and decreasing ne money supply, though debt operations are only one means of acting in nis policy area. Fiscal policy has led to a large public debt because of budget eficits in most years since the beginning of World War II and has grown xtremely large in the 1980s and 1990s. Federal deficits increase federal debt nd affect economic activity. Unfortunately, no macroeconomic theory ade-uately explains and predicts the consequences of monetary and fiscal policy noices.

Fifth, federal government involvement with debt principally concerns poli-es determined through the political process. Further information on par-cular policy issues can be found in writings about macroeconomics and ublic finance in economics; specific policy-oriented writings in economics nd political science, among others; and writings in political science dealing ith the policy-making process.

PUBLIC DEBT CHARACTERISTICS ◆

Public debt characteristics are less difficult to comprehend in themselves nan the terminology used to signify the characteristics. Here, the charac-eristics are described in common language and in terminology commonly sed by those involved with public debt. The characteristics concern the form r appearance, obligation bases, tax status, time periods, amounts, rates, atings, external guarantees, special features, and innovative forms of public ebt.

Form of Debt

The form of debt refers to what controls ownership of a debt contract. The wo forms are *bearer* and *registered* debt contracts. In the bearer form, posses-on is ownership—whoever has one, owns it. In the registered form of debt ontracts, a record controls ownership. The debt contract terms and records f ownership are separate. Registered debt owners may have paper contracts, ut ownership hinges on registration records. Debt that does not involve any aper contract is called *book entry*, whether recorded in books or in some lectronically manipulated medium. Where book entry debt exists, the terms f a debt contract are recorded or published in an easily available fashion.

Obligation Bases

Debt contracts are also called instruments or securities. The term *security* ndicates that repayment is secured by the debt contract. Securing of debt repayment is done by specifying the obligations the debtor has to the debt holder in legally valid terms. Four obligation bases describe the security or liability basis of debt contracts. Securing debt payments is also thought to be a function of creditworthiness and external guarantees (which are discussed later), as well as adherence to all relevant legalities, such as having legal authority to act and following legally prescribed procedures (which are discussed in the public debt process section).

General obligation means that a government with taxing powers has pledged its "full faith and credit," an unlimited obligation to repay the debt from its general revenues. All parts of this definition must be true to say that a debt is a general obligation one. The debtor must be a government; the government must have the power to collect taxes and to pledge the use of general revenues in the particular situation; and the government must pledge its full faith and credit to repayment of the debt. Because issuers pledge unconditionally that they will repay the debt, such debt carries less risk for investors, which makes it more attractive to them and less costly to borrowers. General obligation debt is primarily used for general governmental purposes.

Most limited liability obligation situations occur when the revenue source of debt repayment is specified. The revenue basis for repayment is almost always a central concern. The term *revenue bonds* is common because most bonds use this kind of obligation basis—more than 70% since the mid-1970s. Most often the revenues come from revenue-generating capital facilities, although they can come from other specific revenues sources, including taxes. Because repayment depends on specific revenues, the repayment risk and costs of such borrowing exceed those of general obligation debt.

Limited liability obligation debt differs from general obligation debt in two important respects: Most limited liability debt is not subject to the same debt creation procedures nor to general governmental debt limits. Municipal issuers use limited liability debt to exceed debt limitation laws and to avoid public approval through a referendum election. Still, most limited liability debt receives the same tax preferences as general obligation debt.[2]

Limited liability debt often involves special provisions in the debt contract. For tax-based debt, the debtor generally agrees to levy and collect the relevant tax and not to use the proceeds for any purpose before paying the debt holders. For debt for revenue-generating projects, the special provisions can be so detailed that they require rates, creation and maintenance of a debt reserve fund, prohibitions against free use of a revenue facility or service, and any other aspect of the situation that would be a reasonable concern to the potential investors (e.g., ensuring the value of a revenue-producing facility).

Moral obligation debt is nothing more than an explicit or implied promise to repay debt without a legally binding obligation. This has been used and underlies some federal debt contracts. Federal debt aside, however, there is little to no interest in this obligation basis for debt. People can be so touchy about money.

No obligation debt sounds less inviting than moral obligation debt. No obligation public debt is an oddity, however. Basically, state and local governments lend their names and legal authority to a debt issue for which the true debtor is one or more private parties who are obliged to repay the debt. The government involved presents itself as furthering a public purpose, especially economic development. Governmental involvement secures a preferred federal income tax status for the holders of the debt, which lowers the cost of the debt to debtors.[4]

Tax Status

The tax status of public debt is important because it affects the attractiveness of public debt as an investment. Taxation affects how much investors finally end up with. Other investments are generally taxed, but public debt receives preferred tax treatment. Federal debt is simply exempt from income taxation. Most municipal debt payments are not taxed as income by the federal government or by the state and local governments within the state of the issuing public organization. The importance of this varies with the marginal income tax rate of a particular investor; the higher the marginal tax rate, the greater the value of an income tax exemption. For example, for an investor with a marginal tax rate of 25%, a nontaxable public debt contract yielding 12% is equal in value after income taxes to a taxable investment yielding 16%:

Taxable yield minus (marginal tax rate multiplied by taxable yield)
equals nontaxable yield
16% - (25% x 16%) = 12%
16% - 4% = 12%

Federal income taxation has the most effect because those rates are highest. Municipal bonds can be federally taxed in cases where the purpose is classified as "private activity," primarily with no obligation debt when the debt benefits specific private entities.

Time Periods

Time periods related to public debt are (1) the overall length of time between the point money is borrowed and the debt obligation is contracted to be fully paid off, (2) the time period between any current point in time and the point at which a debt obligation is contracted to be fully paid off, and (3) terminology signifying time periods. Money is always borrowed for some time period. Public debt contracts specify time periods. Federal debt comes in a wide variety of time periods. Federal debt is divided into three time groups: short, intermediate, and long. Short-term debt contracts have a time period of 52 weeks or less and are called *bills,* as in T-bills. Intermediate debt periods range from 1 to 10 years in length and are called *notes,* and long-term periods are more than 10 and as many as 30 years in length and are called *bonds.* Municipal debt is divided into two periods that match the two main purposes for acquiring debt. Short-term debt is usually for cash flow purposes and less than a year in length. Such debt contracts are called *notes.* TANs, RANs, and BANs are acronyms for tax, revenue, and bond anticipation notes. Longer time period debt for capital items is usually called *bonds* whether the time period is for 2 years or 30 years.

The time period between any particular point in time and the point when public debt contracts will be paid off is of interest to participants in public debt markets. These markets establish prices for new debt contracts by establishing prices for common existing debt contracts. Prices are established on debt contracts by the time period to their date of payment. Investors can see the price of buying or selling debt contracts. From the borrower's perspective the cost of borrowing money for various time periods can be determined by observing the price of similar debt contracts with a time period to payment that is the same as the period for which a debt contract is planned. The original term of bonds does not affect their price as much as their time period to payment does. Borrowing costs for a six-year period can be seen by finding out the price of bonds with six years to go before they are paid off. Other factors affecting debt contract prices are discussed below.

More terminology concerning public debt involves time. *Term* literally means the time period of a debt contract from its beginning to end. A term of 10 years describes the time period of the debt contract. A related word is *mature,* which can be used as a verb or an adjective and has a related noun form, *maturity,* which refers to a particular point in time. *Mature* and *maturity* refer to the point in time when a debt contract is supposed to be fully paid. A debt contract matures at a particular point in time, which is its maturity date, and thereafter can be referred to as being mature or matured.

Long-term debt issues are distinguished by whether the debt contracts have the same or different maturity dates. When all debt contracts are due for payment at one time, they are described as term bonds. Where the debt contracts have differing time periods, they are spoken of as serial bonds. Most municipal issues are serial because periodic payment is easier than total repayment at one time.

Amounts

The amounts of debt are referred to in three distinct fashions. First, the total amount of debt of a public organization is referred to as the *amount of indebtedness.*

Second, the amount of debt involved in a particular borrowing at one time is referred to as a *debt issue.* A debt refers to the act of entering into debt contracts and is frequently identified with a particular purpose or project. Usually, a municipal debt issue is sold as a package to an underwriter, a firm specializing in buying and selling debt contracts. Very seldom are individual municipal debt contracts sold separately by the debt issuer.

Third, the amount of debt involved in one of a number of debt contracts is referred to as a *denomination.* The denomination of a debt contract appears in the debt contract as either the initial amount borrowed or as the amount due to be repaid. In either event, the denomination is also called the *face value* or *par value* of a debt contract (e.g., a $5,000 bond or a $10,000 T-bill). The denomination of a debt contract is a starting point for figuring out the price of a debt contract for any parties involved. Most municipal debt is such that an amount close to the par value is paid for a debt contract by its initial buyer, and the par value is paid to the debt holder at the point of maturity. For xample, a municipal bond with a face value of $5,000 is initially sold for about 5,000, perhaps for a few dollars more or less: When the bond matures, the ebt holder is paid exactly $5,000 in principal for the bond along with any nterest payment due. In between those two points in time, the price of a debt ontract varies above or below the par value. A debt contract with a price above s par value is said to be selling at a premium, and one with a price lower than ar is said to be selling at a discount. Both these terms, *discount* and *premium,* lso are used to refer to the exact amount of the difference between an actual rice and the par denomination. The denomination of some debt refers to the mount paid at maturity even though the initial amount borrowed is substanally different from the par value. T-bills are an example of debt contracts nitially sold at a discount. Debt contracts with the initial amount borrowed pproximately the same as the amount paid at maturity have separate, explicit rovisions for the cost of borrowing. For debt contracts initially sold at a iscount, the price of borrowing is the difference between the initial discounted price and the denominational value.

Rates

The term *rates* refers to interest payments made on borrowed money. ypically, interest payments are spoken of and computed in percentages, that , fractions of 100. The two different interest rates are *face interest rates* or *par nterest rates* and *effective interest rates.* The face rate is the explicit percentage pecified in a debt contract (e.g., 8% a year compounded yearly). That rate is ased on the market prices of similar debt contracts at the time they are issued. iscounted debt contracts show no face value interest rate but are sold at a rice reflecting market prices for similar debt contracts.

Effective interest rates refer to the investment returns as percentages. If a ublic debt contract with interest payment provisions is purchased at par alue and held until maturity, the face and effective interest rates are the same. Vhenever a debt contract is purchased at anything other than par, however, he effective rate is different. Investors and debt issuers are interested in ffective rates because they measure the real price of debt contracts. Compuations of effective interest rates can be made using some variation of net resent value equations, which was discussed in Chapter 8, "Cost Analysis".[5]

Two key aspects for rates are the time period or periods involved and hether the interest rates are simple or compound. Time periods for shortrm debt are measured in terms of fractions of a year (i.e., so much per year r that fraction of a year). For contracts one year or longer, the typical time eriod for calculating interest is one half or one year. The distinction between mple and compound interest rates refers to whether a borrower makes nterest payments on only the amount borrowed or also on interest payment mounts. Under simple interest, a percentage is computed for each period nvolved and either paid to the debt holder or added to the total amount due t the maturity of the debt contract. For example, a three-year bond of $5,000 ar value with a simple interest rate of 10% per year with payment of interest t maturity yields $1,500 in interest payments.

$5,000 x 10% = $500 per year
500 x 3 years = $1,500

For compound interest, an interest charge is made on any interest payment not paid to a debt holder for a time period. In other words, a borrower pays interest on interest. Using the same example as above, a compound interest payment for the three-year bond is $1655.

$5,000 x 10% = $500 First year interest charge
$5,000 + 500 = $5,500 Second year principal
$5,500 x 10% = $550 Second year interest charge
$5,500 + 550 = $6,050 Third year principal
$6,050 x 10% = $605 Third year interest
$500 + $550 + $605 = $1,655 Overall interest payments

Compound interest increases interest payments as the length of time of a debt contract increases and as the duration of the period between compounding diminishes.

Although the mechanics of computing interest payments, particularly effective rates, vary, the central concern is actual borrowing costs stated in commonly understood fashion (i.e., an effective interest rate of some percentage compounded annually or semiannually). Where debt is sold on a discounted basis, an equivalent effective rate can be calculated. Such effective rates are used to evaluate debt market prices by both buyers and sellers. This is especially important at the time a debt issue is being designed because that is when a public borrower determines borrowing costs.

Ratings

Independent organizations, most notably Fitch Investors Service, Moody's Investor Service, and Standard & Poor's, issue debt ratings, which indicate those organizations' opinions about the creditworthiness of a particular entity in general or for a particular debt issue. Issuing entities have to pay a fee to be rated and provide the rating organization with all necessary information. Rating opinions are given in two categories: investment grade and speculative grade. An *investment grade* debt contract is thought of as very low in risk of nonpayment or a delay in payment. A *speculative grade* debt contract is thought of as being uncertain of payment or the timing of payment. Debt ratings are important at the point of initial borrowing and within debt market trading generally.

The principal importance of debt ratings is their impact on market access and price, particularly for larger amounts of debt. An unrated or poorly rated debt issue may not be purchased in the public debt markets. Unrated debt issues are most commonly small-scale ones bought and sold within a limited geographic scope, where the purchasers can do the equivalent of rating public debtor and its debt. Small issuers sell debt primarily to nearby financial institutions. Debt with lower ratings, even within the investment grade range, may not be sellable if better grade debt contracts are available. To sell lower rated debt, issuers have to pay higher interest rates to compensate debt holders for a higher level of perceived risk. Also, ratings may change after a debt issue has been purchased to reflect more recent information about a debtor's situation or debt contracts themselves. Ratings on previously issued debt affect new debt issues in two ways. First, previous ratings influence the rating on a new debt issue, unless the new issue is extremely different from earlier ones. Second, a state's bond ratings tend to influence ratings of other entities within the state.

Ratings make millions of dollars of difference in the costs of borrowing for large issuers of municipal debt. This leads to large issuers lobbying rating agencies. Still, investors expect accurate ratings. Rating companies' opinions must match market perceptions or the ratings will attract less attention by investors. Unfortunately, rating decisions in two cases did not work well. In 1975, New York City temporarily failed to pay off investment grade rated short-term debt. In 1983, the Washington Public Power Supply System (known as "whoops"—seriously, we are not making this up!) failed to pay off $2.25 billion of investment grade rated revenue bonds because a court decided that the bonds were not legal obligations. Both events contributed to regulation of the underwriting industry and two new forms of external guarantees, bond insurance and letters of credit.

Except for external guarantees discussed later, the most important factors in debt ratings are economics, debt, finances, and the general government situation. Although each rating organization discusses them differently, the same things concern all of them. The types of details used in analysis for rating purposes can be seen in Chapter 18, "Assessing Financial Conditions." First, the general economic situation for a government is probably the most important concern, which is measured by general economic indicators, such as job, investment, and population growth. A declining economy does not suggest a great ability to repay debt. If the economic wealth is not as easily available for government revenue, then the chances that debt holders will not be paid increase. For revenue bonds, the key economic factor is the economic viability of the service plan that the borrowing is based on because the projects financed by the bonds have to generate sufficient revenues to repay the debt holders.

Second, the use of both short- and long-term debt by the entity is examined to see the overall debt burden and the wisdom displayed in using debt. An overburdened government or population or a government that has done unwise things with debt leads to lower ratings. Third, the entity's handling of its finances is examined. The adequacy of financial administration can be displayed by accurate forecasting, well-developed policies, and timely attention to problem areas. A government that has inaccurate budget forecasts, sloppy handling of financial details, and an operation chronically on the edge of bankruptcy does not yield good ratings.

Fourth, the general government situation refers to the adequacy of a government's powers, relations with other governments, provision of services, and general capacity to succeed. This is probably the least important area and would influence a rating organization to select between only two ratings on a close call.

External Guarantees

One factor with an impressive impact on ratings and marketability of public debt is the existence of an external guarantee, which comes in three forms. First, *bond insurance* is an unconditional guarantee by one of a few bond insurance companies that it will make any debt payments not made by an insured debtor. Bond insurance companies are backed by extremely large financial institutions. This is considered the best guarantee. Second, governmental guarantees are less common. State-run bond banks, which borrow money for their local governments, guarantee the debt by actually borrowing the money. Third, a financial institution issues a *letter of credit,* which specifically obligates the financial institution to loan money to pay off debt holders. Letters of credit are particularly relevant in short-term situations.

Special Features

Three special features of debt contracts afford either the debt issuer or debt holder special rights: options to call, to put, or to rollover. A *call option,* the most common, gives the issuer of debt the right to pay off debt before its formal date of maturity. When the call option is used, the issuer only makes interest payments on the time period the debt contract endured from the date of issuance to the date it is paid after being called. Often, the use of a call option requires a higher interest rate or some other form of extra payment at the time the call option is exercised. Also, a call option can increase the interest rate of a debt contract.

The purpose of the call option is to allow the debt issuer to save on borrowing costs either by paying debt off through use of its ordinary revenues or by borrowing money when the debt market rates change so that borrowing is less expensive. A call option requires a higher interest rate and perhaps other special payment features because the exercise of a call option usually occurs at a time when the rates are better for borrowing and worse for investors.

Call provisions in bonds can specify when and in what order bonds are callable. Calls usually occurs after a minimum period from the date of issuance and on some specific dates or during specific time periods. Which bonds will be called and in what order can be established by shortest to longest maturity or by lot. A preestablished order allows investors to estimate the likelihood of particular bonds being called.

Call provisions are usually exercised through borrowing referred to as a *refunding bond issue,* though such issues can be used to pay for bonds without call provisions. One borrows using a refunding bond issue to pay for previous borrowing only because borrowing costs are less. A refunding bond issue can used for noncalled bonds by investing the newly borrowed money and paying off the old debt as it matures. Refunding bond issues for noncalled municipal debt was rendered unattractive by the 1986 Tax Reform Act, as its provisions generally require a letter of credit with one or more financial institutions.

A *put option* is the exact opposite of a call option and not often used in public debt. It allows debt holders to demand repayment of the principal and interest on a debt contract. Put options have the same sort of timing and ecial payment features as call options. The potential favored party is the debt older, which lowers initial borrowing costs. The problem for a debt issuer is oping with the exercise of put options, which generally requires a letter of redit with one or more financial institutions.

The third special feature of debt is the *rollover option*. This option allows ie borrower to extend a debt contract in time beyond the maturity date as pecified. This means the debt is not paid off until later. Usually, interest rates or periods after a debt contract is rolled over are higher.

Innovation

Innovative forms of debt rise and fall primarily because of legal provisions ssociated with authorization and taxation of public debt. Some innovation simply an attempt to take advantage of market situations. Examples of 1arket situation innovations are sales of mini-bonds with a denomination of 100 by municipal issuers, variable rate instruments, and those denominated 1 foreign currencies. Issuers or their advisors see a market for such bonds nd take advantage of it. The two legal areas relating to authority and taxation rovide two different patterns of innovation.

Innovative debt characteristics concerning legal authority have been evolv-1g during most of this century because of limits on state and local govern-1ent borrowing authority. For example, the Illinois State Constitution of 870 set specific debt limits for the state and its subdivisions that were nrevised until the enactment of a new constitution in 1970. Two paths from onstrictive legal authority were the multiplication of governmental and uasi-governmental units to borrow and creativeness in legal interpretation s to what constituted debt, which led to limited liability obligation debt.

All sorts of lease arrangements are creative debt. A lease in its simple form orders on a debt in being a multiyear financial obligation. It becomes debt hen it involves an advance of money or interest payments. This occurs in 1ost lease purchase agreements involving a public entity implicitly borrowing 1oney to buy something and paying the equivalent of an interest payment in ie lease payments. An example of this occurs in Lincoln, Nebraska, where the tate is constrained from borrowing for most purposes. When the state wants n office building, it enters into a lease purchase agreement with the City of incoln, which borrows the money, builds the building, leases the building to ie state, pays off the debt, and transfers ownership to the state when the debt paid. Lease agreements are debt situations when the initial vendor is not the older of the ownership of the leased items. Leases take two basic forms. First, financial institution buys something for a public entity and leases it to the ntity. Financial institutions can hold or sell rights to lease payments. Second, vendor or a public entity can sell lease-based contracts where the collateral or the money borrowed is the lease agreements, the leased items, or both. The gal authority reason for innovative characteristics of debt has been an ever 1creasing gray area, which can abate only by relaxation or by further tight-1ing of limitations on authority to borrow. Neither is likely to occur, partially ecause some political officials find it to their advantage to borrow without aving the stigma attached to public borrowing.

Debt innovation linked to tax provision varies in cycles. For example massive use of no obligation debt led to stricter federal tax provisions limiting the amount of such debt exempt from federal income taxes in the 1986 Tax Reform Act.

A most innovative example stemmed from legal limitations and federal tax provisions. A city entered into an agreement with an insurance company that was essentially a way of borrowing money to pay for pension obligations. That was the end result; the road there was tricky. Simultaneously, the two entered into contracts; to sell city hall and other buildings to the insurance company, to lease the buildings to the city with ownership eventually going to the city at the end of the lease period, to hire the insurance company to manage investment of the money, and to pay pensions of city employees from the investments. Although this occurred for tax reasons, it also avoided the absence of legal authority to borrow to fund pensions.[6]

◆ PUBLIC DEBT MARKETS

Public debt markets refer to the buying and selling of public debt and not any particular place. The activity of public debt markets is widely scattered. The participants include private individuals, financial institutions, and public organizations. Market activity tends to be concentrated in larger cities, particularly those with financial institutions with a state, regional, or national focus. The markets determine debt costs. Three areas affect debt prices at the time of initial issuance: general investment market conditions, the existence of an active secondary market, and characteristics of the debt itself.

General investment market conditions affect public debt markets because all investment possibilities are alternatives to investors. Among the many factors affecting both debt and equity investment markets are expectations concerning economic growth, general price movements in the economy, specific market price movements, confidence, and security. Expectations of higher rates of economic growth and price inflation favor equity investments, whereas lower rates favor debt. As one area is favored over the other, investors take money out of one area by selling investments and put it into another by buying investments. Generally, the equity and debt investment market prices tend to move in opposite directions for these reasons.

Several other factors can affect public debt markets. Two important factors, confidence and security, are easier to describe than predict. Specific markets do or do not enjoy investor confidence, which makes investors then willing to pay more for an investment. For debt issuers, greater confidence means a lower cost of borrowing. If investors lose confidence in a specific market, rates have to go up to attract investors. When large cities and the Washington Public Power Supply System defaulted on billions, investor confidence in municipal debt plunged, the costs of borrowing rose, and access to investment money diminished. The relative degree of security of public debt makes it an attractive investment during times of general investment market turbulence. When stock markets experience wide swings, some investors move into public debt because of its high degree of security (i.e., certainty of payment of principal and interest).

Finally, all investment markets display specific price movements that are not explainable in a fashion that generates a consensus among observers. Such price movements can be observed, but their prediction is a tricky business. Public debt issuers, along with any financial experts working with them, watch the investment markets generally and specific debt markets in particular to choose the best time to borrow money, which means at the lowest borrowing costs. Analyzing investment markets involves predicting, which is inherently uncertain, and reacting to what appear to be favorable circumstances.

A factor affecting the price of a public debt issue is the existence of an active secondary market. This means debt contracts can be sold before maturity relatively easily by debt holders. Although federal and corporate debt are more actively traded, common forms of municipal debt with investment grade ratings are widely traded. Unusual debt features, lack of a debt rating, or both make it difficult for an initial purchaser of debt to resell it and, therefore, increase the costs of borrowing. Smaller scale or locally issued debt may not require a secondary market for reasonable debt costs; however, large-scale municipal debt is issued with ratings in a common form to make it sellable in a secondary market.

Particular characteristics of public debt contracts also determine the costs of borrowing. Many such characteristics were discussed in Chapter 12, "Investment Administration" (e.g., yield, risk, liquidity, and size of debt issues and denominations). Such elements and others affect borrowing costs. An active secondary market increases liquidity and reduces borrowing costs. Risk is minimized by use of a general obligation basis, higher ratings, and external guarantees, which also reduce borrowing costs. Call and rollover provisions increase costs, whereas put provisions lower costs. Preferential tax status decreases costs also. Larger issues and denominations generally have lower borrowing costs. Otherwise, borrowing costs are basically a function of the cost of borrowing money, which is determined by the market forces of supply and demand in particular situations.

PUBLIC DEBT PROCESS ◆

The public debt process involves steps by a public entity that borrows money and later pays money to debt holders. Municipal debt is discussed here because public administrators are more commonly involved with it than federal debt. Municipal debt issuance is very involved with legalities, technical specialists, and diverse debt characteristics. Legal complexities result from states simultaneously guarding the public against improper use of money and facilitating the proper use of debt. Because these purposes run in opposite directions, laws concerning municipal debt require careful review to ensure that borrowing is done in a legally proper manner. Specialized roles have evolved in the debt industry that are handled by technical specialists. The particular specialists involved in any debt process depend on choices by the debt issuer. The whole process displays many of the decisions that have to be made in issuing debt.

The debt process varies from very simple cases with a few steps to highly complex cases. Short-term debt tends to be simple; commonly, long-term debt is more complex. The process described next is more comprehensive than typical.

The first step is the decision to borrow money. For short-term purposes this can appear without much warning as revenues fall or unexpected expenditures become necessary, though most short-term debt is not unexpected. Short-term borrowing is determined in planning cash flows or in cases where money must be borrowed for capital projects over the short term before long-term borrowing. When officials decide to borrow, they typically explicitly identify the purpose of borrowing. The initial decision to borrow may be reversed later in reaction to political opposition, difficulties in issuing debt and costs of borrowing.

The decision to borrow has to be formally binding at some point in the process. Though deciding to borrow can be interspersed with other steps in the debt process, the decision is discussed here as a conceptually unified issue. The decision to borrow can occur at as many as four decision points in the debt process. The initial determination to borrow has been discussed. A possible second decision point is where a public referendum to authorize debt is required by law; conceptually, this might be divided into a decision to authorize a referendum and the actual referendum voting. A third decision is when a public organization's governing officials formally and officially decide to borrow. The last is the signing of debt contracts, discussed later, which marks the point in time beyond which an entity cannot change its decision to borrow.

The second step in issuing debt is the provision of legal advice to the officials responsible for issuing debt. If the debt is a common form entered into previously, officials may assume that what they are doing is legally correct. Formal legal advice minimizes possible errors, however. In simple or common short-term debt situations, public organizations tend to rely on legal generalists who serve them in all legal matters. In more complex or long-term situations, a bond counsel plays a technical specialist role concerning debt legalities. A bond counsel can be retained to prepare or review documents and to offer opinions. Documents can include various contracts, advertisements, laws, and ones expressing opinions. Contracts can include the debt contracts, contracts transferring debt contracts, and those concerning the performance of certain responsibilities in the debt process by specialists or capital facilities contractors.

Bond counsels offer opinions on two matters: whether debt contracts are legal obligations at the time of issuance and whether they are exempt from federal income taxation. Opinions come in two forms. First, as legal advisors to issuers, they give opinions concerning how to borrow money to achieve these statuses for debt. Second, bond counsels issue formal opinions, which accompany municipal bonds, that state their opinions that a debt issue is a legal obligation of the issuer and, if appropriate, exempt from federal income taxation. Legality of debt issuance revolves around interpretations of pur oses, procedures, and limitations, which are found mostly in state law. This oncern comes first because debt that is not issued legally is not a legal bligation (i.e., the issuer cannot be obliged to pay by legal processes). Federal ax exemption concerns federal law and regulations. Specifics of both con- erns include whether the proposed debt purposes fit particular purposes pelled out in statutory law; the correctness of the calling of public meetings, ne legal action by a governing body to incur debt, and any public referenda; nd limitations in time, amounts, and interest rates. Often, particular proce- ures and limitations, whether unique or additional, are determined by the gal situation concerning purpose. For example, general obligation debt for eneral government purposes is usually required to be submitted to the lectorate for approval or disapproval. Federal income tax exemption is a atter of specific federal laws and regulations, which tend to swing like a endulum between looser and tighter.

Legal advice is important for a variety of reasons. Issuing debt improperly auses difficulties for everyone involved. An entity can have its reputation ained in the debt markets. Responsible officials can be held legally liable dividually for repayment of illegally acquired debt. Technical specialists who re involved in a debt issue may have fewer customers. Investors may not get aid on time or may lose the federal income tax exemption. Two reasons can e given for challenging the legal features of a debt issue: opposition to the se of the debt and insufficient revenue to pay debt. These events happen often nough to make attention to legalities imperative because of the amounts of oney involved.

The third step is to determine how much money to borrow. Generally, the west reasonable amount is best. Short-term debt is estimated on the high de so the borrower avoids having to borrow a second time because a first orrowing was insufficient. Long-term debt is usually approximately equal to ne amount required for the specific capital items. In many cases, long-term ebt amounts are estimated before firm prices are established. The debt rocess and the pricing of capital items may be parallel in time. Where bonds annot be issued until a purchase has been made or work completed, an entity ses some form of short-term financing and later issues long-term debt for ne exact amount.

A consulting engineer can play a technical specialist role in capital project ebt financing. This person estimates the cost of a capital project to determine ow much to borrow and to make sure that prices are reasonable.

The fourth step is the design of a debt issue. Though seldom done in polka ots or bold colors, debt features are chosen to produce attractive debt ontracts from both a borrower and investor perspective. Generally, the debt ssuer chooses features oriented toward minimizing costs as long as the goal f avoiding political opposition is met.

Except for implicit short-term debt that takes the form of unpaid bills, mited period credit for purchases, and registered warrants, short-term debt an be placed privately or publicly. *Private placement,* more common for hort-term debt, occurs when a borrower deals directly with a lender, such as bank or insurance company, by either choosing a lender-designed debt ontract or negotiating loan terms. This generally means only one debt holder.

Public placement means that debt contracts are sold to members of the public. Ordinarily, public placement involves a debtor, an underwriter, and members of the investing public. An underwriter, which is likely to be a group of underwriters as debt issues become larger, buys debt contracts and sells them to investors. In public placement cases, debt design is similar to long-term debt design; however, short-term debt contracts are simpler.

A crucial design issue for short-term debt is whether to use a rollover provision. Ordinarily, a rollover provision is used when short-term debt finances capital projects before long-term borrowing. Rollover options protect against delays in projects and in acquiring long-term debt. They also allow borrowers to choose when to sell long-term debt contracts, which can make a large difference in borrowing costs over a long period. A difficulty common to all markets is buying or selling when the price is right.

Long-term debt offers a full range of design features. Major initial decisions, from less common to most common, are between private and public placement, between direct sales and the use of an underwriter, and between the sale of debt contracts to underwriters on a bid or negotiated basis. Private placement of long-term debt occurs when borrowers directly contact a lender and negotiate terms, usually for relative smaller amounts, less than $1 million.

Public placement means selling debt contracts in a public marketplace. Direct sales by a public entity means the issuer sells debt contracts directly to investors. Issuers expose themselves to shifts in the public debt markets during the period of direct sales, and money becomes available as debt contracts are sold. The other public placement choice is selling debt contracts through an underwriter.

The advantages of public placement through an underwriter include borrowers being shielded from market vagaries and obtaining money without waiting. Also, issuers use underwriters' expertise resulting from buying and selling debt full-time. An issuer using private or direct public placement is more apt to commit a serious blunder than an underwriter. The two ways to sell debt issues to underwriters are competitive bidding or negotiations to set prices.

Where competitive bidding is used, which may be required by law for general obligation debt, the issuer is responsible for designing and advertising all details of a debt issue in a *notice of sale* that contains all relevant details. Usually, a notice of sale is placed in *The Bond Buyer*, a trade publication, and perhaps other financially oriented publications; in addition, it also can be sent directly to selected underwriters. A notice of sale includes much of the information that would be developed later in the process for negotiated issues. Underwriters who are interested in purchasing the debt issue make a bid. The bid can be in the form of a single dollar amount or can include specifications of interest rates on various debt contracts for par interest payments and at what interest rate the underwriter values particular debt contracts. The key to evaluating bids is determining the borrowing cost to the issuer. This is usually measured by an effective interest rate reflecting the difference between what is borrowed and what is obligated in future payments. Underwriters make their profit, after all expenses, by selling debt contracts at a higher price than they pay for them. Formulas used to compute interest costs depend on the particular bid specifications. Of the two commonly used methods of comput-ng interest costs, expert opinion favors a method referred to as true interest costs.[7]

Where prices are negotiated, mostly limited liability bonds, an underwriter cooperatively assists in designing a debt issue. The same measurements of price can be made in a negotiated sale as in a bid sale. Most long-term municipal debt is sold through negotiated sales. Two advantages of negotiated sales are use of underwriter expertise in designing and marketing debt and flexibility in timing the sale of debt to seek favorable market conditions. The primary disadvantage is that underwriters charge for their services through paying less for debt contracts.[8]

Choosing between negotiated or bid sale of bonds is complex. Overall, bid sales have lower average costs than negotiated sales, including some value for the services received from underwriters. The accuracy of this view can be questioned when the value of underwriter services is estimated differently. Negotiated sales are much easier for public officials, which makes price adjustments for underwriter services difficult to estimate from an analytical viewpoint. In one sense, the market price is difficult to estimate from an analytical viewpoint. In another sense, the market price is simply right because that is what buyers and sellers agree on. Other factors are debt issuer credit and reputation. High-credit quality issues and well-known issuers do better with competitive bids, whereas lower-credit quality and little-known issuers do better with negotiated sales.[9]

Much debt design involves choosing sources of expertise to deal with the particular design features. The variety of expertise roles tend to be played by mostly the same actors. Six types of expertise appear in designing municipal debt. First, the principal financial administrators or officers represent the principal debt issuer financial expertise. Second, legal expertise can be represented by staff attorneys but is generally represented by external bond counsels who are hired to carry out particular tasks discussed above. Third, there may be a financial advisor, someone who is knowledgeable about public debt markets. A financial advisor is a consultant on any element of issuing debt. Fourth, though uncommon, an agent in a direct public placement supplies advice on debt features and handles sales details. Fifth, a bidding underwriter's debt market expertise is represented in bids. Sixth, a negotiating underwriter's expertise is complete design advice and purchase of the designed debt issue. The third through sixth areas involve mostly the same people and organizations called variously underwriters, investment bankers, brokers, and dealers. They engage in buying and selling debt and their expertise. Financial advisors generally avoid bidding on issues they design, and the general industry practice is to avoid even appearances of conflict of interest or of taking unfair advantage of debt issuers or customers.

Most design features are a matter of market characteristics and legal validity. The primary design decisions are choice of expertise and specific experts. Beyond those choices, few generally valid things can be said about design features. First, rely on expert advice and get more expert advice where a question is important. Second, set the overall term of a debt issue for capital items at a length no greater than the expected life of the capital item. Third, include call provisions in long-term bonds.

The fifth and sixth steps in public placement are the marketing effort and the development of debt contracts with various particular events intertwining in time. After an municipal issuer decides to borrow money, statements that the issuer is going to sell debt constitute a marketing effort. Various terms are used to describe bond issue advertisements, often published: official notice, official advertisement, and official circular. An *official notice* is more general and indicates that a bond issue will become available for sale; the *official advertisement* and *official circular* contain a prospectus that discloses relevant information about the bond issue and the issuing jurisdiction; in effect, this is a preliminary version of an official statement that is discussed below. Developing debt contracts begins with legal research and continues with debt design. Crucial marketing and contract development activity takes place around the date of sale of debt contracts. The date of sale is the bidding date for bid sales and the date when a negotiated deal is signed by an issuer and an underwriter.[10] The details of debt contracts are completed by the date of sale except perhaps for printing bonds, and issuers' underwriters can make a variety of marketing efforts. The crucial events are the publication of a prospectus, acquiring a rating for an issue, preparing an official statement, finalizing debt contract details, and locating customers.

Before the date of sale, the public issuer has a prospectus published, which describes the debt issue in detail. This can be an advertisement for bids, notice of sale that includes bid specifications, or one with the purpose of attracting underwriters. At approximately the same time, negotiating underwriters can advertise their intention to sell debt contracts. A debt rating is secured as a marketing device; rating agencies are paid to determine and issue ratings. Also, an underwriter can be looking for customers for debt contracts to determine a bid price, to shape a negotiated debt issue, and to sell the debt contracts. Final details are usually precise interest rates and prices, which are determined by bids or negotiations just before the date of sale. Debt contract details are determined last to ensure that the debt contracts are in line with the market prices for debt. The end of debt contract development occurs when a contract is prepared to transfer ownership of an debt issue of debt contracts from a debt issuer to an underwriter. The marketing step continues until the debt contracts are sold.

The seventh step is the actual exchange of the ownership of debt contracts for money. A debt issuer, or an agent authorized to act on its behalf, finalizes the deal by signing a contract transferring ownership of debt contracts to the underwriter, who has already signed the contract. Then, the issuer exchanges the signed contract for the money, which is in some form of a check. Everybody is happy and smiles a lot. After this, underwriters and issuers go their own ways, one with money and the other with ownership of debt contracts. Underwriters continue their marketing efforts. One crucial action is the preparation of the *official statement,* which is patterned after statements required by private-sector debt regulations issued by the U.S. Securities and Exchange Commission that must be filed with the Municipal Securities Rulemaking Board. A notice of sale or a prospectus contains much of the same information. An official statement spells out details concerning the debt contracts and information about the issuer. Though not legally required o

ssuers, underwriters are required to obtain them from issuers when the issue
xceeds $1 million, which means that most issuers wanting to borrow money
eed them. Official statements are an official and legally binding description of
he debt issue. In addition to specific requirements, they have to contain infor-
nation on any major negative concern that an investor would want to know about
he bond issue or issuer. Official statements are pressed on customers both as
n advertising device and as a precise statement of what is being sold. All
isputes concerning representations of a debt issue are referred back to the
fficial statement. In addition, some states specify that certain information
nust be disclosed in relation to a debt issue. Official statements are technically
oluntary disclosures, which are practically required by the debt markets,
specially after the mid-1970s municipal defaults; state disclosure laws man-
ate particular disclosures. Official statements and disclosure laws are mar-
eting efforts in that reliable information is provided to investors.[11]

In 1975, federal law created the Municipal Securities Rulemaking Board
MSRB) to regulate underwriters and other dealers who buy and sell munici-
al bonds. In 1990, underwriters were given the legal responsibility to provide
nvestors with official statements, which are also required to be sent to the
MSRB for bond issues of more than $1 million. Because official statements
re marketing devices of great importance, they have to be strictly accurate.
Misstatements or withholding facts in official statements can be considered
·aud.[12] Official statements are prepared quickly so that underwriters can
esell debt contracts without delay. Holding debt contracts ties up the working
apital of underwriters and exposes them to the risk of a negative shift in the
ebt market. In addition to published advertisements, underwriters make
irect contracts with investors. Underwriters do much marketing work before
he transfer of ownership of a debt issue and may have to finalize only the
eselling of debt contracts. One reason that underwriters prefer negotiated
ales is that they can lock everything into place on both sides of a debt issue
efore the date of sale, which reduces risk.

The eighth step is the administration of the debt that formally is the
esponsibility of the issuing entity. In addition to the debt issuer, one or more
gents or trustees may be responsible. Agents and trustees act on behalf of
ebt issuers. An agent is someone chosen at the discretion of the issuer to carry
ut certain activities, but a trustee is required by the debt contracts to carry
ut particular actions. Who can act as a trustee can be specified in debt
ontracts. Agents do things for issuers because the issuers prefer not to do
hem, and trustees do things for debt issuers because the debt contract
equires trustees. Trustees are used to upgrade creditworthiness and to assure
nvestors that particular actions are handled properly. Trustees are used
articularly for revenue project limited liability debt.

The primary administrative activities are handling the debt proceeds, main-
aining records, and fulfilling debt contract requirements. Also, administra-
on of debt can involve making discretionary choices allowed by debt con-
·acts or not covered in them (e.g., exercise of call options or use of an agent).

Handling debt proceeds means taking money in the form of a check,
epositing it into a public organization's financial account, and using the
noney's time value in the most advantageous manner available. Formerly, this

meant investing debt proceeds as soon as they came into the possession of a issuer; however, elaborate rules developed since the Tax Reform Act of 198 determined in what manner this can occur. If federal regulations are n followed, a debt issue can lose its federal income tax exempt status. Rules at fluid in this area and require a bond counsel opinion. The options includ investing federal income tax exempt debt proceeds, issuing taxable debt tha can be invested without concern for federal income tax regulations, payin vendors as early as possible, and minimizing the handling period. Thes options affect debt design. In handling debt proceeds, safety comes first fo any deposit, investment, or payment of monies to vendors.

Record keeping is an inherent part of debt administration. A record of a debt contracts is required for an accounting system, and all debt transaction should be properly accounted for, especially when there is a need to be able t show that the use of debt proceeds conforms to legal or contractual require ments. Debt records also facilitate budgeting.

One aspect of record keeping is registration of the owners of debt contract which is required by federal tax law. Registered means keeping a record of th ownership of debt contracts; that is usually done initially by underwriter selling bonds to customers. Registration is an issuer responsibility that it ca handle itself or refer to an agent such as an underwriter.

The fulfillment of debt contracts always includes payment of principal an interest in some very specific fashion. Usually, a financial institution in th business of handling money called a paying agent does this. An issuing entit pays money to a paying agent, before or after the debt contract repaymen and the paying agent pays the debt holders, which eliminates debt obligation Often, the paying agent is also responsible for maintaining registration. Othe aspects of debt contracts were discussed previously in debt design. Two ke aspects of debt contract fulfillment are maintaining a federal income ta exempt status for debt contracts and maintaining the debt relationship as legal obligation of the issuing entity. The tax status issue is mostly a concer for future debt but can be contractually specified. The maintenance of the deb relationship as a legal obligation of the issuing entity provisions are meant t force the issuing entity to maintain its obligation status. Prohibitions agains contrary actions in a debt contract force the debt obligation to remain upo the issuer.

Failure to fulfill debt contract terms means the contract is in default an that debt holders can take legal action to force compliance with debt contract Default is avoided by all parties to the extent possible. Three possible form of default can occur. A defaulting entity usually claims that its default is on of the first two rather than the third. First, a technical default occurs when a entity through an error temporarily fails to meet its contractual obligation Lateness of a day in paying something is a technical default. Second, a rea default occurs when an entity cannot or will not meet terms of a debt contrac and negotiates with its debt holders. An issuer typically contends that th default is temporary or nonexistent because of interpretations of debt con tracts. The key here is the issuer negotiating with debt holders because bot fear the consequences of the third default alternative. A third default alterna tive occurs when the debt contract reaches the stage of legal actions in court of law. A debt holder is not paid until legal issues are resolved, and the debt issuer acquires an extremely negative reputation in debt markets. Much of the legal and design efforts are oriented toward avoiding default.[13]

The debt process for a particular debt issue is concluded when all debt contract obligations have been fulfilled. If not normally completed, a debt process is incomplete because of lack of an obliged party capable of being compelled to make contracted payments, or the legal issues are in the process of being resolved.

CONCLUSION ◆

This chapter has served its purpose if it has clarified the purposes of public debt, the multiple federal roles in relation to public debt, public debt characteristics, the workings of debt markets, and the municipal debt process. In addition to focusing on exactly what is involved—A borrows money from B and owes B or another party repayment—the chapter has described public debt briefly. In addition, the legalities and specialized roles have been emphasized because of common importance. Public debt administration is complex and important because of the huge amounts of money being handled over extended periods of time.

DISCUSSION QUESTIONS

1. What are good reasons or situations in which to borrow? Do different people have different preferences for borrowing?
2. Putting aside the large amounts of money involved, how is public debt different from personal loans?
3. What are better debt features to have? What are the advantages of those debt features?

NOTES ◆

1. Wade S. Smith (1979). *The appraisal of municipal credit risk.* New York: Moody's Investors Service, pp. 180-181. This is the strictest definition of a general obligation. A strong but less stringent one is found in Lennox L. Moak (1982). *Municipal bonds: Planning, sale, and administration.* Municipal Finance Officers Association, pp. 41, 351-353, under the terms "general obligation bonds" and "full-faith-and-credit debt."

2. Smith, pp. 181-185; Moak refers to this general category of debt obligations as "nonguaranteed," which tends to be misleading. He notes general confusion in the area of classification systems, pp. 41-43.

3. Smith, pp. 92, 185-188; and Moak, pp. 117-118.

4. Moak, pp. 117-118, 234-235, 253-260.

5. Moak, pp. 181-204, 341-343; and Public Securities Association (1987). *Fundamentals of municipal bonds* (4th ed.). New York: Public Securities Association, 171-186.

6. *City and state: Crain's newspaper of public business and finance.* (1985, July/August). Chicago, 1, 31. Public finance innovations, particularly debt, are one focus of this newspaper,

which is an advertising vehicle for financial service providers marketing to state and local governments, especially in the area of debt.

    7. George G. Kaufman and Philip J. Fischer (1987). Debt management. In J. Richard Aronson and Eli Schwartz (Eds.), *Management policies in local government finance* (3rd ed.; pp. 310-315). Washington, DC: International City Management Association. Also, see note 5.

    8. Kaufman and Fischer, pp. 308-309.

    9. Kaufman and Fischer, p. 309.

    10. Moak, p. 271.

    11. Moak, pp. 277-284; and Kaufman and Fischer, pp. 304-307.

    12. Public Securities Association, pp. 163-170.

    13. Smith, pp. 243-253 specifically. Smith's work is generally oriented to specifying how to analyze municipal credit risk, which is primarily based on the likelihood of default, pp. 6-8.

◆ SUGGESTED READINGS

Girard J. Miller (Ed.). (1996). *Handbook of debt management.* New York: Marcel Dekker.

Lennox L. Moak (1982). *Municipal bonds: Planning, sale, and administration.* Chicago: Municipal Finance Officers Association.

Public Securities Association (1987). *Fundamentals of municipal bonds* (4th ed.). New York: Public Securities Association.

William Simonsen and Mark D. Robbins (1996) Does it make any difference anymore? Competitive versus negotiated municipal bond issuance. *Public Administration Review, 56,* 47-64.

Wade S. Smith (1979). *The appraisal of municipal credit risk.* New York: Moody's Investor Services.

Risk Management

Everyone makes mistakes and is involved in accidents. Individuals make efforts to avoid mistakes and accidents, especially ones that harm people and cause losses or liabilities. Automobile collisions, fires, and injuries from falling on icy sidewalks are all risks that most people deal with by taking sensible precautions. Governments and nonprofit organizations, no less than individuals, are exposed to risks, those "slings and arrows of outrageous fortune." When employees are hurt on the job, a decline in productivity and increased costs in medical and workers' compensation costs can result. Fires, floods, damaging storms, and other natural disasters increase costs, in some cases astronomically. What has been described as an increasing "hyperactivity" in legal system use and decreasing willingness by courts and legislatures to grant individual, governmental, or charitable immunity from lawsuits has greatly increased the costs of government liability. This points to the expanding need for governmental and nonprofit organizations to manage their exposure to losses more effectively, whether those losses occur to real or personal property, because of lawsuits, or through employee injury, illness, or inability to work. Furthermore, Tremper noted that for nonprofits, risk management helps avoid harm, which is key to their mission.[1] This chapter will look at the types of risks that most commonly confront public agencies, review the steps of the risk management process, and review approaches to handling risk in the public sector.

WHAT RISK MANAGEMENT IS ◆

Risk management is often used interchangeably with buying insurance, but this is misleading. Managing risk is much broader in scope than merely focusing on a single element. Managing risk is the systematic organized effort to eliminate or reduce harm to persons and the threat of losses to public organizations. Purchasing insurance can play a role in such an effort. Obviously, the most important thing to consider in risk management is reducing

or eliminating potential harm that individuals can be exposed to within an
outside of the organization. The next most important element is to reduce th
actual or potential cost to the organization through a combination of action
that prevents losses or protects against financial disaster should risks becom
realities. A public agency also wants to stabilize costs—that is, make cos
associated with losses more predictable over time. Such consistency allows fo
planned expenditures and reduces large shocks to the organization's financi
system.

A systematic risk management program includes (1) identifying the risk
faced by the organization, (2) estimating and measuring the frequency an
severity of risks, (3) developing alternatives to minimize risk exposure, (4
choosing measures for funding the costs of unavoidable risks, and (5) admin
istering and reviewing the program to minimize costs.

◆ IDENTIFYING RISK

Risk identification is a systematic and comprehensive way to identify all ris
exposures, including those where persons and property can be harmed o
where financial losses might occur. To identify risks means looking at a
aspects of a public organization, from day-to-day operations to policy makin₃
You must understand where an agency has exposures to loss before plannin
some systematic way of managing risk. One way to identify the losses a
organization can face is by using terminology common to contract law. Thre
different groups or "parties" can be responsible for losses that occur, that i
be required to pay. The first party represents you or an organization you wor
for. The second party represents an individual or organization that you ar
contractually obligated to in some way. The third party is some outsid
individual or group that can be affected by actions taken between the first an
second parties. The following example demonstrates how this classificatio
can help identify risks.

The City of Smalltown has recently decided to contract out its refus
collection to a private hauler. Under this arrangement Smalltown is the firs
party and the private hauler, Dirty Harry and Sons, is the second party to an
action. One day Dirty Harry's son Alphonse is driving the refuse truck an
accidentally drives over the Widow Grouchley's petunia patch. The Widow i
not amused and threatens to sue both Dirty Harry and the City for the loss o
her petunias. She has become a third party in the action. The exposure to los
to each of the parties depends on several factors. Were the Widow's petunia
planted in a public right of way? If so, the loss may have to be absorbed by th
third party, the Widow Grouchley. If the petunia patch was on private prop
erty, it is likely that Dirty Harry, Smalltown, or both will be liable for the loss
State law as well as the contract terms between the first and second partie
determine the liability.

No matter which party participates in a particular action, governments fac
many varying types of exposures to risk. One of the most important i
exposure as a result of liability: "the legal requirement or obligation of ₐ
person, corporation, or local government to restore a value or loss it ha

caused to an injured party."[2] Such risks exist in a myriad of ways. Individuals who are in an accident while operating equipment of a public agency create liabilities for that agency when persons are injured or property is damaged. State and local governments are liable for violations of an individual's civil rights under Section 1983 of the Civil Rights Act of 1871. Cases of this type rapidly increased during the last decade. If state or local governments are carrying out nongovernmental activities, they have the same level of liability as private corporations. These and other cases point to the critical importance of liability as a potentially high-cost risk for public agencies.

Liability exists for accidents that occur either within public agency facilities (on-premises) or on property controlled by or owned by public organizations (off-premises). The collapse of Kemper Arena in Kansas City several years ago would have opened the public owners to enormous liability had it been filled with people. Still, smaller hazards exist. Loose railings, wet floors, exposed wiring, and many other common physical problems can create exposures to injury and loss. Off-premise exposure is common for local governments, where items such as damaged sidewalks, open manholes, potholes, and numerous other hazards created on public rights-of-way increase liability risks. Several years ago, a jury awarded an individual more than $5 million in damages after a dead tree fell on him, causing permanent disability. The tree happened to be in a public right-of-way, and the jury deemed it a preventable hazard. These types of visible dangers are extremely varied, and only a systematic review can begin to identify them.

Personnel represents another risk exposure that can be extremely costly for governments and nonprofit organizations. These exposures can affect the agency in two ways. First, the loss of an employee because of illness or accident can cause delays or inefficiencies in the delivery of services and cost additional money to replace that individual, even on a temporary basis. Fringe benefit costs for disability can increase as well. Second, if negligence by the organization can be shown to have caused the illness or accident, the avenue of suit against the agency can also cause severe financial repercussions. We need look at only some of the recent private personnel suits in the chemical industry to see the potential risk entailed.

A third exposure to loss is property. This includes buildings and equipment that might be lost because of fire, natural disaster, vandalism, theft, or some other cause, as well as loss of use of that property and the contents within those structures. For public agencies, the loss of the use of property could include land, buildings, or equipment. As with any type of exposure to loss, there are varying ways to deal with this problem. Efforts to install more vigilant inspection programs can reduce the likelihood of loss from fire or theft. Stringent construction standards protect property from floods, earthquakes, and other natural disasters. Spreading the location of property to reduce fire risk can greatly decrease the likelihood of major losses in this area. Replacement of outmoded property and equipment can greatly dilute potential property losses. Simple actions such as installing fire detectors and fire alarms can save lives and property.

Public agencies should also distinguish between direct and indirect property losses. Direct losses are those that directly damage or diminish the value of something, whereas indirect losses are caused by a reduction in value through a third-party loss of another person or property. For example, the loss of a machinery part reduces the value of the entire piece of machinery and indirectly reduces collections of a revenue-producing activity. Another example of indirect costs would be a car that is rented to be used while a damaged car is being repaired. Finally, loss of net income occurs when some personnel or property affect the flow of revenue into the organization. If a fire closes a federal park, the federal government loses user fee income normally collected when the park is open.

Vehicular operations represent both a liability and a personnel exposure. Dotterweich listed five typical vehicular exposures: (1) losses from improper or inadequate maintenance, (2) losses from improper driving habits or techniques, (3) damage to government property, (4) injury to government workers caused by others, and (5) unrelated property damage.[3]

The key to identifying risk is using systematic methods for collecting information on exposures. Several sources of information are available. Existing records can show such things as location, use, and condition of all property owned or under the responsibility of an agency. A review of loss histories over an extended period of time tells an agency a great deal about where exposures have occurred in the past. This is no guarantee for the future but it is a starting point. Exposures can be created through actions by the policy board in passing laws and resolutions and entering into mutual aid agreements, or through the basic bylaws or constitution of the organization. In fact, board liability is a key concern of nonprofits. In carrying out their legal responsibilities, the primary area of exposure for boards relates to their treatment of employees.[4] The most common claims are for things such as illegal dismissals, discrimination, and violation of labor laws. For state and local governments and various nonprofit agencies, risk and exposure can be increased by actions taken by other agencies and governments, and such actions should be reviewed and documented. Federal and state governments often pass laws that increase both the responsibilities and the liabilities for local political subdivisions. For example, the Americans with Disabilities Act may have substantially increased risk exposure for some public or nonprofit organizations. The same can be true of the requirements of the Family and Medical Leave Act passed in the early 1990s.

On-site inspections by trained observers looking for areas of potential losses or liabilities are an excellent way to systematically evaluate what risks exist. Such inspections should be done continually, with any changes in physical condition or status reported to whomever is responsible for risk management.[5] Recent inspections by federal, state, and local officials have found, for instance, that almost half of all county bridges are potentially hazardous. In addition, public agencies can use a risk discovery questionnaire which helps provide a comprehensive listing of all possible risks and exposures faced by the organization. Sample listings prepared by various organizations can help provide as all-encompassing a review as possible.[6] Another useful technique is to interview individuals working for the agency to determine what they perceive to be the greatest exposure to injury, damage, or loss. This can provide insights that a risk manager would not have considered. After all,

ABLE 15.1 Categories for Measuring Risk

	Severity	
	Low	High
Low (requency)	1. low frequency/ low severity	2. low frequency/ high severity
High	3. high frequency/ low severity	4. high frequency/ high severity

rho should better know the risks a particular organization faces than the
mployees who work for it?

Risk must be approached from the standpoint of reviewing every possible
ontingency where loss or liability might occur. In other words, loss from an
ccident caused by a government vehicle damaging private property might
ntail not just the loss of the vehicle. Losses from a suit by the owner for
amage to the property, increases to the government's insurance premiums,
oss of use of the vehicle, and personal injury are also strong possibilities. Such
n accident would also have losses because of downtime associated with
mployee time spent filling out accident reports or making court appearances.
: can also be hard to replace that vehicle quickly, resulting in the delay of
ertain governmental services. Any personal injuries caused by the accident
ould also raise costs substantially. Clearly, all the ramifications of a risk
tuation must be considered, not just the immediate impacts of that loss.
inally, even though there is a point where the costs of identifying risks are
ot justified, a thorough effort helps prevent losses the organization simply
annot absorb. Such efforts can also serve as an educational tool of risk
nanagement by alerting members of an organization to risks.

MEASUREMENT OF RISK ◆

Only after risks have been identified can the public organization begin to
neasure the magnitude and probability of those risks occurring. Most organi-
ations look at how often losses are likely to occur and the severity of those
osses. In this way, strategies for handling the risk can be developed. The most
ommon and simplest categories are represented in Table 15.1, which divides
ll risk situations into those high or low with respect to frequency and severity.
osses with the lowest chance of occurrence and those likely to have a minimal
nancial impact on the organization are reflected in category one. An office
rorker who suffers a minor cut or perhaps a "fender bender" causing little or
o damage to property are examples in this category. Category three repre-
ents losses that have a high rate of occurrence but low associated costs. For
xample, many organizations have equipment that is prone to breakdown or
as serious maintenance problems, and they can anticipate this equipment
rill be out of service a considerable amount of the time. The predictability of

this loss makes it possible to plan alternatives such as the purchase of backup piece of equipment or pay t for a maintenance contract to servic the equipment.

The two other categories of risk te more serious problems for manage ment. Exposures to risk that are likely to be the most severe are of mos concern to an organization. Small losses, even if they are unexpected, can ofte be absorbed within the operating budgets of the agency. Large losses ofte cannot be absorbed, however, and must be paid for through revenue genera tion, from incurring debt, or both. One primary function of risk managemen is to protect the organization from such losses.

Category four, losses that happen frequently and have a high cost, can creat serious financial drains for the organization unless steps are taken to eithe reduce the occurrence, avoid the loss, or reduce the size of the loss. If publi workers in a particular department are constantly being injured on duty workers' compensation claims can devastate a budget. Property located in flood plain runs an ever increasing probability of damage or destruction. Th one bright spot in this type of situation is that predicting losses is easy. Th more often a loss occurs, the greater ability the organization has to predic future losses. This allows management to plan courses of action.

Finally, category two perhaps represents the risks that cause the mos problems for public agencies, those that have extremely costly impacts but ar almost impossible to predict because of their infrequent occurrence. Natura disasters provide the best examples of this situation. Who can foresee whe enormous losses of life and property from hurricanes, tornadoes, and flood will occur, when they hit with little or no warning? This is especially true wher no previous history or pattern exists for such a disaster. Although severity i predictable, frequency often is not.

◆ WAYS TO MANAGE RISK

Once risk has been identified and measured, the organization can develo strategies to manage the risk that exists. Options include reducing or elimi nating the risk that exists, absorbing the costs associated with the potential fo loss, or transferring that risk to someone else.

In looking at alternative approaches to avoiding risk, a public or nonprofi organization should evaluate all the potential costs and benefits. For example if a county government finds that one of its bridges is structurally unsoun and thus might collapse under stress, several alternatives are available to dea with the situation. The county can ignore the situation and hope the bridg stays up or close the bridge and thus end the county's exposure at that poin It is important to remember that eliminating one risk can create others however. Closing a bridge can increase hazards at another bridge because c the increased traffic. The bridge can be repaired. The county can buy insur ance from a vendor who will pay for any losses that occur or can fund th exposure in some way other than by paying an insurance company. Eac alternative has benefits and costs associated with it. A successful risk progran would carefully weigh each alternative before deciding which action to take

The county can try to avoid the risk, eliminate the risk, try to reduce it, assume responsibility for the risk, or transfer the risk to someone else. In some instances, the county can combine one or more of these actions to control the financial ramifications that exposure to risk creates. Certain approaches make more sense for the different categories of risk you are facing.

Public and nonprofit organizations can avoid risks in many ways. One is merely to transfer the legal responsibility for providing goods or services to some other public or private organization. When a state government contracts with a construction firm to build a highway, the contract provisions will often transfer any risk of injury or damage that occurs as a result of that construction to the contractor. In this case, the state government would be held harmless from any actions arising from the contractor's actions. If, on the other hand, the state does the highway construction work with its own employees or if such a provision was not written into the contract, the state would be liable for any injuries or damages that might occur. Several charitable nonprofit organizations have been successful in limiting their exposure through the passage of state legislation. Almost 15 states have passed such legislation in recent years.[7]

Another way to avoid risk occurs when other levels of government take over the functions previously carried out by another public organization. For example, cities, counties, and states are constantly arguing about who has responsibility for the various public road facilities within their jurisdictions. Part of the reason for this interjurisdictional squabbling is the cost of maintaining those facilities, but another reason is the liability that is associated with losses that might occur in conjunction with operating those facilities. Any organization considering the options available to it in avoiding risks must consider the possibilities available through such transfers.

Reduction or Elimination

Losses that occur frequently and have high costs associated with them are excellent candidates for risk reduction or elimination strategies. If workers are continually being injured on duty, something must be wrong with either the physical working conditions, the type of work being conducted, or the approach to work being undertaken. Are the workers using unsafe practices? Is the equipment faulty? Are the facilities hazardous? Perhaps one of the weakest areas of past public organizational efforts has been the development of comprehensive safety programs for employees, particularly those in high-risk activities. Many of us are familiar with safety programs such as CPR, which have success in saving lives, but we are less familiar with safety programs that prevent other types of losses. For example, by instituting a back exercise and lifting training program for its refuse collectors, an organization can reduce its time lost to accident and workers' compensation claims. Serious third-party accidents and resulting deaths have been reduced in communities that have established police hot pursuit policies. Training employees in how to avoid fire hazards, and continual inspections of working places or physical structures, are major ways to reduce the likelihood of loss. Among the principal issues faced by organizations in developing an effective safety policy are

- Scope of activities covered
- Who is responsible for implementation of safety programs
- Where and how accountability is fixed
- What rules are to be followed
- What structure is used to implement the safety program

Such a policy not only leads to reduced risk but also to decreased costs. Considerable interdepartmental cooperation is required to develop such a successful program. If no action is feasible to reduce the risk to a manageable level in frequency or severity, the organization may have to consider eliminating a service altogether or transferring the delivery to some other entity. This is especially true if the service being provided is neither legally required nor politically untouchable. Perhaps the agency can have some other organization at least share in its operation so the risk can be spread to a larger group of participants.

Assuming and Transferring the Costs of Risk

The choices in funding risks are assuming the costs of risks or shifting the financial responsibility to another entity. If certain risk losses are fairly common but of little concern in cost, it makes sense to assume the risk within the organization. For example, if an organization's equipment breaks down continually but the cost of repair is relatively minor, most organizations have the financial means to develop some options to deal with the costs internally. The same can be said of those risks that happen infrequently and have no major financial impact. It is cheaper for the organization to buy a first aid kit and bandages for employees who have minor cuts than it is to look for some other alternative. The organization can also find that it has no choice but to assume risk because of legal requirements, lack of affordable insurance, or some other constraint.

Financial assumption of risk can be total or partial. Total assumption can be considered a type of self-insurance. The organization predicts it has the financial resources to pay for losses. This assumption can be systematic and planned, or it can be unplanned and unanticipated. Self-insurance is particularly useful for large public organizations with many employees because their ability to predict losses is greater than small organizations and the funds available to invest for the eventuality of loss are much greater. If a state government could predict with some degree of certainty that accidents on the job site would lead to a number of "injured on duty" claims by employees, the state could identify the types of job most likely to create employee injuries, develop a predictive model to determine the number and size of claims that would be made, and set aside in its budget each year sufficient funds to cover losses that could be anticipated to occur because of such injuries. This would be planned full assumption of risk.

On the other hand, the community that finds itself facing a $5 million lawsuit, with little or no financial resources set aside to pay for that suit and

o insurance to cover the loss, is also self-insured, but in no sense was it
lanned. One major problem with public organizations is building the politi-
al support necessary to adequately fund risks that have been assumed. It is
asy for a political leader, who may not be in office in four years, to raid the
nking funds set aside to cover losses and use the money for more politically
ttractive projects or activities, while hoping that any loss occurs after that
:ader leaves office. Full assumption of risk is a legitimate option for an
rganization to consider, especially for risks that are of low severity. It should
e approached systematically, however, to set aside sufficient resources to cope
ith losses when they occur.

Partial assumption is also quite common among public organizations.
here are several types of partial assumption. An agency can purchase insur-
nce that covers some portion of the potential losses. Another approach,
hich is growing particularly among smaller organizations, is risk pooling.
everal organizations band together to share the risk of loss. This has become
ommon among municipal governments in such areas as unemployment or
orkers' compensation insurance. The local government continues to assume
portion of the risk but also transfers a major portion of the risk to the pool.
his approach is particularly useful for very small public organizations and
here losses are unpredictable and extremely costly. A 1993 survey of pools
und that almost 94% of the more than 400 local government pools repre-
nted entities with populations of less than 25,000. These pools included
ties, school districts, and special districts.[8] Pooling risks with similar organi-
ations reduces the impact that any one loss may have while increasing the
redictability of losses by involving a larger number of organizations with
milar risk exposures. The drawbacks are caused by the lack of control and
exibility available to the small organization, as well as by the administrative
omplexity that can occur when several separate entities try to coordinate
1eir efforts.

Insurance and Non-Insurance Transfer

The most common method of transferring risk is through the purchase of
1surance. Insurance can be required by law, even if the organization believes
: can cope with the potential losses in other ways. Insurance is perhaps the
1ost difficult and least understood element of risk management in the public
2ctor. Terms such as *pro rata distribution, unnamed floater location, waiver of
1urrogation,* and *coinsurance* are enough to confuse anyone unfamiliar with
1surance. Although the terminology can be confusing, the issues facing
ublic managers are not. Insurance is a way of regularizing payments for risk
2sses. In addition to administrative costs, which are a substantial portion of
1surance premiums, insurance premiums are set at a level where they are
ufficient to pay the cost of insured losses over the entire group of entities that
re covered by an insurance policy. Insurance companies manage risk fund-
1g: They figure out probable losses, probable costs, and pay the covered losses
s they occur.

Most insurance plans for public or nonprofit organizations fall into one of
1e following categories:

- Property
- Boiler and machinery
- General employee liability
- General third-party liability
- Vehicle liability
- Public official liability or directors and officers liability
- Fiduciary liability

Property coverage is concerned with both real and personal property and ris associated with property construction. Boiler and machinery insurance cover specific equipment often excluded from general property insurance policie Employee liability coverage relates to exposures to injury and other losses tha might affect employees of an organization, whereas third-party liability con cerns exposures affecting those outside of public employment. Public offici liability is one of the most rapidly expanding areas of exposure. Finall fiduciary liability is a specific type of public official liability that concerns th handling of money within an organization.

This is not meant to be an exhaustive list of exposures. Losses happen i many areas that most of us never think of. Is the organization covered if cannot collect on bills when records of those bills are destroyed? If privat property is damaged or destroyed while in the custody of a public entity, that property insured? If the public organization produces products for sal is it covered by product liability insurance? All possible exposures to risk mu be reviewed to determine the types of insurance coverage needed. Perhaps th best way to review exposures for insurance is to ask the following questions

- What property is covered?
- What persons are covered?
- What losses or risks are covered?
- How long does coverage last?
- What locations are covered?
- What are the limits of recovery?
- Are there any special conditions?

Many state, local, and nonprofit agencies have no comprehensive insuranc procurement process. As a result, they can be overinsured in some areas an totally uninsured in others. One of the first concerns in a risk managemen effort is to systematically inventory existing insurance policies to determin the types of coverages, gaps in that coverage, and areas of duplication.

The variation of insurance coverages is almost infinite. Listed below ar only a few of the major features that may be available.

Deductibles

Deductibles, which range in size and specificity, are amounts an insure party agrees to pay before an insurance company pays. For example, a organization can decide whether to have a deductible for each specific item cost, or for each occurrence of a loss, or for a period. If, for example, a fire sweeps through a state office building, a "per-loss" deductible would require the state to pay a certain amount of the loss over the deductible limit on each item separately listed. If, however the organization had a "per-occurrence" clause in its insurance policy, the organization would have to pay only one deductible for each occurrence of fire loss, no matter how many items were lost. Higher deductibles mean lower premiums and, with a low loss rate, can lead to considerable savings.

Coinsurance

This term refers to a clause contained in many property insurance policies. Both the public organization and the insurance company agree to share a portion of the risk, with the company paying some percentage of the actual value of a loss.

Replacement Coverage

One key to property coverage is whether it is for the replacement value or the actual value. If covered for actual value, an organization receives the depreciated value of that property.

Exclusions

Blanket or specific coverage is another concern with insurance coverage. Specific coverage allows for payment of only those items specifically listed. If an organization purchases new equipment and fails to have it incorporated into the policy and loss occurs, the company is uninsured for that equipment. On the other hand, if the public agency has blanket coverage, any item that is located in a particular building or owned by the insured is covered. This helps avoid disagreements over what is covered and also provides a hedge against failure to update property lists in the policy itself. A word of caution is in order, however. Many blanket policies also have many exclusions, which should be reviewed carefully.

One of the biggest shortcomings of any insurance program is the lack of awareness of what is covered. The organization may have a comprehensive general liability policy, only to find that such things as slander, libel, and defamation of character liability suits are not included. The same situation could occur with public official liability insurance, which protects public employees and officials for actions they take (or fail to take) that in some way injure another party. Directors and officers liability insurance (D&O) is often recommended to cover liability in this area and covers such things as defense costs, settlements, and judgments where an individual or organization has sued the policy board members in challenging a policy decision that the board has taken. If the policy specifically lists the individuals covered and a change in staffing occurs and is not reported to the insurance company, a person who is not listed is not covered by the insurance.

Procurement

Procurement procedures for insurance coverage are extremely important. Many problems stand in the way of a successful procurement effort. Among the most common constraints are political interference, nonconforming insurance policies, statutory limitations, and insufficient expertise. Often, especially at the state and local levels, there is considerable pressure to select an insurance agent or insurance vendor who is known in the community. This local bias can greatly increase costs, especially if the choices available are limited. A public organization may find that few if any local agents have the variety or level of coverage necessary to meet their needs and yet be constrained to purchase locally. The insurance industry is notorious for writing policies that are difficult to understand and that vary greatly from one vendor to the next. This situation has improved considerably over the past several years, but difficulties remain. If a public agency waits for insurance agents to come to them rather than taking the initiative themselves to solicit policies on their terms, it can find itself with costly insurance that does not meet its needs. State and local laws can limit both the types of insurance that public entities can obtain and the process or procedure by which they obtain that coverage. Public organizations can also find themselves without the expertise or knowledge necessary to differentiate between the various insurance carriers and policies that are available, in which case outside assistance may be necessary.

A key issue for procurement is whether to have competitive or negotiated bidding. Competitive bidding has many advantages and disadvantages. The major advantage is the possibility of lower costs. This is not always the case, however. Even if costs are not reduced, the organization is better able to evaluate the positive and negative aspects of insurance vendor proposals and can also find gaps of which they were unaware when bid specifications are prepared. Requirements that place onerous restrictions on carriers reduce the number bidding on an insurance package. Also, if a public organization issues requests for bids for insurance for a relatively short policy life, many carriers will not go through the paperwork requirements of the bid process. Finally, a particular problem for small local governments with a strong desire to allow local carriers to compete for their business is that competitive bidding will place a heavier burden on those carriers than on larger vendors because of economies of scale. Still, if significant savings can be achieved, competitive bidding is the most appropriate approach. The major alternative is negotiated bids: General specifications are issued to a number of carriers requesting information on their qualifications and coverage capacities. Clearly unqualified carriers are eliminated, and the agency can begin formal negotiations with a handful of vendors to select its insurance carrier(s). Vendors can serve as brokers for various insurance carriers or represent only one company. Negotiated bids do not imply less rigorous specifications or procurement procedures. This process can provide, however, more flexibility in meeting the needs of both public organizations and the private carriers.

Major concerns addressed in writing insurance specifications are the structure of their specifications and information that is provided. Specifications should require standardized responses from bidders. This allows an organiza-on to compare carrier cost. If an agency does not offer this structure, carriers ill provide widely disparate information that makes comparisons difficult, not impossible. Public managers should provide a complete listing of their rganization's needs. This allows carriers to provide a complete bid response nd greatly reduces the need for follow-up information requests.

When looking at procuring insurance coverage, public organizations must onsider their administrative costs. Administrative costs include the time and xpense incurred in preparing the bid documents, developing the specifica- ons, reviewing the bid responses, negotiating with insurance vendors, and eveloping the actual policy. Insurance vendors incorporate administrative osts into their proposals. Insurance companies may not be familiar with idding competitively for policies. This increases their costs, which is reflected 1 their bid responses. Administrative costs of insurance policies can exceed 0% of the actual premium costs to the organization. These expenses should e reviewed when avenues for assuming or transferring risks are considered. 1 the final analysis, the success of an organization's procurement process will e tied to the clarity with which it identifies needs and communicates those eeds to private insurance carriers.[9]

ADMINISTERING A RISK ◆
MANAGEMENT PROGRAM

Administering a risk program requires the commitment of top policy and 1anagement leaders. Although such efforts have existed in private organiza- ons for many years, only recently have their public counterparts begun to ike risk management seriously. An organization's size often dictates the types f efforts needed in managing risk. Although exposure to property loss, loss f income, personal liability, and lawsuits of various kinds can affect any ublic organization, the magnitude can be less for smaller organizations than or larger ones. A small nonprofit agency with minimal property or with a ery small staff can face far fewer exposures than a large city or a state; owever, small organizations can have far more serious problems in coping ith losses when they occur because of the impact such losses might have on small budget or the inability to predict with any consistency the frequency r size of those losses. Federal and state governments are the most sophisti- ited in their approach, but even here variation is great. Small local govern- 1ents and nonprofit organizations generally lag behind in their efforts to evelop a systematic approach to handling exposures to risk. No matter what :vel of public administration you are concerned with, certain actions are onsidered important to a successful program. Among the most important ie (1) centralized administration, (2) adequate staffing, (3) effective record eeping, and (4) written policies and procedures.[10]

Most experts recommend centralized administration of risk management fforts. As with many staff functions, risk management crosses all depart- 1ents and bureaus within public organizations. Although some service de- artments are exposed more often to risks (e.g., a local police or fire depart- 1ent), or some elements of government or nonprofit agencies can have a higher risk of loss (e.g., state maintenance facilities where hazardous chemicals might be stored), coordination of risk management efforts by a single office or department allows a systematic and comprehensive approach to risk. Although some organizations create separate departments to perform this function, smaller organizations place the activity under an existing department.

Closely associated with centralization is the question of staffing. In ideal circumstances, one or more individuals hired exclusively for that purpose would have full-time responsibility for administering risk management. This is not possible in small public organizations where budgetary resources simply do not allow for this level of staffing. In those instances, the responsibility often lies with the chief administrator, finance director, or personnel staff. Full-time staffing, however, ensures that adequate time will be devoted to the area without dilution of effort.

Functional responsibilities for a centralized loss control effort might include such things as workers' compensation, safety and accident prevention, insurance procurement and management, and a multitude of data collection and analysis functions. A centralized office can also serve as a processing center for various claims made on behalf of employees or others affected by governmental actions. It is critical that the risk management staff work effectively with other departments and agencies to ensure the most efficient handling of information and claims that occur in this area. Legal expertise is critical when liability issues arise for public agency activities. Certain departments need many more safety-related actions than others. Several departments have major responsibility for capital items and equipment subject to loss if not properly maintained or should hazards not be reduced or eliminated. Those handling revenue sources are more liable for fiduciary violations than other public officials. Many risk management actions are completed by the line agencies, but risk managers must develop a strong working relationship with agencies to implement various policies and procedures to lessen or eliminate risk.

Another concern is record keeping. To know what the risks are and how to meet those risks, the organization has to maintain systematic sources of information that can provide insights into how the organization's activities affect ongoing exposures to loss and what steps have been taken to contend with those exposures. According to Charles Coe, among the most important records to maintain are the following:

- Claims report records that state which claims have been filed and dates for insurance coverage payment
- Loss records identifying sources and causes of losses both insured and uninsured
- Property valuation schedules that list all values of buildings and their contents
- Vehicle and mobile equipment schedules
- Insurance bids and coverage records
- An insurance register of all insurance policies currently in effect
- An insurance manual that provides a guide to an organization's policies and procedures

- An expiration file reflecting when insurance policies lapse
- Premium and loss comparisons reflecting premiums and losses by type of insurance and loss data on uninsured losses[11]

Finally, by providing clear, concise positions on such concerns as (1) what risks will be covered, (2) what risks will be retained, (3) what types of insurance will be purchased, (4) selection procedures for insurance vendors, and (5) what safety policies will be implemented and how, an organization sets standards by which to measure its own performance and greatly increases its chances for implementing a successful program.

CONCLUSION ◆

This chapter has provided the reader with an overview of the major issues surrounding risk management. Many skills are needed by any public organization in developing an effective risk management program. Those responsible must be able to identify risks the organization faces, measure those risks in both qualitative and quantitative ways, and develop strategies and approaches that best enable the organization to minimize its exposure to loss. In the final analysis, such a program saves lives, protects property, and places the organization on a firmer financial footing.

Clearly, the implications that risks present to public agencies are not limited to the financial arena but affect all line and staff functions. Still, the ramifications of how the organization handles risks can directly determine its financial health. A public manager must use the various resources of the agency to see that the threat of loss does not place the organization in a position such that its financial well-being is in danger. Risk management is the tool to help accomplish this goal.

DISCUSSION QUESTIONS

1. Contact two governmental and two nonprofit agencies and determine how they operate their risk management programs. Where are the functions located? How are these functions carried out? Do they have a risk management plan?
2. Compare and contrast a public and a private organization's view of risk management from a human resources perspective. Do they see human resources and risk management in a similar way? If not, how do they differ? What programs do they offer that they see as reducing loss?
3. What factors should a public or nonprofit agency consider in deciding how much to self-insure against potential loss exposures?
4. If you were the manager in a small nonprofit or local government, how would you approach the risk management process compared with managers in larger organizations?

◆ NOTES

1. Charles Tremper (1994). Risk management. In *The Jossey-Bass handbook on nonprofi leadership and management*. San Francisco: Jossey-Bass.

2. William W. Dotterweich, Donald F. Norris, and Robert L. Sinclair (1982). *Local government ris management handbook*. Knoxville: Municipal Technical Advisory Service, University of Tennessee.

3. Dotterweich et al., p. 89.

4. Tremper, pp. 487-488.

5. Charles K. Coe (1980). *Understanding risk management: A guide for local governments* Athens: Institute of Government, University of Georgia, p. 3.

6. Gerald J. Miller and Bartley W. Hildreth (1983). Advantages of a risk managemen program. In Jack Rabin (Ed.), *A reader in local government financial management*. Athens University of Georgia.

7. Tremper.

8. Peter C. Young and B. J. Reed (1995, Spring). Government risk financing pools: An assessment of current practices. *Public Budgeting & Finance 15*(1), 96-112.

9. Dotterweich et al., pp. 119-147.

10. Miller and Hildreth.

11. Coe, p. 10.

◆ SUGGESTED READINGS

Charles K. Coe (1980). *Understanding risk management: A guide for local governments*. Athens Institute of Government, University of Georgia.

Community Risk Management and Insurance. Newsletter produced by the Nonprofit Risk Management Center, Washington, DC.

William W. Dotterweich, Donald F. Norris, and Robert L. Sinclair (1982). *Local government ris management handbook*. Knoxville: Municipal Technical Advisory Service, University of Tennessee.

Public Risk Management Association (1992). *Public risk management: Annotated bibliography* Arlington, VA.

RiskNet (1996). The RiskNet WWW Server. RiskNet Information Services, Inc.

Phyllis Sherman (1983). *Basic risk management handbook for local governments*. Washington DC: Public Risk and Insurance Management Association.

Personnel and
Pension Administration

Despite recent trends toward privatization of public services and uses of technology, labor consumes the largest portion of public expenditures. Public service is a labor-intensive operation, and because of this, costs associated with public employment are a major concern in public financial management.

Traditionally, public finance administrators have had little to do with public personnel administration, with the sole exception of public pension plans. Except for helping to design and administer some pension plans, financial issues arising from personnel administration were handled as if fiscal concerns did not exist. More recently, finance administration has been used in personnel administration to analyze the financial implications of personnel decisions. Pension administration is still a more common finance concern, but cost consequences of personnel decisions are becoming more visible in today's public organization. In this chapter we briefly look at labor costs, associated issues, and the special case of public pension plans.

THREE VIEWS OF PERSONNEL ◆
COSTS AND ASSOCIATED ISSUES

Personnel costs can be viewed from three perspectives. The employee or employees and their representatives see what benefits they receive from working for a public organization. This view may or may not encompass the total range of financial resources provided by that organization to the employee. Cost can also be viewed as a unit of labor. In this instance, the organization is concerned about how much a unit of labor costs and, consequently, what results are produced by that unit of labor cost. This is an especially useful way of looking at costs in negotiating labor contracts and analyzing the cost of labor contract proposals. This approach also provides a different measure of

TABLE 16.1   Selected Employee Benefit Plan Participation, State and Local
Governments, 1994

Type of Plan	Percentage Employees Covered
Flexible benefit plans	5
Reimbursement accounts	64
Child care	9

Source: Bureau of Labor Standards, Report on Employee Benefits in State and Local Governments, 1994.

cost than merely looking at the benefits an individual employee or group of
employees receives.

Finally, we can look at personnel costs from the perspective of the budget
and determine budgetary impacts of personnel on an organization. Adding
an employee adds more than personnel costs. There are also associated costs
such as equipment the employee must use as part of his or her job, and indirect
benefits, such as employee recreational facilities.

Each approach can be useful in evaluating the costs of personnel to the
organization. No matter which approach or combination of approaches is
used, the important point is that the costs that underlie each should be
calculated so management staff can plan effectively for the future financial
condition of the agency. Table 16.1 provides a guideline for the range of
personnel benefits that financially affect the public or nonprofit agency.

Employee Costs

Direct Benefits

The most commonly viewed costs associated with personnel are those tied
to direct salaries and wages. Historically, these are the overwhelming majority
of benefits received by public employees. Employees can be salaried or paid
on a per-hour basis. Salaried employees are paid a flat rate for a pay period
no matter how many hours they work, whereas a per-hour employee is
compensated for the number of hours worked in any given pay period. The
federal Fair Labor Standards Act (FLSA) specifies in some detail which groups
of public employees are in what categories. Generally speaking, management
personnel are paid on a fixed salary basis whereas other employees are paid
on an hourly basis.

How an employee is paid becomes important when public agencies estimate
costs. Employees paid on an hourly basis are guaranteed increased compensation if they work beyond the amount they are contracted to work (often 40
hours in a five-day week). If they work more than 40 hours during this period
or on weekends or holidays, they are paid one and a half times their normal
hourly rate. In some cases, FLSA allows compensatory time, which gives
employees the option of taking time off for every period of time that they
work overtime, or taking an increased hourly rate. Before FLSA's application
to state and local governments, public managers were fairly lax about such

TABLE 16.2 Full-Time State and Local Employees Participating in
Selected Employee Benefit Programs

Benefit Program	Percentage of All Employees
Holidays	73
Vacations	66
Personal leave	38
Funeral leave	62
Jury duty leave	94
Military leave	75
Sick leave	94
Family leave (paid)	4
Family leave (unpaid)	93
Sickness/accident insurance	21
Long-term disability insurance	30
Medical care	87
Dental care	62
Life insurance	87
Retirement	96

Source: Bureau of Labor Standards, Report on Employee Benefits in State and Local Governments, 1994.

things as number of hours worked or overtime. Now, the financial implications of such actions cannot be taken lightly.

Fringe Benefits

Larger and larger portions of employee remuneration are going toward fringe benefits rather than wages. This is true for several reasons. First, many fringe benefits are not currently counted as taxable income. This greatly increases the attractiveness of these benefits because they increase the value of the individual employee's earning power; untaxed benefits are worth more than the money employees would otherwise receive in income. Second, many collective bargaining organizations see fringe benefits as areas where they can obtain more concessions from management. Correspondingly, public policy officials find that providing increased fringe benefits is more acceptable politically than increasing direct wages, especially if those increases are hidden or structured to not become direct outlays for several years into the future. Unfunded liabilities, discussed in detail later, reflect the problem of deferring payment of earned benefits until they come due at some point in the future. Table 16.2 shows the percentage of state and local employees covered by various fringe benefits.

Sick leave provides a good example of long-term costs. Some public agencies allow credits to be developed as a reward for those who do not abuse their sick leave privileges. For every sick leave day that is allocated to a particular employee and not used, one quarter of the daily salary of that employee would be banked and would be paid by the employer at some future date (e.g., end of the year, at separation, or at retirement). This is certainly attractive to an employee because a substantial gain could be developed over a period of time. It can also be attractive to policy and management personnel who believe they can reduce absenteeism and boost productivity through such an incentive system. Management may also find it an easy way to satisfy labor demands while not committing to direct operating outlays that might occur if the benefit were a wage increase.

Still, such an arrangement can cause serious problems. Unfunded liabilities can cause major financial risk. One midwestern community with such a plan never really figured out the implications of this agreement until the city manager retired after almost two decades of service. He had almost $20,000 in sick leave benefits. On further examination, the city found close to $1 million in unfunded liability in its sick leave program. Clearly, such fringe benefit agreements can have substantial costs.

The same problem might develop with unlimited accumulation of vacation time, maternity and parental leave policies, health care benefits, or other fringe benefits that an organization provides its employees. This is not to say that such benefits are not good management policies or that they do not make economic sense. Rather, it is important to examine the fiscal implications of such policies. It may be that the reduced absenteeism and increased productivity the organization gains from a sick leave policy more than compensates for the financial costs of such a program. If this is true, however, the agency should be aware of those costs and put aside or allocate funds each year to cover some portion of the accrued liability of that policy. Nowhere is such a program more important than in public-sector retirement programs.

Overhead

Some personnel costs associated with public organizations do not concern employees. These are often hidden but can be of particular concern to public managers. We will call these overhead costs—costs associated with personnel but not directly tied to employee benefits. The most common such cost in this category is social security. Although employees pay an increasing amount of their income into social security, so do employers, who currently cover one half of the total social security contribution. Federal law requires state and local governments to have their employees covered by social security—it is now mandatory that government employees pay into the system. Some states and localities were able to option out of this requirement, but most agencies have been included. Though this helps the solvency of social security, it has also increased the financial burden of public agencies that pay a portion of both social security and employee pension plans.

Another common overhead cost of personnel is the organization's contribution to unemployment insurance. State governments have been given responsibility by the federal government to manage unemployment compensation programs within their borders, and public agencies do have some flexibility in how these costs are paid. Still, they are responsible for the claims

ssociated with employees who are separated from the organization through
o fault of their own. Many public organizations have developed sophisticated
trategies for handling personnel separations so that unemployment compen-
ation costs can be kept to a minimum. This becomes an issue when a fired
mployee asks for unemployment compensation to which the agency believes
he person is not entitled.

Allied Costs

These are costs that develop simply as a result of having employees. Such
nings as equipment, space, supply needs, and so forth can increase dramati-
ally as additional employees are hired. This is an area too often ignored when
ompanies develop cost estimates for increased personnel. Many public or-
anizations have found themselves rich in people and poor in operating
esources because of this oversight. For a university, for example, hiring one
ew professor increases the need for such things as phone equipment, desks,
hairs, paper clips, copying paper, typewriters, office space, car rentals and
lane tickets, and a multitude of other expenses that are simply a part of the
ost of having people working for the organization.

Where You Stand
Depends on Where You Sit

Clearly, employees are concerned with direct salaries and wages, fringe
enefits, and allied costs. These encompass the direct resources and working
onditions that directly affect them. Employees and their representatives will
ary in which of the three they emphasize the most. As tax costs shift, interest
n shifting benefits will also change. Employees and employers are becoming
nore interested in increasing the flexibility of compensation so individuals
an have more control over where benefits are placed. Employers, on the other
and, are concerned not only about the costs associated with employee
enefits but also with costs that change as the number or level of employees
hanges. We now turn to this issue.

Labor Costs

Employers must concern themselves with all the employee costs described
reviously and how each change in employee status affects those costs. This
ncludes not only hiring personnel but also the change in status of personnel
vithin the organization. Different costs are associated with different employee
ob responsibilities. For example, many governmental and nonprofit agencies
ave successfully reduced the number of middle managers. This was accom-
lished in several ways, including Reductions in Force (RIF), early retirement
rograms, and job reclassification. Many employees of federal agencies were
eclassified from middle management job responsibilities (GS12, 13, and 14)
o job responsibilities that were commensurate with salary grades of a GS 7,
, and 9. Clearly, such action has major financial repercussions for the federal
overnment. The overall unit cost of labor is reduced in particular agencies.

If a city decides to reduce the number of street repair personnel and at the same time increase the number of police on patrol, the per unit cost of labor has changed. First, the basic wage rates may be different. Second, the benefit packages might differ. It is not unusual for police and fire department personnel to have not only different pay scales from other city employees but separate fringe and benefit packages as well. Finally, the allied cost per employee can be quite different. Such cost considerations are important to consider when any such change is contemplated.

Budget Costs

In looking at personnel costs from a budgetary viewpoint, several factors need to be addressed. First, managers need to look at the connection in the budget between the personnel costs for labor and the personnel costs that are associated with such things as operating costs and capital costs. Adding personnel or changing the job responsibilities of personnel without adjusting other parts of the budget can have serious implications for the organization. When managers look at a budget, they should see the linkages between salaries, fringe benefits, overhead costs, and allied costs and how all are affected as personnel decisions are made.

Second, the budget should show the anticipated changes in costs that occur as personnel decisions are made. This is particularly important for such things as merit increase or cost-of-living increase policies, accumulated sick leave and vacation leave policies, turnover rate of personnel by job classification, changes in allied cost levels over time, and personnel pension benefit changes as discussed later in this chapter.

Ultimately, managers and policy officials of a public agency are responsible for the future land mines resulting from the personnel decisions they make today. Financial implications of personnel decisions on present and future budgets are enormous. Without a clear understanding and strategy that incorporates these decisions in a financial context, bankruptcy or future hardships could result. Nowhere is this more clearly seen than in our next topic, pensions.

◆ PENSIONS

The first pension plan in the United States, according to the Employee Benefit Research Institute, was established in 1759. Today, almost 100% of the more than 17 million public employees and millions more nonprofit employees are covered by retirement plans of some type.[1] By latest count, there are almost 2,500 state and local retirement systems and thousands more among the various nonprofit agencies.[2] We define pension plans as programs that provide benefits to individual employees and their families on voluntary or involuntary retirement or unplanned separation from a public organization. Such benefits include retirement benefits, disability benefits, and benefits for the family of an employee who dies before retirement. Pension plans are incredibly diverse and range greatly in types and levels of benefits, employee and employer contributions, levels of funding, financing, and investment policies. Each of these issues has important ramifications for financial managers.

Types of Retirement Plans

Defined Contribution Plans

There are two major types of retirement plans in the public sector. Both are referred to as benefit plans, but they have totally different structures and affect employees in radically different ways. Although still a small percentage of all retirement plans, the most rapidly growing is the defined contribution plan. It does not guarantee any specific level of benefits at retirement but, rather, guarantees a certain level of contribution to a savings plan, generally, a percentage of an employee's salary. In other words, the risk of such a plan is not on the employer but, rather, on the employee. As described by Areson and Kossak, such a plan guarantees that when an employee retires, "the employee receives lifetime payments or annuities whose size is determined by the amount on deposit, the interest rate expected to be earned on funds in the account, and the length of time during which the annuity is expected to be paid."[3]

Most contribution plans are structured around IRS-approved tax deferred compensation plans. The two most commonly used are 403(b) for nonprofit organizations and 457 for state and local government agencies. No longer eligible for use by governmental organizations are 401(k) plans. The 403(b) plans can be used by nonprofits who are organized under 501(c) 3 of the IRS code and by certain publicly sponsored schools and universities.[4] Section 457 used by governments, "allows employees to set aside through payroll deduction an amount up to 33 1/3% of taxable compensation or $7,500, whichever is less."[5]

No one has accurate information on exactly how many contribution plans use 403(b) or 457, but it is estimated that such plans are available to more than 95% of all state and local employees and perhaps equally high numbers of nonprofits. Any IRS-approved tax deferred plan has many limitations and requirements, which are usually tied to such issues as nondiscrimination, maximum contributions, employer contribution levels, and use of the plans for salary reduction.

These plans usually require the employer to deposit retirement contributions monthly based on the percentage agreed to in the plan. Once this contribution has been made (unless it is also managing the investment fund), the organization has completed its obligation to the employee.

Defined Benefit Plans

As can be seen in Table 16.3, more than 90% of all retirement plans in the public sector are defined benefit plans. Under such a system, public employees are promised a certain defined level of benefits based on a predetermined formula. Defined benefit plans also provide many nonretirement benefits as part of the basic package, including survivor's benefits, disability plans, and so forth.

The formula used in defined benefit plans usually includes some combination of factors, most commonly years of service, age at retirement, and salary

TABLE 16.3 Retirement Plans—State and Local Governments

Type of Plan	Percentage Employees Covered
All retirement plans	96
Defined benefit	91
Defined contribution	9

Source: Bureau of Labor Standards, Report on Employee Benefits in State and Local Governments, 1994.

level. As an example, Munnell provides a description of a basic defined benefit plan that might include[6]

1. Number of years of service
2. Average wages paid during the highest three consecutive years

The formula is structured to increase the percentage of the base pension benefits as the years of service increase. An example is 2.0% per year for five years, 2.5% per year for the next five years, and 3% per year thereafter up to a maximum pension of 80% of those highest consecutive years.

An individual retiring after 30 years of service making an average salary of $30,000 over the last three years would have pension benefits calculated as follows:

2.0% x 5 = 10.0%
2.5% x 5 = 12.5%
3.0% x 20 = 50.0%
Total = 72.5% of $30,000 or $21,750 per year

The average annual benefit according to the Government Finance Officers Association (GFOA) for state and local systems was 1.96% of final average salary for those employees covered by social security and 2.29% for those not covered by social security.[7]

These plans have numerous variations that have a major financial impact for the organization. If the formula simply changed so the average of the three highest consecutive years were expanded to five years, it might drop the pension amount considerably. On the other hand, if the salary base is an employee's salary at retirement, it might increase substantially. The risk of operating such a plan is on the employers because they are required to provide the resources necessary to meet the specifications included in the defined benefit formula.

Structure of Benefit Retirement Plans

Defined benefit plans offer a wider range of options and complexity than do defined contribution plans. Like defined contribution plans, concerns over flexibility and employee contribution levels are important. Although defined ontribution plans are usually portable—meaning the retirement investment an be carried to another employer who carries that same investment—it is ess common to see portable defined benefit plans. TIAA-CREF retirement nvestment plans for teachers and the International City and County Management Association (ICMA) Retirement Plan for local public managers are xamples of portable investment contribution plans.

Employees will vest in both contribution and benefit plans. Vesting refers o the point in time when the employee earns employer-supported benefits. mployee contributions to these retirement plans are not usually included /ith vesting requirements. Under defined contribution plans, vesting typially refers to the point at which an employee retains employer contributions o his or her pension investment plan even if the employee were to separate rom that public organization the next day. Defined benefit plans have vesting equirements that often raise important financial considerations for the oranization. Under vesting requirements, employees must be with an organiation for some period of time before they become eligible for employerenerated benefits. This can be as short as a year or as long as 5 or 10 years. or agencies with high employee turnover rates, the costs of a defined benefit lan can be considerably less than for those with low turnover because of esting. On the other hand, if an organization has a rapidly maturing workorce, with many employees reaching retirement age, the costs increase trenendously. This is particularly true of local police forces and state highway atrols where turnover may be lower and seniority higher than among other :ate and local employees. The younger the workforce under a benefit plan, nd the longer the time period before vesting occurs, the lower the accrued osts to the organization.

The formulas associated with defined benefit plans often keep benefits elatively low until a person approaches retirement, at which time they go up apidly. This differs from defined contribution plans, which have higher levels f benefits earlier in employees' careers but much slower increases as they each retirement.

Benefit plans can have cost of living allowances (COLA) built into them. orn found that almost 60% of all state and local plans and all federal mployee plans had COLAs of some sort.[8] This is in sharp contrast to private lans where only 1% have COLAs.[9] In such plans, benefits can continue to icrease beyond the formula amount, depending on inflation. This is usually ssociated with the Consumer Price Index or some other measure of the cost f living. Interestingly, some agencies have even used increased productivity f the organization as a means to increase benefits after retirement, even if the etired employee had little if anything to do with that increased productivity.[10]

Defined benefit plans are also more likely to be integrated with social ecurity. Most federal, state, and local governments and employees are reuired to contribute to social security. Those with defined benefit plans ccount for the amount of social security benefits an employee will receive nd reduce retirement benefit plans accordingly. This integration effort was eveloped to reduce the likelihood of any individual retiring at a combined icome that would be greater than 100% of his or her last year's salary. Some ave criticized integration, however, arguing that it is merely a way for agencies to reduce their costs, which hurts employees' retirement programs. Integration can also be used under the cafeteria fringe benefit plan described earlier. In this way the total amount of fringe benefits provided to any one individual would not exceed a certain dollar level or percentage of some salary amount.

Finally, benefit plans vary tremendously by the factors included in a retirement formula: Years of service, compensation base, and age at retirement are the major factors used. How these factors are measured is the key to determining actual costs to an organization.

Funding Pensions

Defined contribution plans are funded as the liability is incurred. An organization deducts a set percentage from an employee's gross pay, contributes a set percentage, and sends that money to an organization responsible for managing the plan. Pension payments are always current, and no unfunded liabilities are incurred. An unfunded liability is one for which a benefit has been earned (accrued) but for which no funds have been allocated.

Defined benefit plans are more likely to have unfunded liabilities. There is considerable debate about exactly how severe the unfunded liability predicament is. Clearly, the federal government has the most severe problem.

The federal government only pays for retirement benefits at the time they actually are collected rather than when they are incurred, so its liabilities are substantial. The government operates on a pay-as-you-go system, where benefits are paid at the time of retirement rather than when they become legal obligations to the organization. The federal government's pension programs are all pay-as-you-go. Cook notes that the Employee Benefit Research Institute estimates the federal pension liability at $870 billion for nonmilitary federal workers and $1.497 trillion if military pensions are included.[11] A survey sponsored by the GFOA, on the other hand, noted that state and local government ratios of assets to pension benefit obligations have actually gone up from 88% in 1991 to 90% in 1992.[12] There is great disparity among government entities, however. If underfunding is measured as any ratio of assets to obligation falling below 80%, 28 states have been identified as having retirement plans that are "underfunded." Estimates of unfunded liabilities for state and local governments range from $100 billion to $164 billion in the early and mid-1990s.[13]

Those who argue against the need for full accrued funding of public pension plans do so on several grounds. They point to the fact that, unlike private pension plans, governments are permanent structures that will not disappear; therefore, they can more easily justify the pay-as-you-go approach to pension plan funding. Pay-as-you-go advocates also argue that public pension plans are funded through nonvoluntary contributions (taxes); therefore, dollars will always be available to cover the costs of such plans.

Opponents of the pay-as-you-go systems argue that putting off the payment of earned benefits encourages public leaders to carry out fiscally irresponsible policies that only become known when the "chickens come home to roost." They also point to the fact that such actions discourage accountability "by directing the attention of taxpayers [away from the] costs of current employee compensation policy."[14] Intergenerational equity is also a concern with unfunded plans. Future generations will be left to pay unfunded costs incurred by current policymakers. Finally, unfunded plans can create serious problems for states and localities by decreasing their creditworthiness in the municipal bond market.

Employee organizations, alarmed by the huge unfunded liabilities accumulating in state and local governments, have pressed for legislation that mandates full accrual funding of such systems. In Nebraska, police unions helped sponsor a state law that requires accrued funding of their benefit pension plans by local governments. For example, between 1981 and 1990, the State of Illinois retirement plans' unfunded liability grew to $5.4 billion. State estimates made in 1991 indicated that if policies did not change, this amount would increase by $750 million in 1993.[15]

Tax revenues and investment income are the largest proportion of funding for benefit and contribution plans. Tax revenue is the sole source of funding at the federal level. Combinations of tax revenue and investments cover costs at the state and local levels. Other revenue sources, along with investments, make up retirement income for nonprofit agencies. In 1992, investments by state and local governments were divided as follows:

Short-Term Securities	4.6%
Domestic Stocks	39.1%
Domestic Bonds	41.5%
Real Estate	6.9%
International Securities	5.6%[16]

A problem with funding benefit plans is predicting exactly what will be earned and when those benefits will be earned. In most instances, public agencies leave these decisions to actuaries, who look at such things as future experience in yields from investments, retirement rates, death rates, disability rates, termination rates, and rates of salary increases to determine what costs will be incurred by an organization.[17] Even if these assumptions are valid, the costs associated with such plans make it extremely difficult politically for state and local governments.

The General Accounting Office (GAO) provided five potential options to state and local governments concerned about reducing costs of defined benefit pension programs.[18] First, public organizations can reduce benefits. This is politically difficult to achieve, especially when collective bargaining agreements have been made, but this action can be necessary if an organization does not want to continue to incur large costs far into the future.

A second option is to eliminate or control cost of living escalators that are built into a benefit plan. These largely uncontrollable costs can destroy operating budgets in times of high inflation.

A third action recommended by the GAO is to impose tighter eligibility standards. This is particularly important in areas such as time to vesting, eligibility of part-time employees, and disability benefits.

A fourth possibility for controlling cost is to close out existing plans and create a new plan with lower costs. Even though an agency honors the previous commitments made under a defined benefit plan, it might be advisable to "get out while you can" and either introduce a new defined benefit plan with reduced benefits, tighter eligibility standards, or a fully funded contribution plan.

Finally, the GAO recommended integrating social security into the existing benefit plans. If this can be accomplished in such a way as to make retirement benefits no greater than 100% of retirement salary, it can save some costs. If it is used simply to reduce the public organization's retirement costs, however, such a strategy may raise serious objections by employees.

Investment Strategies

Investment strategies for public pension plans are not much different from those for any public investment described in Chapter 12. The long-term nature of such investments and the considerable amount of dollars included in many plans, however, does make such investment decisions particularly important for the organization. One of the first key decisions that must be made is whether the agency wants to contract for the management of pension funds or to keep such responsibility "in-house."

Smaller funds can be contracted to professional pension managers because the administrative costs are simply too high to justify. Larger programs, however, are more likely candidates for internal management. Many state governments manage at least a portion of their own pension plan funds and those of local subdivisions. This can be attractive for several reasons: The organization maintains control of the day-to-day activities and provides more direction of where investments are made, which may prove particularly useful if socially responsible investments are desired. We will return to this concept later. "Do-it-yourself" pension management can also have several drawbacks. Staff expertise has to be hired, and additional costs can exceed the costs of contracting out. Also, more political pressure is likely if the investment decisions remain with the organization. Finally, contracting may avoid investment constraints faced by the public agency.

Whether the management of pension funds occurs internally or externally, fiduciary responsibility ultimately rests with the public agency. This is indirect for deferred compensation funds because the employees may be making specific decisions about where their money is invested. The public or nonprofit agency does have a responsibility to the employee in the selection of "appropriately diverse investment products."[19] This means that an agency is responsible for acting in the best interests of its employees to see that their pension funds are invested wisely so they can be assured of receiving maximum benefits at retirement.

Gertner listed five major functions that fiduciaries of public pension plans should perform.[20] First, they should act solely in the interests of their clients—in this case the employee and any other beneficiaries of the plan. Second, individuals or organizations responsible should perform their duties exclusively to provide increased benefits or reduced expenses. Third, they should bide by the "prudent man rule," which demands that "those investing must exercise the same care that persons of prudence, discretion, and intelligence would exercise in managing their own funds." Fourth, fiduciaries for agency pension plans should make sure investments are diversified to the extent necessary to ensure that no large losses will occur. Finally, Gertner argued that fiduciaries must follow the pension plan that has been adopted by the public agency and make sure that the plan requirements are followed.

Many state and local pension funds have several statutory or constitutional restrictions on their ability to invest. The most common restrictions are

- The percentage of assets held in common stock
- The minimum credit quality of bonds
- The percentage of assets invested in one foreign country[21]

Some states and localities must invest in local businesses or companies. Still, the most common restrictions are aimed at reducing the risk of loss.

Special Issues in Pension Plan Benefits

Several benefits are often attached to a public retirement program that can increase costs. These benefits should be closely evaluated by the public manager to determine their costs and benefits.

Disability Benefits

These benefits are usually provided to an employee who is unable to work because of injury or illness that is job-related. These benefits may allow for early retirement or simply provide payments until retirement. How disability is defined and the requirements associated with the benefits received are extremely important. Munnell lists three major categories.[22] The first is total and permanent disability, which prohibits a person from working in his or her assigned job for at least 12 months. A second category is total disability, which "renders the individual incapable of performing any jobs within a specific organization." A final category is partial disability, which includes individuals who can perform at least part of their duties or other duties within the organization. In some cases (police and fire are particularly good examples), large numbers of employees retire on partial or total disability. Although many such workers obviously deserve such benefits, others receive them simply because the definition of disability is broad enough that almost any injury or illness can be considered. Most disability plans require some minimum length of service for vesting. Commonly, this ranges from 5 to 15 years. The level of benefits is often based on length of service, increasing with service to some maximum amount based on a percentage of salary at the time the disability occurred. These benefits can increase when the person reaches normal retirement age. Some plans purchase disability insurance for their workers rather than operate the program themselves. Others share in the costs of such insurance premiums or merely offer a group discount as part of their fringe benefit package. Commonly, such insurance plans provide a portion c pre-disability wages, often 50% to 75%.

Pre-Retirement Death Benefits

Some defined benefit plans pay a portion of a person's retirement benefit to a family member or dependents if the person dies before becoming eligibl to collect those benefits. This benefit can be quite costly if it is based on defined benefit system or if it includes benefits in excess of those accumulate under a defined contribution system. Many defined contribution plans in clude companion life insurance plans as part of the fringe benefit package Plans can also include additional benefits if the death is work-related.

Survivor's Benefits

Various pension plans may include some provision to provide benefits to spouse or other survivor beneficiary when an employee dies prematurely These commonly are tied to the funds remaining in the defined contributio account or to some formula for a defined benefit plan. Such benefits are ofte allowed only if an employee agrees to reduced benefits at retirement. Som plans provide a lump sum payment on the death of an employee; other continue annuity payments until benefits have been depleted. One issue tha has become a concern in recent years is the rights of spouses to pensio benefits when they divorce before employee retirement. These benefits can b included in a divorce settlement, or they can be taken into account in the plan' design.

◆ CONCLUSION

The financial costs associated with personnel activities within public or ganizations can be enormous. Costs associated with lack of employee produc tivity (absenteeism, for example), salaries, and fringe benefits incorporate substantial portion of all public agency expenditures. Retirement plans car offer the most striking example of such costs, but all direct and indirec personnel expenditures should be included when evaluating personnel deci sions. Overtime, vacation and sick leave policies, health benefits, social secu rity payments, unemployment insurance, and workmen's compensation con stitute claims on the financial resources of public agencies. Only through careful review of personnel policies and a detailed fiscal analysis of the expenditures associated with these policies can public managers understanc the implications of personnel decisions on organizational fiscal condition.

DISCUSSION QUESTIONS

1. Interview three to five employees of any public or nonprofit agency. Ask them details about their pension plans. How many knew whether they had a defined benefit or defined contribution plan? If they had a benefit plan, how many understood the elements of the benefit formula? If they had a contribution plan, how many knew where their annuity was being invested and what return they were receiving on that investment? What questions should this raise to the manager of this organization?

2. Locate an existing public or nonprofit organization. Identify and monetarize all the allied costs for a particular department or division within that organization. Are the allied costs different for different persons in the department? How do allied costs affect the overall costs of the organization?

3. If you were a newly hired manager for a public agency, what five key questions would you ask the human resources department to identify major financial issues affecting the agency? Why are these questions the most important to ask?

4. Should all public pension programs be fully funded? Use the functions, resources, and responsibilities of governmental organizations to support your answer.

NOTES ◆

1. Employee Benefit Research Institute (1995). *Fundamentals of employee benefit programs* 4th ed.). Washington, DC: Employee Benefit Research Institute; and Bureau of Labor Standards 1994). *Report on employee benefits in state and local government.* Washington, DC: U.S. Department of Labor.

2. U.S. Department of Commerce, Bureau of the Census (1989). *Statistical abstract of the United States: 1989.* Washington, DC: U.S. Government Printing Office.

3. Todd W. Areson and Shelley Kossak (1980). *Pension issues for local policymakers.* Washington, DC: National League of Cities, p. 6.

4. Employee Benefit Research Institute, p. 101

5. Kathleen Jenks Harm (1993). *State and local government deferred compensation programs.* Washington, DC: Government Finance Officers Association and the International City/County Management Association, p. 1.

6. Alicia H. Munnell (1979). *Pensions for public employees.* Washington, DC: National Planning Association, p. 3.

7. Paul Zorn (1993). Public Pension Coordinating Council 1993 survey results. Government Finance Officers Association, Gopher Site gopher://pula.financenet.gov.

8. Zorn, p. 2.

9. Gareth G. Cook (1995, January/February). The pension time bomb. *Washington Monthly,* 27, p. 19.

10. Munnell, p. 7.

11. Cook, p. 18.

12. Zorn, p. 3.

13. Cook, p. 18; Zorn, p. 3.

14. U.S. Advisory Commission on Intergovernmental Relations (1980, December). *State and local pension systems.* Washington, DC: U.S. Government Printing Office.

15. Michael D. Klemens (1991, November) State pensions: The truth and the consequences. *Illinois Issues,* pp. 18-19.

16. Zorn, p. 4.

17. U.S. General Accounting Office, p. 5.

18. U.S. General Accounting Office, pp. 26-27.

19. Harm, p. 33.

20. Marc Gertner (1980). Fiduciary responsibility of public employees and employer representation. *Journal of Pensions and Planning,* 6(2), 85-86.

21. Werner P. Zorn (1983, December). Public pensions policy: A survey of targeting practices. *Government Finance,* 12(4), p. 48.

22. Munnell, p. 23.

Auditing

Auditing plays a pivotal role in financial management. It provides mechanisms to review and evaluate what has been done in the past to determine whether public agencies keep accurate records, have adequate internal controls, meet legal requirements, and carry out administrative expectations. This information can be used to correct record-keeping problems; sort out control, management, and planning shortcomings; and in some instances, correct illegal or inappropriate actions taken by a public or nonprofit agency.

The audit function has always been perceived by public managers as akin to a visit to the dentist. Everyone knows it is necessary, but no one likes it. Still, most managers understand the value of the auditing function. The results are sometimes unpleasant. No one wants to hear that they are not doing things as well as they could; however, managers can use audit findings as a way to improve their operations.

Control

The primary purpose of auditing in the public and nonprofit sectors is to ensure that funds are used as they were intended, to act as a control on the financial management system, and, where appropriate, to uncover illegal activity. *Control* is a term we use a great deal in financial management. The preoccupation with control is the result of the unique nature of public organizations. Governments and many voluntary nonprofit agencies depend on the involuntary extraction of resources from the public in the form of taxes. The involuntary nature by which these resources are obtained makes it incumbent on administrative officials to ensure that these resources are used as

specified in the budget of that organization. Expenditures must also reflec
the purposes of the agency, and public officials must be sure that they compl
with all relevant restrictions and requirements. Many activities included i
expenditure administration create a paper trail to follow transactions in orde
to determine such compliance.

The primary way of determining whether a budget has been followed is b
looking at what the organization actually did with its resources. The record o
the "what" occurs through the accounting system. Was the street actuall
paved? Was the day care center actually built? Were new personnel added t
the social services agency? Did elderly and disabled services increase? Fo
financial management, the key is to track the flow of funds in such a way tha
the organization can be reasonably assured that its resources were use
properly. The financial auditing process verifies that the accounting record
accurately reflect what happened.

Management

Audits provide managers with information that can help improve thei
overall operations. By evaluating what the organization has accomplished an
the processes it used to achieve its objectives, an audit can uncover operationa
deficiencies and determine whether it has been effective in accomplishing it
goals. The issues of efficiency and effectiveness are addressed in this part o
the audit process. Managers can then use this information to improve opera
tions of the organization.

Did the particular bidding process used to hire contractors to pave the stree
ensure the lowest cost? Could that process be improved so that less money i
spent in the future? Did a particular street project properly meet the goals an
objectives of the organization? Would another project or activity have bee
more appropriate? These questions might be generated during an audit focus
ing on improved management of the public agency. Such audits can lead t
rules that provide management oversight in a particular area.

Planning

Future directions of an organization depend to some extent on action
taken in the past. Audits assist in planning by providing evaluations of pas
performance with an eye toward planning future activities. Well-designe
audits can help locate problems in the reporting system of a public agency tha
hinder effective planning. What information does the reporting currentl
provide and in what form? Can this information be provided in more deta
or in a different reporting format to assist the manager in making futur
decisions? Are the accounts organized to coincide with a program budgetin
system? Can previous trends in expenditures be determined from the curren
financial reporting system? Audits can help provide information that aids th
manager in better organizing financial and management information fo
planning purposes.

AUDIT CHARACTERISTICS ◆

Pre- and Post-Audits

Pre-audits are generally viewed as a method of internal control in processing expenditures. It is not uncommon for such a pre-audit to be undertaken to evaluate the legal and managerial basis of particular expenditures. Also, such audits can periodically sample purchase orders, vouchers, and other payment records before expenditure to determine whether they fit budgetary appropriations, apportionments, and allotments, and whether they are consistent with existing statutory, regulatory, or management policies.

Post-audits are most often associated with the term *audit*. This form of audit looks at expenditure patterns that have occurred in the agency. As with pre-audits, the concern is with consistency with existing law, budgetary procedures, and management policies. The most common post-audit form is to determine if generally accepted accounting principles have been met. Such an audit uses only the accounting and financial reporting system.

Time Period of Audits

The time period covered by audits varies. Pre-audits are often scheduled periodically throughout the year and can cover expenditure items across an agency or can focus on specific agency activities. Post-audits are usually yearly after the fiscal year financial reports are prepared. In some smaller organizations, post-audits occur less frequently or not at all. The scheduling of post-audits is dictated by organizational policies and procedures and by legal requirements.

INTERNAL AND EXTERNAL AUDITS ◆

Audits can be internal or external. Internal audits are those conducted within the agency by personnel who usually report to the agency's director. External audits are independent audits in the sense that those conducting the audit are outside the agency, either representing private firms or independent entities within the organization, for example, the General Accounting Office (GAO) or a state auditor's office. The major decisions faced by organizations in audits depend on who carries out the audit and the timing with which audits occur.

Internal

Internal auditing departments or agencies help evaluate an organization's internal controls and operations. They are often directly supervised by a chief administrative official. Reports can be issued to the policy-making body of the agency as well as to the chief executive.

An internal auditor has the responsibility to "independently and objectively analyze, review, and evaluate existing procedures and activities; to report on conditions found; and, whenever he deems it necessary, to recommend changes or other actions for management and operating officials to consider."[1]

Internal auditing provides numerous benefits. It offers managers an objective and, it is hoped, independent source of information about the operations of their organizational units. It allows quick responses to real or perceived problems before those problems become serious. It can help point to duplication or inefficiencies that outside auditors are unlikely to notice. Finally, internal auditing allows a focused and extended ongoing review of operations that is not often feasible for external auditors because they lack continuous experience over time with the organization.

Large public organizations often have a formal internal auditing capability. This is particularly useful for organizations that want to track a number of different activities. Informal internal audits are often carried out by management staff.

Internal auditors perform a number of activities. They track internal controls. They are often involved in special projects aimed at resolving specific problems within the organization. For example, internal audits can be used to uncover why interfund transfers occur more frequently than generally accepted accounting principles would call for, or why particular expenditure patterns in one department vary dramatically from other departments. Finally, internal auditors can be extremely important in helping improve management and planning activities for the organization. Whether they focus on financial record keeping or management procedures, such audits serve the manager in ways that expand on those carried out by external audits or cover areas frequently not covered by external audits.

Most federal agencies have some type of in-house audit office for the agency's programs, operations, or activities. These internal auditing responsibilities include a wide range of activities for control, management, and planning. State agencies can also have their own internal auditing staffs, which operate similarly to those at the federal level. Local government's size often dictates the ability to staff an internal audit function. Where no internal auditing capability exists, the responsibility often falls on managers to carry out such activities.

External

External auditors are also referred to as independent auditors and are located outside the public organization. The U.S. Government operates two major independent auditing systems: (1) the GAO and (2) inspectors general. The GAO carries out audits on behalf of the Congress of the United States and operates under the direction of the Comptroller General.[2] GAO audits cover all ranges of audits affecting control, management, and planning of federal activity. A sample of recent GAO audits includes

- Financial audit of federal savings and loan insurance corporations
- Annual report to the House and Senate Appropriations Committees on improving operations of federal departments and agencies

- Financial audit of the House Beauty Shop
- Investigation of alleged fraud in an Air Force contract
- Medicare payments to radiologists, anesthesiologists, and pathologists
- Debt collection: Interior's efforts to collect royalty, fine, and assessment receivables
- Selected tax provisions affecting the hard minerals mining and timber industries
- Consolidated supply contracts for commercial trash compactors
- Use of funds for youths placed in Rite of Passage program
- Information on agricultural credit provided to Native Americans on 14 reservations
- Panama Canal Commission's financial statements

Most large federal departments and independent agencies have an inspector general, who is appointed by the president and confirmed by the Senate. Public Law 95-452, passed in 1978, lists their responsibilities.

Provide policy direction for, and conduct, supervise, and coordinate audits and investigations relating to programs and operations.

Review existing and proposed legislation and regulations and make recommendations concerning the impact of such legislation or regulations on the economy and efficiency of programs and operations or the prevention and detection of fraud and abuse.

Recommend policies for and conduct, supervise, or coordinate other activities carried out or financed by their establishment for the purpose of promoting economy and efficiency in the administration of, or preventing and detecting fraud and abuse in, programs and operations.

Recommend policies for, and conduct, supervise, or coordinate relationships between their establishments and other federal agencies, state and local governmental agencies, and nongovernmental entities with respect to matters relating to the promotion of economy and efficiency, the prevention and detection of fraud and abuse in programs or operations, or the identification and prosecution of participants in such fraud or abuse.

Keep the head of their establishment and the Congress fully and currently informed concerning fraud and other serious problems, abuses and deficiencies relating to the administration of programs and operations, and recommend corrective action and report on the progress made in implementing corrective action.[3]

The inspectors general report both to the head of the federal agency or department and to Congress. State governments have auditors, usually in an agency headed by an elected auditor or in the legislative branch, who are responsible for auditing activities within state agencies and departments as well as local governments. The scope of state auditing offices can be broad, but often they focus on financial control.

Most external auditors used by local government are from the private sector and range from the "Big 6" accounting firms to small, locally owned accounting firms. As mentioned in the introduction, external and internal auditors

are too often seen as the enemy; most provide a highly beneficial service t
public managers.

◆ TYPES OF AUDITS

Audits are classified into four general types: (1) financial, (2) compliance
(3) economy/efficiency, and (4) performance/program results. We will dis
cuss each type and describe its characteristics and its usefulness in publi
organizations.

Financial

By far the most common form of auditing is financial audits, "which consis
of a systematic examination and evaluation of the financial systems, transac
tions, and accounts of an organization in order to offer an opinion on th
fairness or reliability of its financial statements."[4] Financial audits are con
cerned with control. They are directed at determining that money flowing int
and out of organizations goes where it was supposed to go and determinin
whether the annual financial reports accurately reflect the financial conditio
and operations of the organization. The first concern is that the agency meet
generally accepted accounting principles. The second is that budgetary appro
priations were followed.

Most linkages between budgets and accounting systems are tied closely wit
financial audits. When referring to an audit trail, we are generally discussin
the ability of auditors to follow the financial trail among the financial state
ments, ledgers, journals, original documents, and actual financial transaction
by an organization. Financial audits can uncover inadequate documentation
inaccuracies or inaccurate figures, failures to meet generally accepted account
ing principles, or, in the extreme, willful fraud and financial abuse. Mostly
internal controls are associated with fraud prevention. Management letter
help inform administrators about internal control issues that can help addres
problems found through the audit process.

Compliance

Compliance audits are concerned that appropriate laws and regulations ar
followed by the organization in carrying out its duties and responsibilities.
These laws can pertain to financial activities, but they also include nonfinan
cial areas as well. The GAO and inspectors general of various federal agencie
often focus on compliance.

Compliance audits are less common among state and local government
and nonprofit agencies. This is because of the lack of staffing to carry out suc
activities within internal auditing offices and the lack of familiarity of externa
private-sector auditors with state and local laws and regulations. There ar
clear exceptions to this, however. State and federal agencies responsible fo
allocating grants and other intergovernmental revenues to public agencie
often have staff specifically assigned to audit compliance with various rule

nd regulations attached to those grants (e.g., the federally funded Commu-
ity Development Block Grant Program). The federal government audits
ompliance by states and large cities, whereas the states are responsible for
uditing compliance by small cities. The range of compliance audits is exten-
ive and includes such things as federal civil rights laws, regulations associated
with environmental protection, lead paint prevention, acquisition of prop-
rty, and flood control. An increasing trend is the use of unified or compre-
ensive compliance audits, where state or federal audits look at compliance
with federal and state laws across various programs and activities.

Economy/Efficiency

Economy and efficiency audits "determine whether the entity is managing
r utilizing its resources (personnel, property, space, and so forth) in an
conomical and efficient manner and the causes of any inefficiencies or
neconomical practices, including inadequacies in management information
ystems, administrative procedures, or organization structure."[6] In other
words, this type of audit is not concerned with flow of funds but whether the
unds were spent at the least cost to carry out activities required of the
rganization. The major focus is on how things are done. Such audits are also
ometimes referred to as operations audits because they resemble operational
ontrol review procedures carried out as part of financial audits in the private
ector.

These audits often use management-oriented analytical approaches, such
s the various forms of cost analysis, workflow, and time-study analysis, as
art of the process.[7] The Comptroller General of the United States has
pecified several things auditors should look for in carrying out an economy
nd efficiency audit, including the following:

- Procedures, whether officially prescribed or merely followed, that are ineffective or more costly than justified
- Duplication of effort by employees or between organization units
- Performance of work that serves little or no useful purpose
- Inefficient or uneconomical use of equipment
- Overstaffing in relation to work to be done
- Faulty buying practices and accumulation of unneeded or excess quantities of property, materials, or supplies
- Wasteful use of resources.[8]

Performance/Program Results

The newest and least common form of auditing is commonly referred to as
erformance-based or program results auditing. Other adjectives commonly
sed to describe this type of audit are *management, effectiveness,* and *opera-
ional.* This type of audit focuses on the achievement of the organization
elative to its stated goals and objectives. In other words, such audits attempt
o determine if the results an agency is given to achieve are being accom-

plished.[9] One difficulty is that this type of audit requires quantifiable goals
and objectives, clearly stated mission statements, and a strong commitment to
results-oriented budgeting before it can be successful. Otherwise, auditors
spend an inordinate amount of time trying to determine what the organiza
tion is trying to accomplish before beginning to measure what has been
accomplished. The focus of the audit can be on performance in the form o
meeting objectives (e.g., outputs), organizational goals (e.g., program out
comes), or both. For example, if a social service agency states its goal to be
reducing by 10% the number of homeless persons in a particular community
an audit attempts to measure how successful that agency is in achieving this
goal. This requires an accurate measure of who the homeless were; how many
of them would be included in the measure; tracking the disposition of these
individuals' efforts to find decent, safe, and sanitary housing; and accurately
measuring the impact of the social service programs in the transition for such
individuals from a homeless situation to one where they have housing. The
audit can also evaluate how effective a particular action was in reducing the
number of homeless. Such objectives might include several concerns, for
example, the number of rental units that are made available to the homeless
population, or the development of single-room occupancy facilities similar to
hotels or college dormitories where homeless persons have access to individual sleeping rooms while sharing common facilities such as rest rooms and
kitchen facilities. The increased availability of support services such as counseling and medical services could be used as an objective if such support
services help lead to independence and an increased likelihood of homeless
persons finding alternative means of shelter.

Performance audits are less concerned with how efficiently an organization
is carrying out its activities than whether those activities are effectively meeting its mission—the what. An organization can be successful but highly
inefficient in achieving that success.

◆ AUDITING STANDARDS

Standards for governmental and nonprofit auditing come from two major
sources. First, the American Institute of Certified Public Accountants (AICPA)
offers "generally accepted auditing standards" (GAAS) that focus on the
ability of an auditor to determine how accurately financial statements reflect
the financial position of an organization.[10] The AICPA auditing standards list
the process and procedures to be followed by auditors and direct concern
toward "generally accepted accounting principles" (GAAP).

The Comptroller General, the head of the General Accounting Office, issues
"generally acceptable governmental auditing standards" (GAGAS) that reflect
a broader focus than financial and compliance audits, including internal
controls.[11] Factors that concern both the AICPA and the Comptroller General
are

- Professional competence of governmental auditors
- Independence of audit staffs

- The proper scope of the audit itself
- The readability, usefulness, and relevance of the audit report itself
- The role and responsibilities of the auditor in detecting fraud (it is not the responsibility of the auditor to find fraud but, rather, to focus on internal controls and make such fraud more difficult to carry out)
- The application of government audit standards to particular types of audit activities.[12]

AUDIT PROCESS ◆

Whether an audit is being conducted internally or externally, it is essential that both the auditor and the public manager understand the process under which the audit is conducted. Only then can they both ensure that the audit can accomplish what it is intended to. According to Tierney, there are six steps in developing and conducting a public-sector audit.

1. Gaining approval to conduct an audit
2. Developing an audit plan
3. Conducting an audit survey
4. Reviewing and testing
5. Conducting a detailed audit
6. Preparing and issuing an audit report[13]

Step One—Gaining Approval to Conduct an Audit

The first step in the process is to select or empower an individual, group, or organization to carry out the audit. The Government Finance Officers Association (GFOA) and GAO both advocate establishing an audit committee to oversee the design and approval of the auditor, particularly the hiring of an external auditor. A recent survey of federal, state, and local agencies indicated about half use such committees.[14] More than two thirds of the committees review and advise on the selection of external auditors, and half of them review the scope of the external audit.

Such committees may be responsible for advising the policy board about the audit process as well any issues related to internal controls.[15] The committee should include members who have expertise in financial management, legal issues, organizational development, engineering, and so forth. The audit committee should develop and structure the procurement process, work with the policy board to determine the scope of the audit, and have a strong understanding of the basic structure of the organization's financial reporting system and internal control structures.

The benefits of an audit committee include preserving the integrity of the process, facilitating communication between management and the external auditor, increasing the technical expertise included in the process, and providing support for management in pursuing changes recommended by the auditor's recommendations.[16]

Step Two—Developing an Audit Plan

An audit plan, like any plan, requires a clear sense of direction concerning the steps to be undertaken. Issues include scope of the audit, schedule for the audit to be undertaken, kinds of data needs, and personnel requirements. This requires collecting information and increasing understanding about the organization and the scope of what is proposed. State and local laws may specify the minimum scope of the audit. In addition, the federal government can require additional audit elements as required by the Single Audit Act of 1984 and the U.S. Office of Management and Budget (OMB) Circular A-128. The GAO's *GAGAS*, revised in 1994 and often referred to as the yellow book, may also apply.[16]

There must be a clear understanding of exactly what organization or part of an organization is to be included in the audit. Public accounting systems are divided into a multitude of different accounting entities, or funds. Each fund tracks the flow of funds for particular purposes and goals. Different organizational units are responsible for activities included within these funds. It is critically important for a financial audit that the audit plan recognize exactly which funds and account groups are being included within the scope of the audit, who is responsible for each fund, and what organizational units are being audited in relation to each fund. For example, accounting standards require that state governments with public higher educational institutions include them in their financial reporting documents. The general audit of state government may not include colleges and universities, however, because they can be audited separately. Local governments may be required to show public authorities in their financial reports, but audits of these entities (e.g., airport authorities, transit authorities, housing authorities) would be handled separately.

Any audit plan must be developed through discussions with key financial and nonfinancial actors concerning the operations of the organization. This should include all those who potentially can assist in defining the scope and activities to be carried out, including management, policy officials, employees and those outside the agency who might play an important role. Through interviews and discussions, the scope can be further defined to determine the particular type of audit to be conducted. This information can be written into a contract between the organization and the auditing entity itself. Will it be financial and compliance? Will it include all funds or just the general fund? Are there particular areas of concern or interest to be covered in the audit? By becoming specific at this point, misunderstandings and wasted time and effort can be avoided.

Once the scope of the audit has been determined as part of the plan, it is important to determine exactly who is directly involved. Different personnel are involved in different types of audits. Financial audits can be appropriate for certified public accountants to handle, whereas compliance audits might be more appropriately handed by someone with legal and regulatory training.

Information about an organization's financial system must be reviewed to develop a clear understanding of what the audit will accomplish. For example is the financial system completely manual or is it automated? If automated how are records maintained within this system? This knowledge dictates how particular aspects of the audit will be conducted. Auditors also want to know how previous audits were conducted and what information exists from those previous audits. Audit standards often require that auditors keep detailed working papers specifying the process used in conducting their review. These working papers are vitally important to a new audit plan because they can provide important information about how previous audits were carried out.

Finally, an audit plan should specify who will be working on the audit, where the responsibility for various aspects of the audit resides, and the time frame for completion of various parts of the audit. Some type of visual display of due dates and responsibilities can be particularly helpful. Once a plan is completed and disseminated to all participants, there should be little reason for misunderstandings or confusion during an audit itself.

Step Three—Conducting an Audit Survey

Generally accepted auditing standards used for general purpose public agencies and GAGAS specify that an audit survey should be conducted. According to the Standards issued by the Comptroller General, a skillfully performed survey should provide information about the size and scope of the entity's activities and any areas in which there may be weaknesses in internal controls, uneconomical or inefficient operations, lack of effectiveness in achieving prescribed goals, or lack of compliance with applicable laws and regulations.[18]

Among the things that might be included in such a survey are organizational structure, legal requirements, financial information, structure of data process systems, special problems or issues, and specific reporting requirements of the public agency itself. One way to think of a survey is as a game plan for how the audit is conducted and the various elements that are included. To use a football analogy, the survey would include all the offensive and defensive formations, the rules and standards under which the game will be played, and any special concerns that the opposing team can present on game day.

Step Four—Reviewing and Testing

After the survey has been completed, a more specific step is undertaken to determine the criteria for conducting tests and reviews of specific internal controls, data systems, compliance systems, operating procedures, personnel practices, asset utilization, and procurement procedures used by the organization, depending on the type of audit being conducted. Using the football analogy once again, the review and testing process involves criteria for carrying out a particular play. For example, to carry out the play, more specific information is needed such as the actual alignments that each player can use within particular defensive and offensive formations that relate to the play being carried out. By developing such criteria and reviewing each of these specific steps in the process in some detail, the auditor can determine exactly what tests will be needed to adequately review the organization. Among the reviews Tierney mentions are

- Evaluation of internal controls—including tests of financial transactions, systems, subsystems, accounts
- Review of data systems
- Tests for compliance
- Checks for economy and efficiency
- Analysis of tests and review results—preferably in the form of narrative or flowchart descriptions of controls, evaluation of controls . . . and conclusions about whether certain aspects of the system controls can be relied upon and where more detailed tests must be made.

By carrying out these series of reviews, the auditor should "yield the information necessary to develop an audit program to be used for conducting a detailed audit."[19]

Step Five—Conducting a Detailed Audit

Once the plan, survey, and test and review processes are completed, an actual audit is conducted. The components of the audit should demonstrate the importance of verification, cross-checks, detailed sampling, direct observation, inspection, and documentation in the audit process. Verification and cross-checks entail the process of locating documentation that supports the written record, which can be a set of financial accounts or a file describing compliance with a particular statute. Detailed sampling focuses on the decisions used by the auditor in selecting transactions to analyze from all those that have taken place during a particular reporting period. The sampling approach used will determine the generalizability of the audit findings and the overall accuracy of the audit report. Observation, inspection, and documentation all tie to the actual implementation of the audit. Methods of observing records of transactions, inspection of written records, and documentation supporting those records are all central to an audit's accuracy and validity. For example, if the auditor wants to determine that the financial reports fairly represent the financial condition of the organization, how can this best be determined?

It is unrealistic to follow every accounting entry through the accounting cycle. Instead, the auditor selects a sample of entries and traces them through the cycle from original document to journal ledger and finally to the financial reports. Through this sample of transactions and entries, the auditor can determine how consistently and accurately records were kept, how well accounts reflect GAAP standards, and the validity of those findings.

Step Six—Preparing and Issuing an Audit Report

Audits always result in a number of reports and findings by the auditors. Among the most common are the audit letter for a financial audit and the management letter. The audit letter (sometimes referred to as the audit report), in addition to spelling out its scope, notifies the governmental or nonprofit entity of such things as

- Whether the auditor has used generally accepted auditing standards
- Whether the financial statements of the organization present fairly the financial condition of the organization
- Whether the financial statements of the organization are in conformity with generally accepted accounting principles[20]

The audit letter is followed by the financial statements themselves. As discussed in Chapter 3, these statements include a balance sheet, combined financial statement of revenues and expenditures for the reporting period, and a comparison of revenues and expenditures by fund over time.

In some cases, there is a management letter under separate cover. This includes the auditor's various recommendations to improve a public agency's financial management system. Items that might be included under audit recommendations are how to improve such things as internal controls, various reporting practices, interfund transactions, and documentation. These recommendations often are not made public and are meant as guidelines and direction to management of the agency. An audit letter is the most visible part of the audit report, but the auditor's recommendations as communicated orally or in a written management letter can be more useful to the public manager.

Other types of audits are finalized in reports. Audit reports on compliance express whether laws, regulations, and by-laws have been adhered to. Auditors can also make recommendations concerning ways to improve compliance in the future. Audit reports concerning economics and efficiency or program results allow more discretion by the auditor but still use nationally recognized standards and principles as the basis for the findings and recommendations.

CONCLUSION ◆

Auditing is a key legal, administrative, and policy tool available to public agencies to evaluate their financial management performance. Audits should not be perceived as something to be avoided but, rather, as a tool for improving agency operations. Although they are used to uncover inaccuracies, they also provide an opportunity to evaluate organizational activities that affect the agency's efficiency and effectiveness. When an auditing process is approached with a positive attitude, it can be invaluable for management and policy officials in improving their financial operations. The key to achieving this is for the manager to understand the purposes, scope, and processes that constitute an audit program. In this way, managers can anticipate their own needs and requirements and use audits to help meet them.

DISCUSSION QUESTIONS

1. What are the key questions managers should ask before conducting a financial audit?

2. What are the benefits or drawbacks to establishing an internal audit office? How do the duties of an internal auditor contrast with those of an external auditor?

3. How does the auditor use the accounting system to perform the financial audit? How do program, performance, and line item budgeting processes link to their auditing counterparts?

4. Analyze two audited financial statements for similar organizations. What appear to be the major similarities and differences in the audit letters? How do the financial statements compare?

◆ NOTES

1. Felix Pomeranz, Alfred J. Cancellieri, Joseph B. Stevens, and James L. Savage (1976). *Auditing in the public sector: Efficiency, economy and program results.* Boston: Warren, Gorham and Lamont, p. 88.

2. Cornelius E. Tierney (1983). *Public sector auditing.* Chicago: Commerce Clearing House.

3. Tierney, pp. 84-85.

4. Rhett D. Harrell and Richard J. Haas (1984, March). Selecting an external auditor. *Governmental Finance, 13*(1), 3-11.

5. U.S. General Accounting Office (1994). *Government Auditing Standards.* Washington, DC: U.S. General Accounting Office.

6. Pomeranz et al., p. 8.

7. Peter F. Rousmaniere (Ed.). (1979). *Local government auditing: A manual for public officials.* New York: Council on Municipal Performance, p. 19.

8. Tierney, pp. 11-12.

9. Pomeranz et al., pp. 8-9.

10. Tierney, p. 99.

11. U.S. General Accounting Office.

12. Tierney, p. 99.

13. Tierney, p. 136.

14. Stephen J. Gauthier (1989). *Audit management handbook.* New York: Government Finance Officers Association, pp. 7-12.

15. Gauthier, pp. 7-12.

16. Marcia B. Buchan and Deborah A. Koebele (1995, April). What the 1994 yellow book means for auditors. *Journal of Accountancy,* p. 53.

17. U.S. General Accounting Office.

18. Tierney, p. 144.

19. Government Finance Officers Association (1994). *Government accounting, auditing and financial reporting.* Washington, DC: Government Finance Officers Association.

20. Rousmaniere, p. 12.

SUGGESTED READINGS ◆

Government Finance Officers Association (1994). *Government accounting, auditing and financial reporting*. Washington, DC: Government Finance Officers Association.

Felix Pomeranz, Alfred J. Cancellieri, Joseph B. Stevens, and James L. Savage (1976). *Auditing in the public sector: Efficiency, economy and program results*. Boston: Warren, Gorham and Lamont.

Peter F. Rousmaniere (Ed.). (1979). *Local government auditing: A manual for public officials*. New York: Council on Municipal Performance.

Cornelius E. Tierney (1983). *Public sector auditing*. Chicago: Commerce Clearing House.

U.S. General Accounting Office (1994). *Government auditing standards*.

Assessing Financial Conditions

Assessing financial conditions refers to evaluating information related to finances for the sake of making decisions. Most public-sector assessment efforts are concerned with capability in the sense of an organization being able to act in a preferred manner. Two of a variety of views on capacity involve the provision of public services and payment of debt. Those who focus assessment efforts on the provision of public services are concerned with the purposes of public organizations, and those who focus on debt payment generally have an interest in seeing debt payments made. Although service provision is particularly interesting to public administrators, the best known examples of financial assessment are bond ratings, which are capsule descriptions of debt repayment capacity.

Bond ratings show assessments of particular bond issues and issuing organizations as well as any guaranteeing organization. Such ratings reflect the rating agency's informed judgment about the relative degree of riskiness of timely repayment of bonds. Ratings are produced so that the investment community can decide whether to buy bonds at particular prices. Public organizations participate to facilitate access to debt markets and to secure the best possible interest rates. Rating agencies produce the ratings by systematically reviewing relevant data and information that include, but are not limited to, budgets, annual financial reports, special disclosure reports, debt levels and history, available revenue measures, economic conditions of its financial supporters, and measures of social conditions. Bond ratings are one form of public-sector financial assessment.

Formal assessment efforts are necessary in the public sector because of the complexity of public organization finances. The degree of complexity in the public sector exceeds that experienced in the private sector, where the focus is on net worth and profits. Public organizations, in contrast, provide services and do not make profits nor concern themselves with net worth. As service providers, public organizations are necessarily more concerned with their long-term revenue situation and the need for their services. Also, accounting and expenditure administration practices of public organizations, as well as

he political character of public budget decision making, contribute to complexity. The complexity of public organization finances is so great that poli-
ymakers and finance administrators are not likely to understand important
spects of their organizations' financial condition fully unless formal financial
ssessment is undertaken.[1] If the most informed officials can use formal
fforts at financial assessment, then others who concern themselves with a
ublic organization's financial condition will find financial assessment even
nore useful.

Financial assessment is discussed here under the headings of perspectives,
oncepts, information systems, and scoring systems. *Perspectives* signify the
iewpoints from which assessments are done. A rating agency assesses bonds
y looking at public organizations from the viewpoint of whether debt is likely
o be paid and, therefore, looks at things related to that.

Any perspective uses one or more *concepts*. For bond ratings, debt level is
ne such concept. The concepts used are mostly those related to topics
iscussed in earlier chapters.

Information systems are used to categorize, gather, summarize, and hold
ata and information. Data in the form of numbers are not self-evident and
equire a conceptual framework to be useful. Data are usually interpreted in
vords, such as "this is a lot of debt." Information can take many forms without
ecessarily being quantifiable (e.g., a liability suit has been filed against a
overnment).

Assessments are often formalized by a simple measure, which can be called
score. *Scores* are an extremely compact way of compressing information to
ommunicate. The meaning of all scores hinges on the characteristics of the
coring system used. For example, bond ratings range from Aaa and AAA to C
nd D. All the possible scores are related to one another and reflect the rating
gency assessment of risk.

PERSPECTIVES ◆

Perspectives can be divided into external and internal perspectives.[2] Exter-
al perspectives refer to viewpoints from outside an organization; internal
erspectives refer to ones taken by persons in a decision-making position
vithin an organization.

External Perspectives

External perspectives include those of creditor, contractor, constituent,
otential constituent, and policy analyst. External perspectives are typically
ominated by a self-interested concern with how a public organization's
ctions affect particular groups and individuals.

The first perspective discussed is that of a potential or actual creditor.
inancial assessment by the investment community takes the form of bond
atings. Those ratings and other assessments focus on the degree of risk that
n organization will repay debt in a timely fashion. Three areas typically cause
oncern: (1) the legal validity of the debt instrument, (2) the obligation basis,

and (3) the financial condition of the issuing entity. Regardless of all othe factors, except a guarantee by another financially strong entity, the ability o a public organization to pay is most important. Although conceptually dis tinct, we cannot separate analysis of a debt instrument from the entity issuin that debt instrument. This concern for repayment is reflected in a deb industry saying, "No one buys a lawsuit."[3] This means that investors want t be paid without any legal actions, which is more likely when a debtor has greater capacity to pay. In some cases, those who take a creditor perspectiv can act on another basis. For example, in the New York City case of 1975, bank continued to loan money to the city and sell those debt instruments to other long after the city's financial condition deteriorated beyond the point wher reasonable people would judge the city capable of repaying its debts in a timel fashion.[4]

A second perspective is taken by contractors, who assess public organiza tions for their capability to perform contractual obligations. Grantor agencies service purchasers, and vendors of goods and services take this perspective. unique contractor perspective is that of organized employee groups con cerned with the capacity to pay wages, preferably higher wages.[5]

A third perspective is taken by constituents, who can be citizens, residents or group members. This perspective can be further divided into personal an business perspectives. Personal perspectives show a concern for the impact o public organizations' financial conditions on individuals expressed as reve nues collected from and services performed for individuals. A business per spective involves assessing the impact of a government on that business' activity. The key is the cumulative effect on business profitability. Both per sonal and business constituent perspectives form the basis for political activit in general policy making and in budgeting. Constituents attempt to persuad policymakers and administrators of the appropriateness of their preferences Examples of this are most easily seen in specific efforts aimed at tax relief Private property owners, particularly homeowners, seek reductions or mod eration in increases in their property taxes. Businesses seek reductions o moderation in increases in taxes affecting them.

A fourth perspective is that of potential constituents. Potential constituent are choosing whether to become associated with a public organization. Th people involved are usually dealing with one of two questions: whether t locate in a particular governmental jurisdiction or whether to join a nonprofi organization.

Potential constituents differ in their use of assessment in that they us assessments to choose situations rather than to attempt to manipulate situ ations in which they are already involved.[6] Potential constituents are makin a choice, whereas constituents seek to influence an ongoing situation in whic they find themselves. People moving from one area to another who are lookin to buy a house provide examples of this when they ask about schools, services and taxes. Another common example is a business location decision that i made on a formally comparative basis.

The fifth external perspective is that of a policy analyst, a disintereste person who analyzes the consequences of policy choices to provide decisio makers with objective analysis. This perspective is taken by various re searchers: economic analysts, research bureaus, academics, and organizations' staff analysts. Chamber of Commerce studies showing the need for lower business taxes are seldom seen as being disinterested.

Internal Perspectives

Internal perspectives provide information to officials to make decisions about budgets and financial management. Budgetary discussions and decisions benefit from a general overview of an organization's financial position. These assessments inform choices about revenue collection (which and how much to collect) and expenditures (which and how much to make).

Internal financial management concerns focus on analyzing specific areas, for example, changing debt levels, cash management practices, or investment policies. In a sense, these assessment efforts are an extension of the budget perspective because they arise from concern for budget implementation. Different general financial conditions dictate particular actions, such as tight expenditure controls, borrowing, and considering new revenue measures instead of new personnel benefit packages, investment policies, and cost-benefit analysis. Although internal finance perspectives deal with what appear to be mundane and limited concerns, they also deal with original data where any problem a public organization faces is likely to appear first. One study found that local government financial emergencies are caused by "unsound financial management," which suggests that such emergencies could be avoided to some extent by reviewing financial management practices.[7]

CONCEPTS ◆

Despite the multiplicity of perspectives, relatively few basic concepts are used to assess the financial position of public organizations. All the concepts concern capacity to take action. Each concept represents one facet of a public organization's ability to act. Many of the concepts discussed here are already familiar from previous chapters: assets; liabilities; revenues; expenditures; results of operations; solvency; liquidity; flexibility; quality of record-keeping systems, leadership, and financial administration; and the economic and social environment.

Assets are things owned that are fixed or liquid. Fixed assets are physical entities, which are not easily sold for cash; liquid assets are cash or easily converted to cash, which indicates an immediately useable form of assets that can flow to another use. Fixed assets are a measure of past expenditures, and liquid assets are a measure of current capacity to act. More liquid assets increase the current spending capacity.

Liabilities are usually monies owed to others. Debt of all sorts, unpaid personnel fringe benefits, and unpaid bills are common liabilities. Liabilities can be examined in several respects. Long-term debt levels and changes in short-term debt are most commonly reviewed. Due dates of liabilities vary; those that are currently due have more impact than those due at a much later date. An increase in current liabilities shows a reduced capacity for immediate action.

Revenues, along with assets, are the source of monies for financial action. Revenues are most frequently examined for restrictions, dependence, and variability. Restrictions can be placed on revenue rates, rate increases, or uses. Dependence on particular revenue sources, especially revenues from interorganizational transfers, provide evidence of potential vulnerability. Variability of revenues—why they vary—is seen by looking at elasticity, delinquency, and one-time revenues.

Expenditures of particular types create expectations. Besides the total amount of expenditures, particularly relative to total revenues, the two most common concerns are fixed expenditures, which are legally uncontrollable, and rates of expenditure change. Another concern is fully measuring future costs that may not be budgeted (i.e., the legal obligation to make the expenditures is not officially recognized in a budget or matched with resources to make the payments). Here, employee benefits and the social security program spring to mind. Although social security is a clear example of a national public policy issue, unfunded public employee fringe benefits, which include pensions and accumulated paid sick, vacation, and other personal leave, can be found in many states, local governments, and nonprofit organizations. In both cases, unmeasured and unfunded liabilities can represent high future expenditures. Reduced expenditures on capital items and their maintenance often are the first signals of a declining financial condition.

The results of operations, which are the results of expenditures and revenues, are increases or decreases in fixed and liquid assets and liabilities. Revenues become assets; liquid assets are used for expenditures; and expenditures can result in liabilities and fixed assets. These results show up on annual accounting reports. In addition to the previously discussed concepts, these reports are examined for the current and cumulative results, solvency, and liquidity.

The most intuitively intelligible concern is with the yearly and cumulative deficit or surplus position of an organization. A surplus means more money has been collected in a fiscal period or overall than was spent; a deficit means more money was spent than collected. A fiscal period surplus usually results in an increase in liquid assets, a decrease in liabilities, or both. A deficit produces opposite results. Surpluses and deficits are looked at for size (e.g., percentage of expenditures); continuity (e.g., consecutive years of surpluses or deficits); and impact on the entity's fund balances, which are almost invariably positive.

Solvency involves the capability of an entity to pay its bills eventually, as measured by its assets relative to liabilities. A public organization is solvent if its assets exceed its liabilities. Because most public organizations are solvent all of the time, mere solvency is not a big deal. On the other hand, insolvency is a very big deal, especially for creditors. For purposes of financial assessments, the question is whether a public organization is becoming more or less solvent. Solvency is the central focus of the private sector because solvency is associated with net worth and is less relevant in the public sector because the focus is on service provision and the capacity of governments to extract resources rather than accumulate assets.

Liquidity is a characteristic of assets that is often confused with solvency. Liquidity refers to the degree to which assets are usable as or can be converted to money. Cash is an asset that is totally liquid; it can be spent. Other assets, mostly short-term investments, can be converted relatively quickly to money. Other assets cannot be quickly converted to money. Federally owned lands in the United States are large but not liquid assets of the federal government; it would take a long time to sell them.

Liquidity measures the relative capacity of a public organization to spend its assets. Degrees of liquidity are a concern for two reasons. First, financial difficulties can be seen relatively early from declining liquidity. Second, a lack of liquidity increases costs for a public organization. When an organization's assets are not sufficiently liquid to pay its bills, the basic choices are to borrow money to pay bills or to liquidate assets. Both have costs: interest charges for borrowing and losses from the necessity of quickly liquidating an asset.

Flexibility for public organizations, as with dancers, concerns their ability to make moves. Financial flexibility varies inversely with the degree to which public organizations are constrained. If most of the finances, particularly revenues and expenditures, are limited in amount or cannot be changed, then a public organization is less able to respond to new situations. For solvency and liquidity, flexibility is a relative notion. Flexibility is usually analyzed for legal constraints, but political constraints are no less real.

The quality of the record keeping, financial administration, and leadership are all measures of the competency of a public organization. Adequacy and accuracy of records, both accounting and budgeting, provide a basis for sound decision making. The quality of financial administration can be measured by reference to what practices an organization follows (i.e., whether an organization manages its cash flow, takes discounts for early payment of bills, funds pensions, manages risks, and avoids overly optimistic budget forecasts). The quality of leadership of a public organization is difficult to measure precisely; still, leadership qualities are an intangible worthy of notice.

The economic and social environments of public organizations are extremely important. For the most part, the economic environment is viewed with an eye toward revenue collection. More economic activity means that more revenue can be collected. The major exception is government entitlement programs based on economic factors, mostly provided by the federal government, though state governments also participate in welfare and unemployment programs. On the other hand, social conditions are viewed in light of expenditures. Social conditions involve looking at relevant population groups, their characteristics, and their behaviors. Certain characteristics provide a basis for assessing expenditure needs. For example, the demographic configuration of the population of Utah indicates a high rate of expenditure in public education, as that state has the greatest percentage of school-age children in the country.

Finally, productivity is a measure of the financial condition of a public-sector organization. Productivity is measured as a relationship between inputs and results. Inputs can be money spent or input factors, such as personnel and materials. Results can include outputs in the sense of work performed by the

public organization (e.g., miles of streets swept or number of students in
structed) and outcomes in the sense of final effects or goal achievemen
(e.g., miles of clean streets or students with degrees or able to perform a
particular levels of competency). Measures of productivity are typically a uni
cost or other unit measurement, such as $100 a mile for street sweeping o
400 books used by library patrons per each employee day worked. An increas
ing rate of productivity suggests greater financial viability of a public enter
prise, and declining productivity indicates potential financial difficulties.

◆ INFORMATION SYSTEMS

Concepts are applied to public organizations based on information. Fo
example, measures of solvency require asset and liability figures. The source
of information are primary and secondary information systems. Primary
systems are those in which data and other information are initially gathered
and secondary sources use information from primary systems.

Primary information systems include financial record-keeping systems and
governmental reporting systems. Financial record-keeping systems are essen
tially budgeting and accounting systems, which are not created with financia
assessment in mind. Certain information is typically available from these
systems, including assets, liabilities, debt, revenues, expenditures, estimated
revenues, fund balances, and appropriations (estimated expenditures).

Other relevant information is found in reports issued from the Departmen
of Commerce. The Bureau of the Census regularly collects and publishe
information on population characteristics for many government jurisdic
tions. Also, the Bureau of Labor Statistics and the Bureau of Economi
Analysis collect and publish information on the rate of inflation and levels o
economic activity, some of which is available over the Internet.

Other primary information systems are found in a wide variety of places
Social service agencies collect and report various kinds of caseloads by juris
dictions. Revenue offices have geographic and income-level breakdowns o
revenue collections. Criminal justice agencies report various crime and of
fender statistics. The Bureau of the Census reports characteristics of the
housing stock. Such sources can be useful in assessment.

A variety of secondary information systems regularly collect and provide
information. Examples of these systems include census reports on state and
local government finances and information provided by bond rating agencies
Secondary information systems' biggest drawback is that by the time infor
mation is available, it is at least one or two years old.

◆ SCORING SYSTEMS

Scoring systems describe something with many observable features in a few
relatively precise and easily understood symbols. The thing being scored i
observed for some specific quality or qualities. The features being scored are
assumed to be the most important or relevant aspects of the situation. In

sports, the most common purpose of scoring is to determine who wins. The specific quality being observed is whatever involves scoring as defined by the rules of that sport. Even when sports are being played informally or individually, people keep score to determine whether they are doing better or worse. In other cases, scoring is done to describe a situation—for example—99 bottles of beer on a wall. Accounting systems represent this kind of scoring system. Scoring systems for assessing financial conditions of public organizations differ from other scoring systems. They are formulated to be predictive of capabilities to take desirable action. Their predictive character is a distinguishing feature.

Relevant scoring systems are based on perspectives, concepts, and information systems discussed above. From a particular perspective, a person looks to find information in an information system to operationalize the financial condition concepts for one or more organizations. The result is some number of particular scores, measures, or ratings that predict ability to act. The particular measures vary greatly, depending on perspective, information systems, and the precise mode of determining a rating.

Here, scoring systems for assessing financial conditions of public organizations are discussed by scores themselves, common types of scoring systems, and a few particular examples. Scores are discussed to clarify their use as measuring and predictive devices. The common types of scoring systems highlight the use of scores in practice. Finally, particular examples provide a view of scores in actual detail.

Scores

Scores for assessing financial conditions are relative measures because they measure capability. This can be illustrated with a simple predictive scoring system. People can be rated for their capabilities in a variety of ways. One way is the grocery list score. This score is an answer to the question, "How many items would you feel comfortable putting on a grocery list if you sent this person to a grocery store?" Aside from two absolute answers—zero and an unlimited number—answers to this question are only relative measures.

Generally, financial assessment scoring is done as comparisons. The meaning of relative scores depends on one or more comparisons. For example, if you are assessed as a "7" on the grocery list score by someone, what does that mean without some comparison? If the person doing the scoring gives an average score of "3", the "7" is a much better score than if that same person gave an average score of "40." Comparisons are found in three forms: the same entity at different points in time, different entities at the same point in time, or a combination of the two. Comparison requires a common basis, which varies, depending on whether the scoring system is qualitative or quantitative.

Qualitative Scores

Qualitative scores are those for which there is a predetermined set of possible scores or a range of scores that are assigned based on observers' judgments. Bond ratings, course grades, and various judged sports, such as diving, gymnastics, and ice skating, use such qualitative scoring systems. The common factors for the comparative basis are the same conditions, the same observers, and the same scoring system. The key is the common scoring range within which everything is rated. One drawback of such scoring systems is their judgmental character, which requires reliance on observers whose scoring can vary widely. The score, then, is only as good as the scorers. Once the basic scoring is done by judgment, any later mathematical manipulation of the scores does not change the qualitative character of the scores.

Quantitative Scores

Quantitative scores are derived through calculation of actual empirically verifiable numbers. Common bases are provided by efforts at statistical equalization. Such efforts are not particularly difficult to understand if they are followed step by step. Unfortunately, such statistical operations are insufficiently explained in many cases. Here, some of the most commonly used statistical techniques are examined briefly.

First, the variability of the value of money over time is adjusted. That makes it possible to compare dollar figures accurately at different points in time. To equalize money values at different points in times requires that the values be divided by some consistent inflation index. Examples of this are found in Chapter 4 and Chapter 8.

Second, statistical equalization can be carried out using some common base to compare otherwise different entities. The most familiar is percentage. A common base is used to create comparable figures through mathematical computations. In addition to percentage, other common methods include per capita, ratios, and rates. Per capita, used predominantly for governments, involves dividing a government finance figure by its population. Ratios are merely an expression of the relationship between two numbers. Percentages are one example. Another example is raw number ratios, where one number is divided by another (e.g., so much debt per $1 million of assessed valuation for real property). Using this example, the relationship between assessed valuation and debt for two or more entities can be compared. The same relationship could be compared using percentages or raw number ratios.

A third way of expressing a comparison on a common basis is rank order. A rank order can be created by putting entities in a low-to-high or high-to-low order on the basis of some common characteristic or measurement. Then, the rank position of that entity on that quantified measurement provides an ordinal or rank scoring of first, second, and so on to last. A rank order basis provides only a positional ranking relative to the other entities included in the particular rankings. One rank is only higher than those below it and lower than those above it in that particular ranking. Rank orderings are attractive as they are intuitively intelligible to most people in the sense of providing an order of finishing in a race or other contest. Unfortunately, for purposes of financial assessment, they are flawed because they are arbitrary and use less information than is available. Ranking is arbitrary when entities are ranked,

nless all possible entities are included; different selections of entities to rank
esult in different ranking relationships. Ranking takes precise information
nd reduces it. Rankings provide only relative positions. Actual figures pro-
·ide much more precise information. Also, rankings can both mask tremen-
·lously large practical differences and create impressions of greater than actual
·lifferences. The difference between first and last on a particular rank score
·lay or may not be very significant. It is impossible to tell much from rankings.

A telling example of a ranking situation comes from a television program
·vith a mirror and a witch as characters. The mirror responded to numerous
·ccasions of being asked who was fairest of all by the witch with the following
·anking statement: "In my book, you are the fairest of them all." The mirror
·ater explains that his book, which is his ranking basis, includes only the witch
·nd a professional boxer whose face looks like it was hit by a large bag of
·lickels.

The validity of any figures used to create scores is important. In other words,
·e concerned that numbers are not at odds with the underlying reality either
·y being falsified or being nonrepresentative in the sense of creating an
·laccurate impression. These two deceptive practices are most colorfully
·lescribed by the term "smoke and mirrors." Examples in budgeting and
·inance abound. The definition of the federal budget has been changed
·epeatedly to show lesser deficits. Asset sales and proposals for a capital budget
·re other federal-level examples. The State of Illinois used deceptive account-
·ng practices concerning its financial condition.[8] Two large cities, New York
·nd Chicago, systematically falsified financial records in the 1970s to maintain
·ccess to credit markets.[9] Other local governments experiencing financial
·mergencies also display creativity in financial record keeping and report-
·ng.[10] As in any measurement situation, measuring actual things is superior
·o reports of measurements. Reports are easy to manipulate; direct observa-
·ions by outsiders are almost impossible to manipulate.[11]

Common Types of Scoring Systems

Because of the limited number of perspectives, concepts, and information
·ystems, common types of scoring systems concerning financial conditions
·re few in number. The underlying reality is basically the same, though it can
·e looked at in a variety of ways. Common scoring systems can be grouped
·nto those for outside interests and those for the organization itself. Outsiders
·se three types of scoring systems concerning creditworthiness, public policy,
·nd comparative selection. In effect, outsiders use scoring systems to compare
·rganizations. An organization reviewing its financial condition reviews its
·wn financial information over a number of time periods; it compares itself
·t different points in time.

The whole area of financial assessment in the public sector gained much
·mpetus from the events of March 1975, in New York City. Essentially, the
·anks that were the prime short-term lenders to the city told city officials that
·hey could not provide any more short-term loans. The city, subsequently,
·emporarily failed to pay its debt obligations, which created a general panic in
·he credit markets and great concern over the financial condition of American

cities. Subsequent cases of similar character plagued other large cities. Al
though New York City was unique in many ways, its temporary default led t
a generalized concern with assessing the prospect of other cities going int
default. Such scoring systems act as alarm bells signaling fiscal stress. Studie
in this area have attempted to isolate early warning signals. Some commor
measures include liquidity, solvency, results of operation for direction ove
time, and increases in debt and other liabilities.[12] This one case undergird
much of the other work in the area.

Creditworthiness reflects assessment of the underlying reality of debt ratin;
systems. Ordinarily called bond ratings, such ratings also can be given fo
short-term loans or notes as well as debt guarantors. In the same manner a
consumer loan situations, specialized organizations whose business is rating
determine how good a credit risk a public organization is for particular debts
In addition to bond rating organizations (e.g., Moody's, Fitch, and Standar(
& Poor's), other rating services, debt insurers, specialized units of financia
institutions, and individual debt holders do essentially the same thing.

People who relied on the two major rating services and held New York Cit
debt were not terribly amused by the lack of warning concerning its credit
worthiness. This led both to an increased quickness by the rating services t(
downgrade ratings and greater analysis of creditworthiness by other partici
pants in the debt markets, particularly financial institutions. Concern witl
creditworthiness led also to much greater efforts at financial disclosure as
means of showing creditworthiness.

Credit ratings systems are judgmental in character, which does not mear
biased in any way. Judgment bridges the wide gulf between any particular se
of financial numbers and other information on one side and a rating on th(
other side. The factors looked at by the rating services include financia
operations; debt purposes, characteristics, levels, and patterns; financia
analysis of assets, liabilities, revenues, expenditures, results of operations, an(
financial administration practices; economic bases of the organization; an(
administrative and legal aspects of the organization. In addition, for limite(
liability debt, the particular security (a revenue-producing facility that pro
duces a stream of income that pays for the debt) and its associated use ar
scrutinized closely. An extremely detailed analysis results in a rating for
particular public organization's debt issue. Any change in a rating of a publi
organization's debt issue reflects an assessment of increasing or decreasin
creditworthiness.

Policy type scoring systems are concerned with financial assistance and witl
regulation of public organizations as service providers. These concerns ar
related. Analyses for financial assistance look at social and economic condi
tions in particular jurisdictions to determine whether to provide financia
assistance, and if so, how much and to whom. Many federal and state gran
programs include formulas to target financial aid to jurisdictions showin
evidence of greater need.[13] A slightly overlapping but different policy concer:
is the regulation of local governments by state governments. From the stat
perspective, the potential problem is that local officials will do stupid thing
without being bound by regulations evidencing the infinite wisdom of stat
officials. The local officials, on the other hand, tend to see state regulations a

another nuisance to be ignored to the extent possible and otherwise tolerated as best possible. The same sort of logic in the state/local regulatory relationship is found in the federal/state and federal/local relationship when regulations are attached to financial aid. Both types of scoring systems are developed and used by policymakers and those attempting to provide useful information or to influence policy decisions. Much regulatory oriented scoring work focuses on determining early warning signals of local fiscal stress. Such signals would make it possible for state officials to issue regulations to prohibit actions leading to fiscal stress and to get involved in such situations sooner.

A third external type of scoring system is that concerned with providing a comparison between two or more entities for the sake of making some kind of choice. This kind of scoring system has been used to show states' capacity for economic development and to distinguish between the relative tax burden of local governments. These scoring systems tend to be more oriented toward cost factors.

Scoring systems used for organizational self-assessment are either general in character, with measures of many of the concepts, or specific scores focused on one thing, such as the efficacy of short-term investment programs.[14] The two major examples of general self-assessment scoring systems are very comprehensive and concerned with service provision.[15] Both use comparisons of a single entity at different points in time. The scores show what happened over time. They show financial conditions as improving or declining on the different measures. Both scoring systems use graphs with upward or downward trend lines to show the course of the measures over time. The general internal scoring systems can be manipulated to produce misleading results only to the extent problems can be hidden in one or more places in a financial record system.

Example: The U.S. Government

A question of common interest is the condition of the U.S. government. Some relevant scores are exhibited in Tables 18.1 through 18.4 for the fiscal years 1990 to 1992. Three tables show per capita scores for revenues, expenditures, and debt on an inflation-adjusted basis with yearly percentage changes. The fourth table shows debt as a percentage of Gross Domestic Product and yearly changes.

The computations are relatively simple. Revenues, expenditures, and debt for the U.S. government are divided by the Bureau of the Census's annual estimates of population, and those resulting figures are divided by the yearly Consumer Price Index-Urban (CPI-U) figure, a price inflation index that reflects the rate of inflation in the U.S. economy. These two division operations produce per capita inflation-adjusted figures that can be compared across years. Both the population size and currency inflation are adjusted to make the resulting figures comparable. The percentage change figures are based on the inflation-adjusted per capita figures. The debt as a percentage of Gross Domestic Product figures results from dividing U.S. government debt by the reported Gross Domestic Product for each year.

TABLE 18.1 Revenues per Capita Adjusted for Inflation

Fiscal Year	Revenues per Capita	÷ CPI-U	=	Revenue per Capita Adjusted for Inflation	% Change
1990	$4,642	130.7	=	$3,552	0.05 increase
1991	$4,762	136.2	=	$3,496	(1.56) decrease
1992	$4,937	140.3	=	$3,519	0.65 increase

Sources: U.S. Bureau of the Census (1994). *Statistical Abstract of the United States: 1994* (114th ed.). Washington, DC, p. 297 for revenues figures shown and p. 489 for CPI-U. The figures for 1989 revenues used to compute the percentage change for 1990 were drawn from U.S. Bureau of the Census (1993). *Governmental Finances: 1990-1991*, Series GF91-5. Washington, DC: U.S. Government Printing Office, p. 3.

TABLE 18.2 Expenditures per Capita Adjusted for Inflation

Fiscal Year	Expenditures per Capita	÷ CPI-U	=	Expenditure per Adjusted Capita for Inflation	% Change
1990	$5,601	130.7	=	$4,286	3.87 increase
1991	$5,867	136.2	=	$4,308	0.51 increase
1992	$5,988	140.3	=	$4,268	(0.92) decrease

Sources: U.S. Bureau of the Census (1994). *Statistical Abstract of the United States: 1994* (114th ed.). Washington, DC, p. 297 for expenditure figures shown and p. 489 for CPI-U. The figures for 1989 expenditures used to compute the percentage change for 1990 were drawn from U.S. Bureau of the Census (1993). *Governmental Finances: 1990-1991*, Series GF91-5. Washington, DC: U.S. Government Printing Office, p. 3.

TABLE 18.3 Debt per Capita Adjusted for Inflation

Fiscal Year	Debt per Capita	÷ CPI-U	=	Debt per Capita Adjusted for Inflation	% Change
1990	$13,132	130.7	=	$10,047	7.35 increase
1991	$14,605	136.2	=	$10,723	6.73 increase
1992	$16,006	140.3	=	$11,408	6.39 increase

Sources: U.S. Bureau of the Census (1994). *Statistical Abstract of the United States: 1994* (114th ed.). Washington, DC, p. 297 for debt figures shown and p. 489 for CPI-U. The figures for 1989 debt used to compute the percentage change for 1990 were drawn from U.S. Bureau of the Census (1993). *Governmental Finances: 1990-1991*, Series GF91-5. Washington, DC: U.S. Government Printing Office, p. 3.

TABLE 18.4 Debt as a Percentage of Gross Domestic Product

Fiscal Year	%[a]	Changes: Raw %[b] and Yearly %[c]	
1990	58.9%	+4.02%	7.33%
1991	63.8%	+4.91%	8.34%
1992	66.9%	+3.07%	4.81%

Sources: U.S. Bureau of the Census (1994). *Statistical Abstract of the United States: 1994* (114th ed.). Washington, DC, p. 297 for debt and p. 446 for Gross Domestic Product. The figures for 1989 debt used to compute the percentage change for 1990 were drawn from U.S. Bureau of the Census (1993). *Governmental Finances: 1990-1991*, Series GF91-5. Washington, DC: U.S. Government Printing Office, p. 3.
a. U. S. government debt divided by the Gross Domestic Product (e.g., 3,266.1 billion/5,546.1 billion equals 58.9%).
b. Current fiscal year percentage minus the previous fiscal year's percentage (e.g., 63.8% - 58.9% equals 4.9%).
c. Raw as a percentage of the previous years percentage (e.g., 4.02% divided by 54.9% [the percentage in 1987] equals 7.3%).

One key issue in assessing actual financial conditions is the selection of the data to use for calculations. Many different particular sets of information can be used to do calculations. Different sets can lead to different conclusions. Tables prepared for this chapter are based on U.S. Census data; similar but different figures can be found in other data sources (e.g., the federal budget prepared by the Office of Management and Budget and various Department of Treasury and Federal Reserve Board reports). Perhaps the best possible appreciation of how much numbers can vary is supplied by two economists who explain how the federal budget deficit in Fiscal Year 1988 reported as $255 billion can really be understood as being only $3 billion after a few minor accounting and economic adjustments.[16]

The scores allow us to assess the financial condition of the U.S. government. Briefly, revenues per capita adjusted for inflation are almost equal in fiscal years 1990 to 1992, declining very slightly. The expenditures per capita adjusted for inflation, which also are substantially higher than revenues per capita, show the same pattern. The result of the imbalance between revenues and expenditures shows up in a steadily increasing level of debt per capita adjusted for inflation. Debt as a percentage of Gross National Product provides another view of an increasing debt level.

CONCLUSION ◆

This discussion of assessing financial conditions introduced and explained relevant perspectives, concepts, information systems, and scoring systems. Financial assessment predicts future capacity for action, particularly for meeting financial obligations, generating revenue, and providing services.

DISCUSSION QUESTIONS

1. What would you analyze further to assess the financial condition of the federal government?
2. What would financial analysis of your state show?
3. What particular things would you like analyzed in your federal, state, or local government or nonprofit organization?

NOTES ◆

1. International City Management Association (1981, August). *Finance report: An evaluation of the financial trend monitoring system,* submitted to the National Science Foundation as a final project report for the International City Management Association's Assessing Municipal Financial Condition and Improving Financial Management Practices Project, pp. 14-19. This was also one author's experiences when applying that financial trend monitoring system to selected municipalities. See Sanford M. Groves (1980). *Evaluating local government financial condition: Handbook 2, a practitioner's workbook for collecting data, charting trends, and interpreting results.* Washington, DC: International City Management Association.

2. Earlier typologies of perspectives in financial assessment can be found in J. Richard Aronson (1984). Municipal fiscal indicators. In James H. Carr (Ed.), *Crisis and constraint i municipal finance*. New Brunswick, NJ: Center for Urban Policy Research, The State Universit of New Jersey at Rutgers, pp. 3-41; Richard J. Reeder (1984, January). Nonmetropolitan fisca indicators: A review of the literature. *Economic Development Division*. Washington, DC: Eco nomic Research Service, U.S. Department of Agriculture ERS Staff Report, No. AGES 830908 and Roy Bahl (1982, Winter). The fiscal health of state and local governments: 1982 and beyonc *Public Budgeting &Finance, 2*(4), 5-21, which is reprinted in Carr.

3. Wade S. Smith (1979). *The appraisal of municipal credit risk*. New York: Moody's Investor Service, p. 180.

4. Patricia Giles Leeds (1983). City politics and the market: The case of New York City financing crisis. In Alberta M. Sbragia (Ed.), *The municipal money chase: The politics of loca government finance*. Boulder, CO: Westview Press, pp. 119-126.

5. For example, a consultant to the American Association of University Professors has computer software program to analyze university budgets: Larry Gerber (1995, Spring). Alabam AAUP co-sponsors financial analysis workshop. *Alabama Academe*, 1; this follows the much earlier observation that school districts might actually hide money in their budgets as a collectiv bargaining ploy: John P. Hulpke and Donald A. Watne (1976, November/December). Budgetin behavior: If, when, and how selected school districts hide money. *Public Administration Review 36*(6), 671-672.

6. Warren Hirschman (1970). *Exit, voice, and loyalty*. Cambridge, MA: Harvard Universit Press. Hirschman conceptualizes choices in politics and economics as involving exit, voice, an loyalty. In politics, when one is an integral part of a situation, one uses voice to influenc conditions. In economics, when one is an integral part of a situation, one uses exit to chang conditions. Loyalty is a continuation of a part practice, continued support in politics, o continued product purchases in economics.

7. Advisory Commission on Intergovernmental Relations (1985, March). *Bankruptcie defaults, and other local government financial emergencies*. Washington, DC: Advisory Commis sion on Intergovernmental Relations, p. 5.

8. Robert B. Albritton and Ellen M. Dran (1987, March/April). Balanced budgets and stat surpluses: The politics of budgeting in Illinois. *Public Administration Review, 47*(2), 143-152.

9. See Leeds, p. 118 for New York and A. F. Ehrbar (1980, June 1). Financial probity, Chicag style, *Fortune*, pp. 100-102, 104, and 106 for Chicago.

10. Advisory Commission on Intergovernmental Relations, p. 5.

11. Robert Jervis (1970). *The logic of images in international relations*. Princeton, NJ: Princeto University Press. Jervis distinguishes between signals, which are easily manipulated, and indice which are beyond an entity's control insofar as projecting a misleading image. Paper document that are issued by an entity are signals; actual values established or observed by others are indice

12. See Aronson, Reeder, and Bahl for reviews of several relevant studies.

13. J. Richard Aronson and John L. Hilley (1986). *Financing state and local governments* (4t ed.). Washington, DC: The Brookings Institution, pp. 53, 78.

14. For an example, see Carol W. Lewis and A. Grayson Walker III (Eds.) (1984). How t evaluate short-term investment performance. In *Casebook in public budgeting and financia management* (pp. 241-245). Englewood Cliffs, NJ: Prentice-Hall, which was adapted fron Nathaniel Guild (Ed.) (1981). *The public manager's handbook*. Chicago: Crain Communicatior

15. Philip Rosenberg and C. Wayne Stallings (1978). *Is your city heading for financial difficulty A guidebook for small cities and other governmental units*. Chicago: Municipal Finance Officer Association in conjunction with Peat, Marwick, Mitchell & Co. and the Institute of Governmen University of Georgia; and Sanford M. Groves (1980). *Evaluating local government financia condition: Handbook 2, a practitioner's workbook for collecting data, charting trends, and interpre ing results*. Washington, DC: International City Management Association, which was reissued i a moderately updated fashion without the other four handbooks, as Sanford M. Groves an Maureen Godsey Valente (1986). *Evaluating financial condition: A handbook for local governmen Washington*, DC: International City Management Association. A third edition of the same titl and publisher has been issued.

16. Robert Heilbroner and Peter Bernstein (1989). *The debt and the deficit: False alarms/rea possibilities*. New York: Norton, pp. 71-81.

SUGGESTED READINGS ◆

Advisory Committee on Intergovernmental Relations (1986). *Measuring state fiscal capacity: Alternative methods and their uses.* Washington, DC: Advisory Commission on Intergovernmental Relations.

Advisory Committee on Intergovernmental Relations (1987). *Measuring state fiscal capacity, 1987 edition.* Washington, DC: Advisory Commission on Intergovernmental Relations.

Robert Berne and Richard Schramm (1986). *The financial analysis of governments.* Englewood Cliffs, NJ: Prentice-Hall.

Financing
Economic Development

The role of public and nonprofit agencies in financing economic development projects is rapidly changing. This role has become the focal point of increasingly diverse activity, particularly at the state and local levels. Governmental and nonprofit agencies have been involved in economic development for many years. During the past 15 years, direct financing of business has become commonplace.

Similarly, in the past, it was much easier to determine the roles of private and public institutions in creating, expanding, or retaining economic activity. Nonprofit agencies were not active participants in the process. Today, the blurring of roles has increased and the dividing line among the institutions is less clear.

Simply put, economic development financing refers to the conscious and direct use of governmental resources to spur specific project-based private investments. It also refers to use of governmental resources to increase project-specific public or nonprofit investments that directly affect economic activity.

Economics was originally focused on the political economy, the wealth of nations. Adam Smith saw public works activities of government as an important economic development function. The U.S. Constitution was, in part, an attempt to organize the roles of governments and private interests to promote the general welfare through economic activity. Much government activity is purposeful, whereas other actions have unanticipated consequences. Funding for land grant universities, free land for settlers, and advantages to those constructing the rail lines across the country were all conscious efforts to stimulate economic activity on a large scale.

Economic development is policy focused and includes activities that remain close to the traditional public activities of government. Provisions of quality public services and regulation of health and safety concerns to provide an environment where economic investment can occur are examples. Economic development also includes indirect activities such as reducing local crime rates r improving public education. These can have a substantial impact on conomic activity, but they do not directly cause specific activity to take place. conomic development policies are concerned with the big picture, whereas conomic development finance is project focused.

Economic development finance addresses specific situations. It does not efer to macro-level activities to stimulate investment. Actions taken by the 'ederal Reserve Board, for instance, affect business activity throughout the ountry and the world. Instead, economic development finance refers to ctions taken by public and nonprofit agencies that attempt to stimulate ctivity by particular businesses or groups of businesses at a micro level. 'roviding a sewer extension to an industrial park because of an agreement hat a specific company will locate in that park is an example of an economic evelopment finance activity.

Although economic development finance is an element of a much broader conomic development policy, it includes nontraditional functions that focus n direct investment activities. For example, sharing risks has become a tandard practice by government. States and localities become business part- ers with firms that need cash to start or to expand their activities. Such overnments then share the risks of the business and in the profits (or losses) ssociated with that firm. Direct economic development finance activities nclude selling land to a developer for a new shopping center or financing the onstruction of an office building.

GOALS OF ECONOMIC DEVELOPMENT ◆

The goals of economic development generally focus on three areas: (1) job reation, (2) wealth creation, and (3) increasing tax bases.[1] In addition, ttention is often directed at particular locational concerns. Each of these reas will be discussed.

Job Creation

Job creation is often perceived as synonymous with economic development, ut it is actually a residual effect of economic activity. The question of employ- nent is a complex one. Some members of a workforce may be unemployed, /hereas others are underemployed. This simply means that these individuals ave jobs, but the jobs they have represent less pay and fewer skill require- nents than their abilities represent. This is a serious problem as more and nore employers hire part-time personnel to reduce the costs associated with ringe benefits (e.g., health, retirement, sick leave, and so forth). Jobs can be reated that focus on unskilled labor, semi-skilled labor, or highly skilled labor. obs can be temporary or permanent. Jobs can be part-time or full-time. Jobs an be high- or low-paying. Jobs can be focused on a particular geographic rea or on a particular category of individual. Job creation and retention are imed at best meeting the needs of the nation, state, or community.

For states and localities, investments made by public and nonprofit entities an play an important role in job creation. Locational decisions made by the federal government concerning military bases, office buildings, and research and development facilities can often touch off a storm of activity by states and localities because of the economic impact such a decision can have. Similarly state or nonprofit investments in new medical facilities, parks and recreational facilities, or regional offices can often substantially affect where jobs are physically located.

Wealth Creation

Wealth creation may or may not be associated with job creation. A focus of economic development today is in adding economic value to an economy. This is done by increasing economic activity in such a way that goods and services are exported to customers outside the nation, state, or community. Resources, usually money, are then imported, which adds wealth directly to businesses and indirectly to the larger community. Wealth-creating businesses may not be labor-intensive. In other words, increased sales can occur in businesses with few employees. When this occurs, job creation can occur in other businesses that provide goods and services to the wealth-creating business and its employees.

An example shows how this occurs. Pioneer Seed Company in Johnson, Iowa, develops and sells seed products both inside and outside the United States. Increasingly, its markets are overseas. As it sells more and more of its products to foreign countries, it generates wealth. It does so through exporting products to and importing money from these countries. Value is added to the U.S. economy, the economy of Iowa, and the local economy of Johnson. This new wealth in turn allows Pioneer Seed to increase investment in its business and other businesses. It also allows Pioneer to expand its workforce and increase higher-paying jobs, which stimulates increased purchasing power for those employees. These changes result in additional local, state, and national employment. In contrast, a locally owned restaurant in Johnson does not sell its products overseas, nationally, or even throughout the state of Iowa. Instead it sells locally. It does not export products beyond the borders of Johnson, and thus, there is a circulation of dollars within Johnson itself but little net wealth creation. Businesses such as Pioneer Seed provide the wealth that support businesses such as local restaurants.

A good restaurant in Johnson that marketed its products well might lure customers from Des Moines. In this case, it would be exporting a portion of its product beyond the community's border and thus would be importing money from Des Moines. This would do little to improve the economy of Iowa or the United States, however. Similarly, if a company sold products exclusively within the United States but outside its state borders, it would improve the net growth within the state but would do little to help the U.S. economy directly.

Increasing Tax Bases

The final major goal of public agencies is to increase tax bases. Economic development and economic development finance activities that produce jobs and wealth can also expand tax bases. The type of business investment that occurs and its impact on the tax base depends on the characteristics of the business activity. A business that generates a great deal of wealth but owns or uses little real estate will do little to help a community that depends heavily on the real property tax. On the other hand, a business that creates substantial wealth but has few employees can do little to increase personal income or sales taxes. Also, these businesses can have a substantial indirect impact through increasing wealth and employment in secondary businesses (the local restaurant mentioned earlier), which in turn increases the tax base.

Location

Much attention directed at economic investment by state and local agencies is based on a concern with location. Agencies want to see investment occur within their borders, but they also often want to see it occur in areas where the need appears to be the greatest. This is particularly true of local officials who see business investment as a way to reverse the decline of commercial and residential neighborhoods. Denver saw locating its new baseball stadium—Coors Field—in the downtown as a key priority because of the added economic activity the stadium would generate as well as the visibility and psychological impact it would have on the city as a whole.

Federal and state programs are often directed at areas considered blighted, and specific resources can often be used only in areas so designated. This is true of the enterprise zone concept currently used by almost 40 states and recently established by the federal government. Zones are selected based on their deteriorated condition and the level of need of zone residents. Financial and tax incentives then are provided to businesses promising to invest their dollars in the zone.[2]

One major debate among development experts is whether development efforts should be place- or people-oriented. In other words, the concern is whether business incentives should be aimed at helping a geographic area or particular people. Should a business investment be supported only if that investment occurs in a particular area or should that support be based on whom that business hires? Should the public sector care whether a new department store locates in a central business district or on the outskirts of town if the owners agree to hire low-income persons regardless of location? This is an important issue for the public sector because many argue that it is economically inefficient to use tax dollars to entice businesses to locate where they otherwise might not and that the key concern should be creating jobs for those who are in most need. Others believe that improving deteriorated areas serves the public interest.

Specific economic development finance roles are focused on project unique needs (e.g. risk sharing, lower short- and long-term costs, access to credit) that are discussed later in this chapter. Each of these specific roles should relate back to the general economic development policy goals of jobs, wealth, tax base, or location.

◆ PUBLIC ROLES AND RESPONSIBILITIES IN DEVELOPMENT FINANCE

Public-sector agencies take various roles. The range of activities in economic development finance efforts is limited by both legal and philosophical constraints. It is not unusual to find many at the state or local level questioning whether it is appropriate to use tax dollars or resources to help particular private businesses. Should public dollars be used to help build a new hotel if that hotel will then be able to compete unfairly with existing facilities? Why should public tax dollars be used to stimulate private profit? How directly involved should government be in financing private activity? It is one thing to build a sewer line to an industrial park. It is quite another to become business partners with a firm and share in that firm's profits. Should government be involved in business enterprises that are competing with other businesses? How do governments justify such activity? Most efforts at spurring investment occur as a result of a broad definition of the public good.

Public Funds for Private Gain?

States and localities argue that it is appropriate to use public funds to promote the health and welfare of its citizens and that part of that role includes increasing the income, jobs, and tax base for those citizens. This is particularly well accepted when such business activity occurs in blighted or deteriorated areas or where the jobs and income directly improve the condition of minorities or low-income persons. Many federal and state programs directed toward economic development finance activities require that the funds be used to assist the disadvantaged or help restore deteriorated areas of states and localities. Still, many people believe it is an inappropriate role of government to help specific businesses to the perceived detriment of others. They also object to direct public intervention in the private marketplace.

Who is right? No clear answer emerges. The National Chamber of Commerce objects strenuously to economic development finance efforts directed to specific business firms. They argue that governments' role is to "raise all boats," meaning that government policies should be directed at helping all classes of businesses and not directed at specific firms or specific areas of the country. Organizations such as the National League of Cities argue that government financing tools that are made available to states and localities to help the disadvantaged and those areas in severe economic distress are an appropriate use of tax dollars. Federal, state, and local policies vary, depending on how they view development finance.

Legal Constraints

Even if public agencies see their role as appropriate, at the state and local levels they are often constrained by legal barriers. For example, most local governments have limits on general obligation municipal debt that they can use to support specific private initiatives. Many state constitutions restrict the use of public funds for private gain and effectively eliminate the ability of state

or local governments to use resources for such things as loaning money to
private businesses and becoming equity partners in projects or owning,
purchasing, or selling nongovernmental facilities.

Political Constraints

Even where such measures are legal, political constraints can make it
difficult to use local or state tax dollars for such efforts. Some communities
have been able to undertake such activities because of dollars made available
from the federal government. Federal funding is greatly reduced, and political
opposition for use of local tax dollars for such purposes remains strong.

Government Responsibilities

Governments that are involved in economic development finance have a
responsibility to their constituents to be guided by the following criteria: (1)
no incentives are provided to private business beyond those that are absolutely
necessary to make an investment occur, (2) the total costs do not exceed the
benefits produced by that investment, and (3) the costs associated with that
investment provide intergenerational equity. This responsibility is not easy to
achieve. It requires a clear and concise understanding of private investment
decisions and access to the information needed to evaluate costs and benefits.

In determining an appropriate decision, a public agency must ascertain that
the benefits of such efforts are worth the costs associated with them. If, for
example, a state or locality provides free land, tax breaks, the elimination of
various health and safety regulations, and various other incentives to lure a
business to its borders, is that business likely to generate income, jobs, and tax
benefits sufficient to justify the costs such incentives create? The public agency
must know the value of each of those incentives.

- What is the market value of land?
- How much income is produced for the business through the forgiveness of
  various taxes?
- What does this loss of tax revenue cost the government?
- Will the new business investment stimulate economic activity sufficient to make
  up that revenue loss?
- What are the societal costs of deregulation?
- How much will this save the business in additional expenses?
- Correspondingly, how much new business investment is being created?
- How many jobs will be created?
- How much will those jobs pay?
- Are jobs permanent or temporary?
- How many additional jobs will be created in the state or locality as the result of
  this business investment?

Only after these questions are answered or the results reasonably predicted
can the public agency be sure that the incentive costs are justified.

In addition, intergenerational equity, discussed previously, is important. Those who pay the costs of a public decision should also receive the benefits of that facility. In economic development finance, such equity may not exist because the costs are often borne by current taxpayers, whereas the benefits may not accrue until years in the future. If benefits are to be allocated back to the state or community over a number of years, it makes sense to try and spread public costs over a number of years as well. For example, if a business requires a loan to expand its operations, that loan might be made in stages by the public agency so that the economic activity stimulated by the loan is shared by the taxpayers who help underwrite it.

◆ PRIVATE INVESTMENT DECISIONS

Unlike the public sector, which has multiple concerns, the private sector is concerned with one thing: maximizing profits. There is nothing evil about this; our entire society is built on the free enterprise system. What is important is to ensure that the use of public resources to stimulate economic activity does not in turn provide a windfall for private interests such that inordinate profits are created and other private interests are placed at a competitive disadvantage.

The public sector can assist in specific ways, such as by reducing barriers to markets for a business, thereby reducing the costs that business faces. Costs occur in a number of areas controlled by public agencies, including taxes, regulation, availability of money, and operations.

Taxes

All businesses are liable for taxes of some sort. Corporations are now required to pay at least a minimum level of U.S. corporate income taxes. When they buy products, they often pay state and local sales taxes. They share in the costs of social security and support unemployment insurance. In addition, most pay local property taxes in the communities in which they are located. Taxes directly reduce profits and reduce dollars available to pay owners and stockholders or to reinvest into the business itself. Research indicates that taxes affect business investment decisions, particularly on location choices within a region of the country.

When taxes are seen as important, federal, state, and local governments can use tax incentives as a means of stimulating economic development. If they do so for all businesses in hopes of stimulating general growth in the economy, this represents a general economic development activity. The lowering of corporate income taxes is an example. If, on the other hand, specific taxes are reduced to stimulate particular business investments, this activity falls in the category of economic development finance. The use of selective tax reductions to lure business investment to an urban enterprise zone is an economic development finance activity. California, for example, allows the following tax credits for eligible companies locating in such zones:

- As much as 100% net operating loss (NOL) carry-forward. NOL can be carried forward 15 years.
- Firms can earn $19,000 or more in state tax credits for each qualified employee hired.
- Corporations can earn sales tax credits on purchases of $20 million per year of qualified machinery and machinery parts.
- Firms can engage in up-front expensing of certain depreciable property.
- Lenders to zone businesses can receive a net interest deduction.
- Unused tax credits can be applied to future tax years, stretching out the benefit of the initial investment.
- Enterprise Zone companies can earn preference points on state contracts.[3]

Such an approach has several drawbacks. First, whether or not taxes actually change particular investment decisions is difficult to determine. If a company wants to increase profits, it can use the threat of reducing or eliminating investment as a way to reduce tax burdens, even if such a reduction has nothing to do with the investment decision itself. Still, few governments are willing to risk the possible loss of business activity by refusing tax breaks.

Second, providing tax breaks to businesses conflicts with the concern of governments with increasing their tax base. At some point, the revenue losses associated with these breaks are greater than the increased revenue that might be generated from the business investment itself. There is also a trade-off among the various types of taxes. Kansas City, Missouri, granted a major property tax reduction to Hallmark Cards for a commercial and residential development project partly because the city anticipated substantially increased tax revenue from sales and income taxes. Depending on which taxes are reduced, some governments lose more than others. If, for example, property taxes are reduced by a city in hopes of increasing sales tax revenue, that city may see a net increase in tax revenue, but others depending on that property tax (the county, schools, and special districts) may see a net loss in tax revenue.

Regulation

Regulation plays an important part in the costs associated with business development and directly affects the costs of business in a number of ways. Local building codes and state and federal pollution control regulations require that certain standards must be met. This can cost businesses a substantial amount of money. Some argue that myriad regulations create confusion among new business enterprises and stifle the development of new technologies.

A second impact of regulation is delay. The old phrase "time is money" is certainly appropriate in explaining the costs associated with such delays. Projects can become economically unfeasible if regulatory requirements delay the start of a project for an extended period. This is very common in physical development projects such as office buildings and shopping centers, where financing costs can increase dramatically over a period of months. Ohio has established a "one-stop business permit center" that provides direct help and advice to businesses, particularly those starting or expanding a business. Its function is to help facilitate businesses dealing with regulatory requirements of the state. It also acts as a referral agency for technical assistance in dealing with regulations.[4]

Economic development activities involve the overall change or reduction in regulatory requirements. Economic development finance would attempt to reduce the burdens of government regulation to reduce the time necessary to instigate a particular project. In other instances, businesses can be freed from more onerous regulations if they locate in particular areas, such as enterprise zones.

Cost and Availability of Money

A major determinant of a successful business enterprise is the cost and availability of money needed to implement the production of a particular project or service. Money can be obtained in a number of ways. Most new businesses obtain operating capital from savings, friends and relatives, and personal loans.

Money can be obtained by borrowing from a lender. The interest or cost of borrowed money depends on several things. If a business has a good track record of paying back previous loans (credit rating) and has been successful with business ventures of a similar nature in the past, the risk to the lender is less than would be the case when a weak track record existed. This tends to lower the cost.

If the size of the loan is very large, fewer lenders are available to make that loan, or a number of lenders can pool their resources to make a very large loan. In some cases, the risk is so great that no traditional lender is willing to make the loan. Then, a loan can be made only where all or a part of that loan is guaranteed by a third party. Governments and nonprofit development corporations often fill this third-party role. The State of Massachusetts has both loan and loan guarantee programs that cover areas such as long-term debt, equity, and real estate mortgages.[5] Massachusetts also focuses on short- and intermediate-term loans for businesses that cannot secure bank financing.

Micro-enterprise programs have also used loans as a way to stimulate development. The concept, which originated in Bangladesh, focuses on loaning small amounts of money (usually less than $1000) to individuals who plan to start small, labor-intensive business enterprises.[6] Many states, including Arizona, South Dakota, and Nebraska, have developed such funds.

Another way to raise money for a business activity is through partnership with others who bring money to the effort and correspondingly share in the profits or losses associated with the business enterprise. This is referred to as equity financing. Some businesses raise money in this way by selling stock in their business. Businesses solicit partners who serve as investors willing to risk money in the hopes that the business will be successful and produce profits. Unlike a debt lender, there is no set amount of interest earned by an investor. Instead, investors count on businesses making profits so that they gain.

Costs of Operation

No business can prosper unless its costs are lower than its revenues, espe-ially over the long run. Costs vary throughout the life of a business. Early in business, for example, maintenance costs are quite low, but these costs ncrease as equipment and facilities age and need to be maintained or re-placed. Business costs are predominantly tied to labor and maintenance of and, buildings, and equipment. Such costs can also be associated with rentals nd leases if land and improvements are not owned by the business itself. Costs can also be heavily associated with expendable supplies.

To make a profit, businesses must bring in more money than they spend in osts associated with taxes, regulation, daily operations, and financing (debt). Public agencies can assist in helping reduce all or some of these cost areas and thus help a business make investments that otherwise would not be possible.

CLOSING THE GAP: ◆ PUBLIC RESOURCES TO STIMULATE PRIVATE INVESTMENT

Where sufficient private resources are not available to stimulate business ctivity, the public sector can help fill the resource gaps necessary to move that ctivity forward. Four basic resources have been used by public agencies to timulate private investment: (1) direct financing and financing guarantees, 2) tax codes, (3) regulatory relief, and (4) direct service provision. We will iscuss each.

Direct Financing and Financing Guarantees

Direct debt and equity financing of business activities is a popular tool for tate and local public agencies and nonprofit development corporations. This pproach is used for business investments that cannot be funded through raditional financing mechanisms. It is important to understand that debt and quity financing are based on risk levels. Certain business activities are, by their ery nature, highly risky. New technologies or a proposed location can make n activity a high risk. Locating a business in a declining neighborhood area is •ften more risky than locating it in a rapidly growing area. A business project night be more easily financed under one set of circumstances than another.

Business owners are interested in making profits. If financing costs are reater in one location than another, profits are reduced, and businesses locate vhere profits are likely to be higher. Governments can help reduce financing osts to make less attractive locations be competitive, which can be accom-•lished in a number of ways. Public agencies can subsidize the costs of a loan rom a lender so that it is competitive with more attractive investment •pportunities available to the business. In another case, an agency can assist business in receiving a loan from some other quasi-governmental source, uch as the Small Business Administration.

If the cost of money is not the problem so much as the risk of the activit or location, a public agency can "guarantee" a loan from a private lender. Th Small Business Administration is well known for its loan guarantee program States and localities also operate such loan guarantee programs in hopes o assisting specific businesses that otherwise would lack the capital to carry ou their investments. If none of these options appears viable, a public agency ca make the loan directly, thereby serving as a lender of last resort.

Tax Codes

Various tax incentives can be used for business investment. Among the mos common in development finance are tax increment financing, tax abatement and industrial redevelopment bonds. In general economic development changes in tax structure and tax base are common.

Tax increment financing (TIF) and tax abatement are both linked to th real property tax. Industrial redevelopment bonds are linked to federal anc state income taxes, whereas changes in tax structure and tax base are incentive: that can be linked to any particular tax source.

TIF provides a method by which local governments can use increasec property tax assessments to retire bonds issued to help finance project directly linked to some particular business investment. Local government: borrow money to provide physical facilities as inducements to businesses tc undertake particular business investments; the money for repayment of deb comes from the increased value of the property as a result of business investment. Business development finances itself. An example best illus- trates how TIF works. An industry is interested in locating at a specific site in a particular community and believes it needs major capital improve- ments (sewer, water, and road improvement and a rail spur) to be competitive A government could issue TIF bonds to pay for these improvements. The payments to retire these bonds come from increased property tax revenue: gained by this industrial investment. Undeveloped land produces little ta> revenue. When the value increases dramatically as a result of the industria development, the difference between the predevelopment and post-develop- ment tax revenues is used to retire the bonds. Minnesota, California, anc Michigan lead in the use of TIF, and today more than 30 states have enabling legislation allowing its use.[7]

Specific criticisms of TIF focus on the property tax base itself. First, some argue that voters can limit future increases in property tax assessments anc that such limits could threaten the repayment of TIF bonds. This fear has no greatly affected the use of such financing, because these risks can be incorpo- rated into the interest rates paid on the bonds when they are sold. A seconc criticism of tax increment financing is that it diverts future tax revenue away from other uses, an example of opportunity costs. This is true because prop- erty taxes are used to finance local governments providing a wide array o services. Money earmarked for bond repayment is a direct loss of revenue tc support service activities. Recent problems have also developed in Florida where property tax revenue has not kept pace with bond payments.[8] Despite these criticisms, most state and local officials appear to strongly support the use of TIF, which can be seen in its growing popularity in the last decade.

A very popular twist on tax increment financing is the creation of business improvement districts. Although predominantly used in central business district areas, they have also found acceptance in industrial attraction efforts. The concept is quite simple. If state law allows, a number of businesses within a particular area of the community agree to place a surcharge on their current property tax assessments. Revenue derived from this surcharge is then used to help improve the physical appearance and competitive environment of that area. How the funds can be used is determined by state law, but the uses often involve personnel and marketing expenditures as well as physical improvements. Because not all areas of the community or state are eligible for such assistance, it can be considered an economic development finance tool.

Little opposition has arisen from the use of TIF, largely because it is imposed on local businesses rather than on the general public and because it requires a majority of those businesses affected to voluntarily approve its use. Some have questioned its effectiveness in retail projects when funds have been used for cosmetic improvements rather than to implement more tangible investment strategies.

Tax abatement is the flip side of tax increment financing. In this case, the government agrees to "freeze" the property tax assessment for a particular parcel of land at a predeveloped value for a specific period of time in return for business investment. This allows a business to benefit from improvements made to property without paying higher taxes because of those improvements. This tax incentive is used extensively in Missouri and Ohio.

As with tax increment financing, opposition to the use of abatements focuses on the opportunity costs of lost revenue for other property tax-dependent activities. It also is criticized along with other tax incentives for its tendency to give new businesses unfair competitive advantages over existing firms that do not receive such financial assistance. This complaint has been particularly visible for industrial redevelopment bonds.

Industrial redevelopment bonds (IRBs), despite greatly curtailed use as a result of the recent changes in the federal income tax laws, still provide an attractive incentive for development. Simply put, IRBs are approved for issuance by a state or local government, but they are actually marketed and sold by private businesses. Governments give only the nontaxable status to the bonds; the businesses receive the money and are directly responsible for repayment. The bonds are attractive because they are tax exempt and, therefore, cost less than taxable bonds. This reduces the cost of capital to business and thereby serves as an incentive for investment.

IRBs have been among the most highly criticized of all tax incentives—for several reasons. Many believe that these tax-free bonds give unfair advantages to new firms over those who made business investments without them. For example, a hotel firm allowed to issue IRBs could reduce costs sufficiently to offer room rates below those of existing hotels. Another objection to IRBs is their indiscriminate use, which negatively affects the revenue stream of the federal government. Many states and localities have granted permission to issue bonds to any business that requested them, thus providing no control over their use or linkage to economic development goals and objectives. This also makes this less of an economic development finance activity and more of a general economic development activity. Iowa City, Iowa, made headlines several years ago by actually adopting a policy about how IRBs would be used. Unfortunately, it was the exception rather than the rule. These criticisms have led to substantial restrictions on the use of IRBs by the federal government.

For general economic development activity, some tax incentives have developed that help reduce the tax burden on general categories of business firms or their employees. These incentives take many forms: reduced corporation tax rates, corporate tax credits, sales tax exemptions, revisions in how various taxes are computed, and changes in individual income tax rates for higher-income wage earners.

Only Nevada and South Dakota have no corporate income taxes. Many state policies, however, reflect a perceived trade-off between the revenue derived from these taxes and concern that such taxes cause firms to locate outside their borders. Although most literature indicates that taxes do not play a decisive role in locational decisions, many states try to use low corporate tax rates as an incentive to attract industry. This is possibly because taxes are a controllable element of a state's economic development strategy, whereas factors such as natural resources and labor force productivity are largely uncontrollable and thus extremely difficult to change.

Many state sales tax policies reflect concerns about the economic impact taxes have on economic development. Few states have sales taxes on services, at least partly because of the economic impact such a tax would have on service businesses. States can exempt certain products from the sales tax because of the importance of those products to the state. As an example, in agriculturally oriented states, farm equipment is often exempt from such taxes.

In some instances, the definition of a tax base or how taxes are computed can play a role in attraction efforts. The recent furor over how several states computed income for corporations—the so-called unitary tax—was a good example of the use of computation methods as a tax incentive or disincentive. This tax provision required computing tax liability on the basis of worldwide business (sales, payroll, and property) rather than simply on the basis of U.S. business. The net effect was to increase taxes for many multinational firms. Many states such as California and Oregon repealed their unitary tax provisions because of business pressure and threats to relocate or stop investment. Other states have proposed changes to the tax computation formulas so corporations headquartered outside the state would pay a higher rate or have a larger base for taxation than would businesses with headquarters within the state.

In another example, states with highly progressive income tax structures have found businesses with a larger number of highly paid executives to be very negative about increased investment because of the tax liability suffered by those executives. A recent example occurred in Iowa, where the business community advocated substantial reductions in state income tax rates for high-salaried employees because of the perceived reluctance of these individuals to move to a state with such a tax structure.

Regulatory Relief

One area directly controlled by governments is the use of regulations that affect businesses and individuals. Although regulations are meant to protect the public interest, some changes can be made to help stimulate specific private activity. As mentioned earlier, some states and localities have gone to a one-stop shopping concept that helps particular developers, builders, and other businesses affected by local regulation through the maze of red tape in the quickest possible time. Others have developed regulatory ombudsmen who serve as advocates within government to reduce regulatory burdens on particular businesses.

From a general economic development perspective, public agencies have carried out a comprehensive review of regulations to determine their value, costs, and benefits. Business activity is then weighed against the health and safety benefits the regulations provide to determine a regulation's worth. A fiscal note is also used by governments; the costs of particular regulations on citizens, businesses, or other governmental units are assessed before passage to determine their relative worth and importance. All these efforts are an attempt to reduce the regulatory constraints to business development but do not involve development finance for specific businesses.

Direct Service Provision

Governments can use traditional government services, particularly public facility improvements, to induce particular kinds of business investment. Examples are very common, ranging from sewer, street, and water extensions to industrial parks to improving the lighting on Main Street.

In many cases, such direct service assistance has more to do with creating the possibility for development rather than actually causing the development to occur. For example, a sewer line to an industrial park may be a necessary precursor to industrial recruitment, but in and of itself, it cannot cause the investment to occur. For this reason, it is more a general economic development activity than one focused on economic development finance.

NEGOTIATING IN DEVELOPMENT FINANCE ◆

Once a public agency has a clear understanding of the resources it has available, it can begin a specific economic development finance effort aimed at specific businesses or public investment opportunities. At some point that agency will be required to negotiate with potential investors. To negotiate successfully, the public representatives must clearly understand the investors' needs and concerns as well as their own. They must also have a realistic appraisal of the strengths and weaknesses of their position. Boston may be in a much stronger position to negotiate business development in its downtown than is Gary, Indiana.

Public organizations should negotiate to minimize the amount of public resources necessary to stimulate the largest amount of investment possible. The goal should also be to maximize the public benefits associated with the outside investment. This is difficult and requires considerable sophistication, particularly in understanding business operations. It also requires strong interpersonal skills.

Success, then, is based on understanding public and private objectives, obstacles to development, complete information, strengths and weaknesses of each party, and strong interpersonal capabilities. With the proper mixing and matching of public financing resources and business opportunities, negotiations should prove beneficial to both public and private participants.

◆ **CONCLUSION**

Economic development finance is a complex and wide-ranging area. It involves numerous participants from both the public and private sectors. It also requires a clear understanding of the proper roles and responsibilities of public agencies in stimulating business investment.

Increasing sophistication by state and local governments as well as nonprofit development agencies has made this a rapidly growing area of public financial management. It is still a new and rapidly changing field, however, with new tools and techniques constantly being developed. As the needs and demands of both public and private organizations change, so will economic development finance.

DISCUSSION QUESTIONS

1. How do states and localities decide whether a public purpose is served by using tax resources to stimulate private investment? What criteria should be used? How should they be measured?

2. Find at least three businesses in your local community that have used tax dollars (federal, state, or local) to develop, recruit, expand, or retain those businesses. List the various expenditure, tax, and regulatory incentives that were used in each case. What similarities or differences existed in each instance? What positive or negative effects did each investment have?

3. What would make a tax expenditure a more attractive method to stimulate business investment than a direct expenditure of public funds.

4. Why are nonprofit organizations an increasingly popular vehicle for economic development initiatives? Can you find an example in your state or community?

NOTES ◆

1. Alan Borut (1981). *Creating a framework for economic development decision-making: A guidebook for economic development practitioners.* Washington, DC: The National League of Cities.

2. See Empowerment Zone information on the World Wide Web (http://www.ezec.gov).

3. See Enterprise Zones, California State World Wide Web Site, 1995, p. 1 (http://www.ca.gov/commerce/bd.html/#c.1.b).

4. State of Ohio gopher site, 1995 (...ment %20 Programs/The %20 Office %20 of %20 Small %20 and %20 Developing %20 Business).

5. Massachusetts Office of Business Development. Financing Your Venture, 1995 (http://www.novalink.com/mobd/finance2.html).

6. Edward J. Blakely (1994). *Planning local economic development: Theory and practice* (2nd ed.). Thousand Oaks, CA: Sage, pp. 189-190.

7. Richard D. Bingham, Edward H. Hill, and Sammis B. White (Eds.) (1990). *Financing economic development: An institutional response.* Newbury Park, CA: Sage, 86.

8. Penelope Lemov (1994, February). Tough times for TIF. *Governing Magazine, 7*(4), 18.

SUGGESTED READINGS ◆

Richard Bingham and Robert Meier (Eds.) (1993). *Theories of local economic development.* Newbury Park, CA: Sage.

Edward J. Blakely (1994). *Planning local economic development: Theory and practice.* Thousand Oaks, CA: Sage.

John M. Levy (1990). *Economic development programs for cities, counties and towns* (2nd ed.). New York: Praeger.

Index

About the Authors

B. J. Reed is Professor and Chairman of the Department of Public Admini-stration at the University of Nebraska at Omaha.

Before to moving Omaha, Dr. Reed was employed by the National League of Cities, where he directed many of their technical assistance programs for housing, community development, economic development, and transportation. Dr. Reed has also served as the development director of Mexico, Missouri.

During his tenure at the University of Nebraska at Omaha, Dr. Reed has published numerous articles in journals such as *Public Administration Review, American Review of Public Administration, The Journal of Urban Affairs,* and *Rural Development Perspectives.* His major research interests are finance ad-ministration, intergovernmental management, community and economic development, and public-sector budgeting.

Dr. Reed is active in many community activities and currently serves on the Board of the Greater Omaha Private Industry Council, The Omaha Housing Authority Board of Commissioners, and the Planning Committee of the Urban League of Nebraska.

Dr. Reed received his B.A. and M.S. degrees from Fort Hays State University and his Ph.D. in Political Science from the University of Missouri-Columbia.

John W. Swain currently serves as a faculty member in the Department of Political Science at The University of Alabama, where he teaches in the Ph.D., D.P.A., M.P.A., M.A., and B.A. programs. Previously, he was a member of the faculties of Oklahoma State University, University of Nebraska at Omaha, and Southern Illinois University-Edwardsville. In addition to enjoying teaching, he has been involved in off-campus education, training, consulting, applied research, and academic research. In 1983, his dissertation received the Leonard D. White Award ("For the best dissertation completed and accepted in the general field of public administration") from the American Political Science Association. He is currently working on research projects in the areas of public budgeting and finance administration, public policy, and congres-sional elections. His published works include *Managing Small Cities and*

Counties and an earlier version of *Public Finance Administration,* numerous book chapters and technical manuals, and a wide variety of articles in *Public Administration Review, American Review of Public Administration,* and *International Journal of Public Administration.* His major research interests include public finance administration, public budgeting, and local government. He holds a B.A. in political science from the University of New Hampshire and an M.A. and Ph.D. in political science from Northern Illinois University.

CPSIA information can be obtained at www.ICGtesting.com
Printed in the USA
LVOW03*1212261114

415686LV00003B/17/P